Keep Innovation Simple

Lead with Clarity and Focus in a World of Constant Change

Brad Barbera

Inside Keep Innovation Simple...

"Simplicity in innovation will come for your organization when everyone in it is operating with a common understanding of how innovation works: who does what, when, why, and how. Simplicity means that everyone 'gets it.' Simplicity means that no one is *Lost*, wondering why there is a polar bear and a smoke monster on a tropical island."

"Complicated analyses will always use assumptions as inputs. Those assumptions will always be wrong. Some more wrong than others. The precise output of a complex analysis may feel good, but it will still be wrong. Better to be approximately right using simplicity than precisely wrong using complexity."

"Even a well-written and communicated expression of mission will fall flat if the people of the organization, and particularly the leaders in it, don't actually live the mission on a daily basis. For example, part of one company's mission statement was 'Respect, Integrity, Communication, and Excellence.' That company was Enron. Need I say more?"

"Innovation is all about 'I don't know, *but I'll find out*.' There is no better way to capture the attitude of curiosity necessary for innovation. That attitude needs to be a determined part of any individual innovator. That attitude needs to be a pervasive part of an organizational culture of innovation."

"The difficult decisions come when you have to choose between multiple good projects. These choices can be so hard that some have compared it to – and this is not for the squeamish – shooting puppies."

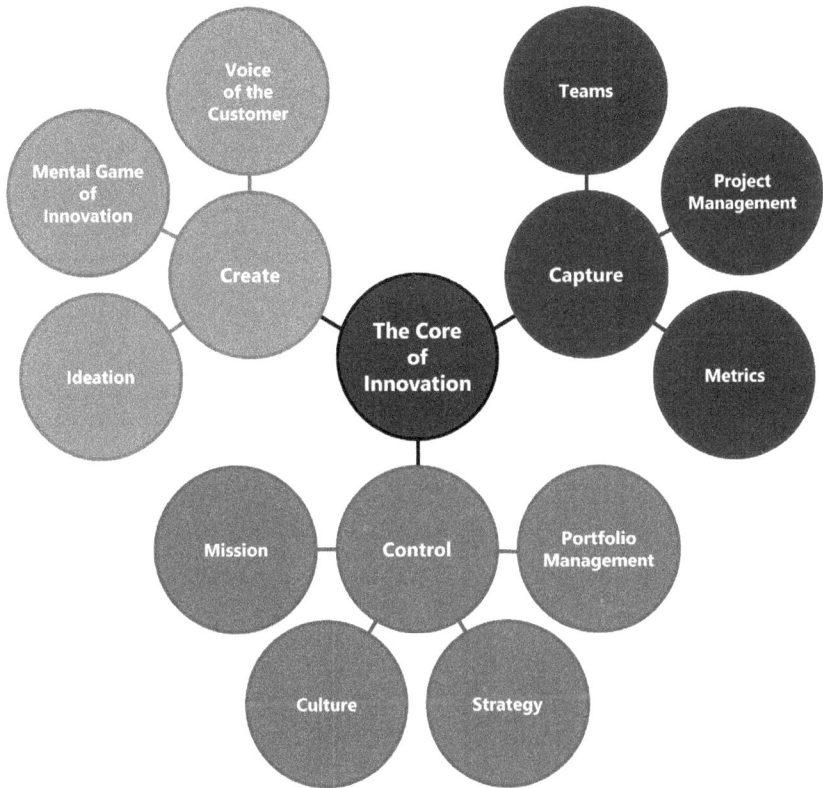

"Simple" does not mean "easy." Innovation is a complex process in a chaotic world. "Simple" brings clarity to the chaos. Clarity aligns and coordinates resources to maximize the return from their efforts. And *that* makes the innovation engine hum.

Keep Innovation Simple

Lead with Clarity and Focus in a World of Constant Change

Brad Barbera

C2D Publishing Ltd.
Chicago, IL

ISBN 978-0-9972021-1-3

Dedications

To my dad, who showed me the path to innovation;

to my mom, who put up with him long enough to have me;

to both of them for the support that made this book possible;

to my sister, a.k.a. "Jello-Head," for motivating me to work hard by always being a little bit smarter than me;

and to my kids, Giancarlo and Sophia, without whom my world would be a much sadder, more boring, and less creative place.

"Innovation is the specific tool of entrepreneurs, the means by which they exploit change as an opportunity for a different business or a different service. It is capable of being presented as a discipline, capable of being learned, capable of being practiced. Entrepreneurs need to search purposefully for the sources of innovation, the changes, and their symptoms that indicate opportunities for successful innovation. And they need to know and to apply the principles of successful innovation."
~Peter Drucker

"Most creative endeavors are somewhat unpredictable. They often seem ambiguous, hit-or-miss, trial and error. And unless people have a high tolerance for ambiguity, and get their security from integrity to principles and inner values, they find it unnerving and unpleasant to be involved in highly creative enterprises."
~Stephen Covey

"You have to go through the falling down in order to learn to walk. It helps to know that you can survive it. That's an education in itself...Comedy is tragedy plus time."
~Carol Burnett

"For about 400 years, it's been widely quoted that 'Knowledge is Power.' Sorry, Sir Francis, it's time for an update. In today's info-saturated world, what you know is power *only if* you know how to use it to help you juggle the too many things that were all due yesterday."
~Bill Jensen

"The number one premise of business is that it need not be boring or dull. It ought to be fun. If it's not fun, you're wasting your life."
~Tom Peters

"If I can get you to laugh with me, you like me better, which makes you more open to my ideas. And, if I can persuade you to laugh at a particular point that I make, by laughing at it you acknowledge it as true."
~John Cleese

"An original play changes every day...it taught me to stop falling in love with my first drafts."
~Chris Rock

"Most of the quotes you find on the internet are wrong."
~Abraham Lincoln

Table of Contents

Note Regarding the Print Version

Keep Innovation Simple was originally written specifically to be an eBook, attempting to take advantage of that digital medium with hyperlinks galore, both to places within the book and to information on the internet: videos, websites, documents, etc.

In preparing a print version, we did what we could to provide a similar experience, with all the referenced URLs spelled out for you. A fantastic innovation would be a print book that allows internet connectivity, but at the time of this printing, that is still just a unicorn. See the section "What the #&%! Is Innovation, Anyway" for an explanation of what I mean by that.

The figures may be a little small to read in print – especially the tools. No worries, though. All of the tools are available in full size (and color) at www.3point14Innovation.com/Toolbox/.

There were already something like a zillion footnotes in the eBook, but now with so many hyperlinks being dropped down into additional footnotes, there are something like a bazillion of 'em. I figure that if you want the info, it's there, and if you don't want the info, it makes each page shorter, so you'll feel like you're reading faster. That's a win-win.

If you want to experience the electronic version, just go online to www.3point14innovation.com/contactus/, and we'll help you get a copy. See, wouldn't it be cool just to tap on that URL and be zipped in mere moments to the site?

I hope that you will still enjoy the reading, and get some useful stuff out of it!

Your humble author,

Brad Barber

Preface: Answering Your Questions Before You Even Ask Them

Will This Book Cure Your Insomnia?

This is a book about systematic innovation in organizations, both for-profit and not-for-profit, and the general principles (what some would call "best practices," but I call "evidence-based practices") that make innovation work more effectively, efficiently, and successfully, blah, blah, yadda, yadda...

Snooze...

Okay, you can wake up again.

I've read too many business books from authors who should be charged with manslaughter for boring their audience to death. I am determined not to let this be another one. If you have insomnia, I feel for you, but I'm not here to cure it.

Is This Book for You?

Here are some folks for whom this book was *not* written: those who like complicated bureaucracy; those who enjoy boredom; and those looking for the latest get-rich-quick scheme. So that's the not-fors. Who, then, is it for?[1]

---

[1] Yes, I know that "For whom, then, is it?" is the grammatically correct way to phrase that sentence, at least as I was taught in school. But c'mon, that just sounds so haughty. I'd rather just write the way I might chat about it with you at a barbeque. Besides, the lexicographer at http://blog.oxforddictionaries.com/2011/11/grammar-myths-prepositions/ (which you could click to read if you had the eBook version) says that whole rule is bogus anyway. If you are one of my former English teachers, or if you are a devotee of *Warner's English Grammar and Composition*, please forgive me.

Figure 1 will help you to determine if you are a good candidate for reading this book. If you are either stupid or evil (or worse – both), then please put the book down and step away. I will not be held responsible for what you might do with it.

But seriously, folks... this book is for those who want to innovate[2] within an organization. That sounds like a straightforward statement, but let me emphasize a couple of things. This is for people who *really* want to innovate. It's not for those who merely want to check a buzzword box. You need to be someone who wants to serve a customer by creating something new that is of value both to them and to your organization.

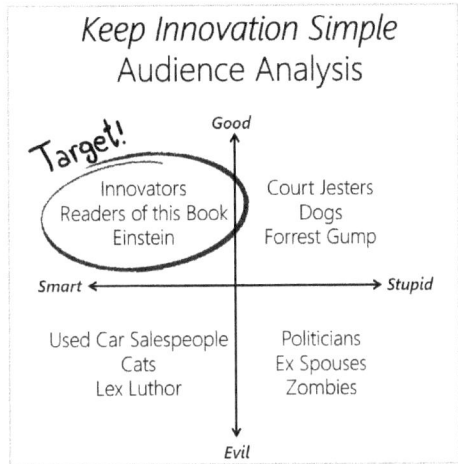

Keep Innovation Simple
Audience Analysis

Figure 1: Make sure you fall in the correct quadrant before you continue to read.

It's not *necessarily* for lone wolf entrepreneurs. It's primarily for people who are working in an organization of some sort, whether a for-profit business, a non-profit charity, or some community of like-minded people wanting to achieve a goal. The target is the manager (or aspiring manager) of an innovation group – whether an executive leader of a complex innovation organization, or a first-time manager of a small innovation team. While some of this book is clearly about tasks and processes, there is much more on the people side than in most innovation books.[3]

Note, however, that I threw in that qualifier "necessarily." I did that because even lone wolf entrepreneurs or inventors are likely to have to work with someone, somewhere, to achieve their goals. That's when this book could come in handy. That's when the lone wolf will become part of a pack, even if

---

[22] For the definition of innovation used in this book, go to the "What the #&%! Is Innovation, Anyway" section, page 4.

[3] Okay, I admit, I don't have quantitative data to support that. From what I read, though, I think it's accurate.

only for a short time. The loner will need to become a leader, able to manage an innovation team.

Innovation is a human endeavor. Innovation is a mental endeavor. To lead and drive innovation requires an understanding of how innovators think, how customers behave, and how teams collaborate. You need to get inside the hearts and minds of all different kinds of people. As Simon Sinek says, "if you don't understand people, you don't understand business."[4]

Effective innovation management requires understanding and working within cultures, at the organizational, local, and global levels. It requires working with people inside and outside the organization. It requires working with individuals and groups. It is a people challenge, even more than a strategic challenge. So if you are someone looking to lead innovation in an organization, whether now or in the future, you are in the target audience.

That does not mean that systems, processes, and structures are unimportant, of course. Research into what separates the best from the rest in innovation practices[5] shows that the best organizations – those who have superior launch success rates, superior new product sales, and superior profits from new products – are those that have more formal processes and distinctive organizational structures. So this book offers simple insights on both sides of the topic.

Are you already one of the best? Congratulations. Keep up the good work. Just don't rest on your laurels. Another thing that separates the best from the rest is that they spend more time and attention keeping their innovation engine well-tuned and up-to-date.

If you believe that you already know how to play the innovation game, I still urge you to read on. Heed the warning of George Bernard Shaw, "Beware of false knowledge. It is more dangerous than ignorance." Make sure you really know what you think you know.

---

[4] Here's another instances where the eBook version has advantages. In the eBook, this is hyperlinked directly to one of Mr. Sinek's talks, where you can see him expound on this short statement. But, since this is print, we can't do that. If you want to see it, get online and go to https://www.youtube.com/watch?v=llKvV8_T95M.

[5] Stephen K. Markham and Hyunjung Lee, "Product Development and Management Association's 2012 Comparative Performance Assessment Study," *Journal of Product Innovation Management*, May 2013.

Kodak once owned the world of photography. They even won an "Outstanding Corporate Innovator" award in 1996. Digital photography was invented there. But they "knew" that photography was a film-based business, so they largely ignored their own invention. Just a decade and a half after their innovation award, they had to file for bankruptcy protection. What they "knew" to be true about their business and their markets proved to be very dangerous indeed.

If It's So Simple, Why Is the Book So Long?

While testing the original manuscript in its beta-version form, I received feedback that confirmed what I had already been asking myself: if this is about being simple, why does it take over three-hundred 8½" x 11" pages to say it?!? Now that it's in print, it's 400+ pages. Holy cow. Why so darn long?!?

Three reasons: 1) there are examples, explanations, and comedy jokes galore to make it more than just an innovation to-do checklist; 2) "simple" does not mean the same thing as "easy;" and 3) I wanted to provide numerous tools to help fill your innovation tool box.

First, you can get the gist of the whole book in just a few pages. It's actually laid out in such a way that you can do that with minimal effort. The first chapter, in fact, is called "The Whole Darn Book in One Simple Chapter." The subsequent chapters provide supporting detail, research, examples, stories, self-assessments, illustrations, tools, and, of course, comedic relief. All of that is there to make it clear and memorable. The first chapter is like the spoiler-alert movie synopsis you get on IMDB.[6] You'll get the main points and know what the movie is about, but it won't be the full experience of seeing the movie in a theater with over-buttered popcorn and a gallon of your favorite carbonated beverage.

If my witty prose is not to your liking, skip it all and just read the "Simple Summaries" that appear at the beginning of each chapter. All of the key points are bulleted there for you. At the end of the book, all of the evidence-based-

---

[6] The Internet Movie Database, IMDB, can be found at www.IMDB.com.

practices[7] are listed out as well. Quick and painless reading. If all you want is the meat of this mental meal, that's where you'll find it. The rest is just there to make the meal all the more delicious and nutritious.

If length is a concern, skip to the "How Can You Best Use This Book" section for other ideas on how to make this book work best for you.

Second, let's talk briefly about what "simple"[8] really is. Simple is about clarity and understanding. That is not always going to come in the form of short and easy. That's why the book wasn't titled *Innovation Made Quick and Easy.*[9]

Simplicity is like an onion – it comes in layers.[10] At the core, there is the simplest essence of the concept. Expanding outward are increasing levels of detail, nuance, and specifics. To learn a subject, you start at the core, master it, and then work your way outward.

For example, to children just learning to count, 2+5=7 is not simple. They have to take off their mittens to count on their fingers. Once they start to get those kinds of problems, then someone asks them 7+8. They find out that they run out of fingers, so they take off their shoes, too. As they learn and master new methods of calculation, then subtraction is introduced – and once again, that's not simple for them. Once subtraction is mastered, then along comes multiplication and division. Then exponents, roots, and logarithms. Then geometry and trigonometry and algebra and calculus and statistics and matrices and imaginary numbers and approximate inequalities and the Riemann hypothesis[11] and stuff I can't begin to comprehend even though I used to be pretty good at math.

---

[7] For what is meant by "evidence-based practices," go to the "'Best Practices' and 'Innovation'" section, page 24.

[8] In the eBook, you can click on the word "simple" to go to a cool TED Talk on the subject. http://www.ted.com/talks/eric_berlow_how_complexity_leads_to_simplicity?language=en

[9] If you ever come across such a title, run. Run away as fast as you can. It's a lie. Innovation can be made simple, but any innovation worth doing isn't going to come quick and easy.

[10] Much like cake, parfaits and ogres. Gotta love Shrek. https://www.youtube.com/watch?v=GZpcwKEIRCI

[11] If you really want to know what that is, get online and go to http://mathworld.wolfram.com/RiemannHypothesis.html

To someone who understands the Riemann hypothesis, differential equations are simple. To someone still mastering long division, such calculus is incomprehensibly complicated. Simplicity in mathematics comes in layers.

Or, if you are not a math person, consider written language. To children learning the English alphabet, distinguishing between the letters b, d, p, and q is not simple, because they are all essentially circles with long lines attached. It takes time, effort, and practice to figure out the difference. Then the letters are put together in words, and that's complicated for them. Once they start to understand how to sound out words, they then discover that the spelling doesn't always make sense. Why does "two" have a "w," but "one" doesn't? Why does "tough" end in an "f" sound, but "though" doesn't? Why does "though" rhyme with "toe," but "bough" rhymes with "cow?"

Eventually, they figure that all out, and read words together in sentences, paragraphs, pages, chapters, and books. To the child who struggles through *Danny and the Dinosaur*, a book like *The Princess Bride* is incomprehensibly complex. To the few people in the world who have read and understood *The Complete Works of James Joyce,*[12] Stephen King's *The Stand* may be mind-numbingly simple. Simplicity in literature comes in layers.

Simplicity in innovation is no different.

So this book comes in layers, too. Figure 2 shows those layers visually. The first chapter is the innermost core. The basics of simple innovation. The next layer out is the innovation engine – three systems that are necessary to drive

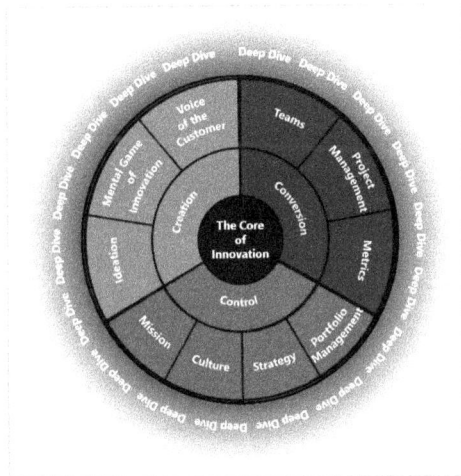

Figure 2: The layers of innovation simplicity in this book.

[12] I considered writing this in stream-of-consciousness style, but I was afraid that it might get censored on the ground that it might cause American readers to have irreverent and innovative thoughts. If this was the eBook version, you could click on that sentence to see that it is a play on the words of the ruling that censored James Joyce's Ulysses. If you really want to see that, get online and go to http://www.nytimes.com/books/00/01/09/specials/joyce-court.html?_r=2

innovation in an organization. The next layer out breaks those systems into their components. That's where the bulk of this book will focus, and where the simple tools that you can use in your organization can be found.

There are layers beyond those components – the deep-dive specifics, where each component can be explored in finer detail, broken into further and further components. Believe it or not, some of the beta-version feedback I got was that I should cover more topics – things like intellectual property, new product launch marketing, recruiting and retaining innovative talent, design for manufacturing, social media research, crossing Geoffrey Moore's chasm, product lifecycle management, customer experience...

Those are indeed important topics in the end-to-end innovation process. That layer, though, is beyond the scope of this book. However, the links and citations scattered throughout the text, especially in all of the footnotes, should enable you to venture into that layer, if you desire. Just make sure that you and your organization have mastery of the outermost layer of this book first, or people may find the deep dive information to be as incomprehensible as the Riemann hypothesis.

Simplicity in innovation will come for your organization when everyone in it is operating with a common understanding of how innovation works: who does what, when, why, and how. Simplicity means that everyone 'gets it.' Simplicity means that no one is *Lost*,[13] wondering why there is a polar bear and a smoke monster on a tropical island.

When the choir is singing out of the same songbook, the music is simply beautiful. But when one person is singing from one songbook, another is singing the latest pop tune being overplayed on Top 40 radio, and another is whistling the original *Mario Brothers* video game with the midi music that you can't forget[14] (no matter how many times you hit your head with a mallet), the combined "music" becomes ear-stabbing noise.

---

[13] The eBook hyperlinks here to a quick synopsis of the uniquely bizarre TV show *Lost*. If you want to see it, get online and go to https://www.youtube.com/watch?v=X0vG5FAnXzs

[14] The eBook lets you click to hear that music. If you want to hear it, get online and go to https://www.youtube.com/watch?v=c7xnsNFN4Ts. Be warned: once this music is in your head, it's awfully hard to get out.

And finally, I've tried to fill your innovation toolbox with enough tools for your people to be solid builders of an innovative organization. These are actual tools that you can use on your job, the day after you've read about them. Heck, if you are ambitious, maybe even the same day that you've read about them.

There are dozens of individual tools and guides to help you in all facets of innovation. There are scores of pictures to help capture the essence of the concepts. There are hundreds of hyperlinks to further explanations, supporting research, clarifying comments, or illustrative videos.

If you have a metaphorical construction problem, this book offers a metaphorical tool to address it. If you have a nail problem, this book offers a hammer. If you have a screw problem, this book offers a set of screwdrivers. If you have a nuts-n-bolts problem, this book offers wrenches and pliers. And saws, and files, and clamps, and...

You get the idea. If there is ever a question you have about any of the tools, just reach out to me at www.3point14Innovation.com/contactus/.

Why Read this Book?

You are investing your time – a resource you can never get back – in reading this book. I hope to give you two things in return: an enjoyable reading experience, and some memorable stuff that you can actually use in your business, charity, association, family, club, or whatever other organization of people that is important to you.

What would it be worth to double your success rate at getting new goods and services to your clients or customers? What would it be worth to cut in half the resources required to get a new project launched successfully? What would it be worth if you could get projects completed in 40% less time?

Those are not just made-up fantasy numbers, by the way. Those are the differences between the performance of the best innovators and the rest.[15] Those are the differences between organizations that embrace the evidence-based practices presented in this book and those that don't.

---

[15] Stephen K. Markham and Hyunjung Lee, "Product Development and Management Association's 2012 Comparative Performance Assessment Study," *Journal of Product Innovation Management*, May 2013.

If you are running a non-profit, how many more people could you serve? How much more financial backing could you get by promising better bang-for-the-donated-buck? How many more volunteers could you get, or how much more volunteer satisfaction could you deliver? How much closer could you get toward achieving the mission that got you into the social sector in the first place? These principles are not confined to business. They apply to any organization, and they work especially well for organizations with a mission.

If you are running a for-profit business, how much more profit could you earn? How much more market share could you gain? How much more would you be able to invest in growth? How much would your cash flow improve? How much closer could you get toward achieving the mission that got you into business in the first place?

Hopefully, whatever you get from these principles will be a substantial return on your reading investment.

What makes this book different from all the others that you could choose to read on the topic of innovation?

Something essential is missing from many of the innovation books that are out there: while all sorts of suggestions and theories and proposals are made, few are grounded in any sort of real, objective analysis.[16] They are long on advice and short on evidence. This book will not follow that path. It will not be the "all-new revolutionary super-cool way of doing things." That's on purpose. The practices I espouse have actual evidence of being effective, from robust, objective, academic research.

As a decades-long student and practitioner of new product development and organizational innovation, I've learned encyclopedias full of knowledge about what works and what doesn't when it comes to making innovation happen. Don't misunderstand that as bragging – as much, if not more, has been learned from failure as from success.

I have had the great fortune of learning from some of the brightest minds in the field. I have a couple of decades of corporate practice, launching hundreds of products in a variety of industries, from consumer packaged

---

[16] Mary M. Crossan and Marina Apaydin, "A Multi-Dimensional Framework of Organizational Innovation: A Systematic Review of the Literature," *Journal of Management Studies*, September 2010.

goods, to B2B industrial products, to social welfare nonprofit services. I've had the chance to serve as Executive Director of the Product Development and Management Association (PDMA) and to become one of the founding members of the International Association of Innovation Professionals (IAOIP). I have been immersed in the thought leadership of people who have written the seminal works in, and founded the practice of, innovation research.

This book is as much a product of their work as it is of mine. I intend to share some of the most critical nuggets of wisdom that I've learned from them, mixed with a helping of personal experience, a side of illustrative stories, and a dash of illuminating humor, to make those nuggets accessible and relevant. What I've done with this book is to share the most important general principles that will enhance the return on your innovation investment. The trick for you will be to figure out how those general principles apply to your organization. To help you in that effort, I'll share some self-assessments for you to ask about your organization, and to keep in the back of your mind as you read.

As a result, you will be better able to deliver what your customers need and want.

Why Did I Write this Book?

I won't lie to you. I love to write. Always have. So that's my selfish motivation for writing this book.

However, I could have worked on a variety of other topics. And not just business topics.[17] The thing is, innovation is important to me. It's been my professional life. For society, innovation drives economic growth, standards of living, job creation, and other social benefits.[18] For organizations, innovation

---

[17] I've had it in my mind to write and illustrate a story I told my baby sister one night, decades ago. Maybe you're thinking "Brad, a children's book is definitely more fitting of your intellect." You may be right.

[18] Nathan Rosenberg, "Innovation and Economic Growth," OECD Centre for Entrepreneurship, 2004.

drives longevity and performance.[19] For individuals, innovation is meaningful and fun.[20]

None of the general principles of innovation are really all that new. It's just that some organizations live those principles, and become magazine-cover worthy innovators, while other organizations just talk about innovation without actually adapting innovative behaviors.

So the question hit me: why do so few organizations actually want to innovate?

Most organizations say they want innovation, but when it comes right down to it, they don't want to *innovate*. They don't want to do the doing. They apparently want innovation to fall in their laps – and wallets – without having to change their approach to business.

Why is that?

Here are the answers I came up with:

1) **They don't know what innovation really is.** They just follow the thinking of US Supreme Court Justice Potter Stewart's thinking on pornography: I'll know it when I see it.[21]

   This challenge will be addressed in "The Whole Book in One Simple Chapter" chapter. Whether you agree with my definition of innovation or not, it will at least start us on common ground.

2) **They don't know how to go about innovating.** They think it is something that just happens, when some creative person has a "eureka!" moment. They think that "innovation management" is just as self-contradictory as "jumbo shrimp" or "Congressional ethics."

---

[19] Ming Piao, "Thriving in the New: Implication of Exploration on Organizational Longevity," *Journal of Management*, November 2010.

[20] At least it should be fun. Look at places like IDEO, Zappos, Threadless...those people are having fun. Unfortunately, for reasons beyond my understanding, many organizations and many managers seem to believe that work wasn't meant to be fun. They think that if anyone is having fun, they must not be working. What a shame. Fight the power!

[21] Referring, of course, to Justice Stewart's famous (or, perhaps, infamous) concurring opinion in *Jacobellis v. Ohio*, 378 U.S. 184 (1964), and does not imply that he actually participated in pornographic activities. Eww.

That may sound like a harsh indictment of businesspeople, but a 2010 McKinsey Global Survey showed that 75% of organizations lack a very formalized process for getting their innovations commercialized.[22] That's 75% who are making it up as they go along.

This challenge will be addressed in the chapters on strategy, portfolio management, voice of the customer, ideation, project management, and metrics.

3) **They don't know how to rally the troops to innovate.** There is plenty of innovation talk, but not a lot of innovation walk. That same 2010 McKinsey study found that over 70% of organizations fail to effectively set formal priorities for innovation.

When something is not formally prioritized, it may as well not exist. All the things that are formally prioritized will eat all the food, drink all the water, and breathe all the oxygen within the organization. Leaders must provide the setting, the means, the direction, and the reason for innovation. Formally. As a priority.

That challenge will be addressed in the sections on mission, culture, the minds of innovators, and teams.

4) **Change is hard.** Few people enjoy doing stuff that is difficult to do. Those who have tried to go on a diet, pick up an exercise program, maintain a New Year resolution, quit smoking, or floss their teeth regularly can probably relate to this. Even those who are successful at dropping bad habits and picking up good habits will tell you that it ain't easy.

Change management will be discussed in the chapter on "Engine Oil."

5) **When it comes right down to it, they simply don't value innovation.**

There isn't much anyone can do to help with this one. If you see no reason to change (or have a compelling reason not to change), if you have no desire to engage in creative problem solving, if you just

---

[22] "Innovation and commercialization, 2010: McKinsey Global Survey results, August 2010." Can be found online at
http://www.mckinsey.com/insights/innovation/innovation_and_commercialization_2010_mckinsey_global_survey_results

want today to be exactly like yesterday and tomorrow to be exactly like today, then this book is not for you. Thanks for reading this far, though!

What Was I Thinking?

Since this is a book about innovation, I need to try to be at least a little innovative with it. So before you jump in and wonder what the heck is wrong with the author, let me explain a few points that I had in mind as I wrote.

First, as you may have surmised from the title on the cover, I believe in simple. Stanford professor Kathleen Eisenhardt and MIT Sloan professor Donald Sull agree: "How can people manage the complexity of the modern world? Our answer, grounded in research and real-world results, is that simple rules tame complexity better than complex solutions."[23]

I'll present a variety of tools and techniques that you can apply to your innovation work immediately. These tools are intentionally made simple. I believe that if you need a 586-page training manual to figure out how to use a single tool, that tool is destined to be a dust collector. I want to give you tools that you might actually use. You can always get more complicated later.

Figure 3: Meet Simpleton. Simpleton and friends will be illustrating many of the principles presented in this book. It doesn't get much simpler than a round head, limbs, eyes, and a mouth.

Second, in addition to simple, I believe in comedy. Let me say that if you are looking for a book written like a congressional budget report or a helicopter technical manual, I sincerely hope that you find this book NOT to be for you.

Even if you're trying to do innovation for dog toothpaste, you should be having at least a little fun. While I present information that comes, as much as

---

[23] Kathleen Eisenhardt and Donald Sull, *Simple Rules: How to Thrive in a Complex World,* Houghton Mifflin Harcourt, 2015.

possible, from rigorous academic research, please be ready for me to do so with a dash of energy and a smidge of humor.

While this isn't intended to be *Dave Barry Goofs on Innovation*,[24] I believe that a thin veneer of levity on the solid structure of academic business research will be the spoonful of comedic sugar that helps the business lesson medicine go down (to thoroughly mix my metaphors). Humor helps to make the information more memorable, and it can give you insights on the truth better than any set of facts can. That's why the Onion News Network[25] is by far "America's Finest News Source" – the most truthful, if not the most factual, news source around.

Figure 4: Why so serious? Innovation is fun...lighten up.

My hope here is to address a need mentioned by Constantinos Markides of the London Business School,[26] who argues that there is a growing gap between what academics are learning through their research, and what actual business managers know and do. The research is rich, and valuable, and relevant, but it's not being used. It's not being transformed into better doing.

Why would that be? Well, if you've ever tried to read an academic article in a peer-reviewed journal, you know that it can be a daunting task. So much paper space is spent on explaining methodologies, data collection procedures, and statistical analyses that by the time a practitioner gets to any information they can really use, their retinas have detached and hung up a "gone fishing" sign in their brains.

Note to all of my academic friends: that was NOT a criticism of your work. On the contrary, I am THRILLED that you can and do follow-through on all of

---

[24] No, that's not a real book. I just made it up. Sorry to disappoint you.

[25] If you don't know The Onion, you can check it out at http://www.theonion.com/. Some say it's satire. Some find it offensive. I say it's funny because it's true.

[26] Constantinos Markides, "Crossing the Chasm: How to Convert Relevant Research into Managerially Useful Research," *The Journal of Applied Behavioral Science*, January 2011.

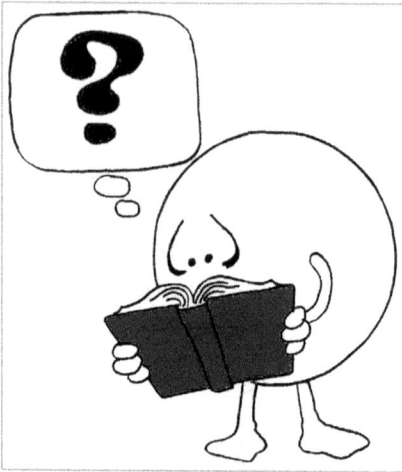

Figure 5: Wait, is that supposed to be funny?

those details, and publish them to the world for critical review. It takes guts and brains beyond what most people appreciate. You stand up before hundreds of your peers and have to prove your point beyond their focused intellectual skepticism, justifying details like why you used a Niedermeyer transformation to calculate the tangent of the Lumbergh curve.[27] I could never do that. That's why I went the practitioner-who-reads-and-learns-from-your-work route.

And as a practitioner, I know that the days of people in the business world are filled with a whole lot of work besides keeping up-to-date on innovation research. Like filling out TPS reports with the right cover sheets,[28] or paying attention to the WENUS[29] while doing a data reconfiguration.[30] You simply don't have time left over to wade through the calculus swamp within academic journal articles.

That's where this book comes in.

You see, I want you to actually read this. There's good stuff in here that just may help you to do things better, make dazzling new products, and save the world with your creations. The least I can do is to write it in a way that you actually *want* to read it.

---

[27] To my knowledge, there are no such things as Niedermeyer transformations and Lumbergh curves. If you'd like to discuss real statistical analysis tools, you'll have to talk to a real academic. I'm not a real academic, I just play one in books.

[28] In the eBook, this links to the foundational scene of Office Space, another fine example of funny-because-it's-true. https://www.youtube.com/watch?v=Fy3rjQGc6lA

[29] In the eBook, this links to a scene with Chandler Bing of *Friends* discussing the nature of his job. https://www.youtube.com/watch?v=o91oclUZr9g

[30] Thanks go out to the writers of *Office Space* and *Friends* for these all-too-close-to-reality creations.

Oh yeah. If the text itself doesn't deliver any entertainment value, there may be a few "Easter eggs" mixed into the footnotes with serious journal citations to give you some occasional comic relief.

Third, this book is not necessarily intended to be read from beginning to end. It kinda starts in the middle, and lets you work your way outward from there. In this hardcopy version, you'll have to do that manually, but I'll try to make that as easy as possible. In the digital format, you can quickly shift from topic to topic, simply clicking to where you want to go.

I'm not arrogant enough[31] to think that every single word I write will be of benefit to every single reader. You can navigate your way through this book the way that is most interesting, most valuable, most timely, or most whatever-is-important-to-you.

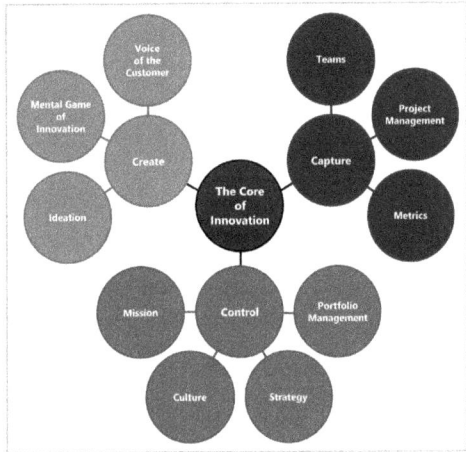

Figure 6: How the book is organized.

Of course, if you want to read it from end-to-end, you are welcome to do so. I promise, I won't complain.

Fourth, I like analogies and metaphors. I think a good analogy can serve to enlighten and enhance understanding, by relating the unfamiliar to the familiar. There is a good deal of research suggesting that we humans learn by building on what we already know.

I recognize, however, that analogies have their limits. No analogy is perfect.

One of my favorite analogies is about the learning process. When you start learning something new, the information can come at you faster than you can take it all in. It can be overwhelming. People often refer to that as "drinking from a fire hose."

While I've never actually tried to consume water from a fire hose, the visceral feeling I get from imagining the experience really captures that feeling of being overwhelmed. It illustrates the reality so much better than "the

---

[31] Close, maybe, but not quite.

information comes faster than you can take it all in." Therefore, I will frequently use such analogies to give you a better feeling for the point.

If you find yourself reading one of my attempts at enlightening metaphor, and you say to yourself, "well, Brad, that's not entirely

Figure 7: If you are new to innovation, this book might feel like drinking from a fire hose.

accurate, because this is different than that in thus and such a way..." do us both a favor, and just let it go. This is a book, after all, and I can't actually have a discussion with you on the point.

I realize that analogies have their limitations. But if you really push me on this, I'll just throw out a couple of quotes from the great statistician George E. P. Box, who said, "Just as the ability to devise simple but evocative models is the signature of the great scientist, so overelaboration and over-parameterization is often the mark of mediocrity." He also said, "Essentially, all models are wrong, but some are useful." There. That oughta put you doubters in your place.

Yes, all of my analogies are imperfect and wrong in some detail or another, but I hope that they prove to be useful in conveying some nugget of value.

Fifth, this is just an overview of the innovation process. Well, maybe a little more than that. If the body of innovation knowledge is a pool, then consider this the shallow end, deeper than the baby wading pool, but not SCUBA certification depth.

In trying to cover the whole end-to-end process of innovation in a single volume, we can't go much deeper. I look on my bookshelf, and I have yards of space taken up by various books on innovation, from grand overview handbooks to highly specific, in-depth topical discussions. There is no way to do a deep dive into all topics, and still make the book readable. Keeping it simple is the theme, after all.

Finally, keep in mind that I wrote this book at a moment in time. Reality, however, is a constantly flowing stream of change. Therefore, if it is to be effective for the long haul, this will need to be a living document. I'm always diving into the academic literature, looking for discoveries that make me say "holy myth-busting, Batman, that's amazing!" Yeah, I'm a nerd, I get it. But that's what I like to do. Then I like to share that information with people who can use it. So this book will be linked to the Pi Innovation website, www.3point14Innovation.com.[32] That way, I can keep the information fresh, and up-to-date. I hate the smell of information that's been in the fridge past its expiration date.

One terminology note: I may slip into using "innovation" and "product development" interchangeably. That may annoy those of you who think of innovation in terms beyond just creating new goods and services to be sold to customers. I happen to agree with you folks (about the scope of innovation, not about the annoyance). Innovation isn't just about making the next nifty widget for which people will camp overnight, just to say they bought it before any of their friends could.

Innovation, as I define it,[33] involves creating something to serve somebody. That could be a physical thing, sure, but it could also be an intangible thing, like a method, a process, or a system. Such methods, processes, and systems can be treated as "products," and can be pursued in the same framework of principles that I describe for goods and services. If I seem to interchange innovation and product development sometimes, that's why.

Do I Have a Foot(note) Fetish?

A note about all of the footnotes. There are hundreds of 'em.

If you are frustrated by having so many distracting digressions, rest assured that the author was duly punished by the work required to write out all of the various citations and URLs.

Many of the footnotes in this book are just jokes, entertaining asides, links to classic TV videos, or *Star Trek* references. Read them at your own peril.

Most, however, are citations to various research works in the field of innovation, cognitive science, psychology, business management, etc. If you

---

[32] For the non-mathematically inclined, 3.14 ≈ π, so 3point14Innovation is Pi Innovation...you get a math lesson with every click. Just kidding.

[33] For the definition of innovation used in this book, go to the "What the #&%! Is Innovation, Anyway" section, page 4.

are a stickler for the formatting of citations, I'm just going to say this: please forgive me in advance.

I tried to be consistent, but not all[34] of the citations of various sources in the literature conform to a generally accepted single preferred citation format. Frankly, such things are irrelevant to me, and the energy required to get everything "right" far exceeds what I perceive to be the resulting value. My cost-benefit analysis was approximately as negative as the state budget of Illinois.[35] This book would never pass Academic Journal or Doctoral Dissertation standards in the citation formatting department.

My citations have two purposes: 1) to demonstrate that I'm not making this stuff up, and 2) to avoid accusations of plagiarism. I learned this stuff from pretty smart people, and I believe in giving credit where credit is due. I also want to give you sufficient information to look up the source material, so that you can reach your own conclusions on whether my points are valid. In fact, most references have hyperlinks that send you right to the material online.

That's it. Those are my only reasons for the citations.

Here's an example to illustrate my utter lack of concern for citation formatting:[36]

- Adams, Ansel, <u>Ansel Adams, an Autobiography</u>. Boston : Little, Brown, 1985.
- Ansel Adams, *Ansel Adams: An Autobiography* (Boston: Little Brown and Company, 1985).
- Adams, Ansel. *Ansel Adams: An Autobiography*. Boston: Little Brown and Company. 1985
- Ansel Adams, *Ansel Adams: An Autobiography*, Little Brown and Company, 1985

---

[34] Actually, none.

[35] It is possible that the only thing Illinois' state and local governments have more of than debt is corruption, but that's for an entirely different book – like this one: Thomas J. Gradel and Dick Simpson, *Corrupt Illinois: Patronage, Cronyism, and Criminality*, University of Illinois Press, February 2015. Hard to believe that "The Land of Lincoln" takes its nickname from someone whose nickname was "Honest Abe."

[36] The first three examples are a blatant cut-n-paste from the website http://users.library.fullerton.edu/cbruns/citationstyles.htm, which details proper use of APA Format, MLA Format and Chicago/Turabian Format. The bottom example is a format I just made up, so let's officially call it Barbera/Pi Format. I hope it catches on.

Do any one of them really offer you a better way to access the source material? If you believe so, please call me and explain why at 1-800-GET-OVER, ext. IT.

Just kidding. I don't even have voice mail on that line.

How Can You Best Use This Book?

Because this book was written from the inside out, you can use it in a variety of ways to meet your needs. Whether you want to read it cover-to-cover for its shear entertainment value, or you'd rather use it as a pick-n-choose innovation reference, or you need to find a good product development joke, you can leverage the format and the built-in links to do it your way.

Some possible approaches:

Method One: Just read it straight through.

Duh. It is a book after all.

Method Two: Read it as if you were a pinball in the rock opera *Tommy*.[37]

Anytime you want to switch subjects, just go back to the Table of Contents and go where you want to go. Many footnotes suggest where you can find information related to what you are reading.

The eBook does this with a variety of hyperlinks, but the paper here just won't cooperate with that.

Method Three: Get the main points quickly, get details later.

Each section of this book starts with a "Simple Summary" that captures the key ideas of the section in a succinct set of bullet points. You'll come away with the important themes, just without all the subtle nuances of deep insight, and all those uproarious comedic comments that illustrate those points so memorably. Or something like that.

Method Four: Really study it with the intent to internalize it.

In addition to the "Simple Summary," each section has a "Simple Self-Assessment," with a set of questions to get you thinking about how your

---

[37] The eBook has a link here to Elton John at his flamboyant best, performing "Pinball Wizard." https://www.youtube.com/watch?v=EK33CY68s1w

organization's innovation engine is currently functioning. Keep those questions in mind as you read. Research in learning[38] has shown that one of the best ways to learn (and possibly *the* best way) is to test yourself. So ask yourself these questions, think about potential answers, then read on and see what the text says. At the end of the section, some study guide questions are available to aid further reflection and retention.

You can also come up with your own questions before reading the section, and then look for answers as you read. Hey, if the answers aren't there, give me a shout. Let me know what the questions are, and I'll either guide you to where the answers can be found in the book, or research an answer for you and give you credit in the second edition (after I give you the inside exclusive, first).

If you are intent on really absorbing this material, repeated testing will make a big difference over just reading, highlighting, and writing comments in the margin. And keep in mind that if you are reading this on a digital screen of some sort, those margin comments wreak havoc on the resale value of your device.

Method Five: However you darn well please.

Enjoy! Let me know what you think.[39]

Wishing you many happy innovations,

BRAD BARBERA

Founder and Principal
Pi Innovation LLC
Oh yeah – author of this book, too

---

[38] John Dunlosky, Katherine A. Rawson, Elizabeth J. Marsh, Mitchell J. Nathan, and Daniel T. Willingham, "Improving Students' Learning with Effective Learning Techniques: Promising Directions from Cognitive and Educational Psychology," *Psychological Science in the Public Interest*, .

[39] In the eBook, a click takes you right to the end of the book, where there are links to providing online feedback. You can flip to the "Help Me to Help You" section (page 427) at the end to see how to get ahold of my ear and tell me what you really think.

THE WHOLE DARN BOOK IN ONE SIMPLE CHAPTER (The Core of Innovation)

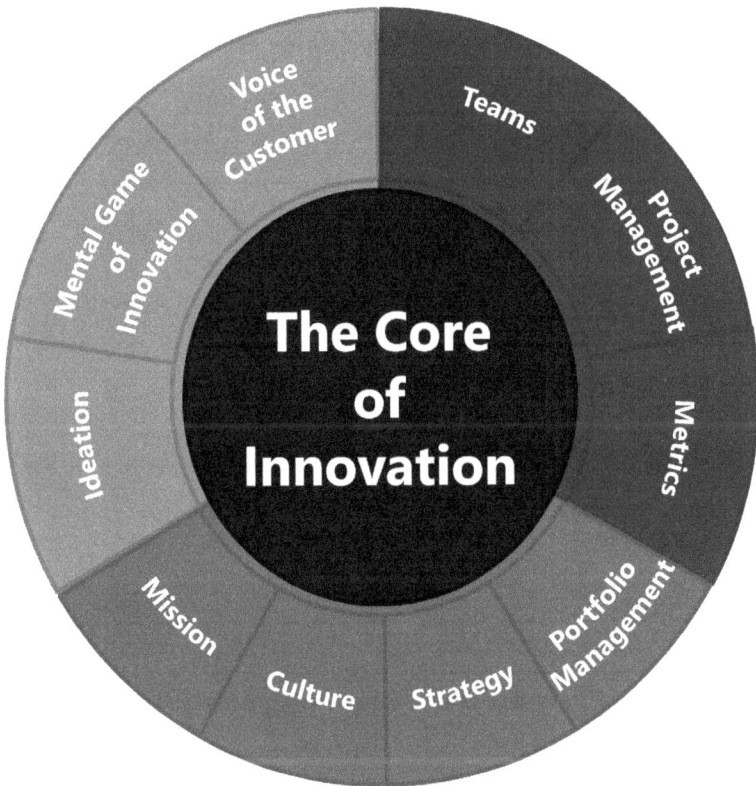

Simple Self-Assessment – The Core

Rate yourself on the following questions. To benchmark yourself against others, go to www.3point14Innovation.com and click the "Self-Assessments" menu.

- **How innovative would you say that your organization is?**

  Innovation? What's That?

  We are "Captain Innovation" in our industry

1	2	3	4	5	6	7	8	9	10

- **Does everyone in your organization agree about what "innovation" means?**

  Nobody has a clue

  Everybody shares a common definition

1	2	3	4	5	6	7	8	9	10

- **How aware is your organization of research into effective innovation?**

  There is such a thing?

  Not just aware...we live 'em

1	2	3	4	5	6	7	8	9	10

- **How up-to-date are your innovation practices?**

  Neanderthal

  Ahead of our time

1	2	3	4	5	6	7	8	9	10

- **How collaborative are the different functions in your organization?**

  Silos that never speak to each other

  A well-oiled collaboration machine

1	2	3	4	5	6	7	8	9	10

- **How clearly defined are your innovation processes?**

  "Throw-against the wall and see what sticks"

  Clearly defined and documented

1	2	3	4	5	6	7	8	9	10

- **How well do you actually follow the defined processes?**

  We always follow it to the letter

  Follow what?

1	2	3	4	5	6	7	8	9	10

Simple Summary – Core of Innovation

Key take-aways you should get out of this section:

- Innovation – done right – drives progress: improved standards of living, quality, and quantity of life; organizational longevity and performance.
- Innovation occurs at the intersection of creativity/novelty, significance/value, and execution/reality.
- "Best practices," has become a cliché, overused and trite. Moreover, what is best for one organization is not necessarily best for another.
- What you need are fundamental guiding principles. Principles with the weight of evidence behind them. Such evidence-based practices are not simply activities that work under specific conditions, in specific industries, at specific times, but rather they can work anywhere, anytime.
- Evidence-based practices are not one-size-fits-all prescriptives, nor are they suggestions for mere imitation. Your job is to understand the principles so that you can apply them to your specific circumstances, and then derive your specific solutions.
- These are principles for innovation that, if you follow them, will help you and your organization deliver more successful innovations, more often.
- Manage your expectations. Evidence-based practices do not promise innovation utopia. *Such a place does not exist.* Practicing innovation is inherently risky. Risk means the possibility – the necessity – of failure. These practices will help you succeed more often, with higher rewards, but will not guarantee success at all times, everywhere.
- It bears repeating: these generally applicable principles must be applied to your specific industry, culture, and capabilities to define the specific systems for your organization. Simply doing what someone else did will not help if it doesn't fit your organization.
- This book uses the "innovation engine" model instead of the classic "innovation funnel" model. Innovation is an intentional act of the innovator, not a passive thing that just happens. The engine model captures the variety of components that must work together to drive innovation forward. The engine model also captures the variety of forms that engines can take to meet the particular needs of the work at hand.

The Whole Book in 10 Bullet Points

These are the simple things you need to do to innovate effectively:

- Align everyone in your organization to a common goal and means of achieving it.
- Understand the people that your organization is trying to serve.
- Solve their problems in new and better ways that you are capable of delivering.
- Understand the people in your organization and how they think.
- Organize your people and processes to make it easy for them to create value.
- Do the best you can with what you've got – don't settle for less, don't demand more.
- Communicate clearly and effectively to all of your stakeholders.
- Don't expect innovation to just happen – it will always be a risky, difficult endeavor.
- Measure the important things that will get you to your goal.
- Change is hard. Even beneficial change. Know how to make it happen. Never stop doing the hard work of changing for the better.

There. It doesn't get much simpler than that, right?

What the #&%! is Innovation, Anyway?

So let's talk about the core topic of this book. What exactly is innovation?

You may be thinking, "Seriously? Do we really have to spend time on that? I know what innovation is!" Well, consider this from an article in *MIT Sloan Magazine*:

> "Faced with slow growth, commoditization and global competition, many CEOs view innovation as critical to corporate success. William Ford Jr., chairman and CEO of Ford Motor Co., recently announced that, '[f]rom this point onward, innovation will be the compass by which the company sets its direction' and that Ford 'will adopt innovation as its core business strategy going forward.' Echoing those comments,

Jeffrey Immelt, chairman and CEO of General Electric Co., has talked about the 'Innovation Imperative,' a belief that innovation is central to the success of a company and the only reason to invest in its future. Thus GE is pursuing around 100 'imagination breakthrough' projects to drive growth though innovation. And Steve Ballmer, Microsoft Corp.'s CEO, stated recently that 'innovation is the only way that Microsoft can keep customers happy and competitors at bay.'"[40]

Then the next paragraph begins with the disconcerting question, "But what exactly is innovation?"

How is it that such modern captains of industry can all be talking about the critical importance of innovation, if we aren't even sure what innovation is?

I get the sense that the business leaders and media pundits of the world aren't all talking about the same thing when they say that word. And the products and services they keep churning out as their "innovations" make me question what they mean, too.

So, before embarking on a journey into the principles of innovation, we should probably establish what innovation is. Let's start where any reasonable person starts when looking for a definition. The dictionary.

The Mirriam-Webster Online Dictionary defines innovation thusly:

Innovation *noun* in·no·va·tion \ˌi-nə-ˈvā-shən\
    1: the introduction of something new
    2: a new idea, method, or device; novelty

When I dug that definition up, I noticed a heading called "Rhymes with Innovation." It cited such words as "abdication," "aberration," "abnegation," and "abrogation," all of which could be applied to whoever came up with this entirely unsatisfactory definition. Noah Webster should be turning over in his casket at that one.

Neither satisfying nor useful.

---

[40] Mohanbir Sawhney, Robert C. Wolcott and Inigo Arroniz, "The 12 Different Ways for Companies to Innovate," *MIT Sloan Management Review*, April 2006.

So I naturally went next to where we all go in the modern world when we need some knowledge. So what does the Google have to say? A search of "definition of innovation" returns about 250,000,000 results (in just 0.47 seconds – consider my mind blown). Readers, I love you and everything, but I just can't go through all quarter-billion pages for you. If you really want to know what they all say, you're just going to have to do that for yourselves.

Most of the satisfying definitions have a good deal of overlap, and vary only by some wordsmithing and nuance. Rather than try to come up with some super definition that trumps all others, I'm going to give you what I see as the definition of innovation in a picture – saving you a thousand words worth of reading.

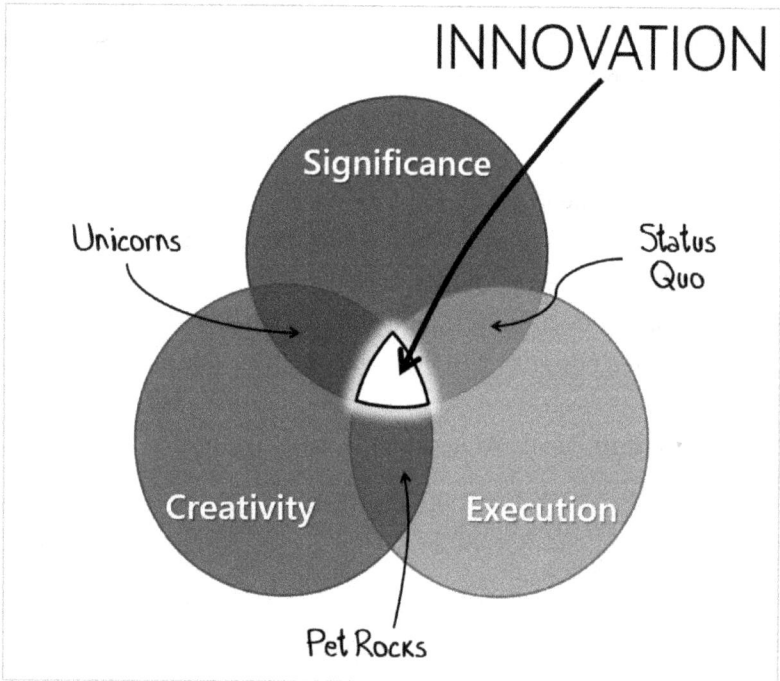

Figure 8: The definition of innovation according to the Pi Innovation picture dictionary

Real innovation comes at the intersection of three elements: creativity, significance, and execution. Or call them "novelty," "value," and "reality." Or use "new and different," "problem solving," and "implementation." I suppose there are many ways to express the general meaning of those three circles. That is why I didn't wordsmith a pithy little definition. Whatever words you choose to describe it, just remember that innovation occurs where those three things all come together.

If any one of those three elements is missing, it's not innovation.

Creativity is the most recognized element of innovation for most people. Being creative and novel gives your product a competitive advantage. Even if it solves a problem for your customer in a way that they value, and you actually deliver it to them in the real world, without novelty, it's nothing more than the status quo. It's an existing commodity. It's not an innovation.[41]

Significance means that it makes a positive difference for someone. If it doesn't do something valuable for your customer (and, in turn, for you), it's also not an innovation. You can come up with a whacky, unique idea and make it into reality, but if it doesn't do something that people value, it's just a useless trinket, like a pet rock.[42] Okay, I'll concede that when they first came out, pet rocks were valued as gag gifts, but that ran its course quickly. Humankind has matured enough since then to recognize their utter lack of value. At least most of us have.

Finally, without the element of execution in the real world, in a way that people can actually experience the value provided, you've got nothing but a unicorn. It may be a fantastical, magical, wonderful concept, with the power to save the world, but if you can't make it into something that actually provides real value to your customers, it's just a fantasy. It is not an innovation.[43]

Innovation must have creativity, significance, and execution. All three.

---

[41] Not surprisingly, research demonstrates that novelty is indeed critically important to new product success and helps drive competitive advantage. See, for example, Subin Im, Mitzi M. Montoya, and John P. Workman Jr., "Antecedents and Consequences of Creativity in Product Innovation Teams," *Journal of Product Innovation Management*, January 2013.

[42] In fact, as Im, Montoya, and Workman point out: "New ideas may be perceived as simply weird or bizarre by the target audience if they are novel or unique but carry no meaning (i.e., the extent to which outputs are perceived as appropriate and useful by the targeted audience) ...novelty in and of itself may imply an unreliable or untrustworthy product." Thus, pet rocks. Note: I slightly rearranged the words to flow better here, but they are all in the paper and consistent with its meaning.

[43] Okay, so I don't have academic research saying that new products that are never executed don't succeed. I suppose they don't fail, either. I'm just going to take it as a statement of the obvious that if it doesn't exist, it can't do much. If you can prove me wrong on that, let me know.

Note also, in this definition, what innovation is not: it's not just about being high-tech. It's not just about generating patents. It's not just about being connected to the interweb. It's not just about coming up with the radical breakthrough that will change the world.

It's also not just about products that go up for sale. Business models can be innovations. The iPod was not just a gadget. It was a rethinking of how media can be distributed and enjoyed.

It's not just about things you sell to people outside your organization. Internal processes and systems can (and should!) be innovations. Finding a new and more efficient means of sharing information than changing the cover sheets on a TPS report (stapled with a red Swingline® stapler, of course) meets the criteria necessary for innovation.[44]

There are many ways to innovate. We can intuitively sense that a new-to-the-world product employing a new and unique technology and delivering market-changing value (like the world wide web) is different than an extension to an existing product set employing existing technology and adding only incremental value to the market (like adding rutabaga-kumquat to a line of iced tea flavors). Some innovations will land you a guest spot on the *Tonight Show*. Most will not. But they can all add value to the world, and that's not a bad thing.

Since the word innovation by itself covers a wide range of possibilities, let's break innovation down to a few types. As we do, though, let's be clear that there may not be clear lines distinguishing between them. That's okay. Just as the colors of a rainbow don't have clear lines distinguishing between them, we can still name all the colors after Roy G. Biv.[45]

---

[44] Thanks to the brilliant movie *Office Space* for illustrating the potential value of business process innovation so poignantly.

[45] In case your grade school science teacher didn't teach colors that way, Roy G. Biv is a mnemonic for red, orange, yellow, green, blue, indigo, and violet. Now you'll ace that colors-of-the-rainbow exam.

There is no single means of classifying innovations,[46] so I'll share how I like to think of it.[47] Once again, I'll define the terms with a picture, rather than getting bogged down in wordsmithing the perfect definitions. Just take a look at Figure 9.

An innovation can either apply a novel technology to a problem, introduce a novel solution to a market, or both.

Consider "the market" to be the people for whom you are doing the innovating, those who will derive value from it. This can be the market in the sense that most people think about it, where goods and services are exchanged for money. However, it need not be just external to the organization. Internal innovations can be just as valuable, so think of your internal customers as well.

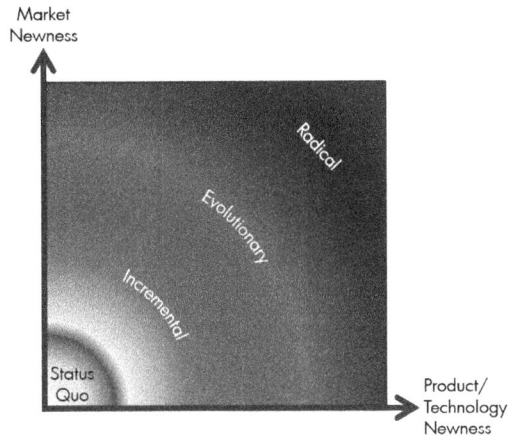

Figure 9: The categories of innovation according to the Pi Innovation picture dictionary

Fixing the way cover sheets are placed on TPS reports could be an innovation (incremental), or replacing TPS reports with direct mind-link devices among all employees would be an innovation (radical...and dangerous...I don't want everyone knowing what I'm thinking in some of those meetings).

---

[46] Rosanna Garcia and Roger Calantone, "A critical look at technological innovation typology and innovativeness terminology: a literature review," *The Journal of Product Innovation Management*, September 2003. I'm glad someone is trying to narrow the number of definitions out there.

[47] I know I said I wouldn't just try to sell my own ideas, but there is research support for this. My classifications of "Incremental," "Evolutionary," and "Radical" roughly correspond to Garcia and Calantone's "Incremental," "Really New," and "Radical." I just don't like the term "really new," and I don't think the lines between them are quite as definitive as they strive to make them. They have a different purpose – academic research clarity and consistency. I'm just trying to keep the understanding and execution of innovation simple for the rest of us. Feel free to call the categories whatever seems meaningful to you and your organization. My feelings won't be hurt.

As for technology, don't think of it as just referring to digital-internet-electronic-computer-laser-quantum types of stuff. Technology simply means how something gets done. That will include digital-internet-electronic-computer-laser-quantum things, but it will also include seed-planting methods for farmers, ratchets on wrenches, and scissors for cutting pizza.[48]

For both market newness and technology newness, the degree of novelty falls on a continuum. It can be as small as changing a product color from black to red, yellow, and blue,[49] to as big as creating the industrial revolution with a practical steam engine.[50]

Incremental innovations involve small changes to existing products, with existing technologies, and within existing markets. The level of novelty is limited to enhancements, feature additions, and the like. Examples could include a cost reduction by switching to a new and improved component supplier, bundling existing services together into a new single offering, or adding a pumpkin spice fragrance to a line of men's deodorant.[51]

Evolutionary innovation involves breaking into a new market, or leveraging a new technology. The Sony Walkman, for example, created a new market with an existing technology by making that technology portable. The Canon LaserJet leveraged a new ink application technology in the existing paper printer market.[52]

Radical innovation involves both new markets and new technologies. The steam engine. The internet. The warp engine, replicator, and transporter that

---

[48] No, really. https://dreamfarm.com/us/scizza/

[49] The only time this was a big innovation was when General Motors teamed up with DuPont to make inexpensive colored cars a reality, and taking market leadership from slow-reacting Henry "any customer can have a car painted any color that he wants so long as it is black" Ford. Yes, even the great innovators have blind spots.

[50] In the information age, we tend to forget about such life-altering events from past centuries. Fortunately, there are historians who appreciate and can tell a good historic story. Check out William Rosen, *The Most Powerful Idea in the World: A Story of Steam, Industry, and Invention*, University of Chicago Press, 2012.

[51] I've always wanted my pits to smell like Starbucks in the fall. Not really. Just a comedy joke.

[52] Both examples were taken from Garcia and Calantone, "A critical look at technological innovation typology and innovativeness terminology: a literature review," *The Journal of Product Innovation Management*, September 2003.

haven't been invented yet, but soon will be according to Gene Roddenberry's team.[53]

I won't be using the very popular term "disruptive" to classify innovation. Why not? After all, it's a very popular word in the popular press. Did I mention that it's popular?

The problem with talking about "disruption" and "disruptive innovation" is that there is a conflict between the narrow definition of Clay Christensen in *The Innovator's Dilemma*, *The Innovators Solution*, and *Seeing What's Next*, and what the average ordinary mortal business person means by disruption. In the former sense, a particular innovation must fit a specific set of criteria to be considered disruptive,[54] and not all dramatic, industry-altering innovations fit those criteria. In the latter sense, pretty much anytime a businessperson feels blind-sided by a competitive move that they failed to foresee, they consider themselves disrupted.[55]

Don't get me wrong. The concept of disruptive innovation (under the narrow academic definition) is important. I'm not dismissing it. I'm just going to declare it beyond the scope of this book to discuss in detail. For now, just understand that "disruptive" in the Christensen sense is not the same thing as

---

[53] Less than fifty years to go, unless the Borg successfully travel back to our time and assimilate us all.

[54] Those characteristics are: "(1) the innovation initially underperforms on the attributes mainstream customers value; (2) the new features offered by the innovation are not valued by the mainstream customers; (3) the innovation typically is more simple and cheaper and is offered at a lower price than existing products; (4) at the time of its introduction, the innovation appeals to a low-end, price-sensitive customer segment, thus limiting the profit potential for incumbents; and (5) over time, further developments improve the innovation's performance on the attributes mainstream customers value to a level where the innovation begins to attract more of these customers." Courtesy of Vijay Govindarajan and Praveen K. Kopalle, "The Usefulness of Measuring Disruptiveness of Innovations Ex Post in Making Ex Ante Predictions," *Journal of Product Innovation Management*, January 2006.

[55] This is not just sarcasm on my part. As Erwin Danneels says in "Disruptive Technology Reconsidered: A Critique and Research Agenda," *Journal of Product Innovation Management*, July 2004, "A question that remains is whether a technology is inherently disruptive or if 'disruptiveness' is a function of the perspective of the companies subject to it." That's academic-ese for "if someone hands you your lunch in the marketplace, you will say you've been disrupted." And almost two decades after Christensen introduced his concept of disruptive innovation, articles in *Harvard Business Review* continue to argue whether innovations are disruptive (see, for example, "Tesla's Not as Disruptive as You Might Think," May 2015). Clearly, I'm not going to resolve the issue in this book.

"radical," "breakthrough," "revolutionary," or any other word that you chose to use for that third category.

Innovation is NOT an Expense

There's one other component in the definition of innovation that I haven't yet mentioned. Innovation is an investment. It is *not* an expense. If you see me at a cocktail party, don't get me started on how annoying it is that most innovation expenditures are treated by generally accepted accounting principles as expenses. It's one of my bigger professional pet peeves.

As I said, innovation is an investment. Like any investment, it is one that involves risk and uncertain payoff. The evidence-based practices discussed in this book will help you to do your innovation investing wisely.

Remember the financial market collapse of 2008? Although the causes of the collapse were numerous and complex, a significant contributor was too many people investing too much money in innovative but unproven financial instruments. When those instruments proved to be far riskier than believed, bad things happened.

Remember the dot.com tech bubble burst of 2001? Warren Buffet kept arguing for real, fundamental value investment, while the tech investors laughed at his outdated failure to recognize the "new economy.". But as the BBC reported right after the crash, "Warren Buffett took a pasting for ignoring the 1999 surge in dot.com stocks. Now he is enjoying the last laugh."[56]

The intent of this book is to help you invest in innovation like Warren Buffet, not like an innovation day trader.

If you think of innovation as an investment, then the investment advice you get in this book will not be to dump all of your money in the latest real estate derivatives, nor will I use a sock monkey to convince you to invest in Pets.com. Rather, I'm going to tell you to do the hard work of creating a diversified portfolio of investments that matches your risk profile and time horizon, using well-understood and proven investment strategies.

Think of it like this. Say you have $100,000 to invest. You could go to a roulette table in Vegas, put it all on double-zero, and hope for a $3,500,000

---

[56] BBC News World Edition Business, Tuesday, 13 March, 2001.

payout. And you just might get it...after all, it does happen 2.6% of the time. Of course, 97.4% of the time, you go home broke.

Alternatively, you could stick the money under the mattress. You may not get anything for it, but at least you won't lose it. Just stick with the status quo, and be safe. Take out a little at a time to pay a bill here and there, or to cover an unexpected rainy day expense. Until the day that you reach under the mattress, and find only enough loose change to buy yourself a can of pop at the local convenience store (or soda or coke, depending on what part of the world you're from).

Or, you could invest the money in anything from a simple savings account to precious metals to government bonds to corporate stocks. You could create a portfolio that aims at the return you need within an acceptable level of risk. You grow your returns, and over time, build something to retire on, so that you don't have to work as a Walmart greeter when you are 87 years old.

The same is true for innovation investments.

You could place your bet on that one big idea. After all, you just read the "How I Did It" issue of *Inc.* magazine, and that's how the new rich-and-famous entrepreneur did it. Unfortunately, you will likely find out the hard way that such hits don't happen very often. For every entrepreneur that made it big on their one great idea, there are fifty, a hundred, or five-hundred that ended up filling out grill master job applications at the local Burger Barn.

You could just keep doing what you and everyone else in your industry are already doing. It was successful before; why wouldn't it continue to be successful? You're good at it, so stick with it. Until, that is, better services and better products are offered by someone else, and your old reliable customers start lining up at that someone else's shop door.

Or, you could look into how to invest your innovation dollar wisely. Understand the investment principles that have been proven to work. Devote the time to figuring out how those enduring principles apply to your industry and to your organization. Make the investments that will ensure a return now and into the future, for you, for your investors, for your customers, for all the stakeholders involved.

The purpose of this book is to share the general principles and best practices of wise innovation investment, in a way that you can apply to your organization immediately. If you implement these principles, you will improve your innovation outcomes – success rates, returns on investment, customer satisfaction, revenue, profitability, mission fulfillment – whatever measures[57] are meaningful for you.

Will every effort be a home run? No. But you will win more ballgames, guaranteed.

Why the #&%! Should You Innovate?

If things like profitability, return on investment, return on assets, return on sales, topline sales, sales per employee, employment growth, EBITDA, market share, margins, and sustainable competitive advantage are important to you, then you should innovate. More innovative organizations deliver more of all of those things.[58] If you are a nonprofit, finding ways to innovate and adapt is critically important to delivering against your mission – and the financial soundness from metrics just mentioned will help sustain your organization to pursue its mission on into the future.[59]

Those are the visible benefits of innovation. Less obvious is the intangible value of having a reputation as an innovator. Companies that develop such a reputation have more loyal customers. They have customers that are more involved with and excited about the organization. And their customers are even more tolerant of their failures.[60]

Imagine that – the more innovative you are perceived to be, the more forgiving your customers are. Your innovation risk profile goes down as your innovation reputation goes up.

If you are a non-profit, don't think to yourself that you don't have "customers." You do. The people you help with your services are customers.

---

[57] For more on innovation metrics, go to the sections on "Innovation for Fun and Profit" (page 389) and "Innovation for Fun and Not-for-Profit" (page 403).

[58] Mary M. Crossan and Marina Apaydin, "A Multi-Dimensional Framework of Organizational Innovation: A Systematic Review of the Literature," *Journal of Management Studies*, September 2010.

[59] Mark H. Moore, "The Public Value Scorecard: A Rejoinder and an Alternative to 'Strategic Performance Measurement and Management in Non-Profit Organizations' by Robert Kaplan," Hauser Center for Nonprofit Organizations Working Paper No. 18, May 2003.

[60] David H. Henard and Peter A. Dacin, "Reputation for Product Innovation: Its Impact on Consumers," *Journal of Product Innovation Management,* 2010.

Your volunteers are customers. Your donors are customers. People of the community are customers.

Peter Drucker stated it well: "Because the purpose of business is to create a customer, the business enterprise has two – and only two – basic functions: marketing and innovation. Marketing and innovation produce results; all the rest are costs."[61] And don't let the "business" word make you think that it doesn't apply to nonprofits. It does.

In the time since Drucker wrote those words, the study and teaching of marketing took off, with practically every business school on the planet featuring extensive coursework on the subject. *US News and World Report* has been annually ranking which schools are best at teaching it. Meanwhile, "innovation," has almost been an afterthought. Perhaps it would get mentioned in one lecture of one of those marketing classes. For me, it was in a class on operations management.[62]

I wonder how many businesses would still be in operation if innovation had received equal attention in that time span.

Remember Blockbuster Video?[63] If you don't, the Onion News Network[64] can help you to relive history.

In just ten years, Blockbuster went from having 9000 outlets and dominating their market, to closing all of their stores and declaring bankruptcy.

---

[61] Peter Drucker, *The Practice of Management*, Harper Business Reissue Edition, 2006.

[62] Fortunately for me, my operations class was taught by Dr. Abbie Griffin, one of the renowned thought leaders and researchers in the field of product development and innovation. I owe a great deal to her, not only for teaching me then, but continuing to teach me much of what I know about the subject today. Thanks, Abbie!

[63] You probably do, since reading this book implies that you are old enough to have been around in the early 2000s, when Blockbuster Video stores were as ubiquitous as coffee shops and Burger Barns.

[64] The "news" network that comes closest to sharing the *truth*, even if not sharing any actual facts.

This dramatic fall of the mighty was largely due to lack of innovation in a changing marketplace. Blockbuster could have benefited from some innovation education.

That's any easy statement to make, of course, with the benefit of hindsight. It's easy to ridicule the strategic miscues made by Blockbuster's leadership. How could

Figure 10: Watch this ONN video at http://www.theonion.com/video/historic-blockbuster-store-offers-glimpse-of-how-m-14233.

they be so myopic? Thank goodness that never happens in any organization I know of.[65]

I had the good fortune to speak with someone involved in Blockbuster's 2007 strategic decision to focus on physical, brick-and-mortar video rentals and avoid entering online media streaming.[66] This individual was smart. Darn smart. The other people involved in the decision were just as smart. The reality is that they made a decision that made sense, corresponded with the data at hand, and yet still proved to be wrong. And that's one reason so many organizations get beaten by innovation.

The point here is that innovation is hard. Innovation goes against our bias to maintain the status quo.[67] It goes against our preference for acting according to the certain now rather than the uncertain future.[68] Unless you are enabled to act in a conscious, deliberate, and systematic way, creating the future rather than becoming victims of it, you just may find yourself to be the target of that "how could they be so stupid" ridicule as people in the not-too-distant future look back on what you are doing today.

---

[65] Yeah, right. I've seen this happen in numerous organizations. Did you catch the references to Virgin Records and Borders Books at the end of the video? This kind of thing happens all the time, everywhere.

[66] Whose name is withheld to protect the innocent.

[67] For more on cognitive biases, go to the "Cognitive Biases" section in the "Mind of Innovation" chapter, page 224.

[68] Jennifer S. Mueller, Shimul Melwani, Jack A. Goncalo, "The bias against creativity: Why people desire but reject creative ideas," *Psychological Science*, January 2012.

Keeping Innovation Simple

Ah, the KISS principle.

Kelly Johnson, the creator of and lead engineer at the Lockheed Skunk Works back in the days of developing the U-2 and SR-71 Blackbird spy planes, developed the KISS principle (an acronym for "Keep It Simple Stupid"). This became a popular way of expressing that "simple" generally works better than "complicated." "Keep It Simple Stupid" eloquently and humorously captured a beautiful design and development philosophy.

Then somebody decided that the word "stupid" was offensive.[69] Since it's become socially unacceptable for anyone to be offended anywhere at any time,[70] sensitive folks looked for new words to fill the same acronym just as memorably. I suppose "Keep It Simple, Simpleton," both failed to resolve the personal offense issue and was redundant,[71] so further efforts were required. Polite variants of "Keep It Simple, Silly" (because using the cute 3-year-old word "silly" is obviously less offensive than the more forceful 8-year-old word "stupid"), "Keep It Simple, Soldier," "Keep It Simple and Straightforward," and "Keep It Simple, Solipsist"[72] have all been tried.

I toyed around with ideas for a second "S" to complete the acronym in my book title. All variants fail to capture the wit and wisdom of the – dare I say it? – simple and straightforward original. I eventually gave up, and just deleted the last "S" to end up with just "Keep It Simple." The acronym may not be as pretty, but the principle is just as valid. Keep it simple.

And in this case, the "it" is "innovation." Organizations should keep their innovation efforts simple.

Yet we overcomplicate things all the time. It's as if Rube Goldberg[73] himself were designing not only the products we offer, but also the work systems we

---

[69] The spectacular success of the *[Insert Subject Here] for Dummies* books indicates that not everyone is offended by a jab at readers.

[70] I sure hope that statement doesn't offend anyone.

[71] And repetitive.

[72] I made that last one up. No one really says that. Even if you are an advocate of egocentric epistemology, the reference is purely coincidental and should not be taken as directed at you.

[73] For more on the brilliant work of Rube Goldberg, get online and go to https://www.rubegoldberg.com/

use to create them. In the name of communication, we have too many reports and too many meetings with too little clarity and too many PowerPoint slides.[74] In the name of maximizing return on investment, we pursue so many potentially valuable projects that we can't do any of them well. In the name of decision-making, we waste time, money, and energy collecting and analyzing nonactionable data on spreadsheets with more formulas than Dr. Jekyll's laboratory.

Yet even feeling the frustration of any or all of those things, you may find yourself resistant to change. Change is hard. We have a natural preference for the status quo. We have a natural preference for information that agrees with what we already think. We have a natural preference to resist information contrary to our preconceived notions. So if you think complex issues require complicated solutions, you might dismiss this simplicity message out of hand.

If you are such a simplicity denier, I will simply ask that you keep an open mind as you read.

Why Simple?

The human brain is an amazing thing. It can think about mixing the chicken noodle soup while feeling worry about a sick child and wondering where the thermometer is to see if that same child has a fever. And while prioritizing the fourteen things that need to be done at work by the end of the day tomorrow. And while humming the latest catchy tune said child plays repeatedly on their iPod so loud you can hear it in the next room. And while considering whether to schedule a hearing test for them. And on, and on.

Amazing as it is, though, it is not an all-knowing, all-powerful computer. It is limited and fallible. It has only so much capacity. It can do only so many tasks. When we over-complicate things, we waste valuable mental resources. Making the effort to find the simpler way can free up those resources to do more valuable things.

C. S. Lewis captures this well in *Voyage of the Dawn Treader*: "One day the cat got into the dairy and twenty [men] were at work moving all the milk out; no one thought of moving the cat."

---

[74] And no, using Prezi instead of PowerPoint to make cooler visual transitions between mini data dumps is no better.

Meeting complexity with complexity breeds more complexity. That means more work than necessary. That means wasted effort. That means lower returns – or even negative returns. Finding ways to simplify enables us to do more, and achieve more.

As Bill Jensen, author of *Simplicity*, puts it, "Simplicity – the art of making the complex clear – can give us the power to get stuff done. Power to work smarter. It's a prerequisite if we want to leverage the untapped energy, innovation, creativity, and ideas that already exist in our organizations."[75]

That definition is important. Simplicity is the "art of making the complex clear." To make the complex clear, you need to do two things – avoid over complicating the system, and communicate in a way that your organization understands.

When confronted with complexity, we tend to respond with complicated solutions. If the problem has ten moving parts, the solution must have eleven. We move the hundreds of milk pails instead of the one cat. The trouble is that the more moving parts, the more likely failure becomes. The more resources are wasted. The more coordination between parts that is necessary. The more likely breakdown is to occur. The more likely customer disappointment, disillusionment, dissatisfaction, displeasure, discontent, disenchantment, distress, disgruntlement... Stop dis-ing your customers with unnecessary complications.

Once you have a system defined, make it easy to understand. Speak with a common language for the whole organization. If you need to teach a new vocabulary, make sure to teach it well *before* trying to implement anything new.

Imagine a doctor who tells you that "your emesis was caused by veisalgia; administer 500 mg of acetylsalicylic acid buffered with calcium carbonate, followed by eight hours of left and/or right ventral decubitus with somniation, then electronic transmission of post-therapeutic modality data." Hearing something like that, you might barely have the courage to ask, "How long have I got, Doc?"

A better communicator tells you exactly the same thing in a way you can understand: "You tossed your cookies because of a hangover; go take two

---

[75] Bill Jensen, *Simplicity: Working Smarter in a World of Infinite Choices*, Basic Books, 2001.

aspirin and call me in the morning." See how great clarity can be? Making the complex clear is what simple is all about.

Simple is not about lazy. It's not about easy. It's not an excuse to avoid the work involved with complex solutions to complicated problems. You may find this hard to believe, but making something simple is hard work. Maybe even harder work than making things complicated. But simplicity can outperform complexity, even in matters as complicated as econometric forecasting.[76]

No, "simple" does not mean "easy." Seeking simplicity in innovation is particularly challenging. Innovation is a complex process in a chaotic world. "Simple" seeks to bring clarity to the chaos. Clarity aligns and coordinates resources to maximize the return from their efforts. And *that* makes the innovation engine hum.

"Simple" is the coxswain[77] of the innovation boat. The rowers still have to row their arms off to make the boat go, but the boat goes in the right direction and a whole lot faster than when every rower just rows blindly on their own.

Innovation is a complex process in a complex world. Bringing simplicity to it is hard work. So why pursue simple if complicated is easier?

Innovation involves learning. Learning is done best when it's kept simple.[78]

Innovation involves coordinated decisions and actions of diverse people. Such coordination is best done when the guidelines are simple.[79]

---

[76] Kesten C. Green and J. Scott Armstrong, "Simple Versus Complex Forecasting: The Evidence," *Social Science Research Network*, March 1, 2015. From the abstract: "Our review of studies comparing simple and complex methods...found 97 comparisons in 32 papers. None of the papers provide a balance of evidence that complexity improves forecast accuracy. Complexity increases forecast error by 27 percent on average in the 25 papers with quantitative comparisons...Nevertheless, complexity remains popular among researchers, forecasters, and clients. Some evidence suggests that the popularity of complexity may be due to incentives: (1) researchers are rewarded for publishing in highly ranked journals, which favor complexity; (2) forecasters can use complex methods to provide forecasts that support decision-makers' plans; and (3) forecasters' clients may be reassured by incomprehensibility. *Clients who prefer accuracy should accept forecasts only from simple evidence-based procedures.*"

[77] Note: "coxswain" is not a dirty word.

[78] Jacob Feldman, "The Simplicity Principle in Human Concept Learning," *Current Directions in Psychological Science*, December 2003.

[79] David J. Snowden, "Multi-ontology sense making: a new simplicity in decision making," *Informatics in Primary Care*, February 2005.

Innovation involves prudent investment, and the best investors follow simple rules. As investment guru John Bogle has said, "When there are multiple solutions to a problem, choose the simplest one."[80]

Keep in mind that we are talking about simple — *not* simplistic. You do need to be careful not to cross the fine line between them. I believe strongly in the paraphrase of Einstein, "Make things as simple as possible, but not simpler."[81] As design genius Don Norman puts it, "The mark of the great designer is the ability to provide what people need without excessive complexity, without feature bloat. [But] simplicity [alone] should never be the goal."[82] Simple, but not simplistic.

Simple is empowering. Simplistic is debilitating. Simple is taking into account the myriad of complexities in the world and coming away with a cohesive understanding of how it all works together. Simplistic is focusing on one small piece of it all and thinking that's all there is. Simple is seeing the whole animal and saying "elephant." Simplistic is seeing just the tail and thinking "fuzzy snake without a face."[83]

If you didn't read the preface/answers to your questions,[84] well, shame on you. I wrote that just for you.

For those of you who did read it, thank you. The fact that you continued to read after that is either a testament to the value of the material in this book, or a testament to your ability to endure suffering. In either case, bear with me for a moment while I fill those other folks in.

---

[80] John C. Bogle, *The Little Book of Common Sense Investing: The Only Way to Guarantee Your Fair Share of Stock Market Returns*, John Wiley and Sons, 2007. *Fortune* magazine named him one of the four investment "Giants of the 20th Century," along with Warren Buffet, Peter Lynch and George Soros. So he might know what he's talking about.

[81] Apparently, what Einstein actually said was "It can scarcely be denied that the supreme goal of all theory is to make the irreducible basic elements as simple and as few as possible without having to surrender the adequate representation of a single datum of experience." Others then paraphrased that into the more eloquent, and ironically simple, quote used in the text.

[82] From Don Norman's blog post "Why is 37signals so arrogant?" published on his website, jnd.org. I added the "but" and "alone" to better capture the meaning of the article as a whole.

[83] If you are unfamiliar with the parable of the Blind Men and the Elephant, get online and check out the story here: http://www.allaboutphilosophy.org/blind-men-and-the-elephant.htm

[84] You can always go back and read it now...just flip to page ii.

For those that didn't read it in the first place, and didn't go back and read it even after discovering my hurt feelings, I'll fill you in on a part of what you missed. Stanford professor Kathleen Eisenhardt and MIT Sloan professor Donald Sull have done research on managing complexity.[85] They say, "How can people manage the complexity of the modern world? Our answer, grounded in research and real-world results, is that simple rules tame complexity better than complex solutions."

So there you go.

Here are their rules for making things simple in a complex world:

1) **Identify bottlenecks that are both specific and strategic.** When opportunities exceed the resources available for investment, you have a bottleneck. Avoid feel-good resolutions to such bottlenecks like "recognize and reward good innovation practices." Instead, be specific, like "Innovation projects should leverage existing technology platforms when possible."

2) **Let data trump opinion.** Recognize that nobody has enough time, money, talent, or brain capacity to do everything they want to do. Choosing between opportunities is hard,[86] and can be emotional. But you must focus. Prioritize only a couple of key areas where simplicity will have the greatest impact. Let data determine what those areas need to be – not somebody's pet project preference.

3) **Users make the rules.** Command-and control rules for simplifying are a big mistake. The people who will actually have to use the rules are better at creating them than executives directing from a distance will be. The people close to the action can test and adjust the rules based on actual experience, rather than on even the most well-intentioned assumptions from above.

---

[85] Kathleen Eisenhardt and Donald Sull, *Simple Rules: How to Thrive in a Complex World*, Houghton Mifflin Harcourt, 2015. For the *Reader's Digest* (actually *Harvard Business Review*) condensed version, check out https://hbr.org/2012/09/simple-rules-for-a-complex-world.

[86] For a graphic representation of just how hard such choices are, go to the "Tough Choices" section, page 154.

4) **The rules should be concrete.** Simplicity avoids abstractions and buzzwords. Simplicity is easy for the people who do the work to understand. Eisenhardt and Sull offer the example of the intense statistical analyses done by the Oakland A's, made famous in the book and movie *Moneyball*. The results of these regressions were presented as simple, easily-understood rules, such as "don't draft high school players," and "no players with problems that the club can't fix."

Note that being concrete is different than being precise. Avoid requiring things that appear to be simple but are actually analytically complex (like insisting that a project have a positive net present value). That might sound crazy. How can you make decisions without knowing if something is going to be of value? The thing here is that complicated analyses will always use assumptions as inputs. Those assumptions will always be wrong. Some more wrong than others. The precise output of a complex analysis may feel good, but it will still be wrong. Better to be approximately right using simplicity than precisely wrong using complexity.

I experienced this first hand working with an organization that lacked comfort with ambiguity.[87] While evaluating a project, we offered some rough estimates of future sales, based on comparisons to similar product launches. I was then asked what the marketing expenditures would be in years two and three to justify the forecasts. Now, this company had just gone through a mid-year budget adjustment, which changed all the planned expenditures for that very year. It wasn't even the first mid-course adjustment of that year. Yet they demanded precision on what was going to be spent three years down the road. That is what I mean by wasted effort in the name of precision.

5) **The rules should evolve.** Simplicity adapts to a changing world. The simple guidelines that work today may not work tomorrow. Check on your approach to simplicity every now and then, and update that

---

[87] A very large, bureaucratic, command-and-control style company that shall remain nameless so that I don't get beaten if I run into any of their employees or shareholders. Comfort with ambiguity is a key element of an innovator's mindset (see page 258).

approach as necessary. Learn from your successes and failures,[88] grow and adapt. No simple rules—not even the good ones—last forever.

So those are the simple rules I used to write this book. Innovation efforts are a strategic bottleneck for many organizations. My guess is that you wouldn't be reading this if it wasn't a bottleneck in yours. You are not alone.

I leveraged as much data as I could find in offering the recommendations of this book. If you haven't picked up on it yet, there are a lot of footnotes. When they aren't hilarious comedic asides,[89] they are references to solid, data-based research done by brilliant people. Click the hyperlinks to delve into them, if you dare.

Keep in mind that I am a user. No, that's not meant to be an introduction to the group in a twelve-step program meeting. I am a practitioner of these innovation principles, and have been doing this for longer than I can believe. I have the gray hairs to prove it.

As much as possible, I try to offer concrete suggestions, with simple tools that you can actually use. Today. I'm always annoyed when I read a business book or see a speaker at a conference and I think "Hey, that was great...but now what?!?" In here, you will find the "now whats."

As for evolution, the brilliant people mentioned above continue to conduct and publish their research, and I continue to read and digest it. I intend for this book to evolve[90] as the body of innovation knowledge expands.

"Best Practices" and "Innovation"

In here, you will find a collection of the evidence-based practices that drive innovation effectively in any organization. Yes, any.

---

[88] For more on how to learn from your innovation efforts, go to the "After Action Review" section (page 382).

[89] Like this one.

[90] While planning for future editions before the first one has even been published may seem a bit cocky, the real intent is to keep updates current through blog posts, newsletters, and website updates. And through the miracle of the internet, that is all possible at www.3point14Innovation.com.

How can I make such a claim? After all, the pharmaceutical industry is a bit different than a local laundromat, which is a bit different than a nonprofit serving the homeless. They can't all be run the same way, can they?

Of course not.

But that doesn't mean that the evidence-based practices presented here can't apply to each situation. When I talk about such practices, I am talking about general principles that transcend industries, objectives, regulatory environments, and operational models.[91]

Notice that I am avoiding the term – or cliché – "best practices." I am doing so consciously.

Robert Camp of the American Society for Quality (ASQ) defined a best practice as "that technique, method, process, or activity that is more effective at delivering a particular outcome than any other technique, method, process, or activity within that domain."[92] Is it really possible, particularly with regards to the creative practice of innovation, to know what practice is more effective than any other? Such a claim would be dubious at best.

I'm going to stick to "evidence-based practices." These are methods, techniques, processes, etc. that have solid research demonstrating their effectiveness when it comes to innovating. These will serve as solid, adaptable principles that you can apply in your work, no matter what you do.

I will fully admit to you that there might be organizations out there somewhere who have identified better practices than those that I'll be sharing. So why don't I go out looking for them to share with the world? Because I can't identify them. And no one else can, either.

Without the rigor of objective analysis, what any one organization identifies as "best" can't be known as truly "best." Even if they had spectacular success with some practice or another, it is possible that the success came *in spite of* the practice, rather than *because of* it. It's possible that the practice works because it fit a particular set of circumstances – timing, talent, market

---

[91] All of the principles are briefly summarized in the "Principles" section of the Change Management chapter, page 420.

[92] Camp, Robert C. (1989) *Benchmarking: The search for industry best practices that lead to superior performance*. Milwaukee, WI: ASQ Quality Press.

emergence, customer trend, weather patterns, sunspots – that don't apply to anyone else, anywhere else.

Look, just because someone wins a $500-million-dollar lottery doesn't mean that buying lottery tickets is a best practice income strategy. The same is true for innovation practices. Just because someone, somewhere, claims success with a practice doesn't mean it is actually a best practice.

If you are a business daredevil thirsting to try the next new thing and see if it works, then God bless you. You could create the next practice that is someday proven to be superior to the evidence-based practices found here. That is how these things advance. That's innovation, and I obviously encourage it!

Innovation is not, however, to be done in a vacuum. Innovation is not about returning to the Stone Age to see if you can come up with something better than the wheel. Innovation is built on the foundations laid by those who have gone before. Sure, you may overturn what the earlier evidence suggested was true, like Einstein overturning Newton's physics. But remember that Einstein didn't do so without thoroughly understanding the current state of the science first.

Grounding yourself in evidence-based practices will help you, whether you are a novice looking to do things better, or an expert looking for the next advance in the art and science of innovation.

I've heard some people object that if you try to apply practices that others have already proven to work, then you can't be innovating. As Seth Godin has supposedly put it,[93] "The only thing all successful people have in common is that they're successful, so don't waste your time copying 'the successful strategies' of others."

Actually, another thing all successful people have in common is that they breathe. I don't see anyone recommending that you don't waste time breathing.

---

[93] This is a quote attributed to Seth Godin in about a thousand lists of quotes on the internet. I could not find an original source for this, though. Some people even attributed it to the *Bhagavad Gita*, but since my Sanskrit is a little shaky, I didn't try to find out if that was more accurate than the attribution to Mr. Godin. By the way, I'm actually a fan of Seth Godin. I just think this quote is taken out of context and twisted to mean something it shouldn't.

The thing is, evidence-based practices are not about imitating, copying, mimicking, replicating, or impersonating. You can do your own thing, in your own way, while still following proven success principles.

Or, think of it this way. There are many ways to succeed, but far more ways to fail. Why not save yourself some unnecessary failure time and learn from others' experiences?

A word of warning, though, about learning from the experience of others. Much of what you see in the business section of your local book store – if you bother going to a brick-and-mortar bookstore anymore – essentially boils down to case studies. How many times have you seen articles or books that could be interchangeably titled "Innovation the Google/ Apple/ Toyota/ Amazon/ Tata/ Disney/ Siemens/ Facebook/ Samsung/ 3M/ IDEO/ P&G/ GE/ NASA/ George Washington Carver/ Joy Mangano/ Ron Popeil Way?"[94]

To be sure, we all can learn something from these stories. But consider this statement of the obvious: unless you work for one of those organizations, you don't work for one of those organizations. Seriously, consider that.

Doing things their way works for them. That doesn't mean it will work exactly the same way for you.[95] They have their own cultures, markets, supply chains, capabilities, resources, etc., none of which belong to you. Such case studies serve only one valuable purpose: stimulating thought about fundamental principles. No matter how great their success, no matter how compelling the story, the only way you get any value out of reading about their work is to figure out how the underlying principles of their success might, or just as importantly, might not, apply to your organization.

There's another major problem with learning from the way successful organizations innovate. Let me illustrate that problem with an example. I'm a runner. Not an elite one, but competitive enough that I wanted to learn how

---

[94] Maybe I should have called this book *Innovation the Pi Way*. Or maybe *My Way or the Pi Way*. Hmmmmm...

[95] Floortje Blindenbach-Driessen and Jan Van Den Ende, "Innovation Management Practices Compared: The Example of Project-Based Firms," *Journal of Product Innovation Management*, September 2010. Straight from the abstract: "The implication [of their findings] for the innovation management literature is that 'best' practices for innovation management are firm dependent."

to be faster than my competition. I set out to learn from the great runners of history.

With speed as my goal, I looked first at the fastest men alive. Everyone from Jesse Owens to Carl Lewis to Usain Bolt. I noticed from pictures and movies that there was something all of them did. I went all the way back through every Olympic 100m final, and saw that all of them did the same thing – even Thomas Burke in 1896!

I felt like I was onto something. I looked at the women's 100m race history. Sure enough, everyone from Anni Holdmann in 1928 to Wilma Rudolph to Evelyn Ashford to Florence Griffith Joyner all did the same thing that the male winners did. Digging even deeper, I found that they all did it, not only in races, but in their training routines as well.

If you are a runner, you might be dying to find out what I discovered. I'm thinking that I might write a "Secret of the Speedsters" article for *Runner's World* magazine. But I'll give you an exclusive preview of what I found here. Every single one of these world's fastest people did the same thing. The photos and videos prove it. That thing is...

They all wore shoes.

Okay, so right now you may be thinking to yourself, "Brad is either of questionable sanity or an idiot. Maybe both. Of course they all wore shoes! What a disappointment." True as that all may be, I tell this silly little story to illustrate a point. It isn't enough to look at what the winners do. It isn't even enough to look at what all of the winners do the same. You have to look at what differentiates the winners from the also-rans.

Yet we make the winners-wear-shoes mistake all the time. I believe that this is the kind of thing that the earlier Seth Godin quote is railing against. Books, articles, and infographics abound, proclaiming to know the secret habits of the wealthy, the successful, the athletic, the productive, the intelligent, the talented. Precious few of those ever bother to see if those "secrets" are different from the practices and behaviors of the not-so-muches.

The evidence-based practices cited in this book are supported by research that makes that differentiation. These practices separate the most successful innovators from the unicorn and pet rock peddlers of the world.

The Innovation Engine

Now that you've dipped your toes into the warm waters of innovation, it's time to wade in a little deeper. This book will provide you a metaphorical mask and snorkel that will enable you to dive in and see beneath the surface of the various parts of a complete innovation system.

It is impossible to cover every topic in complete depth – and that would defeat the purpose of keeping innovation simple. To overuse the swimming metaphor, this book is not intended to provide SCUBA certification, diving to the full depths of each topic. That may come in future publications. For now, if you find yourself interested in a deeper dive, please contact Pi Innovation at www.3point14innovation.com/contactus/.

The following chapters divide an innovation system into various components. This is done for clarity, not because there are clean breaks between those components. The components of an innovation system are highly interlinked. One part depends on another, which depends on yet another, which feeds back into the first.

Don't get too hung up on the complexity diagrammed in Figure 11.

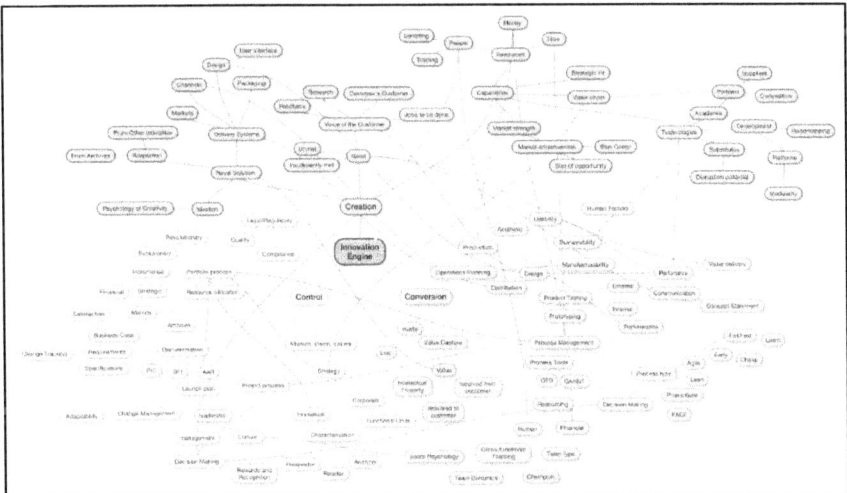

Figure 11: Even this overview Innovation Engine diagram doesn't get at the full complexity. But it should help to convey why we don't try to cover everything all at once.

Embrace the chaos! This book will clarify things, and show you how the pieces work together. That's what true simplicity is – making the complex clear.

Shifting gears a bit (pun intended – you'll see what I mean in a moment), let's look at another analogy for an innovation system. I call it the Innovation Engine (there it is...gears, engine...punny, right?).

Traditionally, innovation has been modeled as a funnel. The wide end represented the many ideas that you start with, which, over time, are narrowed down to the few ideas that are actually executed. This model has been built upon and modified over the years to address different aspects of innovation, but conceptually, it's been basically the same thing for decades.

The Innovation Funnel

Figure 12: The funnel model of innovation - start with a whole bunch of ideas, and whittle them away as time goes on.

I've used the model myself in my career, but the more I've thought about it, the more I have a problem with it. It's way too limited to really help conceptualize a system that an organization can follow. I've seen groups try to force fit it into defining their processes, and it ended up either confusing people or being utterly ignored.

The key problem with it is that it is passive. Think about it. A funnel doesn't do anything of its own accord. It relies on the outside force of gravity to pull stuff through it. This is especially ironic for the innovation funnel, which is more often than not represented horizontally. Have you ever tried to pour something through a horizontal funnel? Stuff either just lays there, inert and motionless, or it makes a big ol' mess on the kitchen counter. Sadly, that is all too accurate a representation of many innovation systems in may organizations.

It is far more useful to imagine the innovation system being an engine. Something that you control and use to drive your organization forward. Something with a variety of components that operate together to make desirable work happen. Something that exists in a variety of forms that can be adapted to the particular needs of the work they are designed to do.

Figure 13 offers examples of a variety of engines, from that on a rubber-band airplane, to a modern rocket engine. The questions to you: which type of engine is the best?

[Cue "Final Jeopardy" theme music while you mull that over]

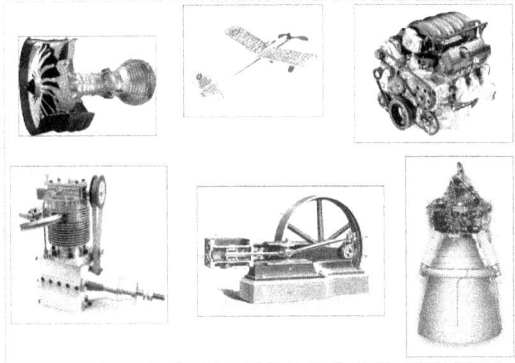

Figure 13: Engines come in a variety of forms, sizes, and levels of complexity

Ready to check your answer? The correct answer is: it depends.

You may have thought "well, Brad, the Rocketdyne F-1 engines used in the first stage of NASA's Saturn V rocket design remain the most powerful and complex such engines ever built, so I'm going to go with that." Answering that way would make you a nerd (which I offer as a high compliment, and I find to be very endearing). It would also make you wrong.

The reason it is wrong is that the best engine is the one that serves its purpose best. Yes, the rocket engine is incredibly powerful and fast and can get huge payloads to escape earth's gravity. However, if your purpose is to provide entertainment to an eight-year-old, you will find that the rubber band airplane engine makes a far better choice.

And that provides a good illustration of how this book works: start with a universal theme (you need an innovation engine to drive your organization into the future), then determine how that fundamental principle can be applied to your specific circumstances (design that engine against the capabilities, objectives, and resources of your particular organization).

To generalize what an engine is, I've broken it into three components, all of which begin with C to make it easy to remember: Creation, Conversion, and Control. Clever![96]

---

[96] How about that? Another word beginning with C. I can sense how impressed you are.

Each of these systems will be further broken down into their components. Again, this is not because such components exist independently of one another. Just like the starter system, fuel system, exhaust system, and cooling system are all interconnected in a car engine, so are the systems of the innovation engine. If any individual system breaks down, the whole engine stops. However, it's much easier to

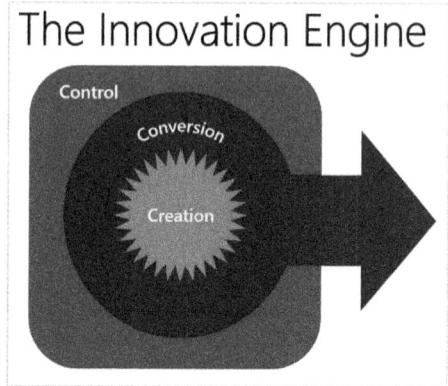

Figure 14: The three components of an Innovation Engine.

describe and understand all that is going on when the systems are broken into their parts. And simplicity, as we know, is about clarity and understanding.

As each part is discussed, you'll see that there are links to other parts of the book available. These links are there to help you quickly jump between components and sub-components that are linked together. You can choose to jump around from topic to topic, or to read straight through. Do whatever helps your understanding the most. It's your book after all.

The Control System

You'll notice that the discussion starts with the control system. That may seem counter-intuitive if you are expecting things to start with the creation system. Please don't assume that starting with the control system means that I advocate a top-down command-and-control approach to innovation. I absolutely don't.

The reason for starting with the control system is the nature of the components. These components – Mission, Culture, Strategy, and Portfolio Management – offer the guidance required to channel innovation energy in the right direction. It bears repeating that these sub-components do not fall exclusively under "control," but are inextricably linked to all parts of the innovation system. They can best be understood in their parts, but must be assembled together as a whole to be effective.

Mission is the whole reason for doing the innovation work in the first place. It is the ultimate goal that you want to achieve. It connects everything else together. If something is not relevant to the mission, it shouldn't be done at all.

Simple Mission Tool: The Mission Definition Template (page 49).

Culture is "the way we do things around here." If your organization were a computer, culture would be the operating system. Everything you try to do must fit the organizational culture, or it will not work any better than a PlayStation game will work in an Xbox. Culture can be changed, but it is a long, slow, and difficult process. In the short run, your efforts need to match your culture. In the long-run, though, you can (and should) adjust your culture to best serve your mission.

Simple Culture Tools: Competing Values Framework (page 66), Change Management Guide (page 82).

Strategy is the plan for achieving the mission. In the context of this book, we will focus on the innovation strategy specifically, which is one of the pillars of an overall organizational strategy. Like an architectural pillar supporting an overarching roof, the innovation strategy must support the overarching organizational strategy, which, in turn, supports the organizational mission.

Simple Strategy Tools: The SWOT Matrix (page 115), The Five Forces PLUS (page 116), Product Life-Cycle Map (page 118), Attribute Opportunity Map (page 119), Blue Ocean Canvas (page 120), Innovation Radar (page 122), Ten Types of Innovation (page 124), Value Web Mapping (page 125), Innovation Roadmapping Template (page 128), Simple Innovation Plan (page 129), Open Innovation Strategy Matrix (page 138).

Portfolio Management is where the strategy talk meets the execution walk. It's where resources are allocated against efforts. Without effective portfolio management, confusion and over-extension will rule.

Simple Portfolio Tools: Strategic Buckets Map (page 160), Risk/Reward Map (page 163), Project Type Map (page 164), Time Horizon Map (page 165), Urgency Assessment Map (page 166), Project Scorecards (page 171).

The Creation System

Next, the Creation system will discuss customer understanding, the mental game of innovation, and idea generation and refinement.

Customer understanding means deeply empathizing with the real needs of those you are trying to serve, and using those needs to guide your innovation effort. It is also known as "Voice of the Customer" in innovation circles – although that name is a hotly debated topic. Delivering something people really need is not up for debate. What is hotly debated is the way in which those needs are identified. There is violent agreement, though, that the one way *not* to identify a customer need is to merely ask the customer and expect a reliable answer.

Nonprofits have a unique customer challenge. They need to be aware that if they want their innovations to be successful, they have two very separate and distinct customers to consider – those that receive from their services, and those that give to their services. Both must be recognized and treated as customers.

Simple Customer Understanding Tools: Design Thinking Approach (page 182), Problem Definition Process (page 185), Simple Customer Survey (page 195), Affinity Sorting (page 199), House of Quality (page 203).

The mental game of innovation – now that might be a scary topic. If, however, you are going to engage in innovation, you have to recognize that innovation is primarily a mental game. To play it well, you need to know how the mind works when it comes to innovating. You need to know what helps people to innovate, and what gets in their way. You need to know what conditions create a fertile field for innovation and what conditions are toxic to innovative growth.

Simple Innovative Mind Tools: The Dirty Dozen Cognitive Biases (page 224), Six Thinking Hats (page 245), Innovator Mental Model (page 250), The Mindfulness Drug (page 264), Conditions for Flow (page 270).

Idea generation and refinement is where the solution process begins. Ideas are the seeds planted in innovative fields. Randomly throwing miscellaneous seeds on the ground is far less effective than planned, controlled, and targeted planting of high-quality seeds. That's as true for innovation as it is for modern farming. The old brainstorming routine doesn't work well. You should use more advanced (yet still simple!) techniques, proven to be more fertile.

Simple Ideation Tools: Brainwriting (page 294), HIT (page 296), SCAMPER (page 297), TRIZ (page 299), Cumulative Voting (page 302), Value Proposition Template (page 305), Simple Concept Worksheet (page 306).

The Conversion System

Finally, the Conversion system will consist of Teams, Project Management, and Metrics.

Innovation teams are a requirement for organizations looking to innovate. The lone inventor who experiences the brilliant epiphany one morning in the bathtub is a myth. Cross-functional, collaborative, and diverse innovation teams are the effective reality.

Simple Team Tools: Five Levels of Teamwork (page 316), Three Teamwork Roles (page 317), Octopi Model (page 323), CLEAR Communication (page 329), RAPID Decision-making (page 334), Transformational Leadership Model (page 340), Conflict Management Tool (page 342).

Project management for innovation is different than managing construction projects. The degree of uncertainty is several orders of magnitude higher. The flexibility and adaptability required are several orders of magnitude higher. And the necessity of managing the project as a part of a complex collection of interrelated projects is several orders of magnitude higher. It takes constant focus on the holistic mission and strategy to do it well.

Simple Project Management Tools: Stage-Gate vs. Lean/Agile Overview (page 353), Simple Project Charter (page 357), Delphi Forecasting (page 367), Simple Pre-Mortem (page 369), Simple Meetings (page 377), Oobeya Room (page 379), After Action Review (page 382).

Metrics are important because what you measure is what you will affect. Metrics are the measures used to guide projects and programs while they are in progress, and the measures used after the fact to determine if those projects and programs were successful. Metrics should always be used in combinations, often with conflicts between them, to ensure that the overall performance is optimized. Non-profits need to follow similar metrics to for-profit organizations, but with an added twist given their differences.

Simple Metrics Tools: Dashboard Development Guideline (page 393), Potential Metrics List (page 399), Nonprofit Considerations (page 406).

Theory and Application

So as mentioned earlier, my goal in writing this is to give you evidence-based practices that are general principles. The key is to understand these principles, and then to apply those principles to your specific situation.

How do you do that? Well, without knowing your specifics, I can't exactly say. But maybe an analogy will help.

Think of it this way. If you want to stay healthy, an evidence-based practice is to eat a nutritious diet and to get sufficient exercise. That is a fundamental principle. However, that does not mean that every single person needs to eat the same specific meals every day. It does not mean that everyone must follow exactly the same exercise training plan. Everyone will have their own individual preferences for how to eat and exercise.

I recently found out that there are actually people in the world who enjoy eating Brussels sprouts. Seriously. I always thought that the only good use for Brussels sprouts was as compact and easily throwable ammunition in a food fight. After my first ever bite of one, I was convinced that they couldn't possibly be intended for human consumption.

Thus, I will need to apply my specific culinary taste in a different way than members of the Brussels Sprout Appreciation Society.[97]

Exactly the same is true of innovation as a practice. All the new technologies out there, all the acceleration of change, and all the globalization in the world's economies, do not free an innovator-to-be from the fundamental principles described in this book. So read them, absorb them, and apply them. You'll be glad that you did.

Simple Study Guide – The Core

- What is "innovation?"
- What is an "innovator?"
- How should expenditures on innovation be managed? Why?
- Why innovate?
- What is the funnel model of innovation?
- What is the innovation engine model?
- What does it mean to be "simple?"
- Why is simplicity important for innovation?
- Can you really have "best practices" for something like innovation?
- What does "evidence-based practices" mean?
- How do you apply fundamental principles to specific situations?

---

[97] Yes, there really is such a thing on Facebook (www.facebook.com/The-Brussels-Sprout-Appreciation-Society-136773149712101/). I couldn't believe it either.

Where do you want to go from here?

Control	Creation	Conversion
Mission (page 40)	Voice of the Customer (page 175)	Innovation Teams (page 310)
Culture (page 58)	Minds of Innovators (page 217)	Project Management (page 347)
Strategy (page 92)	Ideation (page 279)	For-Profit Metrics (page 389)
Portfolio Management (page 146)		Nonprofit Metrics (page 403)
Change Management (page 411)		

Or just turn the page to keep reading...

THE CONTROL SYSTEM

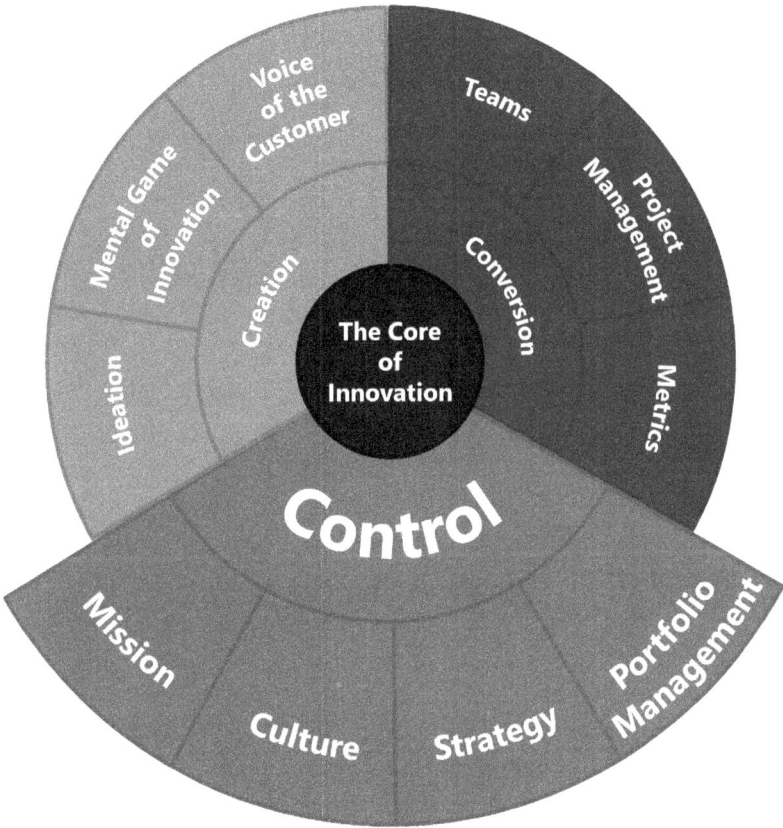

More than Just Making a Statement (Mission)

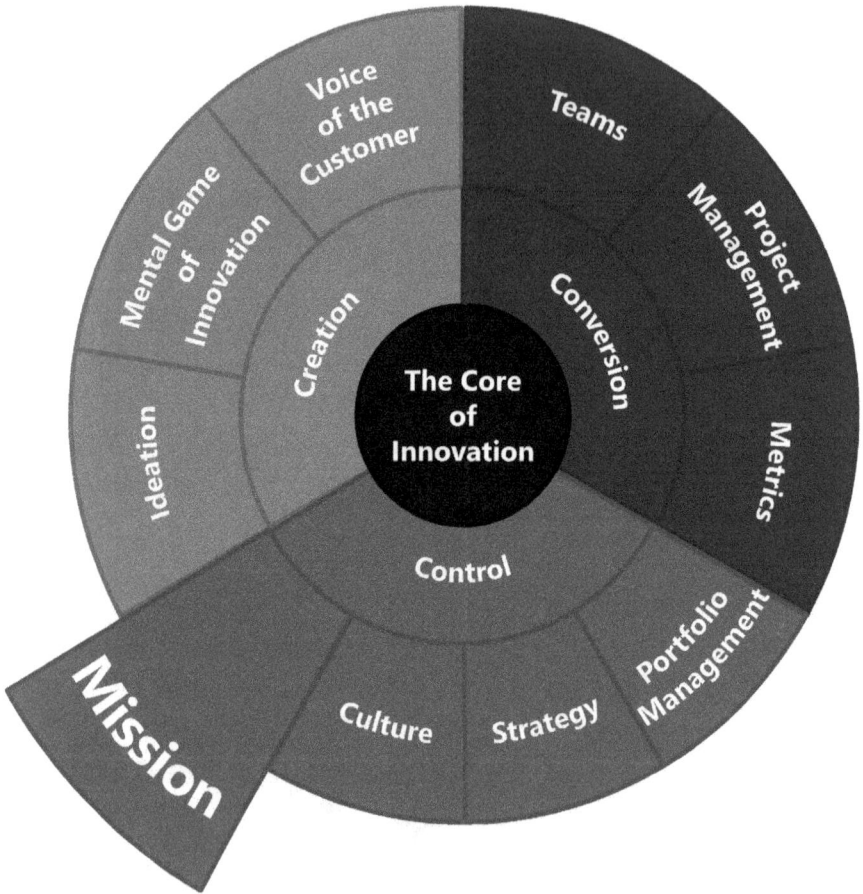

Simple Self-Assessment - Mission

Rate yourself on the following questions. To benchmark yourself against others, go to www.3point14Innovation.com and click the "Self-Assessments" menu.

- ### Do you have a mission for your organization?

What's a mission?!?

Of course! Why else would we come to work?

1	2	3	4	5	6	7	8	9	10

- ### Is your mission clearly understood by everyone in the organization?

Does anyone understand it?

Everybody can recite it by heart.

1	2	3	4	5	6	7	8	9	10

- ### Do the actions of the people in your organization reflect the mission?

Forget that mission stuff and do as I say.

They go together like peanut butter and jelly.

1	2	3	4	5	6	7	8	9	10

- ### Are you clear about what BHAG your organization wants to achieve?

I'm telling mom you said "BHAG!"

Audacity is our middle name.

1	2	3	4	5	6	7	8	9	10

- ### How unique is your mission statement to you?

We got ours at Missions-R-Us

It identifies us better than a fingerprint.

1	2	3	4	5	6	7	8	9	10

- ### Can you state your mission concisely?

It's only a little longer than this book.

It's as short and sweet as the Lollipop Guild.

1	2	3	4	5	6	7	8	9	10

Simple Summary - Mission
Key take-aways you should get out of this section:

- A strong mission contributes to improved innovation for both nonprofits and for-profit companies. It will also contribute to overall organizational performance.
- To be effective, a mission needs to help direct the behaviors of the people in the organization – the decisions and actions they take to execute on those decisions.
- To impact behaviors, the mission must be clearly communicated to all parts of the organization. Since "actions speak louder than words," leaders must pay particular attention to living according to the mission, and to ensuring everyone else does as well.
- The organizational structure, systems, and processes should be aligned to the mission, enabling rather than hindering its achievement.
- Your organizational mission should be able to clearly communicate:
  - ✓ What it is you want to achieve;
  - ✓ Within what constraints you want to achieve it;
  - ✓ Why you want to achieve it (and why others should, too).
- A strong statement of mission will guide strategic development, align resources, and attract people who share the values of the organization.
- When first developing a statement of mission (or revising an existing statement), involve as many stakeholders as possible. The degree of participation may vary, but involving everyone will help to ensure support for the mission, and inspire action to achieve it.
- If you are going to create a mission, do it right. Creating the kind of pseudo-mission statement that is viewed with cynicism rather than commitment is not only a waste of time and money, but can actually have adverse impact on the performance of the organization.

To the Moon

On September 12, 1962, US President John Fitzgerald Kennedy spoke at a podium before a large crowd gathered at Rice University, laying out a mission for the country:

> "We choose to go to the moon. We choose to go to the moon in this decade and do the other things, not because they are easy, but because they are hard, because that goal will serve to organize and measure the best of our energies and skills, because that challenge is one that we are willing to accept, one we are unwilling to postpone..."

And, as you may have heard, people went to the moon and back with 160 or so days left in 1969.[98]

The speech JFK gave that day became famous for galvanizing the nation with a clear competitive purpose, inspiring millions to support a project that would require a coordinated effort of scientists, inventors, manufacturers, designers, doctors, managers, adventurers, pilots, engineers, politicians, and others, the likes of which the world had never seen before.

A big part of the success of that project had to do with the fewer than 100 words quoted above. Granted, in the previous year, Kennedy had proposed to the US Congress that "this nation should commit itself to achieving the goal, before this decade is out, of landing a man on the moon and returning him safely to the Earth," but that statement was incomplete. The words spoken on that hot Houston afternoon served as the *inspirational* communication of what, when, and why:

What to achieve:	Go to the moon;
Within what constraints:	In this decade;
Why it should be achieved:	Because it would be an amazing achievement with benefits to all humankind.

It serves here as a model for stating a mission. One you should follow.

---

[98] Note to any moon hoax conspiracy theorists out there: don't express your doubts to Buzz Aldrin. See him punch out a doubter here: https://www.youtube.com/watch?v=wptn5RE2I-k.

Effective Mission Statements

Let me come right out and say it: I hate "mission statements." I hate them because most of them are meticulously crafted papers more worthy of fireplace kindling than of inspirational reading. I hate them because most of them are justifiably ignored by anyone who needs to be motivated by them. I hate them because most of them are simply bullshit.[99] Please excuse the language, but saying that most of them are "nonsense," "baloney," or "drivel" is just not sufficient to convey the full meaning of what they are.

You know the type: the framed corporate mission statements that hang in beige conference rooms featuring photos of soaring eagles or daring rock climbers summiting a scenic mountain peak. The words, if anyone ever bothers to read them, are

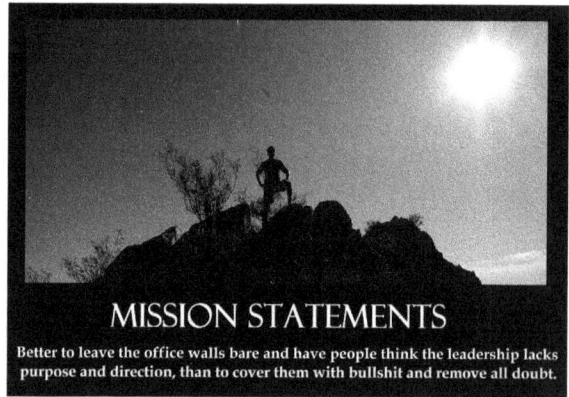

MISSION STATEMENTS

Better to leave the office walls bare and have people think the leadership lacks purpose and direction, than to cover them with bullshit and remove all doubt.

either meaningless malarkey, uninspiring bloviation, or over-written sleep inducers. Such mission statements inspire more cynicism than commitment. Such mission statements hurt more than they help.

If all you want to do is create some useless office wall covering, go to an online Mission Statement Generator[100] and have it do the work for you. It's free, takes practically no time, and it's not entirely worthless – it does have comedic value.

Look, if you can't say your mission simply and sincerely, don't say it at all. Better to leave the organization directionless than to have everyone doubt the direction. In the former case, people may actually ask, "Where are we going?" In the latter case, they won't bother asking because they won't believe the answer, anyway.

---

[99] Check out the brilliant essay "On Bullshit" by Princeton University philosophy professor Harry Frankfurt for a full exploration of what it is and why it's so prevalent in modern society.

[100] Go online and find a great one here: http://www.lotta.se/mission-statement-generator/

Now, if you are going to put the effort into creating a mission statement that will align and inspire, then you should probably make sure that you do it right. What I am advocating is a clearly communicated purpose for what the organization aims to do. Best is something that inspires people to supportive action. At the very least, it should be something on which people can focus when issues arise. In the face of conflict or uncertainty, every discussion should revolve around the question, "what will best help us achieve our mission?"

Someone who was pretty effective at achieving his mission was Mohandes K. Gandhi. He eloquently captured the need for a single "Attitude," a unified reason for being that guides all action: "When the Attitude ceases to be one and undivided and becomes many and divided, it ceases to be one settled will, and is broken up into various wills of desires between which [people are] tossed about."[101] If people in the organization are feeling tossed about, it's likely due to lack of clarity in, agreement on, and alignment to a common mission.

Missions must be lived by people of the organization – most especially by the leadership. They must be used as the lighthouse that guides organizational decisions and activities safely into port. Anything that is posted on the walls but is not lived by the doers of deeds is a waste. But a real mission drives performance.

I have already discussed at length that the practices mentioned in this book have evidence behind them. So what is the evidence behind mission statements? Are they really necessary for improving innovation outcomes? Would I ask the question if the answer wasn't "yes?!?"

In nonprofit organizations, a focused statement of the organization's mission has been demonstrated to drive innovation and overall organizational performance by keeping innovation efforts clearly and strategically targeted at a particular purpose.[102]

---

[101] Mohandes K. Gandhi, *The Bhagavad Gita According to Gandhi*, translated by Mahadev Desai, Wilder Publications, Inc., 2011. I modified it for gender neutrality and applicability to the mission discussion.

[102] Robert E. McDonald, "An Investigation of Innovation in Nonprofit Organizations: The Role of Organizational Mission," *Nonprofit and Voluntary Sector Quarterly*, June 2007.

In for-profit businesses, having a strong innovation mission is one of the differentiating factors between innovative firms and the not-so-muches. Serving a clear mission not only makes organizations generally more innovative, but also helps to drive the success of individual new product launches.[103]

As previously and unequivocally mentioned earlier, we all know that there are some mission statements that have a less-than-positive impact on their organizations. Avoid them like you'd avoid an annoying close-talker[104] with halitosis. Mission statements need to influence the people within the organization if they are to do any good. That influence needs to support commitment and alignment.[105]

The mission needs to be something that people can live, and not just read. As Ralph Waldo Emerson so eloquently put it, "Your actions speak so loudly, I cannot hear what you are saying." Even an eloquent and well-communicated expression of mission will fall flat, if the organization – and particularly the leaders in it – doesn't actually live it on a daily basis.

Need an example of failing to live the words? See if you can guess the company that included "Respect, Integrity, Communication and Excellence" in its mission statement. That company was Enron. Need I say more?

Back to what the research says. There is general agreement[106] that an effective mission statement provide several important benefits to an organization:

- Helping to keep all stakeholders informed and aligned with an organization's objectives;
- Serving as a guide for strategic planning;

---

[103] Chris Bart and Ashish Pujari, "The Performance Impact of Content and Process in Product Innovation Charters," *Journal of Product Innovation Management*, January 2007.

[104] Get online and watch this scene from *Seinfeld* to understand the close-talker: https://www.youtube.com/watch?v=NGVSlkEi3mM

[105] Christopher K. Bart, Nick Bontis, and Simon Taggar, "A model of the impact of mission statements on firm performance," *Management Decision*, 2001.

[106] Consider, for example, Linda Stallworth Williams, "The Mission Statement. A Corporate Reporting Tool with a Past, Present, and Future," *Journal of Business Communication*, April 2008, or Darwin L. King, Carl J. Case, and Kathleen M. Premo, "Current Mission Statement Emphasis: Be Ethical and Go Global," *Academy of Strategic Management Journal*, July 2010.

- Providing a foundation for decision-making and resource allocation.

If you communicate your mission well, you will draw the right people to you – employees, volunteers, customers, donors, partners, suppliers, and supporters. They will serve as references, living testimonials to your cause. You will move forward more easily because everyone is pushing or pulling in the same direction.

Consider the words of Dee Hock, founder and former CEO of the Visa credit card association:

> "I believe that purpose and principle, clearly understood and articulated, and commonly shared, are the genetic code of any healthy organization. To the degree that you hold purpose and principles in common among you, you can dispense with command and control.[107] People will know how to behave in accordance with them, and they'll do it in thousands of unimaginable, creative ways. The organization will become a vital, living set of beliefs."

As we shall see in the chapter on culture,[108] it is important to "dispense with command and control" when it comes to innovation. Command and control does not work well for a mission. To be most effective, the mission must be motivational. Inspirational. Aspirational. And it needs to be developed in a transparent, participative process with the people in the organization.[109] Otherwise, it is likely to end up just another wad of paper in the round file bin.

So what is your mission? If you want to communicate it, you have to know it. I hope that you got into your business, whether for profit or nonprofit, for a reason. If not, I hope you can come up with a reason for staying in your business – besides just paying off some bills.

Once you have that reason firmly in mind, it's time to state it. Simply.

---

[107] "'Command and control' style is just another way of saying 'run bureaucratically by people who don't spend time dealing with tasks.'" ~Shakespearean scholar Francis Boyle.

[108] If you just can't wait, the chapter on culture is starts on page 58.

[109] Chris Bart and Ashish Pujari, "The Performance Impact of Content and Process in Product Innovation Charters," *Journal of Product Innovation Management*, January 2007.

A Mission Statement How To

Thousands of ways to create an effective mission statement are out there. Personally, I recommend keeping the process – surprise! – simple. Remember that, as always, "simple" does not necessarily mean "easy." To do it well requires some good, hard, thought work.

Here are three questions to help guide you in defining your mission:

1. **What is it that you want to achieve?**

   What cause do you serve, or what impact do you want to have in the world? What do you do? For whom do you do it? What do those people want or need? Focus on satisfying customer needs, not on a product or service you want to provide. Studies show that mission statements focused on satisfying the needs of the customer drive both innovation and overall performance.[110] How can you do that better than anyone else? What unique contribution can you make?

   Jim Collins, in his book *Good to Great*, referred to this as the BHAG. No, that's not the latest insulting street slang to scream at the guy who cuts you off in traffic. BHAG stands for "Big, Hairy, Audacious Goal." The kind of goal that will make people ask "Is that even possible?!?" Putting a human foot on the moon. Eradicating small pox. Seeing The Chicago Cubs win the World Series. Your mission should be to achieve such a BHAG.

2. **Within what constraints will you operate?**

   Who are you? What are your strengths? What can you do better than anyone else? What do you aspire to be able to do? Be realistic while also stretching yourself. Kennedy first proposed the moon mission before the US had even put a man in orbit around the earth, so getting to the moon and back in just eight years was a big stretch. However, it was achievable with the resource commitment put behind it. Seek the balance between focus and aspiration, and between near-term and long-term.

3. **Why should anyone want to help achieve what you want to achieve?**

---

[110] Chris Bart, "Innovation, mission statements and learning," *International Journal of Technology Management*, 2004.

What value will you create and for whom? Think about their WIIFM – "what's in it for me?" What will people get out of what you want to do? Avoid making it all about revenues, profitability, or return on investment. Think about how the mission contributes to people's lives. Money counts, don't get me wrong. It just doesn't usually inspire for the long haul. Meaning and purpose do that.

Ultimately, you want this to be inspirational, but you can always do the wordsmithing later. First, just get your thoughts down about those three questions. Check in with others throughout the organization. Once you've got some sort of clear consensus, then you can go about the hard work of making it pithy.

Your mission should feel good when you read it and say it. Yes, *feel*. Even in the business world, people are emotional creatures. We are motivated by emotion, and make even our most reasoned and rational decisions with an emotional component.

Simple Mission Definition

What BHAG do you want to accomplish?	
What are your constraints?	
Why should anyone want to help accomplish that goal?	
State Your Mission	

Figure 15: It may not be as easy as an online mission statement generator, but it's far less full of cow patties.

Your mission should capture, in a few succinct sentences, the essence of your business's goals and the philosophies underlying them. It signals what your business is all about to your customers, employees, suppliers and the community.

Keep it brief. I suggest keeping it under a hundred words, and preferably under fifty. Being able to speak your mission in a concise way makes it more memorable and effective for all involved in the organization, from employee to customer. There's no need to make it overly complicated; in fact, complexity makes it worse. A real stretch goal would be to be able to express your mission on Twitter.[111] Google can do it: "Organize the world's information and make it

[111] Be careful not to go overboard here. Imagine JFK's call to action going out in a White House tweet – "we go 2 moon cuz its not ez #inthisdecade." Not quite as good as the original.

universally accessible and useful." And every Trekkie can recite in their sleep the mission of the starship Enterprise: "to explore strange, new, worlds; to seek out new life, and new civilizations; to boldly go[112] where no one has gone before."

I'm pretty sure this is the exact method that Gouverneur Morris used to draft the preamble to the US Constitution:[113]

What to achieve:	Ordain and establish a constitution;
Within what constraints:	For the United States of America;
Why it should be achieved:	In order to form a more perfect union, establish justice, ensure domestic tranquility, provide for the common defense, promote the general welfare, and secure the blessings of liberty to ourselves and our posterity.

Keeping it clear and concise is important, but be careful not to take the brevity advice too far. For example, the chocolate company Hershey's old mission statement was "Undisputed market leadership." What does that mean? I'm happy to say that they have since changed it. Three words is certainly concise, but even Willy Wonka couldn't get his Oompa Loompas to rally around that one.

The mission must have meaning for *you*. For *your* organization. Anyone who knows you should be able to guess that your mission statement is yours. Check out this mission fail: "To create a shopping experience that pleases our customers; a workplace that creates opportunities and a great working environment for our associates; and a business that achieves financial success." Anyone have any idea what company wrote that? What industry they are in? What they actually do?[114]

---

[112] Stick that in your split-infinitive, grammar police!

[113] Which I will never, ever be able to recite without singing the Schoolhouse Rock song: https://www.youtube.com/watch?v=yHp7sMqPL0g

[114] The answer is Albertson's, a grocery store chain in the eastern US, according to "The 9 Worst Mission Statements of All Time," *Inc.*, November 15, 2013.

Perhaps most importantly, be honest. Crafting eloquently-phrased BS won't cut it. Awkwardly crafted gold is more valuable than expertly carved cow pies. Nothing leads to cynicism and disdain for an organization's mission statement faster than something that obviously isn't meaningful. You'd be better off not communicating a mission statement at all.

Ernest Shackleton over a century ago provided a great example of an inspiring mission with the famous (although perhaps apocryphal)[115] advertisement to recruit adventurers for an exploration of the Antarctic:

> "Men wanted for hazardous journey to the South Pole. Small wages, bitter cold, long months of complete darkness, constant danger. Safe return doubtful. Honor and recognition in case of success."

Over 5000 men applied to go on the expedition.

Why does this serve as a model communication of mission? It provides clear, understandable answers to the three mission questions in just thirty words.

What to achieve:	Journey to the South Pole;
Within what constraints:	Small wages, bitter cold, long months of darkness, constant danger;
Why it should be achieved:	Honor and recognition.

This ad was recognized in 1949 by Julian Lewis Watkins as one of the *100 Greatest Advertisements* of the previous century. Just thirty words of brilliance that convey an inspiring message with a clear objective. It also speaks directly to a clearly defined target audience, even though it does not explicitly state who that audience is. It's directed at those who seek adventure for adventure's sake, and who are willing to sacrifice all personal comfort for a chance at heroic

---

[115] As quoted in the book *Quit You Like Men* by Carl Hopkins Elmore, 1944. A search for the original advertisement, including a $100 reward to anyone that can find it, has, however, turned up nothing to date. Whether factual or not, it is still a darn good expression of mission. If you have any evidence about the quote, and you need a $100, get online and go to http://www.antarctic-circle.org/advert.htm.

glory. It screens out those who are looking for an easy paycheck, or who lack the physical, mental, and emotional fortitude to survive the unavoidable hardship.

A Mission Statement How NOT To

Compare Shackleton's ad to this mission drivel– almost certainly posted in a gilded frame on every white wall of the corporate cubical farm – from General Motors:[116]

> "G.M. is a multinational corporation engaged in socially responsible operations, worldwide. It is dedicated to provide products and services of such quality that our customers will receive superior value while our employees and business partners will share in our success and our stock-holders will receive a sustained superior return on their investment."

If you were able to stay awake through all that, would you feel motivated? Would you feel like you knew what you had to do to achieve the mission? GM makes cars and trucks. The mission doesn't even mention transportation. Apparently, you could help GM achieve their mission by making rubber clown noses or providing grape peeling services, so long as you did so with "such quality that customers receive superior value," whatever that means. And there's nothing more motivating to the average Jane and Joe than sustaining superior returns for stockholders so they can spend more time on their yachts, right?[117]

Look, I'm all for free enterprise and delivering returns to the shareholders who were willing to invest their hard-earned money in my organization. There's nothing wrong with owning a yacht. Just don't expect that the rest of the world is going to wake up every morning anxiously awaiting an opportunity to help

---

[116] I could find no reference to this mission in official General Motors materials, but found several online sources attributing it to them, and it is quoted in William Pride, Robert Hughes, Jack Kapoor, *Business –Ninth Edition*, Thomson South-Western, 2008.

[117] Okay, I know not every GM shareholder has a yacht. Just the ones who got TARP funds. It's hard to believe they needed a bailout given such an inspiring mission. #sarcasm

somebody else get rich. Some people will work hard to help others escape poverty, but no one works tirelessly to help nameless others achieve the spoils of wealth.

GM could have had a mission statement like "We make kick-a** cars and trucks that people around the world crave to own and drive." Now *that* might have given people a reason to go into work.

Exposing Myself

Let's walk through a real example of the process. When starting Pi Innovation, I had to develop clarity for my own mission. As with the other principles in this book, I try to practice what I preach. I can't expect anyone to drink my Kool-Aid if I don't take a sip myself.

So at the risk of exposing myself to public scrutiny,[118] here is a quick summary of my mission development process.

When I first started out in consulting, I was fortunate to really know what my employee – me, that is – wanted from this work. I didn't need to conduct surveys or have town hall meetings or coffee talks to learn from and engage with people that worked for me. I already talked to myself over coffee every morning, anyway. If you are not so fortunate, then you need to do what it takes to understand the people you work with. You need to work with your leadership team, staff, and other stakeholders, to develop your mission with common understanding, agreement, and buy-in.

As a self-employed organization of one, I was also fortunate to really know what my shareholders – me, that is – wanted from the work. Mostly that involved paying the bank for a house, the grocer for some food, and Saucony for some running shoes. Oh, and feeling like I was making a positive difference for people who work creatively to make their part of the world a better place.

As a solo pilot of the company plane, though, I was unfortunate in that I didn't have a leadership group and staff to help develop the mission with me. I lost the benefit that multiple intelligent opinions and collaborative discussions can bring. If you find yourself in such a situation, put together an advisory board that can provide those perspectives. Assemble a team of

---

[118] If you ever get the idea to write a book, be warned: publishing one is completely exposing yourself to public scrutiny.

people that are willing to listen to your ideas, share candid feedback, and offer insightful perspectives. The right path is better lit by multiple lanterns.

Enough preface[119]...on to the process.

First step: address the questions.

1. What is it that I want to achieve?

I've been working in the innovation space for my entire career. I began developing new products in my first job, working as a fat-free mayonnaise engineer (no, really) for Kraft Foods. When I got my name on my first patent, and later saw a customer at a grocery store buy a product that I helped launch, I was completely hooked on the innovation drug. I want others to experience the same high. My cause, my purpose, is to help the world to innovate.

Being one who enjoys studying academic research, I want to combine the knowledge from that study with my professional experience to help people bring innovations to life. I want to help people who have ideas on how to make the world a better place to live, but are uncertain of how to go about making those ideas real. I want to help drive employment and quality of life by giving those who would contribute to innovation-driven growth the tools they need to make it happen more consistently and successfully.

2. Within what constraints will I operate?

I enjoy teaching and solving problems, and I've got skills and experience in doing them both. Consulting, then, is a good way to serve all of those objectives, getting to a wide variety of people, training and problem-solving so that they can serve their diverse clients in ways I could never do on my own.

I have a passion for serving mission-driven organizations (as if you didn't already know that from reading this chapter). I wanted to help smaller organizations that may not have established systems for driving innovation, and I could do that better than others. I aspired to become globally recognized as an end-to-end innovation expert with such clients in the next 5-10 years, while launching and operating a successful new business in the first 1-3 years.

3. Why should anyone want to help achieve what you want to achieve?

---

[119] Perhaps the public scrutiny thing is making me procrastinate as I type.

In addition to being a chemical engineer way back in my undergraduate days, I was also an economist. While I never pursued that field professionally, I have remained an amateur devotee of the subject. I have seen research estimating that *50-80% of economic growth is due to innovation*. That's HUGE. By practicing the best methods for delivering innovation to the world, we can drive economic growth that creates jobs, improves quality of life, and relieves social ills like poverty and disease. How cool is that?

On a personal level, innovators will feel the giddy joy of seeing their work impact the lives of others. On a business level, those who pursue these practices to mastery will gain more customers, drive more revenues, employ more people, and reward their stakeholders better. To paraphrase the ancient proverb, give the world an innovation, and feed it for a day; teach the world to innovate, and feed it for a lifetime. That's what's in it for everybody.

With such reflection done, it was time to cut those hundreds of rambling words into something simple.

I reviewed my notes, and thought about the things that were most important. I highlighted key words that were priorities to include (if not the actual word, at least the concept). I crossed out words that either weren't as important to me, or could be incorporated into other phrases that I preferred.

It was not a clean process. It was iterative, and continues to be so as my business grows and changes. There were fits and starts and revisions. I got pretty good at tossing crumpled sheets of paper into the recycle bin.

At the moment, the Pi Innovation mission is: "to help mission-driven organizations to design, build, maintain, and repair their innovation engines, so that they can make their parts of the world better places to live." Not quite tweet-sized, but concise and descriptive. Is it perfect? Is it even exemplary? Heck, no. But for now, it's working for me.

And executed adequately is better than merely contemplated perfectly.

It expresses the three elements of a mission statement that I want:

What to achieve:	Helping mission-driven organizations achieve what they set out to do;
Within what constraints:	Designing, building, maintaining, and repairing their innovation engines;

Why it should be achieved: So their worlds become better places to live.

But as I said, this is the "at the moment" mission. It's a work in progress. In fact, it's the third or fourth iteration so far. You see, another finding in the research on organizations with mission statements is that those who continually work on them are better performers. Since I'm not one to be satisfied with mediocrity, I'll keep an open mind to adapting the mission, and making changes on a regular basis.[120]

If only I had Kennedy's speech writer, or Shackleton's advertising firm.

So go to it. Get your organization involved in the mission. Make it something your innovators can leverage for motivation and direction. And if you really need a push in the right direction, just imagine Samuel L. Jackson staring you in the eye and saying, "I'll ask you again...what's in your mission?"

Simple Study Guide – Mission Review

- What are the simple elements of a good mission statement?
- Why worry about creating a mission statement?
- What are the benefits of a good mission statement?
- Who should be involved the creation and articulation of a mission?
- What questions should you ask yourself to create a mission?
- What mission mistakes should you avoid?

---

[120] Perhaps the second edition of this sure-to-be-best-seller will contain the story of the Pi Innovation mission update process. Stay tuned!

Where do you want to go from here?		
Control	**Creation**	**Conversion**
Mission (page 40)	Voice of the Customer (page 175)	Innovation Teams (page 310)
Culture (page 58)	Minds of Innovators (page 217)	Project Management (page 347)
Strategy (page 92)	Ideation (page 279)	For-Profit Metrics (page 389)
Portfolio Management (page 146)		Nonprofit Metrics (page 403)
Change Management (page 411)		

Or just turn the page to keep reading...

The Power of Ignorance (Culture)

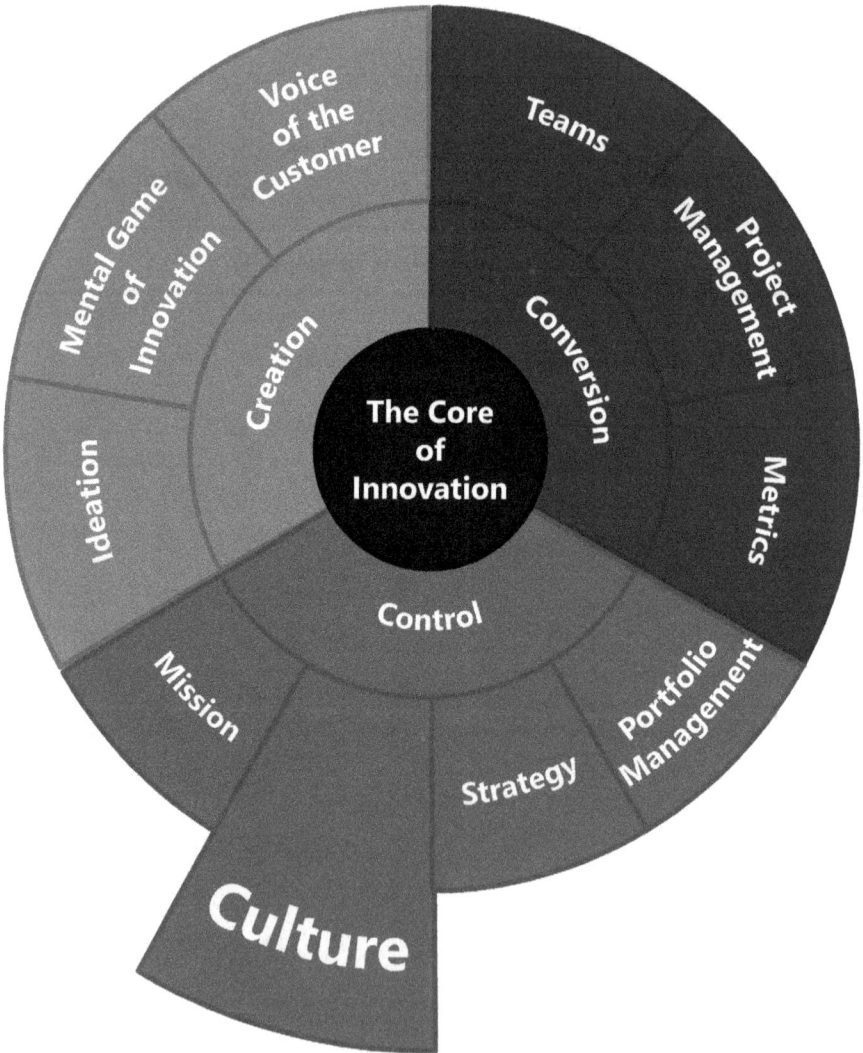

Simple Self-Assessment - Culture

Rate yourself on the following questions. To benchmark yourself against others, go to www.3point14Innovation.com and click the "Self-Assessments" menu.

- ### Do you actively manage your organizational culture?

Cultures can't be managed   As much as possible

1	2	3	4	5	6	7	8	9	10

- ### How well do you leverage fear to drive innovation?

Heads of non-innovative employees   Is that a trick question?
are displayed on pikes at the entrance.   Fear can't drive innovation!

1	2	3	4	5	6	7	8	9	10

- ### How well does your innovation strategy fit your culture?

Like a whale in a bathtub   Like a key in a lock

1	2	3	4	5	6	7	8	9	10

- ### How clearly can you define your culture?

It's a riddle wrapped in a   As clear as the
mystery inside an enigma   queen's crystal

1	2	3	4	5	6	7	8	9	10

- ### What happens in your organization when someone fails?

A good flogging for all   Learning for all

1	2	3	4	5	6	7	8	9	10

- ### How candid and open is the communication in your organization?

We don't discuss   As honest as the summer
that. Ever.   solstice day is long

1	2	3	4	5	6	7	8	9	10

- ### Is thoughtful risk-acceptance encouraged?

Only if we are   Go big or
wearing helmets.   go home.

1	2	3	4	5	6	7	8	9	10

- ### Is healthy conflict encouraged in your organization?

No conflict allowed   Scars are a badge of honor

1	2	3	4	5	6	7	8	9	10

- ### How curious would you say that your organization is?
  Curiosity kills cats.   Good question...
  We don't allow it.   let's explore that.

1	2	3	4	5	6	7	8	9	10

- ### Do you base hiring decisions in part on how they fit the culture?
  No, that psychobabble   Personal fit is as important
  is nonsense.   as professional fit.

1	2	3	4	5	6	7	8	9	10

Simple Summary - Culture
Key take-aways you should get out of this section:

- Choose to consciously manage your organizational culture, and ensure that it supports the mission you are pursuing.
- Use tools to assess and define the culture you have, and want.
- Your culture will trump your strategy when the two come into conflict. In the short term, fit your strategy to your culture. In the long term, work to develop and maintain the culture that supports your mission.
- Culture can be defined according to the Competing Values Framework. This four-quadrant chart plots internal or external focus, against flexibility or control. The four quadrants formed define four cultural types: hierarchical, clan, market, and adhocracy.
- An adhocracy culture is the most innovative, particularly for breakthrough radical innovation. A market culture may have strengths in incremental and evolutionary innovations. A clan culture can also support innovation. A hierarchical culture tends to inhibit innovation.
- Fear is the enemy of innovation. Drive fear out of your organization. Balance an environment that is safe for accepting appropriate risks, while maintaining accountability for behaviors and results.
- You don't have to celebrate failure, but you do have to celebrate thoughtful risk-accepting behaviors, strong efforts to do something extraordinary, and the knowledge gained in the organization even when failure occurs.
- Characteristics of a culture that supports innovation are failure tolerance, effective communication (both internal and external), risk acceptance, healthy conflict, curiosity, and humility.
- Cultural fit should be an important part of any hiring decision. You need to be careful in termination decisions, and anticipate their impact on those who remain in the organization. On one hand, removing poor performers demonstrates that you value the strong performers, and you don't want to saddle them with a detrimental teammate. On the other hand, seeing people terminated may make remaining employees more risk-averse and fearful, eroding innovation performance.
- Leverage subcultures within the organization, with the help of "diplomats" who can work within both the subculture of a group and the broader culture of the organization.

Magic Words

In their book *Think Like a Freak*, journalist Stephen Dubner and economist Steven Levitt provide us with the three most important words that few people use enough. They are rarely heard in board rooms, meeting rooms, or classrooms. They are never heard in political debates.

As Dubner describes in an interview with Wharton management professor Adam Grant, "A really basic rule of thumb or a basic MO that happens very frequently now is a firm will say, 'We need to come up with a plan or a solution. Let's get our top 20 people together in a room for an hour' — that's 20 person hours — 'and let's come up with the best one, the best idea, and then put all our resources into that and go.' What are the odds? If this were science, what are the odds that that would bear a good result? Almost none."

Almost none.

Yet we do that all the time? Why?

In a word: fear.

One of the biggest anti-innovation phobias we have is the fear of three magic words: "I don't know." Even though these three magic words can help us break free of the status quo, people fear saying them. Worse, people ridicule those who do dare to speak them. Yet they may be the most important words to help us actually make real progress in this world.

Levitt and Dubner demonstrate how we are usually over-confident about what we think we know. They recommend that a healthy dose of "I don't know" can be of real benefit.

This is not new wisdom. When asked why the Oracle of Delphi declared him to be the wisest man in Greece, Socrates replied, "because I admit that I know nothing."

Thomas Fuller, a 17th century English writer, noted that "A man is never nearer to ruin than when he trusts too much to his own wisdom."

Ben Franklin, speaking about ratification of the newly drafted US Constitution, said "Most men, indeed... think themselves in possession of all truth, and that wherever others differ from them, it is so far error ... I cannot help expressing a wish that every member of the convention...would, with me, on this occasion, doubt a little of his own infallibility."

Robert J. Sternberg, a prominent researcher and theorist of human intelligence, wrote an entire book called *Why Smart People Can Be So Stupid*.

Jokes about people being stupid when they think they are being smart abound. Check out the musings of medieval barber Theodoric of York:[121]

> "You know, medicine is not an exact science, but we are learning all the time. Why, just fifty years ago, they thought a disease like your daughter's was caused by demonic possession or witchcraft [crowd chuckles]. But nowadays we know that Isabelle is suffering from an imbalance of bodily humors, perhaps caused by a toad or a small dwarf living in her stomach..."

If there's a small dwarf in my stomach, I want it out.

There is a great saying that captures the danger of failing to admit our ignorance. "It isn't what we don't know that gives us trouble. It's what we know that just ain't so."[122]

"I don't know" is liberating. You don't have to know everything, all the time. None of us do, anyway. Hearing someone else say those words frees us to say them ourselves. Hearing us say them frees others to say them.

"I don't know" is inspiring. Those words should earn respect. Keep in mind that those who act as if they know it all are generally thought of as being full of horse droppings by the rest of us.[123]

"I don't know" is empowering. It allows us to challenge conventional wisdom, which, in turn, allows us to learn, grow, and get better at things.

"I don't know" is enabling. It allows our ears to truly hear, without distorting what our customers, clients, stakeholders, and markets are telling us. It eliminates our inclination toward confirmation bias, because there is no "I know" to confirm.

---

[121] You can see Steve Martin perform his Theodoric brilliance online at https://www.nbc.com/saturday-night-live/video/theodoric-of-york/n8661

[122] This aphorism has been variously attributed to Will Rogers, Mark Twain, and Josh Billings, and I really don't know which one came up with it. At some point, I'm sure the internet will start saying that it came from a slew of others as well. I don't know the truth of who expressed it first, but I do know the truth of the saying itself.

[123] Unfortunately, this is not always true, especially if they speak their horse pucks with enough confidence. Still, being a "know-it-all" is never a compliment.

"I don't know" is necessary. It allows organizations to develop and maintain powerful innovation engines.

But fear keeps us from ever admitting that we don't know.

Fear: The Anti-Innovator

Fear is one of the most basic human emotions.[124] It has contributed significantly to mankind's survival. Without it, our ancestors would have all been eaten in the Stone Age.

> Cronk: "Hey, didn't that saber-toothed cat just eat Grog?"
> Thag: "Yeah, but look how cute it is...here, kitty, kitty..."

So fear can be a good thing. Fear helped drive us together into social clusters through a strength-in-numbers survival strategy. And when groups of people get together, culture develops.

So fear helped us form culture.[125] It's no wonder that fear is so much a part of so many corporate cultures. It's no wonder that the FUD factor[126] is a part of sales training.

But so what? Does culture really matter?

Yes, it matters.

Fear is not usually an emotion that drives creativity and innovation.[127] New and different, to many, is synonymous with dangerous and deadly.[128] An organization with a culture formed out of fear and fed by fear is unlikely to be the most innovative of places.

---

[124] Or at least it appears on most of the theoretical lists of basic emotions. See Andrew Ortony and Terence J. Turner, "What's Basic About Basic Emotions?" *Psychological Review*, July 1990.

[125] Brad Barbera, "Fear Helped Us Form Culture," *No Peer-Reviewed Journal Anywhere*, Pure Speculation Press, Sometime in 2015.

[126] FUD=Fear, Uncertainty, and Doubt. Check out the FUD sales training video at https://www.youtube.com/watch?v=Ig5pYmqY5Ig to see how sales people leverage FUD.

[127] Matthijs Baas, Carsten K. W. De Dreu, Bernard A. Nijstad, "A meta-analysis of 25 years of mood-creativity research: Hedonic tone, activation, or regulatory focus?" *Psychological Bulletin*, November 2008.

[128] Expressed beautifully in the opening of this trailer for the movie *The Croods*. Get online and see it at http://www.anyclip.com/movies/the-croods/.

The saying "culture eats strategy for breakfast" was recently popularized by Mark Fields of Ford Motor Company,[129] where a framed version of that saying hangs in the company's "War Room." The point here is not that you don't need a strategy (you do), but rather that you need to have a strategy that can be supported by your culture. If your culture and your strategy are at odds, strategy is going to lose every time.

There is a chicken-and-egg issue here. Should your strategy be fit to your culture, or should your culture be fit to your strategy? The answer is...yes.

Culture and strategy are like earth and water. In the short term, the earth will dictate where the water flows. Over time, though, the water will wear away the earth and shape it to conform to the direction it wants to flow.

In the short term, you absolutely must fit your strategy to your culture. A strategic plan that goes against the culture will get pushed aside. If, however, that culture is not conducive to the long-term survival of the organization, the culture needs to be strategically changed. That takes a great deal of time and energy, but it can be done.

So if innovation is to be part of your strategy, and part of your means of achieving your mission, then you absolutely, positively, must have a culture that can support it.

What is Culture?

But what is culture? Professor Geert Hofstede, one of the leading researchers and theorists on the subject, defines culture as "the collective programming of the mind, distinguishing the members of one group from others." It's "the way we do things around here." You can think of it like the operating system on a gaming machine. All the different strategies and tactics, programs and processes you try to implement are like the games. If you try to play a PlayStation game on an Xbox machine, it's just not going to work, no matter how great the game may be.

Unfortunately, most organizations are not consciously managing their cultures. Few are even aware of what their culture is. As a result, many

---

[129] Fields attributes the quote to Peter Drucker, and it's all over the internet with Drucker's picture next to it, but I can't find a solid source for the original quote. So Fields gets the credit for now. Better to be a stickler for accuracy than a contributor to misinformation, right? I know. I've got issues.

otherwise worthwhile efforts fail because of a mismatch between the culture and the program. And usually it's the program that gets blamed. But that's just like saying the PlayStation game stinks because it didn't work on the Xbox or Wii.

So even though following evidence-based practices can make your organization more innovative, you won't necessarily succeed by just tacking on some innovation program that doesn't actually fit within your culture.

Types of Culture

How do you know what kind of culture you have? There are at least a dozen different ways of measuring and defining an organizational culture. I recommend using a simple tool called the "Organizational Culture Assessment Instrument," originally developed by Kim Cameron and Robert Quinn. It's simple, validated, and effective. With just a handful of questions, you can determine which of four types describes your organization's culture, based on the Competing Values Framework.

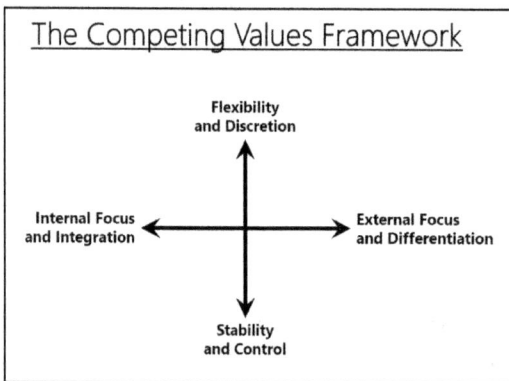

The Competing Values Framework (CVF) plots cultures against two axes. Each axis represents an aspect of organizational culture. On the vertical axis, you plot how an organization is managed and structured. On the horizontal axis, you plot where an organization focuses its attention. The opposing directions of the axes represent competing values – thus, the name "Competing Values Framework." Clever, huh?

Figure 16: The Competing Values Framework for defining an organization's culture

The management/structure axis runs from the value of stability and control on the lower end, to flexibility and discretion on the upper end. The focus axis runs from internal focus and integration on the left to external focus and differentiation on the right.

Notice that those are all valid business values to possess. This is not a plot of good vs. evil and smart vs. stupid. On such a chart, you know which end of the spectrum you want to be on.

Every organization needs to embrace each of the competing values to some degree. Innovation requires both flexibility and control.[130] There must be some level of control and stability, or the organization can't even be called an organization. Driving an idea to reality requires execution processes to guide and coordinate efforts effectively and efficiently. At the same time, there must be some degree of flexibility and discretion – even machine parts have tolerances built into them, and human beings, no matter how well trained and closely supervised, are not machine parts. Sorry, Fredrick "Speedy" Taylor.[131]

Both internal and external focuses are required for effective innovation. There must be some internal focus to keep any team of individuals rowing in the same direction. There must also be some external focus to keep the team from rowing over a waterfall.

Different organizations will have different levels of concentration on each of these four values. Those differing intensities are what allow the CVF to distinguish four types of cultures. Those four types are displayed in Figure 17.

Again, notice that these are not ranked on a good-to-evil scale. All of these cultural types have pros and cons. All

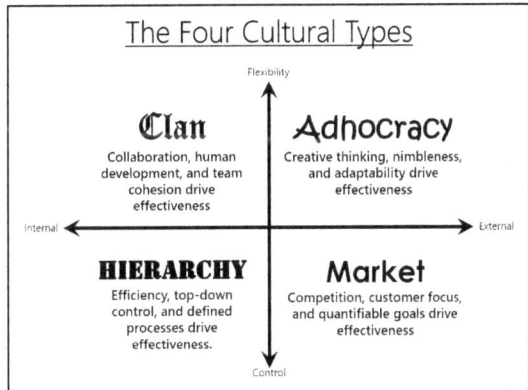

The Four Cultural Types

Flexibility

Clan — Collaboration, human development, and team cohesion drive effectiveness

Adhocracy — Creative thinking, nimbleness, and adaptability drive effectiveness

Internal ← → External

HIERARCHY — Efficiency, top-down control, and defined processes drive effectiveness.

Market — Competition, customer focus, and quantifiable goals drive effectiveness

Control

Figure 17: The Four Cultural Types defined by the Competing Values Framework

of them work well at some times and in some places, and not so well at other times or in other places.

---

[130] Michael Song and Yan Chen, "Organizational Attributes, Market Growth, and Product Innovation," *Journal of Product Innovation Management*, November 2014.

[131] For more about Taylor and his excessive belief in measurement and imitation, get online and go to http://lcweb2.loc.gov:8081/ammem/amrlhtml/intaylor.html

The names of each cultural type are probably readily understandable, except maybe for that one in the upper right. What the heck is an "adhocracy?" I'll let Cameron and Quinn explain for themselves:

> "The root of the word adhocracy is ad hoc," they say in their book *Diagnosing and Changing Organizational Culture*, "implying something temporary, specialized, and dynamic. Adhocracies ...have been characterized as 'tents rather than palaces' in that they can reconfigure themselves rapidly when new circumstances arise. A major goal of an adhocracy is to foster adaptability, flexibility, and creativity where uncertainty, ambiguity, and information overload are typical...It is an organizational form that is most responsive to the hyper-turbulent, ever-accelerating conditions that increasingly typify the organizational world of the twenty-first century."

Got any guesses on which organizational culture best supports innovation?

Culture of Innovation

Recent research has demonstrated that an adhocracy culture best supports innovation,[132] and is most correlated with positive innovation outcomes such as sales from new products, profitability of new products, time-to-market, and similar metrics.[133] But things may not actually be quite that clear. Earlier research had demonstrated that a market-oriented culture produced the best innovation outcomes.[134]

But, perhaps surprisingly, this makes sense. Both the adhocracy culture and the market culture have an external, differentiation focus. That external focus gives an organization insight into the problems out there in the world, and into the solutions that the world will value.

---

[132] Thorsten Büschgens, Andreas Bausch and David B. Balkin, "Organizational Culture and Innovation: A Meta-Analytic Review," *Journal of Product Innovation Management*, July 2013.

[133] For more on innovation metrics, go to the sections on "Innovation for Fun and Profit" (page 389) and "Innovation for Fun and Not-for-Profit" (page 403).

[134] Rohit Deshpandé and John U. Farley, "Organizational Culture, Market Orientation, Innovativeness and Firm Performance: An International Research Odyssey," *International Journal of Research in Marketing*, March 2004.

For an adhocracy, the flexibility and adaptability enable creative and collaborative exploration of novel solutions. For a market culture, the stability and control enable efficient execution of the solutions devised. The former is more likely to support radical or breakthrough innovations, while the latter may better support incremental or evolutionary innovations.

Because of the flexibility and adaptability factors, the clan culture can also have positive impact on innovation outcomes,[135] though significantly less so than with adhocracies. Their lack of external focus may put them in a reactionary position, but if they do need to react to changing circumstances, they are able to do so efficiently.

Hierarchical cultures, not surprisingly, tend to have negative impact on innovation outcomes.[136] Command-and-control not only fails to promote innovation well, but actually *inhibits* an organization's ability to innovate. Focusing internally narrows the field of vision on problems and solutions, and the high degree of structure and control inhibits the ability to adapt to change.

Look, if you are a command-and-control sort of person, don't shoot the messenger here. I know the message is hard to hear. If it helps, you may be comforted to know that some objectives are still best served by a hierarchy. Such a culture can be incredibly efficient at producing volumes of the same thing repeatedly. It's just not, on average, going to be very innovative compared to the other types of culture.

Now, if you doubt that an organization can operate effectively without structured, hierarchical controls. I'd suggest you consider a couple of counter-examples that prove it's at least possible.

Look at Haier, a Chinese home-appliance manufacturer. In the mid-1980s, their predecessor, the Qingdao Refrigerator Co., was near bankruptcy. As part of the turn-around effort, incoming CEO Zhang Ruimin established a radically flexible organizational structure. The overall organization essentially consists of thousands of small business units, some as small as a single individual.[137] Each has its own culture and systems. Each is its own profit center, bearing the

---

[135] Büschgens, et. al.

[136] Ibid.

[137] Martin Reeves, Claire Love and Philipp Tillmanns, "Your Strategy Needs a Strategy," *Harvard Business Review,* September 2012.

fully-loaded costs of all of its operations. Even functions that are normally centralized, like finance or human resources, operate as individual profit centers, selling their services to the other business units. Talk about accountability! To make it, everyone needs to constantly deliver value.

Did it turn things around? Well, they are now the world's largest home-appliance company, with a most recent twelve-month EBITDA of $3.5 Billion.[138] Yes, I would call that a successful turn-around.

Alternatively, look at the example of W. L. Gore & Associates, whose structureless organization was made famous by a *Harvard Business Review* case study in 2012. Gore, best known among consumers for the Gore-Tex® material in their winter coats and gloves, is a leading manufacturer of electronics, medical devices, sealants, and all sorts of other high-tech materials and applications. They have a team-based, flat, interconnected organization that fosters personal initiative. They have no traditional organizational charts. They do not have a defined chain of command. What they do have is $3.2 Billion in annual revenue and a place on the 2015 Forbes list of largest private companies.[139] But this is not some whacky new-aged attempt to try out a creative org structure. They have been doing this since Bill Gore founded the company in 1958. When Eisenhower was the POTUS. A decade before hippies danced to music on that farm in Woodstock, New York.

Now, before commanding and controlling that your organization adopts an adhocratic[140] culture, be aware that the national/local culture has an impact, too. Your corporate culture should have alignment with the local culture (unless, perhaps, you are able to – and want to – pick out the oddballs in your area that don't fit the local culture). If you internationalize your innovation operations, you will have to pay strong attention to the local culture, and take steps to align your local corporate culture with it.[141]

---

[138] According to Morningstar Financials in September of 2015.

[139] And a place on the Forbes 2015 list of America's Best Employers at the same time.

[140] I just made that word up, but I think it works.

[141] Martin Eisend*, Heiner Evanschitzky and David I. Gilliland, "The Influence of Organizational and National Culture on New Product Performance," *Journal of Product Innovation Management*, published online May 4, 2015 (Online version published before inclusion in a physical issue).

So, what do you think is the least common organization culture type of the thousands that Cameron and Quinn have evaluated?

If you guessed "adhocracy," you win the prize, and get to continue in the *Innovation Games*. If you guessed anything else, we have some lovely parting gifts for you.

Okay, even if you guessed wrong, don't go away. We can still help you out if you want to pursue innovation.

You've seen how an external focus is key to developing innovative solutions, while flexibility and adaptability help organizations to adjust to a changing marketplace. Are there any other particulars of a culture that support innovation? What else separates the successful innovators from the not-so-muches?

Culture of Innovation Characteristics

The PDMA's CPAS study[142] identified important cultural components that separated the innovation winners from the innovation mediocrities:

- Failure is understood to be a natural part of the innovation process;
- Innovation values are effectively communicated, both internally and externally;
- Risk-taking is valued for career development;
- Constructive conflict that occurs within the innovation process is accepted.

Two other characteristics demonstrated to enhance innovation capabilities in individuals are curiosity and humility. A culture that values those elements will attract people with those characteristics, and help them to thrive.

Let's take a moment to understand these points a little better.

---

[142] Stephen K. Markham and Hyunjung Lee, "Product Development and Management Association's 2012 Comparative Performance Assessment Study," *Journal of Product Innovation Management*, May 2013.

Failure Tolerance

Let's face it: nobody enjoys failure. It hurts. Managerial behaviors that promote fear just make that pain all the worse. Such behavior is what I call Homer Simpson management, which tells the organization, "You tried your best and failed miserably. The lesson is – never try."[143]

It's a cliché thrown around by innovation pundits that 90% of innovation efforts result in failure. While the research doesn't back this up (accurately measured new product failure rates are consistently found to be roughly between 35% and 45%),[144] it still shows that if you don't have a backbone for failure, you're not going to be an innovator.

Why do we waste so much time trying to avoid mistakes instead of learning from them? We'd be so much better off if we could find a way to extract value from our failures, rather than let them extract value from us. It's like Lucille Ball said when asked about how her groundbreaking TV show *I Love Lucy* came into being: "We [she and her husband, Desi Arnaz] decided that instead of divorce lawyers profiting from our mistakes, we'd profit from them."

Mistakes are going to happen in an unpredictable world. Taking on risk, by definition, means that failure is a possibility. You and your organization must be prepared to fail. The biggest failure of all is the failure to fail well.

It is important to distinguish, however, between two types of failure. There is "good failure," and there is "bad failure."

Good failure comes from daring greatly. When you stand up to innovate, you do so knowing that a fall is possible. As Brené Brown puts it on the cover of her book *Rising Strong*, "If we are brave enough, often enough, we will fall." The attitude before a good failure is one of recognizing risk, taking appropriate precautions, considering the potential consequences, and then courageously

---

[143] If you were reading the eBook, you could click to see the video. Since this is print, though, you'll just have to get online and go to https://www.youtube.com/watch?v=NwVNuyfhF0Q.

[144] There are many reasons for the disparity in conventional wisdom and researched results. One lies in the definitions used to do the measurements, which only involve marketplace-launched innovations, so all those projects that get resources applied and hard work done but end up not being launched are not counted as failures. But that's not the only reason. Steve Markham and George Castellion in "New Product Failure Rates: Influence of *Argumentum ad Populum* and Self-Interest" (published in *Journal of Product Innovation Management*, October 2012) show how much human psychology plays a role in perpetuating the myth of massive failure rates.

accepting the challenge. If the effort fails, good failure involves extracting value from the effort anyway, by learning something that will lead to future success in the process.

Bad failure comes from carelessness or stupidity. Bad failure starts with an attitude of nonchalance. "Whatever, let's get this over with." No courage is required, because no consequences are considered. After the failure, there is not only no effort to learn, but there is often great effort to hide. That is bad failure.

The problem in many organizations is that they treat both types of failure the same way – with systematic punishment. Those who try and fail are relegated to professional gulags, while those who play it safe are given Lucite awards and 4.9-star performance appraisals. When organizations systematically punish both forms of failure equally, risk acceptance and employee effort are stymied.

Figure 18: My son's t-shirt would suggest a third category: "epic failure."

The best innovation organizations find ways to reward "good failures."

I used to be an advocate of celebrating failure, but I've changed my mind. Failure stinks. Failure hurts. Celebrating it seems like a denial of those basic facts. However, celebrating strong effort against the odds, celebrating new knowledge, and celebrating the behaviors that the organization values are all things that I continue to strongly advocate. People should know that the behavior of trying, failing, and getting up to try again is not only acceptable, but encouraged.[145]

---

[145] If anyone needs some motivation on this point, hand them Teddy Roosevelt's famous "Man in the Arena" passage (with apologies to modern gender sensitivities – he wrote this over a hundred years ago, so please forgive him): "It is not the critic who counts; not the man who points out how the strong man stumbles, or where the doer of deeds could have done them better. The credit belongs to the man who is actually in the arena, whose face is marred by dust and sweat and blood; who strives valiantly; who errs, who comes short again and again, because there is no effort without error and shortcoming; but who does actually strive to do the deeds; who knows great enthusiasms, the great devotions; who spends himself in a worthy cause; who at the best knows in the end the triumph of high achievement, and who at the worst, if he fails,

This does not mean that you give up on holding people accountable for their actions. You need to *fully* embrace accountability, which means doing the difficult work of understanding what happened, and handling it effectively, as opposed to resorting to some thoughtless zero-tolerance policy that makes reward-and-punishment decisions easy, but counter-productive.

Communication

Both internal and external communication are critical in all forms: spoken words, written notices, and, most importantly, observed actions.

Everything said and done among a group of people contributes to the perception of what that group stands for, what constitutes acceptable behavior, and what expectations are to be for members of the group.

Just as we discussed in the chapter on mission,[146] actions will speak jet-engine decibels louder than your words. At times, you may have to explain those actions to ensure a common understanding of your reasons, motivations, and desired outcomes. If you don't explain the meaning of your actions effectively, people will assign them their own meanings. You don't want those meanings to be wrong.

There is a simple trick that will help you to convey the meaning that you want people to understand with the actions that you take. It's based on neurological science and psychology.

It's called – get ready for it – honesty.[147]

It goes by other names, too, such as authenticity, sincerity, being real, truth. Look, I don't mean to be preachy or holier-than-thou. I'm just calling out the need for organizations to deal with reality. Real reality. You don't have to be a saint to honestly face a situation, and get those around you to do the same.

---

at least fails while daring greatly, so that his place shall never be with those cold and timid souls who neither know victory nor defeat." Bully.

[146] For more about the topic of mission, go to page 40.

[147] If you are not one of the nearly ten million people to watch it already, I recommend checking out Julian Treasure's TED talk "How to speak so that people want to listen." https://www.ted.com/talks/julian_treasure_how_to_speak_so_that_people_want_to_listen?languag e=en

You do need courage, especially in organizations with a hide-and-seek sort of culture.[148] The risk is reduced (and the courage requirement decreased) when the culture is one of open, candid collaboration.

Some people are really good at BSing,[149] but no one is perfect at it.[150] Human beings all have evolutionarily honed BS-detectors, and some people are exceptionally good at sniffing it out. In the ever-expanding information age, the ability for someone, somewhere to detect your BS and tell the world about it is accelerating exponentially.

Innovation is difficult work. When things are difficult, the truth about people tends to be uncovered even more quickly. As General Dwight Eisenhower said about the European theater of World War II, "This is a long tough road we have to travel. The men that can *do* things are going to be sought out just as surely as the sun rises in the morning. Fake reputations, habits of glib and clever speech, and glittering surface performance are going to be discovered."[151] So don't fake it with glib and clever speech.

Staying honest, aligning your actions with the organizational mission, living the values of the culture you desire... that all works better than extensive lie-telling, and it saves you from having to remember all of your own distortions.

Forget the spin. How many people believe the word "opportunity" anymore? When someone says to me, "Brad, I have an 'opportunity' for you..." I know immediately that I must be in the wrong place at the wrong time, and my life is about to get painful.

If it really is an exciting prospect, then be excited. If it's really a life-threatening challenge, then express that. Remember the Shackleton ad?[152]

---

[148] No, that's not part of the official Competing Values Framework (page 66), but you probably know what I mean.

[149] See Princeton University philosophy professor Harry Frankfurt, "On Bullshit." The information age increases the BS potential. My experience of seeking quote verifications for this book proved that.

[150] Paul Ekman, *Telling Lies: Clues to Deceit in the Marketplace, Politics, and Marriage*, W. W. Norton & Company, 2009.

[151] Letter to Vernon Prichard dated August 27, 1942, published in *The Papers of Dwight David Eisenhower* edited by Alfred Dupont Chandler, Johns Hopkins Press, 1970.

[152] The Shackleton ad appears on page 51.

That's the kind of honesty I'm talking about. Such honesty will draw the right kind of people to you, in abundance.

Eloquence is great, but eloquent BS will lose to bumbling honesty most of the time.

Note that you can maintain confidentiality and still be honest. Honesty does not mean public declaration of detailed strategic plans or revelation of trade secret intellectual property. It simply means genuinely aligning what you say with what you do. And it works especially well for innovation, where trust is a critical component of creative collaboration and execution.[153]

Risk Acceptance

What is risk? Let's not get overly complicated here. Taking a risk is simply making a decision to do something that has a chance of failing.

There are ways to quantify and evaluate risk that are beyond the scope of this book. For now, it's sufficient to make just a couple of points.

First, keep in mind that all risk is personal risk. Whether you go through a complicated and rigorous mathematical evaluation of an investment decision, ultimately an emotional and personal transaction takes place. If everyone were rational, Las Vegas wouldn't exist. The math says you can't beat the house, and the real wealth that is accumulated in that desert is by the owners of the houses. Everyone knows that. But people keep on tossing their chips on the green velvet.

Innovation requires taking some smart risks. Some of those risks will be of the standard business decision variety: should we invest in this equipment? Should we use supplier A, supplier B, or both? Should we do this ourselves or get outside help? These seem to be straightforward, rational decisions we must make, but when professional reputations are impacted, when raises and promotions are at stake, when business relationships come into play, even these become personally risky.

Other risks are more obviously personal: Should I make this design suggestion in front of the whole team? Should I tell the executive team about

---

[153] For more about the critical components of team effectiveness, go to the "Marriage Counseling" section of the Team chapter, page 335.

the latest hiccup or hope that we can fix it before they find out? Should I commit to getting that task done by that date, considering all the other stuff I have to get done?

The biggest problem when assessing personal risk is that we humans are fundamentally irrational creatures. We have a host of "cognitive biases"[154] that impact our decisions in ways we aren't even consciously aware. We are biased toward the status quo.[155] We are also biased to avoid loss, even when potential gains rationally outweigh the potential loss.[156] No wonder innovation is hard.

Understanding these biases and working with your team to overcome them is critically important. Providing personal safety to support thoughtful risk acceptance, while still holding people accountable, is an important balancing act for innovation managers.

Conflict

By far, the most successful teams that I have ever worked with had a significant amount of conflict between members. The opposite has also been true: some of the most disappointing results came from teams that agreed on virtually everything.

It's the difference between the Bay of Pigs invasion and the Cuban missile crisis.

In case you aren't up on your 20th century American history, The Bay of Pigs invasion and the Cuban missile crisis were two major events that occurred during the presidency of John F. Kennedy. They make a wonderful pair to learn from, because they involved the same group of people, working together to make decisions that impacted world security at the height of the Cold War. The Bay of Pigs Invasion has gone down in history as one of the most bone-headed and poorly managed decisions in history. Within just eighteen months, though, the team recovered to set a high benchmark in effective team collaboration under severe stress during the Cuban missile crisis.

---

[154] For more on cognitive biases, go to the "Cognitive Biases" section, page 224.

[155] William Samuelson and Richard Zeckhauser, "Status Quo Bias in Decision Making," *Journal of Risk and Uncertainty*, March 1988.

[156] Richard Thaler, "Toward a Positive Theory of Consumer Choice," *Journal of Economic Behaviour and Organization*, March 1980.

Without going into historical detail, the Bay of Pigs invasion was a botched mess. It is the premier example of the dangers of "groupthink," in which team members, for any variety of reasons, never bother to challenge or confront each other. They fail to express different viewpoints. They defer excessively to the will of the team or to that of prominent team members. Everyone gets along, and every team meeting goes smoothly...until they embarrass themselves before the entire world.

The team regrouped from that catastrophe, though, and instituted procedures, behavioral norms, and expectations that mitigated the possibility of groupthink. During the Cuban missile crisis, under extreme duress, the team managed to make the decisions that diffused a situation as close as the world has yet come to World War III.

Team conflict was the key. Respectful but passionate debate, conscious review of multiple scenarios and alternatives, creation of sub-teams intentionally chosen to have conflicting opinions, selective exclusion of the ultimate decision-maker to avoid biasing the direction of debate, all contributed to rapid but well-thought out decisions, even when the consequences could not have been higher.

Of course, unhealthy conflict does not lead to effective decision outcomes, either. Unhealthy conflict turns the arguments personal. Don't make arguments about "I'm right and you're wrong." If emotions heat up like an Easy-Bake Oven, take a break, drink an iced green tea, and revisit the issue later. Anger can lead to risky and destructive decisions,[157] so avoid letting conflict, which is naturally unsettling, devolve into being infuriating.[158]

If you are uncertain as to how to argue effectively, consider taking a course of ten lessons at the Argument Clinic.[159] Just make sure you go to the right room.

---

[157] Marc L. Resnick, "The Effect of Affect: Decision-Making in the Emotional Context of Health Care," *Symposium on Human Factors and Ergonomics in Health Care*, Human Factors and Ergonomics Society, Baltimore, MD, 2012.

[158] For more about how to effectively manage conflict and keep it healthy, go to the "Marriage Counseling" section of the Team chapter, page 335.

[159] Arguably (pun intended) one of the best among many great Monty Python sketches. Get online and see it at https://www.youtube.com/watch?v=kQFKtl6gn9Y

Bring healthy conflict to your innovation teams. It is one of the best of all evidence-based practices. Dare I call it a "best practice?"

Curiosity

Remember at the beginning of this chapter, discussing the power of the words "I don't know?" Well, "I don't know" is necessary – but not entirely sufficient. "I don't know" gets us only halfway there.

Theodoric of York[160] once again can help us understand a critical component of an innovation culture. After being confronted by a grieving mother of one of his less-than-healed patients, Theodoric considers a possible future...

> "Perhaps I've been wrong to blindly follow the medical traditions and superstitions of past centuries. Maybe we barbers should test these assumptions analytically, through experimentation and a 'scientific method.' Maybe this scientific method could be extended to other fields of learning: the natural sciences, art, architecture, navigation. Perhaps I could lead the way to a new age, an age of rebirth, a 'Renaissance!' [thinks for a minute] Naaaaaahhh!"

Oooooo, he was so close for a second there. If only he had followed up his "I don't know" moment with the other critical piece of innovative inquiry.

And what is that piece?

I was fortunate enough to take a managerial accounting class from Professor Roman Weil at the University of Chicago. The most important and most memorable lesson that he taught me had nothing to do with Generally Accepted Accounting Principles (GAAP).[161]

---

[160] Steve Martin's Theodoric can be seen online at https://www.nbc.com/saturday-night-live/video/theodoric-of-york/n8661.

[161] One of the few things that I still remember about GAAP is that R&D expenditures are counted as expenses, not investments. That, philosophically, is wronger than a llama in lederhosen. Spending on innovation is an investment. Economic Value Added accounting gets it right, where innovation expenses like R&D are capitalized (see Galen R. Hatfield, "R&D in an EVA World: As a

In his class, he liked to have class participation. He kept you awake through the drudgery of double-entry bookkeeping by maintaining the constant threat of being called upon to answer a question in front of the whole class. And that's where the life lesson came in.

He told us in the introduction to the class, in minute one of day one, that if he called on you, there were two, and only two, acceptable answers. One was the correct answer. The other was "I don't know, but I'll find out."

If you were called upon and provided the correct answer, you breathed a sigh of relief. If you ever gave the wrong answer, your ego received a jab to the nose from Dr. Weil's quick wit, and you immediately launched into a relentless search for the right answer. You were never let off the hook.

The search for the correct answer took place while the rest of the class continued on. Mind you, this was in the days before smart phones and the Google. Few of us even owned laptops, and we generally didn't bring them to class if we did. We had to scour through pages of text in a book, our own illegibly scribbled notes, or whatever such archaic resources we had to get the answer. Once found, we'd raise our hands until he called on us again. We'd have to remind the class what the question was, and then announce the correct answer to the question. If we were wrong, the whole process began anew, including another Weil wit-jab to the intellectual ego.

This was not a lesson about accounting. This was not a lesson about paying attention in class. This was a lesson in innovation.

Innovation is all about "I don't know, *but I'll find out.*"

There is no better way to capture the attitude of curiosity necessary for innovation. That attitude needs to be a determined part of any individual innovator. That attitude needs to be a pervasive part of an organizational culture of innovation.

Valuable Financial Metric, Economic Value Added Reinforces the Role of R&D as an Investment in the Future of the Corporation," *Research-Technology Management Journal*, January, 2002).

Humility

To be able to live "I don't know, but I'll find out" requires genuine humility.[162]

That does not mean false modesty. Genuine humility means an honest assessment of your skills, capabilities, and knowledge. It means recognizing not only what you lack, but also what you possess.

The power of humility to innovation can be illustrated in the rise of a new game: freestyle chess. Ever since computers surpassed even the greatest human chess players, chess programs have been leveraged to learn and understand the game better than ever before. In freestyle chess, human players are free to use computer programs to assist them in making their moves, leading to what chess enthusiasts have called the most beautiful games ever played.

You might expect that, out of the gate, the best freestyle chess players would have been the highest-rated human players assisted by the highest-rated chess programs. That's not how it turned out, however.[163] The best freestyle players turned out to be those who were strong on their own, but not necessarily the best. They did have a characteristic that the highest-rated players lacked: a large dose of humility in their psyche. The humble Davids were able to defeat the more confident Goliaths, even though both had access to the same software. How could this be?

The humbler humans were less likely to override computer suggestions, while still being able to add an element of creative human judgment that the computers lacked. The higher-rated, but more arrogant players would believe that their skills and intuition were stronger than the software...until, of course, defeat proved them wrong.

These winning freestyle players demonstrated powerful innovation skills that can be helpful to anyone looking to improve their organization's innovation capabilities:

---

[162] Don Emerson Davis, Jr., and Joshua N. Hook, "Measuring Humility and Its Positive Effects," *Association for Psychological Science Observer*, October 2013.

[163] Tyler Cowen, *Average is Over: Powering America Beyond the Age of the Great Stagnation*, Dutton Penguin Books,2013.

- They are able to accept expert input that may or may not agree with their own thoughts. They make good decisions based on all of the inputs, not just on those that confirm their own bias.[164]
- They can direct the experts to look down particular paths, before selecting the one they believe to be best. The best innovators know both how to focus the analysis and when to stop the analysis and make the move.
- They seek out multiple opinions, knowing that the points where expert opinions diverge present the real opportunities for brilliance. Those are the places that the insightful innovators can contribute the most with their own expertise and judgment. Strong innovation leaders will encourage healthy disagreement in their team of experts.

To be able to live "I don't know, but I'll find out" requires both risk acceptance[165] and tolerance of failure. Admitting you don't know will feel to many like an admission of failure. There is also risk required to go "find out." Finding something out is not always as easy as googling a few keywords on your smartphone. The most potentially rewarding "finding out" is the kind that requires exploration into new areas, creating new knowledge. But, like all explorers sailing into the unknown, it is also the riskiest.

As the saying goes, "Good judgement is born of wisdom. Wisdom is born of experience. Experience is born of bad judgment."[166]

If you aren't willing to make a mistake, then you aren't willing to innovate. And that would be the biggest mistake you could make.

Cultural Change

Okay, so we know what kind of culture we need to have if we want to support innovation. Now, how do we get there?

---

[164] For more on cognitive biases, go to the "Cognitive Biases" section, page 224.

[165] For more on risk acceptance, go to the "Risk Acceptance" section, page 76.

[166] Variations on this aphorism have been attributed to everyone from Will Rodgers to Simon Bolivar to Omar Bradley to Christian Slater. My apologies to whoever first stated this brilliance for lacking a citation.

First, recognize that changing a culture is a challenging undertaking that requires non-stop effort and vigilance. There are things you can do to change your culture to better support innovation, but expect the effort to be a marathon, not a sprint. It may even be more like the Badwater Ultramarathon[167] than just a marathon. If innovation is what you want, though, you have no choice but to create and nurture a culture that supports it.

Second, create subcultures within your organization as necessary. This has some nice advantages, but it also has some unique challenges that we'll need to address.

Let's start with addressing the overall organizational culture.

There are almost as many approaches to cultural change as there are to defining culture in the first place. Fortunately, most of these approaches have several common themes on which they agree. Rather than present a single prescriptive method, I'll just touch on those areas of agreement.

1) Leaders must consciously define and buy into the culture they want.

Even those experts who advocate a bottom-up approach to culture change recognize that without top-level support, such efforts will be wasted. Management must not limit cultural support to lip service, either. It must be lived. The entire collection of organizational eyes will be on the leadership, and any perceived deviations of the walk from the talk will halt any progress.

Consistent adherence to the new desired norms is critical. Most people do not like change, and they will be looking for any rays of hope that change won't be necessary. You'll be dealing with the psychology of the slot machine.

Why do people keep pumping change into slot machines until they go broke? Because the slot machine pays off every once in a while. That reward, coming at irregular, unpredictable intervals, is psychologically addicting. One successful pull at the one-armed bandit – even with a tiny payoff – outweighs twenty pulls that lose.

The same will be true for any inconsistencies in cultural change management. Every little reward someone experiences for doing things the old way will reinforce sticking to the old ways, and will do so far more than many little "punishments" intended to encourage new behaviors.

---

[167] An event not for the faint of heart. See http://www.badwater.com/event/badwater-135/

Also remember that in order to plan the route to where you want to go, you have to know where you are now. Evaluate not only what the culture needs to be in the future, but also what it is in the present. Decide exactly what needs to change, and what won't change. Prioritize the changes, because they won't take hold all at once.

2) Cultural change takes a long-term, sustained effort, not a one-time declaration.

Jerry Levin, the CEO of Time-Warner before their merger with AOL, decided that a change of culture was necessary in his company.[168] He made a 45-minute video of himself outlining the new culture that was necessary, distributed it to the employees, and overnight, the organization became exactly what he wanted.

Oh wait. Scratch that. Actually, nothing changed.

There was no follow-up, there was no effort to build support, there was no change management. Not surprisingly, there was no effect, either.

In addition to monitoring their own behaviors, leaders must recognize the appropriate behaviors of others throughout the organization. That recognition must be done visibly and extensively. Staff needs to be influenced to adjust their behaviors to the changes, not just told to change. Think about it – it is self-contradictory to try to move from a command-and-control culture by commanding and controlling the change!

Find influential staff members, and secure their buy-in. Such people will often be even more influential than the highest-level managers will be in creating and sustaining the change.

Cultural change does not happen overnight. Nor in a fortnight. Not to scare you or anything, but honestly, it is not a process that is ever truly finished. It must be constantly monitored, assessed, re-evaluated, and nurtured. It is not a program, but a way of living in the organization. Change programs are the means, not the ends themselves.

---

[168] Jerome H. Want, *Corporate Culture: Illuminating the Black Hole*, Macmillan, 2007.

3) Hire slowly.

Make sure that the right people who can effectively fit in the culture you want are on your team. Treat each hiring decision as an adoption into a family rather than just as an economic transaction. Involve peers in the hiring process, as they have a stake in knowing the people with whom they'll be working. This will hasten the onboarding process as well, since peers will have already accepted new hires before they arrive.

You must be committed to the culture you want. Hiring people who don't naturally fit the existing culture will arouse the corporate antibodies, which will then try to drive out the intruder. If you allow those antibodies to defeat your newly hired change agent, you will strengthen that immune response system, much like a vaccine does in children. This can potentially wreck your external reputation, making it that much more difficult to get the change agents you want. You must provide ongoing support for them, including hiring more people that fit the desired culture.

Do not expect that hiring just one person, regardless of what level they may be, will deliver a magical transformation of the culture. You need a chain reaction, and chain reactions require critical mass.

4) Fire slowly...or maybe quickly.

No matter how good the hiring process is, some who do not fit will make it through the screening process. It is important to remove such forces from the organization, so as not to allow them to infect others who do fit.

There is disagreement, however, among experts as to whether to fire quickly or slowly. There are two opposing forces: keeping a bad fit on board too long can erode team performance and drive good performers away; firing too quickly can erode individuals' senses of security, eroding risk acceptance and hindering innovation performance – and good performers leave out of fear for their jobs.

Personally, I recommend erring on the side of firing slowly, while paying close attention to team dynamics. However, there have been many vocal and valid opinions I've heard expressed to the contrary. Use your best judgement based on the impact you want to have for your team, and on ensuring progress toward the culture you want.

5) Communicate, communicate, communicate. When you're done, communicate some more.

Keep your communication simple – clear, complete, consistent and concise. Follow a simple communication model[169] that helps everyone who gets your message to know unambiguously what you expect of them. And remember, be real. Or authentic, honest, genuine, etc. However you want to describe it, just be it.

Communication is an ongoing process. It is a dialogue, not a monologue, involving at least as much listening as speaking.[170] Words are only a small fraction of communication as well. Tone and behavior will drive your message far more than words alone. And, like everything in the change process, communication must be an ongoing behavior, not a one-and-done event.

6) Establish new rituals and ceremonies. Real ones.

Not like the corporate award program I once experienced. I worked on a major project that had dozens of people making significant contributions. The team won a corporate award, but the rules limited the recipients to just five people. The managers got it, the rest of us didn't. That was hard enough to take, but the following year made it worse – when I did win an award. I had been transferred to a small team just a few weeks before award time. The two guys who had worked all year on a big breakthrough earned the team an award. Even though I had contributed bupkis to the effort, I was given the same recognition they got.

That is exactly the wrong way to create recognition and ritual. Unless, of course, you want a cynical culture.

Effective rituals must be sincere. Effective rituals must be perceived as a fluid part of the behavioral norms. Effective rituals must support the culture. If you have a cultural objective of team cohesion, the rituals should be team oriented. Encourage team members to evaluate and reward (or sanction) each other based on conformance to the values and beliefs of the team – NOT based

---

[169] For more on a simple communication model, go to the "CLEAR Communication" section, page 329.

[170] In addition to his "How to Speak so People Listen" talk, Julian Treasure covers the topic of listening in another excellent TED talk: "5 Ways to Listen Better."

on particular outcomes. Celebrating outcomes is okay, but rewarding outcomes alone will lead to their pursuit by any means necessary, including those that violate desirable cultural norms.

Defining and engendering a strong and effective corporate culture is the hardest effort that an innovation leader can undertake. It will also prove to be the most durable and rewarding.

Subcultures

Within a single organization, different cultural environments can and should exist as circumstances require. We simply need to adapt to the requirements of the moment.

As an individual, you may be thinking that rapidly changing between subcultures is impossible – that's just not how humans work. You'd be wrong.

Think of this example: I can go to my church on Sunday morning, adapting to the cultural norms without much effort. I dress in appropriate attire, greet others pleasantly and calmly, and sit attentively during readings and sermons. I pretend to sing the hymns (trust me, you don't want me to *actually* sing anywhere outside of a soundproofed shower). After the services end, I can calmly and politely remind the friends who also attended services that I will be visiting with them in just a few hours, to support our football team in their latest gridiron adventure.

I then head home, throw on some beat-up jeans and the replica jersey of my favorite player, run over to my buddy's back yard, pop open a can of beer, spill some as I yell at the TV announcer for clearly being an idiot if he thinks my team's defense really misses that sorry excuse for a linebacker that we got rid of last year, all while using colorful expletives to articulate my point and chewing a bite of hot dog freshly pulled off the grill.

Same day, same guys around me, totally different subculture, totally different norms of acceptable behavior. Yet we transition between them seamlessly, without conscious thought.

The same is true in our organizations. We can go from an executive presentation to a water-cooler discussion with teammates met in the hallway, and we adjust to these subcultures without thinking about it.

There are three different situations that lead to the rise of subcultures. These situations can be defined by how the people involved are momentarily separated from the rest of the world. These separations can occur in space, in time, or in context.

A group separated in space is defined by geographic boundaries. These boundaries can be on a global scale, such as the Singapore office of a company headquartered in New York City. They can also be extremely local, like the team that works on the third floor being isolated from the team on the fourth floor. Don't underestimate the cultural barriers that can crop up from seemingly insignificant physical barriers.

A group separated in time is defined, obviously, by when they are gathered. The same team operating during a time of crisis will need to operate under different behavioral norms than a team casually celebrating an important accomplishment.

A group separated by context is defined by their social or professional expectations. For example, a marketing department will have a different subculture than an accounting department, and they will both be different than an engineering department. In a non-profit, those responsible for fund raising will have a different subculture than those responsible for service delivery.

In the hypothetical church/football example, all three separations are in play. The church is a different space than the backyard barbeque; the morning church time is different than the afternoon game time; and the context of being gathered as worshipers is different than the context of being gathered together as football fans.

You have to be conscious of these subcultures, as well as being conscious of the overall culture. Use the separations to your advantage.

For example, the armed forces are probably the first thing you think of when coming up with an example of a Hierarchy (although that may no longer be as true as it used to be). However, when engaged in strategic planning, or conducting an After Action Review (a critical innovation tool we'll visit later), it is more beneficial to have a climate of open collaboration. Creating separations in time, space, or context can make this happen. As former Chairman of the Joint Chiefs of Staff and Secretary of State Colin Powell said, "When we are debating an issue, loyalty means giving me your honest opinion, whether you think I'll like it or not. Disagreement, at this stage, stimulates me."[171]

---

[171] Colin L. Powell and Joseph E. Persico, *My American Journey*, Random House LLC, 1996.

Then, when facing combat or some other job to be executed immediately, the situation is different. A clear chain of command, from the Commander-in-Chief down to the lowest-ranked enlisted man, governs every action. Boot camp training is designed to ensure that every soldier is going to immediately follow orders and do their duty even under fire. As Powell goes on to say, "Once a decision has been made, the debate ends. From that point on, loyalty means executing the decision as if it were your own."[172]

Innovation is no different. As we've seen, some cultures serve innovation efforts better than others. If you are in a Hierarchy organization, but want to support innovation efforts immediately, you can do so by creating an innovation-supporting subculture. To do so, you must create a wall between the overall organization culture and the innovation team subculture.

Perhaps you could create a separation in space by locating an innovation team off-site from the rest of the organization, as in the Lockheed Skunk Works model. Perhaps you could create a separation in time by designating certain hours as innovation hours and the rest as execution hours. Perhaps you could create a separation in context by designating one group to be responsible for innovation full-time, while other parts of the organization remain devoted to execution.[173] However you create the separation, allow the boundaries to provide protection to the innovative subculture, so that it does not get overrun by the overall organizational culture.

Of course, you must also beware of the potential downsides of subcultures. They can divide people that need to work together as a team. They can create animosity between teams, or between a team and the mother ship.

To manage these downsides, find people who can play the role of diplomat well. These people are the chameleons of your organization, able to blend into a variety of environments. It's not that they change themselves, or merely agree with whomever they are speaking They simply adjust their communication to fit a consistent message to the ears of the audience. Whether you call them diplomats or chameleons, they play a critical role in helping to maintain an

---

[172] Ibid.

[173] Warning: this particular means of separation can lead to an in-group/out-group bias that may not be good for the organization! For more on such biases, go to the "Cognitive Biases" section of the Mental Game of Innovation chapter, page 224.

innovation subculture within an overall culture not-so-supportive of innovation.

What is a diplomat? I've always loved these definitions: "A diplomat is a person who can tell you to go to hell in such a way that you actually look forward to the trip,"[174] and "Diplomacy is the art of letting other people have your way."[175] Such skills come in handy when working on an innovation project.

These critical people need to be adept at identifying and understanding various cultures, and help those cultures work together effectively. The role does

Figure 19: Organizational chameleons are the diplomats that help innovation teams fit into their surroundings. They are needed both in the broad organization and on individual teams.

not need to be played by a single person, but it does need to be played if potential cultural clashes are going to get in the way of progress.

Consider the case of General Dwight D. Eisenhower being selected as the Supreme Commander of the Allied Forces in Europe. He was not selected because of his proven strategic abilities, nor for a history of combat success. Prior to World War II, his had a rather undistinguished military career. But in that career, he demonstrated skills in organization and diplomacy that were absolutely critical for the task at hand. He had to manage differences between national cultures and powerful personalities, often with dramatically opposing perspectives, including such people as Roosevelt, Churchill, Patton, Montgomery, de Gaulle, and Marshall.

Had the invasion failed – and the odds of failure were high enough that Eisenhower had prepared a speech in advance to take responsibility for it – the last 70 years of world history would likely have been very different. Never underestimate the role of a diplomat to the success of an undertaking.

---

[174] Caskie Stinett, *Out of the Red*, Random House, 1960.

[175] Daniele Varè, *The Laughing Diplomat*, Murray, 1938.

So embrace ignorance, encourage exploration, and consciously manage your culture (or subcultures) to support innovation efforts. Don't let your strategy get devoured for breakfast, lunch, dinner, or midnight snack by your culture. Your culture should be a pillar, not a pillager, supporting the hard work you are doing to accomplish your mission.

Simple Study Guide - Culture

- What is the Competing Values Framework (CVF)?
- What are the four types of organizational cultures according to the CVF?
- Which comes first – strategy or culture?
- What types of culture fit best with an innovation strategy?
- What are characteristics of an innovation culture?
- What six things are required for establishing and maintaining a desired culture?
- What role is most critical for a subculture?

Where do you want to go from here?

Control	Creation	Conversion
Mission (page 40)	Voice of the Customer (page 175)	Innovation Teams (page 310)
Culture (page 58)	Minds of Innovators (page 217)	Project Management (page 347)
Strategy (page 92)	Ideation (page 279)	For-Profit Metrics (page 389)
Portfolio Management (page 146)		Nonprofit Metrics (page 403)
Change Management (page 411)		

Or just turn the page to keep reading...

To Do or Not to Do, That is the Question (Strategy)

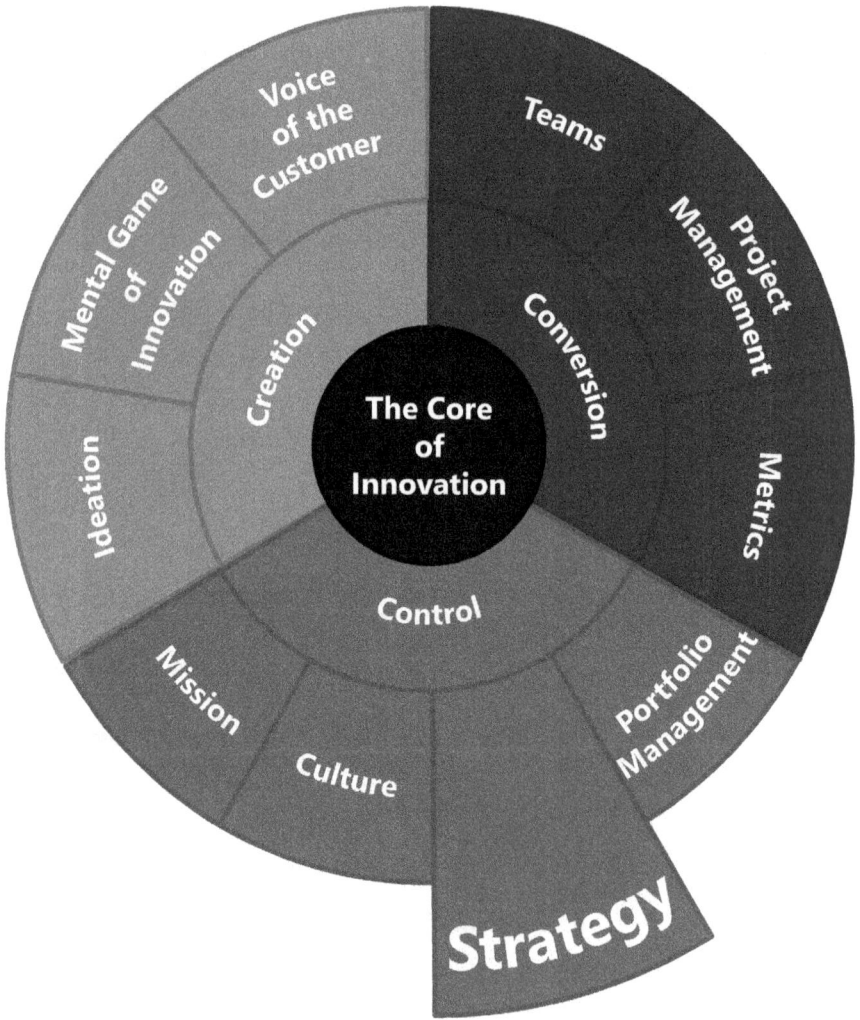

Simple Self-Assessment - Strategy

Rate yourself on the following questions. To benchmark yourself against others, go to www.3point14Innovation.com and click the "Self-Assessments" menu.

- ***Does your organization have a strategic plan that everyone understands?***

  Um, there used to be a binder
  around here somewhere...   It guides our every action.

1	2	3	4	5	6	7	8	9	10

- ***Does everyone share a common understanding of the strategic plan?***

  We argue about it   Our ducks
  constantly   are in a row.

1	2	3	4	5	6	7	8	9	10

- ***How many words does it take to lay out the basics of your strategic plan?***

  More than you   Just enough to share
  have in this book.   in the elevator.

1	2	3	4	5	6	7	8	9	10

- ***Does the strategic plan clearly link resources and objectives to the mission?***

  Are they supposed
  to go together?   Like a solid chain

1	2	3	4	5	6	7	8	9	10

- ***Does your innovation strategy support the overall organization strategy?***

  Like a straw house   Like a brick house
  built on sand.   built on bedrock.

1	2	3	4	5	6	7	8	9	10

- ***Does your innovation strategy have technology and marketing components?***

  Components?   Of course!

1	2	3	4	5	6	7	8	9	10

- **Does your organization use a variety of tools to guide strategic planning?**

  We only use Hammers.

  You should see the size of our toolbox!

1	2	3	4	5	6	7	8	9	10

- **Does your strategy include behavioral norms and expectations?**

  That doesn't belong in a strategic plan.

  Yes, definitely.

1	2	3	4	5	6	7	8	9	10

- **Has your organization thought through contingency plans?**

  No need. Everything will go perfectly.

  We are ready for anything.

1	2	3	4	5	6	7	8	9	10

- **How open is your innovation approach?**

  Closed and locked like a bank vault door.

  As open as the great outdoors.

1	2	3	4	5	6	7	8	9	10

Simple Summary - Strategy

Key take-aways you should get out of this section:

- Strategy is a leader's plan for the use of available resources to achieve a specific objective that supports a higher mission.
- The greatest value of a strategic plan is the planning process itself. Done well, the process will uncover critical information, identify possible futures, and prepare contingencies for those possibilities.
- An organizational strategy should have an innovation component, and an innovation strategy should strongly support the overall strategy.
- There are four types of innovation strategies organizations can follow: *prospector* (first-to-market with breakthrough offerings), *analyzer* (fast-follower, adaptive to changing conditions), *defender* (striving for high efficiency and low cost operations), and *reactor* (basically operating without a plan).
- The SWOT analysis (strengths, weaknesses, opportunities, and threats) is a simple means of summarizing the critical information that should be considered in developing strategic plans.
- Michael Porter's five forces (supplier power, customer power, threats from substitutes, threats from new entrants, competitive rivalry) should be analyzed within the context of environmental conditions, such as general economic forecasts, broad changes in technology, social trends and emerging concerns, changing demographics, the political environment, and the legal or regulatory framework in which you operate.
- You must know where your products fall in the product life cycle. New-to-the-world technologies should receive different kinds of investment than mature technologies ripe for replacement.
- Competing where everyone else is competing leads to everyone getting beaten up. Use tools like the blue ocean strategy canvas, the innovation radar, and the ten types of innovation to expand your thinking, and to discover new arenas for serving customers without having to slog through a fight.
- In order to plan effectively for the future, create a roadmap that identifies the routes required to achieve your future vision. The roadmap will not only help guide what you need to do today to achieve a goal for tomorrow, but it will help identify how realistic your objectives are, what gaps exist in your plan, and what hurdles need to be overcome.

- Capture your strategy simply. Use the one-page simple strategic plan document to provide a common language, guidelines for behavior, and metrics for success. This simple communication tool will then serve as a guide to decision-making for the organization to follow. It sets the boundaries within which innovators can explore and operate.
- Use multiple metrics of success to maximize overall performance.
- Open innovation leverages the involvement of external parties – customers, suppliers, experts, people from other fields entirely – to identify and execute the highest value innovations. Open innovation is not like an on/off switch. It's not a matter of being either open or closed. Open innovation falls on a continuum. You need to understand the costs and benefits to opening your innovation efforts, and determine just how open you can and should be.
- Once the strategic planning is done, you need to communicate it effectively to all that are involved in its execution. *Simply.* Then communicate it some more. Ensure that the plan is commonly understood by all, and considered by all in their day-to-day decisions.

Planning is Everything

As touched on in the chapter on culture,[176] perhaps the greatest example of strategic planning in military history, code-named Operation Overlord, was the invasion of Normandy on D-Day, June 6, 1944. It involved coordinating not just multiple military branches, but multiple military branches of multiple countries. It involved the coordination of efforts of powerful and opinionated personalities. It included the use of a general respected as "the best" by the German army,[177] George Patton, as a mere decoy. It involved precision at a time when equipment and munitions were far less precise than they are today. It involved over a year of planning and deception that could be overturned by the fickleness of Mother Nature, and the winds and weather she would send through the English Channel on the day of execution.

For all the complexity of the actual work to be done, the strategic outline was really quite simple. It's an excellent example of being simple without being simplistic.[178] The idea was to find suitable beaches in natural harbors, amass the men and equipment necessary for an effective landing force, prevent defensive reinforcements by attacking key bridges and roads between the landing site and other German troops, then establish a beachhead through which supplies for a sustained offensive could flow. That took about fifty words to state. Like a good mission statement, you should be able to capture the essence of your strategy in just a few words that all can remember. It doesn't take a 379-slide PowerPoint deck to do it.

---

[176] For more on culture, go to the "Culture" chapter, page 58.

[177] At least according to *Old Blood and Guts: Chasing Bandits and Nazis with General George S. Patton* (by Providence Research, Wikimedia Foundation, U.S. Senate, Office of the Federal Register), in which a variety of German leaders are quoted with similar statements to the one by Field Marshal Gerd von Rundstedt: "Patton, he is your best." A variety of other books suggest that such respect and admiration on the part of the Germans for Patton was not, however, the case. This is a book about innovation, though, not World War II generals, so I won't get into that debate. Suffice it to say that Patton had a good deal of demonstrated success on the battlefield (more than most prior to D-Day), but he was held behind as a decoy, which was a pretty bold strategic move. And George C. Scott's *Patton* movie speech remains one of the great scenes in movie history. See it online at http://www.dailymotion.com/video/x156uvg_patton-s-opening-speech-to-the-troops-george-c-scott_shortfilms

[178] For more on the definition of simple, go to the "Why Simple?" section, page 18.

A simple strategy can help make the complex manageable. We'll revisit that point when we talk about portfolio management[179] and project management.[180]

Don't get me wrong, preparing for complexity is good. Knowing how to make all the moving parts fit together is critically important. But just as a simple mission statement provides a foundation for an organization, a simple strategic plan provides the framework on which to build all the activities of that organization. Remember, simple is not about avoiding complexity, but about making the complex clear and understandable.

What is Strategy?

When it comes to strategy, much of the discussion has to do with the military. You are as likely to hear the statement "We are going to outflank them and seize the high ground" in a corporate boardroom as at the Pentagon. However, don't take that as a sign that strategery[181] is of necessity about adversarial conflict. It isn't.[182]

Military history has some important characteristics that make it easy to reference. Great individual leaders, and, for that matter, blunderers, emerge. Their decision processes are often well-documented, and the actions taken are recorded in detail for posterity. What works and what doesn't can be and have been analyzed from a wide variety of perspectives. Lessons from those analyses are available for all to see, even if learning from history is not a human forte.

However, key differences between military strategy and organizational strategy include the fact that not all organizations have "enemies." This is especially true for non-profits. Think about it. Let's say you are running a non-profit to feed the poor. Unless you are doing so in Somalia, it is unlikely that you have opposing organizations actively trying to prevent you from feeding

---

[179] For more on portfolio management, go to the "Portfolio Management" chapter, page 146.

[180] For more on project management, go to the "Project Management" chapter, page 347.

[181] Yes, I am well aware that this is a made-up word to poke fun at former POTUS George W. Bush. But it's such a good word, I can't pass it up.

[182] This point is well-articulated in a *Harvard Business Review* blog post by Frank V. Cespedes, "Stop Using Battle Metaphors in Your Company Strategy," December 19, 2014. While there is much to learn about effective strategies from military history, it is equally important to understand that there are important differences as well.

the poor. While you could say that poverty itself is the enemy, it's not one that is consciously plotting against you. Lyndon Johnson's War on Poverty is not the same as Napoleon's War on Europe.

Still, much can be learned from the millennia of thought that have been put into military strategy, and the millennia of experience we have in seeing which strategies work and which ones end up in a bad checkmate.

The Difference between Mission, Strategy, and Tactics

Before proceeding further, perhaps some definitions are in order. It is easy to confuse mission,[183] strategy, and tactics. In many cases, they seem to be used interchangeably. That's because the difference between the three is largely a matter of viewpoint. One woman's mission is another man's strategy, which in turn is another woman's tactics.

In general, the mission for a group is the big objective that they want to achieve. Strategy is the broad plan of how the mission is to be achieved. Tactics are the more specific actions taken to execute the strategy. The thing is, depending on the size and scope of the group, the strategy for one team may be the mission of another.

Take the D-Day example. For Eisenhower, the mission was to defeat Germany, the strategy was to do so by establishing multiple fronts to overstretch the capacity of the German army, and Operation Overlord was a tactic to establish one of those fronts.

On D-Day, commanders of armies had the mission to establish a beachhead at their particular point of attack, such as Omaha beach. Their strategy was to leverage air and sea superiority and the element of surprise to overwhelm entrenched German defensive positions. The tactics used included shelling German bunkers with 14-inch artillery fired from the decks of battleships stationed outside the range of German artillery.

For a particular group of infantrymen, their mission may have been to capture a particular machine-gun nest. Their strategy may have been to soften the defenses with mobile artillery fire and a constant hail of covering fire from the front, while soldiers with grenades and bayonets sneak up from the flanks.

---

[183] For more on the topic of mission, go to the "Mission" chapter, page 40.

The tactics could have been to crawl from one safe spot to another, rather than run and risk being spotted.

So the difference between mission, strategy, and tactics is often a matter of perspective. And that's not just my viewpoint. The great military historian and theorist B. H. Liddell Hart referred to "grand strategy" and "pure strategy" to distinguish between the overall purposes of a nation (grand strategy) and the specific military plans of a general trying to deliver against those purposes (pure strategy). The grand strategy is a higher-level viewpoint than the pure military strategy. To the warrior contemplating pure strategy, the grand strategy is the mission. To the politician contemplating grand strategy, the pure strategy is a tactic.

This is why I started by talking about mission.[184] Defining the mission for your group will establish the boundaries for your strategies and tactics. It will also serve as the collective conscience of the organization to keep it moving through inevitable struggles. To paraphrase Viktor Frankl, those who have a "why" can bear with almost any "how."[185]

The mission is the "why." The strategic plan is the "what." The specific tactics are the "how."

Defining Strategy

So how, then, should we define strategy specifically?

Liddell Hart defines strategy as: "the practical adaptation of the means placed at a general's disposal to the attainment of the objective in view."[186]

This is a powerful and simple statement. It considers the planning (or "practical application") for use of limited resources (or "means placed at the general's disposal") and focuses on achieving the mission (or "objective").

---

[184] For more on the topic of mission, go to the "Mission" chapter, page 40.

[185] "A man who becomes conscious of the responsibility he bears toward a human being who affectionately waits for him, or to an unfinished work, will never be able to throw away his life. He knows the 'why' for his existence, and will be able to bear almost any 'how.'" Viktor Frankl, *Man's Search for Meaning*, Rider Publishing, 2011. Considering this philosophy got him through Auschwitz, it should at least help a team get through some business challenges.

[186] Sir B. H. Liddell Hart, *Strategy, Second Revised Edition*, Faber and Faber Ltd., 1967.

Generalizing "general"[187] beyond a military leader to mean a leader of any group pursuing a mission, this is a great place to start understanding the nature of strategy.

To get clearly into the business realm, we have to check out Michael Porter, the godfather of business strategy. He says, "Competitive strategy is about being different. It means deliberately choosing a different set of activities to deliver a unique mix of value."[188]

Differentiation and value. Sounds a lot like innovation to me.[189]

Leveraging another definition found in the academic literature, "Business strategy is the pattern or plan that integrates a firm's major objectives and action sequences into a cohesive whole."[190]

Putting those three definitions together provides the basis for understanding strategy as it will be discussed in this book:

> *Strategy is a leader's plan for the use of available resources to uniquely create value that supports a higher mission.*

That's a simple definition, but it carries a good deal of nuance. Let's unpack it in some detail to ensure clarity of meaning.

Strategy is:
- a leader's
- plan
- for the use of available resources
- to uniquely
- create value
- that supports a higher mission.

---

[187] You gotta love how English can use the same word to have completely different meanings.

[188] Michael Porter, "What is Strategy," *Harvard Business Review*, November 1996.

[189] For more on how I define the term innovation, go to the "What the #&%! Is Innovation, Anyway" section, page 4.

[190] Henry Mintzberg, Joseph B. Lampel, James Brian Quinn, and Sumantra Ghoshal, *The Strategy Process: Concepts, Contexts, Cases, Fourth Edition*, Prentice-Hall, 2002.

Leadership. Why "a leader?" Setting a strategy requires a decision, and ultimately, all decisions are made by an individual. Even group decisions are just a collection of individual decisions to support a common choice. Yes, teams, teamwork, and collaboration[191] are absolutely important. Focusing the strategy decision on an individual is not a call for dictatorial power. It is rather a call for accountability. If everyone is responsible for the decision, then no one is.[192]

Plan. In the end, a strategy is a plan, and strategery[193] is the act of creating that plan. As discussed with regards to project planning,[194] life almost never goes according to plan. So why bother?

You should bother because the planning process prepares you for the inevitable plan derailment. The analytical process is about learning, foreseeing possibilities, and considering alternatives. Later, when in the heat of the fray, you can react quickly, leveraging that foresight, rather than having to figure everything out all over again.

Limited resources. Truly being in touch with the resources available is an underappreciated challenge. It's easy to both over- and under-estimate the resources available. Time, money, and brain capacity are all finite things if you have not yet achieved complete oneness with the universe.

A good strategic plan does not pretend to have infinite resources. You must maximize what you can get out of what you have, of course, just don't assume that you can feed 5000 with a loaf of bread and a couple of fish. First of all, it's been done, so it really isn't

"Hello, I'd like to place an order for delivery, please..."

---

[191] For more on innovation teams, go to the "Teams" chapter, page 310.

[192] That is NOT an endorsement for command-and-control leadership of innovation teams. That should be obvious from the rest of the text, but just in case someone is suffering from a regrettable cognitive bias that led to reading such an endorsement into that sentence, I want to make explicitly clear that they ain't reading me right.

[193] There I go again with the "strategery" thing. Last time, I promise.

[194] For more about managing innovation projects, go to the "Project Management" chapter, page 347.

innovative, even if you could do it. Second, unless you've got access to the hotline to heaven, you may find the execution falls a little short.[195]

Now, part of your plan could include securing future resources to get to where you want to go, and that's fine. But again, even that has to be grounded in the reality of what current resources you have to be able to get what you want. You can't expect to hire the talent you will need if you don't have a way to compensate for that talent. You won't have the production capabilities you will need if you don't have a way to invest in either infrastructure or partnerships.

Frequently, though, we also miss the opportunities to fully leverage the resources that we do have. Faced with a sulfuric acid leak? Fill it with chocolate![196] Need to storm a castle guarded by sixty men to save your one true love from the clutches of an evil prince? Don't forget to tell your project planner about the wheelbarrow and the holocaust cloak.[197]

Okay, joking aside, we really do miss out on opportunities because we fail to see the possibilities of how things could come together. We have a cognitive mental bias[198] that tells us "this is the way to do things, because that's the way we've always done them." When we don't have the resources we've always used to get things done, we tend to say "oh well, we can't do it," rather than seek out ways that we can.

So don't underestimate the challenge of knowing what your available resources can get done. And, for that matter, don't overestimate it, either.

Unique. Every individual is different. Every organization is different. Every customer is different. The only way to have an advantage is to leverage those differences. As the classic Wendy's commercial said, having no choice is no

---

[195] Okay, I realize that this reference is a little risky, with the potential to offend Christians, members of other religions, and atheists alike. But hey, as Steve Martin said, comedy is not pretty.

[196] Performed on the pilot episode of *MacGyver*, and later proved plausible on *Mythbusters*.

[197] One of the many brilliant scenes from the most quotable movie of all time, *The Princess Bride*. Check it out online at https://www.youtube.com/watch?v=yokQ0_8_ts, or better yet, get the DVD and watch it until you have the whole script memorized. And next time you see someone go off to do something, shout out to them "Have fun storming the castle!"

[198] For more on cognitive biases, go to the "Cognitive Biases" section, page 224.

fun.[199] There is no reason for anyone to take what you have to give if it's just like what everyone else has to give.

Moreover, even if you choose to imitate what others are doing, you can't really be *exactly* the same as others, anyway. You and your organization are going to have different sets of skills, capabilities, and resources available. You have to do things differently. So why not take advantage of your differences, leverage your particular strengths,[200] and deliver unique, differentiated value to the world?

Value Creation. Creating value for someone, somewhere, is the ultimate reason for organizations to exist. Creating value – even potential value – must precede receiving value. The organization comes together to conceive, create, and deliver that value to those who value it.

If you are a farmer, you raise food that people value. If you are a medical professional, you develop healing skills that people value. If you run a water mission charity, you provide clean water that both the people who drink it and the people who give time and money to your organization value. Every organization first and foremost creates value. It is the fundamental reason for being.

Supporting the Mission. Always focusing on the ultimate objective is the thing that separates good planning from bad. It's what enables people to get around unanticipated roadblocks. It's what keeps the execution from failing due to diluted resources spread across too many distractions.

When innovating, it isn't enough for a team member to know what they are supposed to do. They need to know why they are supposed to do it. They need to know how their part helps to move the whole team forward. A focused objective, clearly communicated, enables each member of the team to function better together, to adjust to inevitable changes, and to support one another under changing demand loads.

There is a reason you are doing all of this planning stuff. There is a reason you want to accomplish a given objective. That reason is always and

---

[199] An all-time classic television ad – "is next: day wear!" See it online at https://www.youtube.com/watch?v=5CaMUfxVJVQ

[200] Did you know that "strengths" is the longest word in the English language with only one vowel? Now you do.

everywhere to achieve the mission of the organization. That's why a clear and powerful mission is so important. Know the mission well, and ensure that everyone involved in the planning is focused on that mission throughout the planning cycle.

Organizational Strategy versus Innovation Strategy

There are over 115,000 books listed on Amazon.com about business strategy. The combined weight of that collection would roughly equal that of the space shuttle *Endeavor*. That's a lot of trees and ink.

Clearly, there are already many tools available for guiding strategic planning. Some may be better suited for some organizations and cultures. Some may be effective under certain conditions and not-so-much under others.

Innovation is going to have to be part of any successful strategy. Without it, you'll be doing the same thing as everybody else. At least you will until someone else comes along and does it better. Then you'll be doing it worse.

I'm going to assume that you have an organizational strategy in place. I know, I know, that may not exactly be a safe assumption. But overall strategy is beyond the

Figure 20: Innovation is one of the pillars that hold up the strategy of any organization. Yes, any.

scope of this book. If you need help there, please consult one of those other 115,000 books that are available.

For the purposes of this book, rather than looking at overall corporate strategy, let's focus here on how to tie your innovation strategy to your overall strategy. On the corporate level, innovation may be one of the tactical pillars holding up the overall strategy. For the innovation organization, that tactical component becomes a strategy in itself.

Now, hopefully the innovation organization, whatever it may look like, was intimately involved in the overall strategic planning process. Much of what follows should be going on simultaneously, as part of that broader process.

That may mean doing a few iterations, but as an innovator, you should be used to that.

Strategies that Drive Innovation Success

What aspects of an innovation strategy really drive innovation success? Is there one thing about a strategic plan that will ensure delivering impactful solutions to the marketplace?

Yes. Kind of. If you can call it just one thing, that thing would be "balance."[201]

Of course, balance means being able to manage several things at once, so it's hard to call it just one thing. For innovation practices, the things to balance are technological prowess, market orientation, product "fit," and finding "blue oceans."[202]

Technological prowess does not mean that you have the best computer coders and high-tech electronics engineers working in your organization (unless, or course, you are an electronic hardware or software company). It means that you have sophistication with the technologies that enable *your* products, in *your* industry. In insurance, that might mean prowess in statistical analysis. In pharmaceuticals, it might mean sophistication in biochemistry and engineering scale-up. In reducing hunger in rural Africa, it may be high skill in distribution without infrastructure. In novelty toys, it may be expertise in polymer manufacturing that makes rubber chickens look more realistic.

Market orientation is about your ability to identify, focus on, and satisfy customer needs – making relevant product solutions, building awareness of those solutions among your target audience, and getting the solutions to them in a way that they prefer.

Product "fit" means developing products that connect to your customers and to your organization. That doesn't mean you should only develop variations on existing products for existing customers. You can be "radical" and

---

[201] Robert G. Cooper, "New Product Strategies: What Distinguishes the Top Performers?" *Journal of Product Innovation Management*, September 1984. This theme is true not just for the strategic plan, but for its execution as well, in the form of portfolio management.

[202] For more about Blue Ocean strategy, go to the "Blue Ocean Strategy Canvas" section, page 120.

still be connected. Google can develop driverless cars because of their connection to leading edge information technology. Toyota can develop driverless cars because of their connection to automobiles. But neither is likely to do very well developing rubber chickens, because there is no "fit." Leave that to Loftus International.

In essence, you need "permission" from your customers to provide them the products that you want to provide them. They have to believe that you can do it. It doesn't matter how well you actually do it – they will have their pre-conceived notions of you that will impact their perceptions of the products that you provide. When it comes to product performance, *if they don't believe, they won't perceive.*[203]

Finding "blue oceans" is a term that comes from the work of Renée Mauborgne and W. Chan Kim, originally presented in their book, *Blue Ocean Strategy.*[204] The basic idea of Blue Ocean Strategy is to compete where others aren't competing. Those waters are blue because there isn't blood being shed in fighting over the same space. Such fighting is what Mauborgne and Kim call "red ocean strategy." It's what most organizations do. It's difficult for them to think that there might be other ways of doing business, so they just keep beating each other up.

Types of Innovation Strategy

Much research has been done to determine what types of strategies are successful, and what types are, well, not so much. To do that research, you have to start with a way of categorizing strategies. One long-used and useful strategy classification system is known as the Miles and Snow Strategy Typology.

---

[203] This is a blatant use of the irrational "Rhyme as Reason" bias against you. For more on this and other cognitive biases, go the "Cognitive Biases" section of the "Mental Game of Innovation" chapter, page 224.

[204] Renée Mauborgne and W. Chan Kim, *Blue Ocean Strategy*, Harvard Business Review Press, 2005. Note, however, that Cooper identified the success factor of choosing "high potential, high growth, and non-competitive markets" way back in 1984. What Mauborgne and Kim did best in their work was to show *how* organizations can and do make such choices, and they provided good tools to help.

Don't get intimidated by the academic-sounding name. It's really a simple model. They defined four strategic types out there in the business world (and one of them is really a non-strategy strategy). Since each strategy type has a memorable descriptive name, the framework is very easy to use.

The strategic types are prospector, analyzer, defender, and reactor. We won't really consider the type described as "reactor," since that approach consists of crossing your

Figure 21: The Miles and Snow Strategy Typology, complete with cute pictures to help you know who they are.

fingers and hoping everything works out. Reactors wait to see what happens in the world, then hope that they will be able to react appropriately. In reality, they almost always react inappropriately. It's such a non-strategy that the original paper didn't bother to even list characteristics of reactors, although it provided great detail for the other three. It's a type that is doomed to failure, especially as global change becomes more rapid and dramatic.

The Prospector is the kind of organization that goes out and creates change in an industry, market, or community. It grows by developing new products, services, and markets, so growth can come in surges. It approaches problems with multiple solutions, and flexibly adapts to changing environments. It's the type to take a chance and look for the gold nuggets before anyone else can claim them. With innovation, Prospectors use a first-to-market approach.

The Analyzer is the kind of organization that seeks to be efficient in stable parts of the business, but adaptive in changing parts of the business. It tries to achieve steady growth by expanding within markets with "normal" competitive efforts, while monitoring and analyzing the environment for important changes that will require attention. With innovation, Analyzers use a fast-follower approach.

Defenders focus on stability, trying to protect a segment of the market from change, so that they can efficiently deliver a fixed set of products to a fixed set of customers. Growth is incremental, generally pursued by fighting for market share within established segments. As for innovation, it is primarily focused on internal cost reduction and efficiency. Any external product/service/market innovation is done begrudgingly, and only after change has been absolutely proven to be necessary beyond reasonable doubt.

Okay, so we have some strategic types defined. So what strategy is most successful?

Like so many things with innovation, it depends. In this case, it depends on how you define "success." Research has demonstrated that organizations will define their own success measures based on their strategic type. This should come as no surprise. An organization is likely to base its strategy on what it values, and then determine whether the strategy was successful based on those values. That's fine...until the organization decides it ought to value something that it is not set up to deliver. That's the Reactor mode, and it causes loads of confusion. Avoid it.

A Defender strategy will work well in an environment where change comes at a geologic pace, perhaps due to industry maturity or regulation. Such industries are most susceptible to disruptive innovation.[205]

A Prospector strategy will work well in an environment of high turbulence and rapid change – either in the market, technology, or both. In such situations, risk-taking, addressing emerging markets, and embracing new technologies is critical to survival.

An Analyzer strategy is a hybrid between the Defender and the Prospector, so it works well in an environment of evolutionary change. This strategy can be very rewarding, by saving investments in high-risk projects that fail, and concentrating investment on more likely winners. However, that security comes at a price. Analyzers risk falling behind prospectors or getting disrupted like defenders when change happens faster than they can manage.

---

[205] For a discussion about the term "disruptive innovation" and what it means, go to the "What the #&#! Is Innovation, Anyway?" section, page 4.

A Reactor strategy generally does not work well in any environment. The inconsistencies and lack of clear direction make execution challenging at best, if not impossible.

Now, I have yet to see a strategic plan that explicitly says, "We will follow a [Prospector/Analyzer/Defender/Reactor] innovation strategy." If you want to put a strategy into one of those categories, you'll need to figure it out yourself, based on the stated objectives (is "first to market," mentioned?), and the resources allocated (are they going to fundamental research, new product development, or cost reduction and maintenance?).

Knowing the strategic type can help guide innovation planning. Understanding the willingness of the organization to accept risk, and knowing what defines success, will guide what objectives to prioritize, and how to allocate resources to various projects.

There are a few other things you need to know from the overall strategy. You should be able to identify:

- The markets to target
- The resources available
- The role innovation is to play

From that information, your job is to put together an innovation strategy that fulfills the role, solves the problems of the target market,[206] operates within the resource constraints, and fits with the strategic type. Piece o' cake.

The innovation strategy will need to have two pieces: a technology component and a marketing component. The technology component involves the decisions around what technologies will be used to solve customer problems, and where those technologies will be sourced (homegrown or brought in from outside). The marketing component includes decisions about the product lines, customers to target, and responses to competitors.[207]

Guess what? Rarely are organizations set up so that the same people who do the marketing are also the ones who do the technology. That means that there needs to be strong coordination, cooperation, collaboration, and maybe

---

[206] For more on problem definition, go to the "Defining a Problem is Hard" section, page 185.

[207] Harry Nyström, "Product Development Strategy: An Integration of Technology and Marketing," *Journal of Product Innovation Management,* March 1985.

even cohabitation[208] between these folks, to ensure that the strategic plan is carried out effectively. And that generally means some strong coordination at the executive levels.[209]

Creating Your Strategy

So that's all great. Now we have a neat little definition of strategy: a leader's plan for the use of available resources to uniquely create value that supports a higher mission. And we have the requirements of an innovation strategy to address both the technology aspects and the marketing aspects of bringing new products to life.

Now, how do you create a strategy that will deliver against your mission?

The formal nature of the strategic plan must, like everything else covered in this book, be tied to the specifics of the organization. Smaller, more resource-constrained firms should have a less formal, more flexible strategy. More formal and rigid strategic plans in such organizations can actually *impede* the ability of the organization to innovate.[210] For this type of organization, a rigid strategic plan gets in the way of improvisational development, taking away the small-team advantage of nimbleness and responsiveness to the marketplace.

Note that this does not mean that small businesses and start-ups should proceed without a strategy in place – numerous studies have demonstrated that strategic plans enhance firm performance, both overall and with regards to new product development and innovation. Planning helps to make cycle times faster, failure rates lower, levels of innovation higher, and returns on investment greater.[211] Having a strategic plan is critical, but what kind of

---

[208] In an office area...c'mon, get your mind out of the gutter.

[209] Steven C. Wheelwright and Kim B. Clark, *Revolutionizing Product Development*, The Free Press, 1992.

[210] Michael Song, Subin Im, Hans van der Bij, and Lisa Z. Song, "Does Strategic Planning Enhance or Impede Innovation and Firm Performance?" 2011, *Journal of Product Innovation Management*, July 2011.

[211] These points come from several different studies from researchers in academic innovation research, including Abbie Griffin, Robert Cooper, Elko Kleinschmidt, Mitzi Montoya-Weiss, Roger Calantone, Michaels Song, Tony DiBenedetto, etc. See the references cited in "Does Strategic Planning Enhance or Impede Innovation and Firm Performance?" for a long list of examples.

strategic plan you create needs to be aligned with your organization's characteristics.

Larger, more highly resourced organizations, on the other hand, will benefit from a more structured, formalized strategic plan.[212] In these organizations, the clarity of direction helps align broad and overlapping resources, keeping them focused on a common goal. It helps facilitate common understanding when complex communication flows could create confusion.

What about mid-size organizations? Effective strategic plans will be somewhere in between, less formal than Microsoft or Exxon/Mobil ought to be, but more formal than that of a ten-person start-up.

One last thing about creating your strategy: take some advice from the world of chess.

Chess is perhaps referenced even more than war when it comes to strategy. If you google "strategy" and look at the images that come up, half of them involve chess pieces.

So let's consider the advice of chess teachers Lev Alburt and Larry Parr. They advocate a system of analysis that starts with evaluating the position, creating a general plan based on the strengths and weaknesses of both you and your opponent, considering move options that will help you achieve your plan, then selecting the best option.[213] This is not unlike a sound strategic approach to business strategy. The final step before actually making the move, though, is to look at the board "with the eyes of a beginner."

How can thinking like a beginner help you make better strategic decisions? Well, in chess, the idea is that you look for blunders – moves that could either lead immediately to a losing position (or even checkmate), or moves that utterly fail to capitalize on your opponent's blunder.[214] You see, even as you get better at the game, you can still get so caught up in the intricacies and nuances of your analysis, that you end up overlooking the simple things. So

---

[212] Ibid.

[213] Lev Alburt and Larry Parr, *Secrets of the Russian Chess Masters: Fundamentals of the Game (Volume 1)*, W. W. Norton and Company, 2003.

[214] It is said that the winner of a chess game is the one who makes the second-to-last mistake.

Alburt and Parr suggest taking one last look with fresh eyes before making the actual move.

Do the same thing with your strategic plan. Look at it like a beginner. Ask yourself the stupid questions, and make sure that you have smart answers for them. Heck, even bring some beginners in to look at it and ask those questions. Just make sure that you didn't overlook the obvious before executing an action. Many a major strategic mistake might have been avoided by doing such a review.[215]

An Innovation Strategy Toolkit

There are some simple (surprise!) tools that can guide you to generate an effective innovation strategy. For copies of the tools that follow please, go to the Pi Innovation Toolbox.[216]

Among the tools that are offered here, you will find numerous four-quadrant charts.[217] Full confession: I love four-quadrant charts. I find them to be simple ways to generate powerful insights. As you read on, you'll be getting a steady diet of such charts.

The most famous of these, at least in business circles, is probably the Boston Consulting Group's strategy matrix. If four-quadrant charts were Japanese movie monsters, this one would be Godzilla.

In that matrix, which appears in virtually every B-school strategy class and text, the axes are market growth and market share. Plotting a business or

---

[215] The 2012 JCPenney strategic debacle – in which new CEO Ron Johnson chose to do a radical change in the retail philosophy of the stores, in every store all at once, without test marketing first, making questionable assumptions about attracting new customers without alienating the loyal customers – may have benefited well from looking at the plan with the eye of a beginner. Jennifer Reingold, "How to fail in business while really, really trying," *Fortune*, March 20, 2014.

[216] You can find the toolbox at www.3point14Innovation.com/Toolbox/. Getting into the toolbox requires that you be a registered user of the site. But what if you don't want to give me your email address? After all, who knows what a guy like me will do with it? Since you went to the trouble of reading my book, I'll give you an out: instead of signing up, you can sign in with the email "KeepInnovation@Simple.org," and the password "Simpleton." Of course, if I get your email address, I can send you wonderful stuff like newsletters, articles, updates, and comedy jokes. You're the customer, it's your call.

[217] I'm not the only one who likes four-quadrant charts, either. Check out Alex Lowy and Phil Hood, *The Power of the 2 x 2 Matrix: Using 2x2 Thinking to Solve Business Problems and Make Better Decisions 1st Edition*, Jossey-Bass, 2010.

product on the matrix gives you a sense for what you should do with it. If it's in a rapidly growing market and has high share, it's a star that deserves star treatment. If it's got high share but in a stagnant market, it's a cash cow that ought to be milked. A low share in a low growth market is a dog – and not of the Ol' Yeller or Lassie variety.[218] Low share in a high growth area is a question mark, meaning you have lots of thinking to do while you play The Clash's "Should I Stay or Should I Go"[219] in the background.

The reason this chart has endured since its appearance in the 1970's is that it is useful. It helps get perspective on businesses and products in an impartial way. If you've been working on something that was once a star but is now a dog, it can be hard to recognize that things have changed. A chart like this can wake you up like a splash of ice cold water.

So it has a place as a tool for strategic thinking.

That does not mean it is the be-all and end-all of strategic thinking.

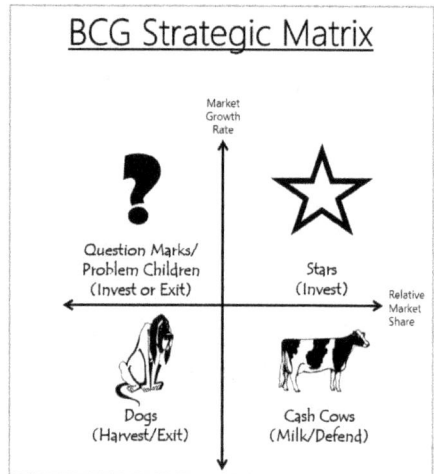

Figure 22: The Godzilla of four-quadrant charts, used in strategic planning and taught in strategy classes for almost half a century.

This chart, like any four-quadrant chart, is simple. It offers a perspective. But only one perspective. A good one, but only one.

Before going further, another quick word about keeping it simple, but not simplistic.[220] Some of the tools, used by themselves, may be simplistic. That doesn't mean the tool lacks value, though. It just means you shouldn't use it alone.

---

[218] Being a dog lover, I'm not fond of this classification name, but that's what BCG called it. I would have gone with "socks with holes in the toes" or maybe "tapeworm." But that's just me.

[219] The video for which can be found for your listening pleasure online at https://www.youtube.com/watch?v=xMaE6toi4mk

[220] For more about what simplicity really means and why it works, go to the "Why Simple?" section, page 18.

Hammers are valuable tools when you need to drive nails. Just make sure you have other tools in your toolbox if your job includes screws, bolts, electrical wiring, dry wall, PVC piping, and 30 weight ball bearings.[221]

So, yes, these charts can be and have been overused and trivialized. And yes, four-quadrant charts are easy to make fun of.[222] I get it.

That doesn't mean using them, when used properly, is simplistic. Using these tools is simple. But using just one, and taking it as the truth, the whole truth, and nothing but the truth, may be simplistic. So be sure to use them in their proper context. That's when they can provide some real eye-opening insights.[223]

Whatever you do, make sure you are using the right tools to get the insights you need. *Use multiple tools to get multiple perspectives.* With each one being simple, you can do so without wasting too much time, money, and mental energy.

The SWOT

Among the tools, you will find some of the old stand-bys of strategy development. Let's start with: The SWOT (Strengths, Weaknesses, Opportunities, and Threats) analysis.

It's a simple tool to capture at a glance what is going on in your world, good and bad, inside and outside.

Full disclosure though: the SWOT tool doesn't do a heck of a lot on its own, unless you are a

SWOT Analysis

	Positive	Negative
Internal	Strengths	Weaknesses
External	Opportunities	Threats

---

[221] If you don't get the reference, see a young and funny Chevy Chase as "Fletch" online at http://www.funnyordie.com/videos/3b7bfc0da3/fletch-mechanic-from-fletchfan?_cc=_d__&_ccid=ximkes.o0uz5d.

[222] Dilbert does it best: http://dilbert.com/strip/1997-03-05.

[223] Especially when you get to the portfolio management section, page 146.

naturally holistic strategic thinker with a full mental catalogue of details who never gets distracted by the urgencies of the moment. I am not such a person.

So to make the SWOT analysis of greater value, there are other tools to help you fully identify your strengths, weaknesses, opportunities, and threats. You probably have a good feel for them, but these will provide support to your intuition. Use the SWOT as the summary for the deeper explorations done with these other tools.

The Five-Forces of Michael Porter Plus

I am a big fan of Porter's Five Forces analytical model.[224] It provides a great framework for considering how your organization gets pushed and pulled in different directions. The variety of forces that Porter categorizes are common to all organizations trying to achieve a mission.

Even if you are a nonprofit, don't fool yourself into thinking that you don't live in a competitive landscape. There are limited resources to do the work you want to do. You are competing for those resources against others who want to do good things, too. If you doubt that, just wait until your fund raising efforts run into "sorry, I just gave what I could to the rescue efforts where the volcano erupted," or "I'd love to give you something, but I have been challenged to pour a bucket of ice water on my head for a different charity, and I

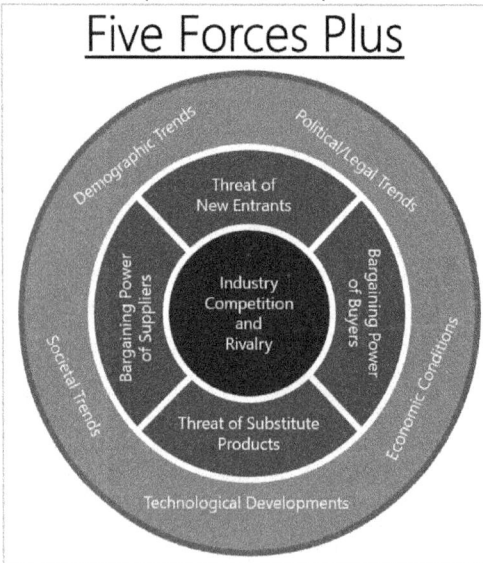

Figure 23: Michael Porter's original five forces, PLUS general environmental conditions.

---

[224] Michael Porter, *Competitive Strategy*, The Free Press, 1980. The structured analytical approach he recommends is excellent. His generic strategies that follow have been much maligned lately, but are still worth consideration, as long as you don't look at them as hard-and-fast, black-and-white concepts.

can't walk away from a challenge."[225]

So it's a competitive world. Whether you are Coke and Pepsi, McDonald's and Burger King, the American Academy of Surgeons and the American College of Surgeons, or Food for the Poor and Food for the Hungry, you are in a competitive environment. You should be familiar with the rivalry among competitors and their tendencies.

On the input side, you need to be aware of the bargaining power that your suppliers have. Are you in a weak or strong position with them when it comes to negotiating prices for their products?

On the output side, you need to be aware of the bargaining power of your customers. Are you in a weak or strong position with them when it comes to negotiating prices for your products?

On the competitive front, are there other products out there that might be a substitute for your product? For example, if you are a pancake manufacturer, is there a waffle manufacturer out there that you should be aware of?

Are there new entrants to your industry that will add competitive pressure? As the lone pancake maker in town, are you aware that IHoP[226] might be opening a place down the street?

Those are the five forces that Porter first proposed. Now for the "plus."[227] Look at the general environment in the world. How might it effect you? That environment could include general economic conditions and forecasts, broad changes in technology that are impacting society, social trends and emerging concerns, changing demographics, the political environment, and changes happening in the legal or regulatory framework in which you operate. All of those global forces will have an impact on the specific local forces in Porter's model.

---

[225] Yes, I took the challenge. If you feel like laughing at me, you can see it online at https://www.youtube.com/watch?v=UnCS4-7ZkGE. The bandwagon effect made me do it.

[226] The International House of Pancakes. I don't know who came up with that name for a restaurant chain, but God bless 'em.

[227] One of the big criticism of Porter's original forces is that they don't take into account general environmental conditions. No, I'm not talking about Global Warming, although that may enter into the analyses of many organizations, especially if you work in industries like Green Energy or Polar Bear Rescue. So the "plus" fills in that gap.

As you think through these questions, capture important answers to them in your SWOT chart.

The Product Life Cycle

To better direct how you ought to approach your innovation investment, it's wise to know where you stand in the natural life cycle of a product category.

Technology development tends to follow an "S Curve," as depicted in Figure 24. At first, when a technological breakthrough has occurred, performance is low. The Wright brothers first flight was only twelve seconds long, and they only got it about ten feet up in the air. Progress in performance may initially be slow, but as awareness of the breakthrough builds, more people contribute to advancement. As people become familiar with and interested in the technology, it improves rapidly during a growth phase. Finally, when the low-hanging fruit has all been plucked from the technology tree, the technology enters a mature phase of slow, incremental improvements.

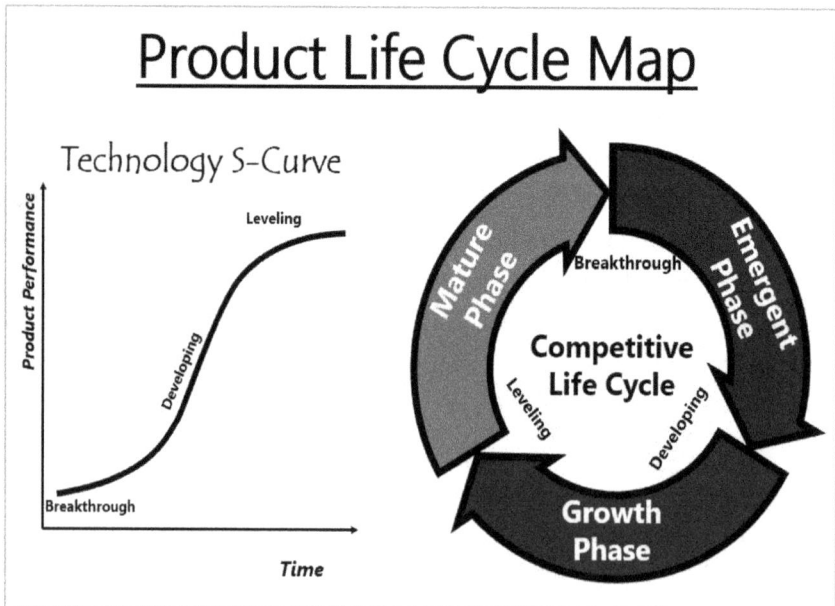

Figure 24: The Product Life Cycle Map depicts where you are on the technology S-Curve for a product category. When the competitive life cycle clock strikes midnight, your technology turns back into a pumpkin.

Why is this important to strategy? Because you will want to invest differently if you are competing in product categories at different stages in the life cycle. If the category is young, you may choose to invest in research to drive large changes in performance and seize a competitive advantage. Doing so in a mature phase, though, would not make much sense. If your strength is in research, investing in the next breakthrough would be the wiser move. Or if your strength is in operational efficiency, investing in cost reductions could be the best choice. In any case, knowing where you are on the S-curve, and therefore where you are in the product life cycle, is important to making the right investment decision.

The Attribute Opportunity Map

Since we are wired to sense threats more than opportunities,[228] you may find it easier to identify a long list of threats that fill in the lower right quadrant of your SWOT sheet, and find the neighboring box to the left relatively empty. The Attribute Opportunity Map is designed to stimulate thinking about where opportunities may lie, given what you know about your customer and about your business.

What's an attribute, you ask? It's a quality or feature of your product. For example, what are the attributes of your favorite Burger Barn French fries? Thin, hot, crispy, delicious, golden-brown, greasy, salty, cheap, fast, fattening... Get it? Got it. Good.

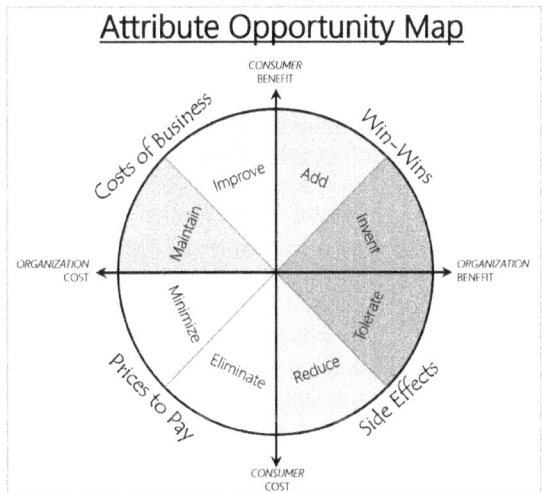

Attribute Opportunity Map

CONSUMER BENEFIT

Costs of Business
Win-Wins
Improve
Add
Maintain
Invent
ORGANIZATION COST
ORGANIZATION BENEFIT
Minimize
Tolerate
Eliminate
Reduce
Prices to Pay
Side Effects
CONSUMER COST

Figure 25: The Attribute Opportunity Chart is a fancy way to think about what attributes of your product should be changed, and how you should change them, given the costs and benefits to both your customer and to your organization.

---

[228] For more on this and other hard-wired cognitive biases, go to the "Cognitive Biases" section, page 224.

Yes, it's four quadrants. It's drawn in a circle to impress you, and to give pretty pie wedge graphics. Okay, not really just for the visual impression. Within each quadrant, there are a couple of options to consider. Depending on where you are within the quadrant, you may want to consider one of those options a little more than the other.

The vertical axis depicts a continuum from high consumer benefit on the top to high consumer cost on the bottom. The horizontal axis depicts a continuum from high organizational cost to high organizational benefit.

It's up to you to figure out what those axes mean for your business. Every organization will have its own "right" answer.

Now think about where those attributes fall on the map. "Thin" might be something the burger-barn customers love in their fries, but it's a cost to the organization because cutting them so thin takes more time than cutting them thicker. So "improve' may be an opportunity – find the best thickness that minimizes costs while maintaining liking.

"Fattening" is something that may be a significant consumer cost, but a slight company benefit – after all, deep-frying is quick, easy, cheap, and contributes not a little bit to the "delicious" attribute. Depending on how much your target consumer feels it's a cost, you could either decide that it's something to be tolerated (if it's low consumer cost) or something to be reduced (if it's a high consumer cost). For most Burger Barns, the answer is "tolerate." But if your target is shoppers at the nearby health food store, you may want to look at that reduce option.

And what if a new regulation comes out (which you identified using the Five Forces Plus tool) that adds a "fat tax" to such foods in the name of improving public health? Now that attribute flips to the lower left of the chart, where it's a cost to both the organization and the customer. You now need to consider minimizing or eliminating the attribute of "fattening."

That's an example of how these tools work together.

The Blue Ocean Strategy Canvas

In general, people tend to prefer fighting the devil that they know, rather than the devil that they don't know. And sailing into uncharted waters means there's a chance of meeting a devil they don't know.

That can be great news for innovators. Since most people have the status-quo preference, they will tend to fight over the same space – creating a bloody red ocean. They leave open plenty of blue water where no one is fighting. That gives you the chance to find a good fishing spot without all of the cannons being fired at your boat.

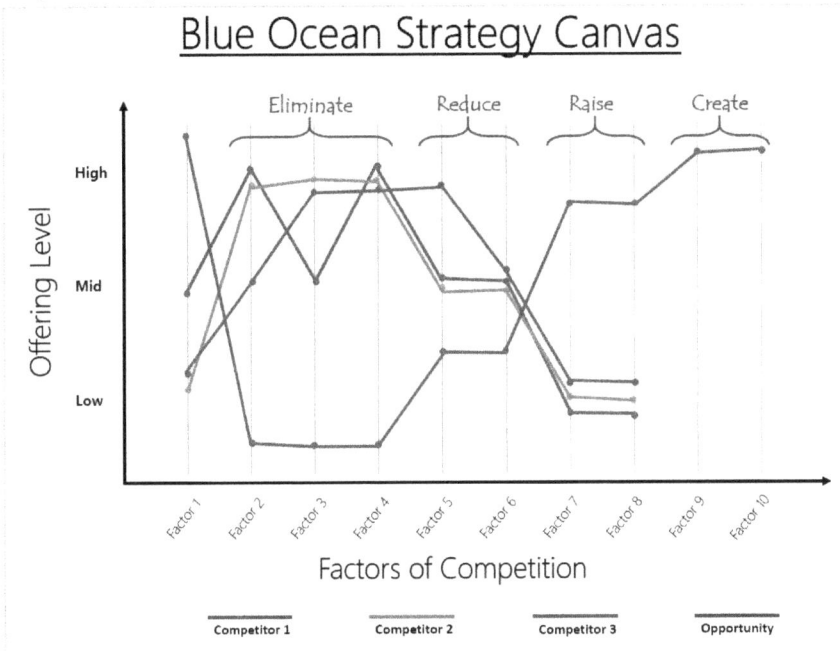

Figure 26: A hypothetical Blue Ocean Strategy Canvas. Or is it "an hypothetical?"

How do you find such a fishing spot? The Blue Ocean Canvas can help.

In the example of Figure 26, the competitive factors for three companies are plotted onto a chart. Competitive factors could include price, location, services offered, varieties available, etc. Each competitive product is rated as to how much of each factor it offers. Where the competition bunches up on the chart, you look for ways to leverage opportunities in the white space. When everyone is making a high-level offering in a factor, you see if you can reduce or eliminate that factor in your offerings. If everyone else is low or non-existent in a factor, you look for ways to raise or create that factor.

Basically, when everyone else zigs, you zag.

Mauborgne and Kim offer the example of Cirque du Solei. Before they came around, circuses traveled around competing on big name stars, animals on exhibition, concessions sold in the stands, death-defying thrills and humorous clowns.[229]

Cirque du Solei eliminated the big names, the animals, and the concessions. They reduced the thrills from death-defying to merely breathtaking. They don't move around, but stay in one place, where they can tailor the theater to their performance. And they eliminated packs of rubber-nosed imbeciles emerging from tiny cars.

Cirque du Solei has been a tremendous success be redefining a category for themselves. Is it circus? Is it theater? Is it performance art? Who cares, it's entertaining and successful. And, you guessed it – it's innovative.

So leverage the blue ocean strategy canvas to identify potential opportunities to break away from the rest of your competitors.

The Innovation Radar

The goods and services you produce for the market are only one arena in which you can innovate. The innovation radar is a concept developed by Mohan Sawhney, Robert Wolcott, and Inigo Arroniz[230] to help visualize opportunities for innovating, not just on goods and services, but in a variety of other ways as well.

The "real" version of this requires that a group of managers from an organization complete an online profile, which then gets mapped on the radar for insights. The "simple" version takes the radar and does a "best guess" as to where the organization currently competes. It's not as formal (and probably not as accurate), but it can still provide valuable insights.

The radar diagram has four primary axes, much like the four directions on a compass. The four axes are "Offerings" (meaning what goods and services the organization offers to the market); "Customers" (whom the organization is trying to serve; "Process" (how the organization goes about creating,

---

[229] Humorous, that is, only if you don't suffer from coulrophobia. Go ahead, look it up. You know you want to.

[230] Mohanbir Sawhney, Robert C. Wolcott and Inigo Arroniz, "The 12 Different Ways for Companies to Innovate," *MIT Sloan Management Review*, April 2006.

producing, and delivering their offerings); and "Presence" (where the organization operates throughout its end-to-end operations). In between are secondary axes that combine elements of the primary axes, including platforms, solutions, customer experience, value capture, organization, supply chain, networking, and brand.

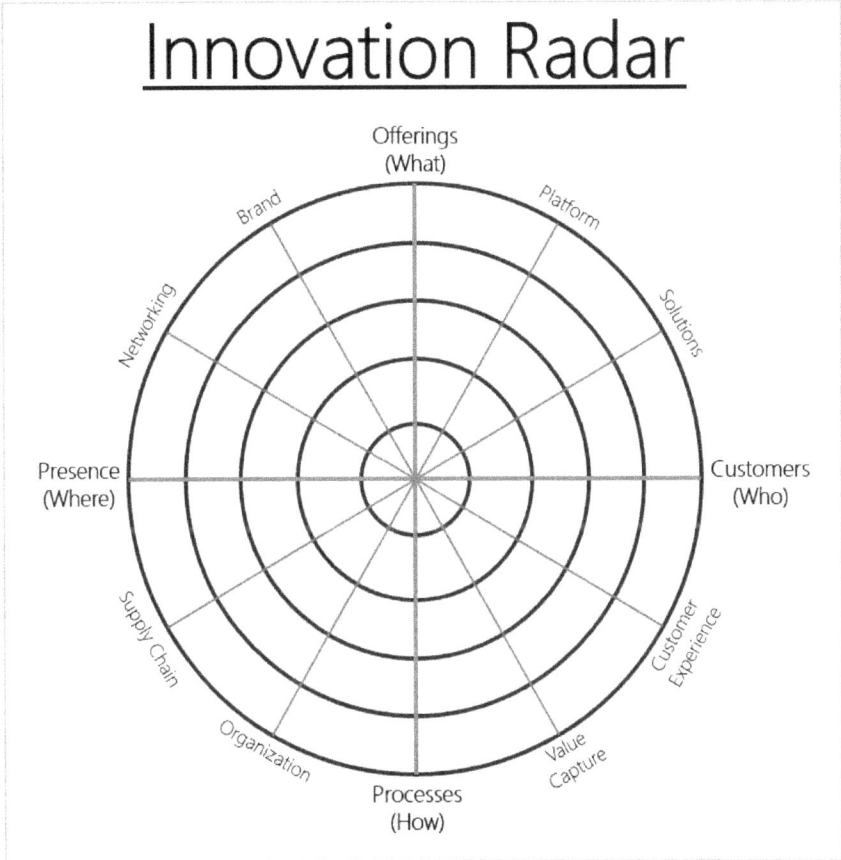

Innovation Radar

Offerings (What)
Platform
Brand
Solutions
Networking
Presence (Where)
Customers (Who)
Supply Chain
Customer Experience
Organization
Value Capture
Processes (How)

Figure 27: The Innovation Radar

By seeing where the organization is strong (further out on the radar) and not-so-strong (closer to the center of the radar), and by comparing your organization's map to those of competitors, you can identify opportunities for innovation that leverage your strengths, address your weaknesses, and move into blue-ocean-like space.

The Ten Types of Innovation

Authors Larry Keeley, Helen Walters, and Ryan Pikkel also want to encourage you to think of innovation beyond the goods and services you offer.

In their aptly named book, *Ten Types of Innovation: The Discipline of Building Breakthroughs,*[231] they outline ten areas to consider when looking to create value differently.

Figure 28 shows the list of ten opportunity areas that Keeley, Walters, and Pikkel came up with. It is worth looking into all of these areas, and consider how you may be able to do things better.

Ten Types of Innovation

	What to Innovate	How you...
Configuration	**Profit Model**	...make money
	Network	...connect with others to create value.
	Structure	...align your talent and assets.
	Process	...use signature or superior methods to do your work.
Offering	**Product Performance**	...employ distinguishing features and functionality.
	Product System	...create complimentary products and services.
Experience	**Service**	...support and enhance the value of your offerings.
	Channel	...deliver your offerings to customers and users.
	Brand	...represent your offerings and business.
	Customer Engagement	...foster distinctive interaction with customers.

Figure 28: The Ten Types of Innovation

---

[231] Larry Keeley, Helen Walters, and Ryan Pikkel, *Ten Types of Innovation: The Discipline of Building Breakthroughs*, John Wiley and Sons, 2013.

While both the Innovation Radar and the Ten Types of Innovation provide similar stimulus to look beyond just new products when seeking to innovate, experiment with both of them to see which best suits your needs.

However, don't let your choice be "neither," unless you have some other means of stimulating and expanding your thinking. Taking a diverse approach to innovation strategy has been shown to add value to businesses, and to improve survival rates of organizations.[232] Strategies that derail while operating on a single track invite disastrous consequences.

The Value Web

Although it is said that it is better to give than to receive, if you don't receive something in exchange for your product offerings, you won't be able to provide them for long. How do you determine how to get that value returned?

Value web mapping is a tool that can help stimulate thought around who gets value from your offering, and who can best pay for it. And yes, the tool is simple.

Start by considering someone who will benefit directly from the innovation you bring to them. For a business, this would typically

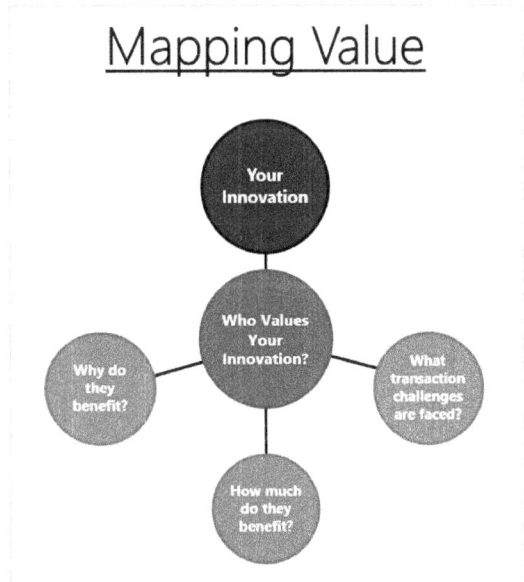

Figure 29: Mapping the value that your innovation brings to the people who will benefit from it.

be a customer with whom you have direct transactions. In the nonprofit world, this could be someone that your services directly help, such as someone

---

[232] Ithai Stern and Andrew D. Henderson, "Within-business diversification in technology-intensive industries," *Strategic Management Journal*, May 2004.

suffering from a particular disease for which your organization is seeking a cure.

Ask yourself three questions about this person or group that will receive value from you:

1) **Why do they benefit from your innovation?** What is it about your solution to their problems that brings them value? What physical, mental, emotional, or social impact does it make? Does it help them directly, or does it help them to serve someone else? Does it create new possibilities for them? Does it free up resources that they can then devote to other things?

2) **How much do they benefit?** Is it something critical to their lives, or simply a nice-to-have? How much value do you deliver in comparison to other alternatives that they can consider for solving their problems? How easily can they switch from one solution to another? Is the benefit long-lasting (even permanent) or short-term? How much of the benefit will they perceive versus what can be physically measured?

3) **What transaction challenges do you face with this person or group?** Do you have the ability to interact directly with them? How easily can they obtain your solution versus alternative solutions? What resources do they have to offer you in exchange for your innovation (which will typically be money, but could also take the form of "in kind" exchanges of goods, services, volunteer time, etc.)? What complexities exist around the transaction, such as legal/regulatory issues, storage and delivery, or measurement of value?

Note that one customer is just a start. You will (or at least should) have particular customers in mind as you create your innovative solutions, but there will never be just one customer or set of customers that get the exclusive benefit of your product.

That's where mapping out the full value web comes into play.

As you can see in Figure 30, the value web consists of repeating the initial exercise for all of the people or groups who benefit from your innovation. Go through the steps above for not only the primary beneficiaries, but also for secondary or even tertiary beneficiaries. Consider not only your customers, but also your customers' customers. Consider not only your customers, but also the producers of both complementary and substitute goods and services that will go along with your innovation. Consider not only your customers, but also those who will benefit from your customers' benefits.

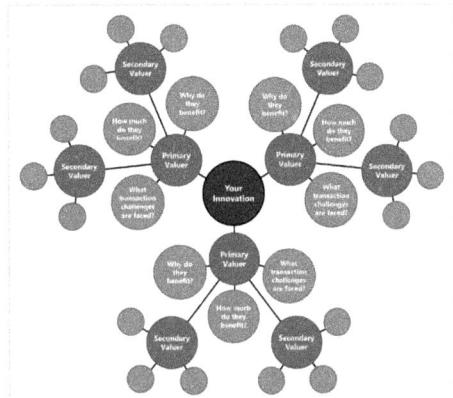

A direct customer transaction of value for value is obvious, but perhaps the other considerations merit some examples. Let's say you are a Brussels sprouts producer. You've come up with an innovation that makes them taste better than their current sweaty-shoe-insole

Figure 30: Value web mapping helps to create a structure around the complexities of the market for your innovation.

flavor. Your first thought may be about the grocery stores that you sell to. You'll be offering them a better product, which they should surely value, right?

But you must think also about their customers. After all, your product is just a means for your customer to serve their customers. Those people will benefit from having a new source of all the nutritional benefits of Brussels sprouts, without the nauseating agony of eating the original variety. Might there be a way for you to get value from them directly?

And what about the producers of complementary and substitute products? Perhaps those that made a variety of flavorings in a vain attempt to mask the flavor of the original will be hurt by your innovation – will they fight against you, perhaps by scaring potential consumers with fears about what ungodly science you performed to make such a vegetable taste like actual food? Or what about chefs who have been searching for the next big thing after the beet and kale fads... your delicious new ball of green leafy goodness may be just the thing, and they are willing to support you in efforts to further refine your product.

And what about those who benefit indirectly from your product? Previously, few would eat Brussels sprouts on any occasion other than a triple dog dare,[233] but now there is potential for so many people to eat them that

---

[233] If somehow you have missed the 24-hour broadcasts of the classic holiday movie *A Christmas Story*, you can catch this boys-will-be-boys scene at https://www.youtube.com/watch?v=ZLZj3zOUZNs.

the whole community would be healthier. Perhaps there is a grant from a heart disease nonprofit or the Brussels Sprout Appreciation Society that can return value to you?

In the process of developing a value web, you can uncover opportunities and business models that may prove more rewarding than restricting yourself to the narrow view on just a direct customer.

This is particularly important for nonprofits. Often, the customer being directly served by their products lacks the means for paying back a reasonable value. Other sources, such as donations, grants, bake sales, and dunking booths need to be explored. The value web exercise will help to do just that.

Innovation Roadmap

Finally, one last tool to help your planning process is the Innovation Roadmap. Like a roadmap for traveling,[234] the innovation roadmap helps you to identify how you want to get to where you want to go.

The concept is simple. Starting with where you believe the consumer is going to be at some time down the road,[235] you plan backward to where you are now,

Simple Innovation Roadmap

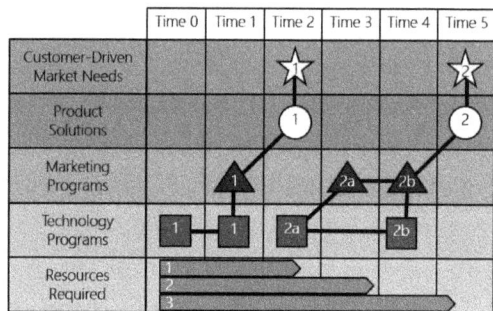

Figure 31: Use the Innovation Roadmap to plan your journey from where you are now to where you (and your customers) want you to be.

---

[234] Hopefully the various GPS navigation systems have not caused you to forget the days of using roadmaps to figure out how to get someplace. Ah, the joys of trying to find 308 Hickory Street in section D7 of a tattered paper too big to hold flat with outstretched arms, printed in 3-point font, and covered in grease stains from the burgers, fries, and shake spilled on it during long road trips. Oh, and the refolding! Kids these days will never have such visio-spatial brain challenges to keep them mentally sharp.

[235] I'm specifically avoiding the tempting but clichéd quote so overused in business today: Jason Kirby, "Why businesspeople won't stop using that Gretzky quote," *Maclean's*, September 24, 2014. Oh wait. Does this link count as using that quote?

identifying the key activities that need to happen and milestones that need to be achieved in order to reach your destination.

Working backward from the anticipated need, you identify the product solutions that you will want to create, the marketing and technology programs that need to be executed, and the resources required to execute those programs.

The roadmap helps you to identify what you need to do right now in order to achieve your long-term innovation objectives. Don't be like the stereotypical student who waits until the night before it's due to write that term paper comparing and contrasting Herman Melville's *Moby Dick* with Tom and Jerry's Dicky Moe.[236]

Plan your work, then work your plan.

Creating the Innovation Plan

So now you've done all this great analysis and forward thinking. Time to put it all together into a cohesive plan.

Full confession: this is a blatant rip-off of the "Business Model Canvas" of Alexander Osterwalder and Yves Pigneur,[237] but adapted to the specific needs of an innovation organization. Hey, the sincerest form of flattery is imitation, right? The original is a great tool, no doubt. One that I've used myself. If you used it to develop an organizational canvas/business model/strategy, you could then use the Innovation Plan[238] to help develop your innovation strategy.

---

[236] The Tom and Jerry Show was one of my favorite after-school cartoons to watch in the days of having only five channels to choose from. Although this was not among my favorite episodes, the spoonerism "Dickey Moe" from Moby Dick cracks me up. https://www.youtube.com/watch?v=VXkq3MNpNeA

[237] I highly recommend getting online and learning about the original Business Model Canvas, if you don't know it already. It can be found at http://businessmodelgeneration.com/canvas/bmc?_ga=1.99839067.438960691.1444597246

[238] I avoided the use of the word "canvas" even though the original uses it. No need to create confusion with other canvases. What's the deal with all these tools getting named for an art medium?

This tool gives you a simple means of thinking about and capturing the key elements of an innovation strategy:[239]

- The objectives of overall innovation efforts;

Simple Innovation Plan

Input Management	Technical Requirements	Strategic Objective	Market Requirements	Output Management
• Who are the key suppliers? • Are there external partners involved? • What resources can these partners provide? • What are the roles and responsibilities for all the players? • Who has what decision-making authority? • Who funds what? • How are the funds secured?	• What technical challenges need to be overcome to meet the strategic objective? • What technical development is required to overcome those challenges? • What time constraints are involved?	• How will innovation efforts deliver against the strategic plan? • What customer/client problems are we trying to solve? (Unmet needs) • What current solutions are we offering? • What current competitive solutions are out there? • How can we provide unique and superior solutions? • What are the top priorities of problems to be solved? • What is the urgency for solving each problem?	• What customer segments are involved? • How are these segments different? • Is the end user of the product the same as the customer? • Who is the customer's customer? What are their needs? • Wen do they need the solution you are offering?	• How do the products and services deliver value to the customer? • How do customers want products delivered? • What are the relationships with customers? • How do we communicate with customers?
	Resource Requirements • What functions of the organization need to be involved in development? • What customer involvement is required? Is possible? • What market knowledge is needed? • What external help is needed? Is available? • What time, money, and people are available?		**Distribution Requirements** • What distribution channels are available to reach the customer? • What channels are most effective for meeting strategic objectives? • What are the costs of various means of distribution? • What time frames are involved for different means?	

Delivering Value	Receiving Value
• How does the organization deliver value to the customer? • What is the cost to the organization of providing that value? • How are costs distributed among required resources? • What channels are most effective for meeting strategic objectives?	• For what products are your customers willing to pay? • What is the customer willing to pay for that value? • How does the customer return value to the organization? • By what method would your customer prefer to return value to the organization? • How are revenues distributed among various sources?

Figure 32: the one-page Simple Innovation Plan

- The role of innovation as part of the overall strategy;
- The human, financial, and time resources available and allocated to the plan;
- A diverse portfolio of strategic projects;
- The scope of innovation efforts (target customers, applicable technologies, and product categories);
- Planning over both short- and long-term.[240]

The plan should flow from the overall organizational strategy. The organization wants to achieve something, and has put a plan in place to

---

[239] Robert G. Cooper and Scott J. Edgett, "Developing a Product Innovation and Technology Strategy for Your Business," *Research-Technology Management*, May-June 2010.

[240] We'll focus on these last two points in the chapter on portfolio management (a.k.a., cat juggling), page 146.

achieve it. The question to be answered with this tool is how innovation will contribute to achieving that objective.

Notice that this is a one-pager. One page. *One*. Keep it that way.

Remember, a big part of why simple works[241] is that it will actually be used. If you turn this thing into a 9-box version of the complete works of Marcel Proust,[242] it will not be used. By anyone. Ever.

As Donald Sull and Kathleen M. Eisenhardt put it:

> "Where does strategy live in your organization? If the answer is on a shelf, you have a problem. Strategies don't live in thick binders—that's where they go to die. Simple rules, in contrast, represent the beating heart of strategy. When applied to a critical bottleneck, carefully crafted, and used in a mindful manner, simple rules can guide the activities that matter. In a world of hard trade-offs, they are one of the few ways managers can increase alignment, adaptation, and coordination all at once."[243]

It will be tempting with this and other tools to make them complicated. You'll want to capture subtle details that somebody somewhere might ask about. You'll want to make sure you haven't missed anything, so in addition to including the kitchen sink, you will want to add the refrigerator, oven, coffee maker, and combination egg-slicer/grape juicer. Don't do it!

Keep it simple. Focus on the important few points that must be captured, not the trivial many points that won't really matter. Just enough to be useful at focusing efforts. There will always be other ways to capture the excruciating detail.

---

[241] For more on what simplicity is and why it works, go to the "Why Simple" section, page 18.

[242] "Taking on his seven-volume novel, *Remembrance of Things Past*...is the reading equivalent of running a marathon." Jimmy Guterman, "In Search of Proust: Actually, It's Easy to Find the Verbose French Novelist, The Question Is, Why?" *Chicago Tribune*, February 14, 1999.

[243] Donald Sull and Kathleen M. Eisenhardt, "Simple Rules for a Complex World," *Harvard Business Review*, September 2012.

The simple strategic innovation plan can be used as what some people call a Product Innovation Charter (PIC). Personally, I don't like that name, because it causes confusion with the Project Charter that is so important to project management. However, I'll refer to PICs here for a moment, because that is how the academic literature refers to it.

PICs provide the three Cs necessary for strong strategic execution: Clarification, Codification, and Common Language.[244] To achieve this, the most innovative firms get specific in their PICs. There is a clear connection to the vision and mission of the organization. There are standards of behavior established. The language used has clearly defined common meaning for everyone in the organization.

Several components of PICs have been found to differentiate between highly innovative organizations and the rest.[245] Components of the strategic objectives will include concern for employees, concern for society, concern for shareholder, concern for suppliers, and concern for customers.[246] Strategic components of the PIC should also include metrics[247] of success (both financial and nonfinancial) and the technology arenas to be leveraged.

A strong new product development strategy consists of both a technology strategy (the "execution" part of innovation[248]) and marketing strategy (the "significance" part of innovation).[249] So the simple strategic plan clearly captures both. Here's how it works.

Start in the center with this tool, in the box called "Strategic Objective." Working from the center outward is a good way to ensure that things stay connected to the strategic imperatives.

---

[244] Chris Bart and Ashish Pujari, "The Performance Impact of Content and Process in Product Innovation Charters, *Journal of Product Innovation Management*, January 2007.

[245] Ibid.

[246] Looks to me like the best innovators are the best corporate citizens. Just sayin'.

[247] For more on innovation metrics, go to the sections on "Innovation for Fun and Profit" (page 389) and "Innovation for Fun and Not-for-Profit" (page 403).

[248] For more on how innovation is defined in this book, go to the "What the #&%! Is Innovation, Anyway?" section, page 4.

[249] Harry Nyström, "Product Development Strategy: An Integration of Technology and Marketing," *Journal of Product Innovation Management*, March 1985.

In this box, *briefly* capture what's important about questions such as:
- How will innovation efforts deliver against the strategic plan?
- What customer/client problems are we trying to solve? (Unmet needs)
- What current solutions are we offering?
- What current competitive solutions are out there?
- How can we provide unique and superior solutions?
- What are the top priorities of problems to be solved?
- What is the urgency for solving each problem?

That will serve as your starting point for the rest of the document.

To the left, then, you'll look at inputs and their associated costs – the technical side. To the right, outputs and their associated revenues – the marketing side.

Working out to the left, *briefly*[250] capture what's important about questions such as:

Technical Requirements
- What technical challenges need to be overcome to meet the strategic objective?
- What technical development is required to overcome those challenges?
- What time constraints are involved?

Resource Requirements
- What functions of the organization need to be involved in development?
- What customer involvement is required? Is possible?
- What market knowledge is needed?
- What external help is needed? Is available?

---

[250] Is the message of brevity getting through? It's important to be brief. Brevity is the essence of wit. Keep in mind that keeping things brief, to the point, and impactful is hard work. "Short" and "easy" are not synonymous. As Woodrow Wilson said about his speeches, "If I am to speak ten minutes, I need a week for preparation; if fifteen minutes, three days; if half an hour, two days; if an hour, I am ready now." It's easy to just rattle off a bunch of words, but to be concise and clear takes thoughtful effort. Maybe I should have put more such effort into this footnote!

- What time, money, and people are available?

Input Management
- Who are the key suppliers?
- Are there external partners involved?
- What resources can these partners provide?
- What are the roles and responsibilities for all the players?
- Who has what decision-making authority?
- Who funds what?
- How are the funds secured?

Delivering Value
- How does the organization deliver value to the customer?
- What is the cost to the organization of providing that value?
- How are costs distributed among required resources?
- What channels are most effective for meeting strategic objectives?

Working out to the right, *briefly*[251] capture what's important about questions such as:

Market Requirements
- What customer segments are involved?
- How are these segments different?
- Is the end user of the product the same as the customer?
- Who is the customer's customer? What are their needs?
- When do they need the solution you will offer?

Distribution Requirements
- What distribution channels are available to reach the customer?
- What channels are most effective for meeting strategic objectives?
- What are the costs of various means of distribution?
- What time frames are involved for various means?

---

[251] Consider the brevity horse dead and beaten.

Output Management
- How do the products and services deliver value to the customer?
- How do customers want products delivered?
- What are the relationships with customers?
- How do we communicate with customers?

Receiving Value
- For what products are your customers willing to pay?
- What is the customer willing to pay for that value?
- How does the customer return value to the organization?
- By what method would your customer prefer to return value to the organization?
- How are revenues distributed among various sources?

So now you have a one-page innovation strategy capturing all the key points of your analysis, backed up by some simple tools that stimulated your thinking. Time to take a coffee break. Right?

Nope.

Do it again. Yep, that's right, do the Innovation Model exercise again. Do it with a different perspective, with a different set of assumptions. Think about what could go wrong with your plan, and think of a different approach that might avoid those issues.

Remember, "plans are useless, but planning is indispensable."[252] It is this kind of planning process that will help you in the actual execution. Preparing multiple plans in the strategery[253] process will give you two distinct advantages over stopping at one.

First, you may discover that the first plan, as drafted, was not the best plan. Either another plan turns out to be superior, or additional thinking from a new perspective helps to modify and improve on the original.

---

[252] One of the famous aphorisms of Dwight D. Eisenhower, as quoted in Richard Nixon, *Six Crises*, Doubleday, 1962.

[253] There I go again, using that made-up word, even after I promised not to. Such a fun word.

Second, you have contingency plans in your pocket. The best-laid plans of mice and men often go awry,[254] after all. Best to be prepared for the going awry in advance, rather than doing the impromptu[255] scrambling at the time of going awry.

So while redundant effort may not seem simple, in the long run, it is.

A Word (or a Thousand of Them) on Open Innovation

Since Henry Chesbrough's book *Open Innovation: The New Imperative for Creating and Profiting from Technology* a decade ago, open innovation (affectionately or derisively known as OI, depending on your perspective) has been a hot topic in innovation and product development circles.

Procter & Gamble has served as a primary exemplar on the topic. They launched their "Connect and Develop" program, and for years there were articles galore about the successes they were having, and how they did it. In 2009, P&G was named by Business Week as one of the 25 most innovative companies in the world, touting their Connect & Develop as a key reason for their success.

More recently, the articles have been about their failures and where they went wrong. In 2012, a Business Week headline read "At Procter & Gamble, the Innovation Well Runs Dry," pointing out that companies with more "traditional" (meaning internal) R&D structures were beating them in the marketplace.

Or look at Quirky. Started in 2009, Quirky leveraged an open innovation crowdsourcing model to come up with innovative new products. As late as 2013, *Wired* magazine was hailing their partnership with GE as a way to "conquer the internet of things."[256] Less than two years later, Quirky filed for

---

[254] But even strategery isn't as much fun to say as putting on my best Mike Myers Scottish brogue and saying "Tae a Moose," the title of the Scots poem that provides this oft-alluded to line, at least in the English translation called "To a Mouse." See Mike Myers in "All Things Scottish" online at http://www.nbc.com/saturday-night-live/video/scottish-shop/n9938.

[255] I can't help but think of Mark Twain's witty lead time requirement for an impromptu speech. I wish it was easily captured in a pithy quote, but according to the Quote Investigator, the internet has it wrong, and I'm a stickler for getting those right. If you are also a quote stickler, go online and read http://quoteinvestigator.com/2010/06/09/twain-speech/.

[256] Read it online at http://www.wired.com/2013/11/how-ge-and-quirky-want-to-smarten-up-your-home/.

bankruptcy protection, raising "questions about how far the crowd-based model of innovation and product development can go."[257]

What gives? Does "open innovation" work or not?

Well, first I suppose we need to know what we are talking about. Chesbrough expressed the closed innovation paradigm as "companies must generate their own ideas and then develop them, build them, market them, distribute them, service them, finance them, and support them on their own." In the open innovation paradigm, "firms can and should use external ideas as well as internal ideas, and internal and external paths to market."[258]

So basically, a closed innovation system is a do-it-yourself approach, and an open innovation system is an it-takes-a-village mindset.

But all real innovation systems lie somewhere in between those extremes.

Being closed has its advantages. You control everything, and you own the whole pot of gold at the end of the internally-developed innovation rainbow.

Being open has its advantages. No matter how smart and talented the people in your organization are, there is someone, somewhere who is at least as talented, at least as smart, and has a different, perhaps better, solution to the problems you face. You don't and can't know everything internally. Looking outside gets new and superior ideas into your organization.

So a key consideration of any innovation strategy is how open to make it. Notice I didn't say whether to make it open or not. Open innovation is not a binary choice.[259] It's not an on/off switch. An innovation system is never either open or closed. Rather, there is something more like a continuum of openness.

As you are thinking about your strategic opportunities, and wondering how open innovation might fit in, consider the OI strategy matrix shown in Figure 33. If your identified strengths play well in a market that is attractive to you, then do it yourself. If your strengths play well in a market that is unattractive to you, consider looking for partners that may want to use what

---

[257] Read it online at http://www.nytimes.com/2015/09/23/business/the-invention-start-up-quirky-files-for-bankruptcy.html.

[258] Henry Chesbrough, *Open Innovation: The New Imperative for Creating and Profiting from Technology*, Harvard Business School Press, 2006.

[259] That reminds me of one of my favorite nerdy jokes: There are 10 kinds of people in the world—those who understand binary, and those who don't. If you get it, congratulations! You're a nerd.

you have. If there is a market that is attractive to you, but it doesn't play to your strengths, consider looking for a partner who is strong in that arena, and who would be willing and able to help you get there. And it should go without saying[260] that you should avoid getting into ugly markets where you have no strengths. If you are already there, get out before that market goes all *Amityville Horror* on you.[261]

Note that "partnerships" come in all shapes and sizes. It can come from customers, suppliers, universities, online collaboration tools, or organizations in different industries. It might even be an archrival that you join to take advantage of your mutual strengths.[262]

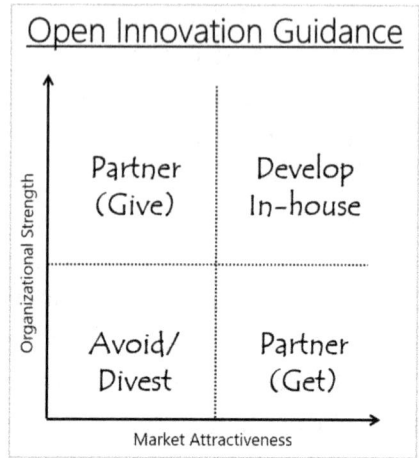

Figure 33: A thought stimulator when it comes to figuring out the resources you need, what's available, and where to go from where you are.

Think of it like a door. Some doors are closed most of the time, only opening for rare access. Some doors are rarely closed, and only for special circumstances. Other doors have screens that let fresh air and light in while keeping annoying pests out. Some doors have mail slots or little doggy doors. Some are "Dutch doors" where the top and bottom open separately. There are lots of different kinds of doors, and they can all be opened or closed to varying degrees. Such is true for OI – lots of types and degrees of openness.

Open innovation efforts will take different forms depending on whether you are developing new services or developing new physical goods.[263] New

---

[260] But I'll say it anyway, for the sake of thoroughness.

[261] If a house tells you to get out, listen. https://www.youtube.com/watch?v=H08yYqGCTiM

[262] A great example of this is Glad Force Flex trash bags and Glad Press-n-Seal plastic wrap, which leveraged Clorox's brand and technical capabilities in flexible films with some of Procter & Gamble's proprietary technology developed for their diaper business. Perhaps there is hope for all bitter rivals to one day find such peace.

[263] Stephanie C. Schleimer and Arthur D. Shulman, "A Comparison of New Service versus New Product Development: Configurations of Collaborative Intensity as Predictors of Performance," *Journal of Product Innovation Management*, July 2011.

service development requires collaborations built on mutual trust (a relationship and ownership sort of dimension), while new physical product development requires joint operations based on mutual engagement and shared responsibilities (more of a system and process dimension).

Such is the state of open innovation. Crowdsourcing. Co-creation. Expert networks. User communities. Collaboration sites. Grand challenges. Tech scouting. All sorts of open innovation doors.

All innovators everywhere and always have done some sort of open innovation. Okay, maybe the cave dweller who invented the first wheel did it all alone,[264] but no one has since. We are always learning from others, borrowing from others, speaking with others, partnering with others, selling to others, buying from others, collaborating with others.

Suppliers bring ideas to manufacturers. Consumers write letters with ideas or complaints. Consultants are brought in to help with technical or business issues. Patents are mined and intellectual property is licensed. Joint partnerships are established. All of that can be part of open innovation, and it's been going on since genies were being put in oil lamps at Arabian bazaars.

That's why innovations have historically been concentrated in cities. Large groups of people packed together in a confined space are naturally going to interact with one another more. The opportunities to bump into someone, learn from them, connect with them, and partner with them is naturally going to happen more often in Tokyo than in Greenland.[265]

The difference now is that the ability to connect with others has exploded in recent years. With the ever-increasing opportunity to interact with people not just in your neighborhood, but practically anywhere on the planet, you are no longer limited to talking with your neighbors. Communities aren't limited to geographic locations, but now exist for all sorts of common interests and

---

[264] But I doubt it.

[265] To find out more about where you should go to stimulate more innovation, check out David B. Audretsch and Maryann P. Feldman, "Knowledge Spillovers and the Geography of Innovation," *Handbook of Urban and Regional Economics, Volume 4*, 2003.

activities. I mean, if there can be a Brussels Sprout Appreciation Society,[266] there can be a virtual community for anything.

Perhaps even more important than the exponential increase in serendipitous encounters is the ability to seek out expertise through social media and open innovation websites. It's easier than ever before to learn the needs of your consumers, to generate ideas to solve their problems, and to find people with the expertise to bring those solutions to life.

It's beyond the scope of this book to go into detail on each and every type of open innovation program out there. But reading this, you may be thinking, "If this open innovation thing is so great, why doesn't everyone open their innovation processes up to the max?"

Because, like all good things, open innovation is not all dancing ponies and cupcakes with sprinkles on top.

Anything that has value also has costs, and open innovation is no exception. And the costs can be complex, given the variety of forms that open innovation can take.

First, there is culture.[267] Yes, I am a broken record on culture, culture, culture. Remember the competing values framework? The horizontal axis represented internal focus and integration versus external focus and differentiation. Guess which side is more likely to embrace an open innovation model? Clan and hierarchy cultures with a strong internal focus will face a good deal of resistance trying to collaborate with the outside world. Understand the impact your culture will have before embarking on an open innovation program (or any program for that matter).

Even if you can fit an open innovation approach within your organizational culture, you need to design the organization and processes in a way that they can effectively handle OI efforts. Fill the OI part of your organization with people who are entrepreneurial and collaborative. Diplomats with good communication skills. Networkers who can see possibilities. Simply telling the

---

[266] No, seriously, there really is such a thing. https://www.facebook.com/The-Brussels-Sprout-Appreciation-Society-136773149712101/

[267] For more on culture and the Competing Values Framework, go to the "Culture" chapter, page 58.

existing organization to go forth and openly innovate will generally lead nowhere.

Then there is the challenge of customer ideas. Customers have limited ability to truly innovate.[268] Simply offering customers a suggestion box won't get you far. You'll get uncountable numbers of suggestions for "innovations" like making your blue widget green, adding chicken to the Caesar salad on your restaurant's menu, or adding guinea pigs to your pet adoption shelter. The equivalents of Henry Ford's "faster horse."[269]

The problem-solvers have their own interests, too. Who owns what, and who owes whom what, are negotiation and legal challenges that must be worked out. In the US, recent changes to patent laws (and further proposed changes) add another layer of complexity, as inventors and organizations adjust to the new approach.[270] And more change is likely on the horizon, with high-profile challenges to an "outdated" system.[271]

Opening up your innovation efforts can pay big dividends, but as with all reward opportunities, there are associated risks. Proceed with cautious optimism.

What to Do with Your Strategy

Okay, so you've created a strategic innovation plan. Congratulations!

Now what?

Now, communicate it. Then execute it.

That's when problems can arise. If the measures of success don't align with the real values, capabilities, culture, systems, and/or mission of the organization, the internal conflict will make achieving your objectives impossible.

---

[268] For more on how to get at the Voice of the Customer, go to the "VoC" chapter, page 176.

[269] For more on Henry Ford's famous quote and how it applies to really understanding your customer, go to the "Voice of the Customer – What it Isn't" section, page 186.

[270] Lisa Shuchman, "Patent Litigation Will Never Be the Same Again" *Corporate Counsel*, October 26, 2015.

[271] Steve Lohr, "Samsung's Patent Loss to Apple Is Appealed to Supreme Court," *New York Times*, December 14, 2015.

Take the example of IBM under Lou Gerstner. Among the numerous changes made to turn IBM around, one of the most critical was a change in the compensation system. While demanding that business units be more cooperative and customer-focused, the compensation system encouraged internal competition and operating within silos. Until that conflict was identified and resolved, the stated objectives remained unachievable.

Similarly, if you are in a Hierarchical culture with a Defender strategy type, but you decide to measure how radical your innovations are, you are likely to be severely disappointed. Similarly, if you are in an Adhocracy with a Prospector strategy type, but set out to achieve the efficiency measures of a high-volume, low-product-diversity manufacturer, you are likely to be severely disappointed.

This situation usually arises when a competitor, industry rival, or well-known organization has some success publicized, leading other organization leaders to think, "We must do that, too." Somewhere, someone releases an innovation, and a hierarchy shouts to the masses, "Thou shalt innovate radical breakthroughs," enshrining the commandment on stone tablets, or at least on motivational posters in the hallways.

But the hierarchy also commands that the breakthrough must meet all the same requirements of a short-term productivity investment, with a virtually guaranteed return on investment in a fixed period of time. Failure to achieve objectives will be met with the standard floggings and rolling of heads.

Sign me up for that!

Look, if your organization wants to retain its hierarchical culture, and pursue a defender strategy, that's fine. Just don't expect radical, breakthrough innovations to come out of it. They don't happen by fiat.

For now, the focus is on aligning your expectations with your strategy. A Defender strategy is going to produce high efficiency, with slow, incremental change at a deliberate pace. Presumably if that's what you want, if that's what fits your mission, if that's what fits your capabilities, then go for it.

Just don't measure your success based on innovation.

The worst thing you can do is to choose a strategic course and then express frustration that you're not delivering something you aren't set up to deliver. That's like embarking on a cheesy puff and ice cream diet and getting frustrated that you aren't looking and feeling healthy.

How do you choose the strategy type to follow?

Rather than worry about categorizing yourself into one of Miles and Snow's four categories, make the conscious choice of whether to be a leader or a follower. Clearly define the target market you are after, and whether you are going to try to dominate it or accept a smaller share of it. Then define your strategy in terms of what types of innovation will deliver against the objectives – whether it is incremental or radical, whether it is a product or service, whether it is a business model or internal system change that benefits the customer and the organization.

Communicating for Execution

Disseminating a strategic plan throughout the organization is both critical and daunting. It is critical, because the strategy cannot be executed effectively without the alignment, coordination, and collaboration of all parts of the organization.[272] Alignment ensures everyone understands and agrees to pursue the same objective; coordination ensures that all the individual parts are working together as an effective whole; and collaboration ensures that communication and feedback between parts drives efficiency and continuous improvement in the execution.

It is daunting because any strategic plan will be open to interpretation by different business units and functions, based on how things have been done in the past, resource availability and capability, and differences in managerial involvement.[273] A host of cognitive biases[274] will also interfere with clear interpretations of even the most eloquently stated strategy.

What can you do to ensure strategic alignment?

Focus on the simple strategic plan document.

---

[272] Although this seems to be a statement of the obvious, here's some verification: Donald Sull, Rebecca Homkes, and Charles Sull, "When Strategy Execution Unravels, – and What to Do About It," *Harvard Business Review*, March 2015.

[273] Serdar S. Durmuşoğlu, Regina C. McNally, Roger J. Calantone and Nukhet Harmancioglu, "How Elephants Learn the New Dance When Headquarters Changes the Music: Three Case Studies on Innovation Strategy Change," *Journal of Product Innovation Management*, July 2008.

[274] For more on cognitive biases, go to the "Cognitive Biases" section, page 224.

The simple strategic plan, once completed, will help guide project and portfolio decisions. The planning document provides the opportunity to empower execution teams with "bounded autonomy" – the authority to make decisions within defined limits. Bounded autonomy is a little like driving a car: you are free to choose where you go (autonomy), within legal limits, like driving on actual roads and not through people's backyards, across school playgrounds, or inside shopping malls[275] (bounded). Bounded autonomy can be a powerful lever for driving well-targeted strategic innovation.[276]

A tightly defined and well-communicated simple strategic plan will define the boundaries for innovation, which minimizes the need for managerially-imposed ad-hoc decisions. That, in turn, means that teams can make their own decisions, freeing management to more strategic tasks. Not a bad deal for anyone.

One trick for good strategic execution is to use multiple metrics.[277] These metrics must be captured in the simple strategic planning document.[278] As John E. Jones, the leadership guru, said, "What gets measured gets done. What gets measured and fed back gets done well. What gets rewarded gets repeated."[279]

Metrics to which the organization pays attention and for which people feel consequences are the ultimate determinant of what your strategy really is. Your strategy is not really what you put into words. It's what you translate into actions through decisions, measurement of performance, and consequences for actions. Saying you want to do one thing, while rewarding people for doing

---

[275] The use of deadly force in the apprehension of the Blues Brothers has been approved: https://www.youtube.com/watch?v=IldGxR-aU6o.

[276] David S. Bedford, "Management control systems across different modes of innovation: Implications for firm performance," *Management Accounting Research*, September 2015.

[277] For more on innovation metrics, go to the sections on "Innovation for Fun and Profit" (page 389) and "Innovation for Fun and Not-for-Profit" (page 403).

[278] Serdar S. Durmuşoğlu, et. al. "Elephants" article.

[279] My search for a source of this quote yielded only a bunch of repetitions of the quote online. Even published books citing this quote referenced online sources that were not subsequently referenced. So it is entirely possible that John E. Jones, leadership guru, never said this. Also, don't confuse this John E. Jones with US District Court Judge John E. Jones, who ruled that teaching intelligent design in public schools is unconstitutional. That John E. Jones has entirely different quotes for an entirely different book.

another, means that "the other" is your real strategy, while what you say is just your façade strategy.

Simple Study Guide - Strategy
<ul><li>What is the definition of strategy?</li><li>What are the four strategic types according to Miles and Snow?</li><li>What is a SWOT analysis?</li><li>What is a "blue ocean"?</li><li>What is the Five Forces Plus analysis?</li><li>What is the Innovation Radar?</li><li>What are the Ten Types of Innovation?</li><li>How does a strategic roadmap work?</li><li>How do you go about communicating a strategic plan?</li><li>What is the most important outcome from creating a strategic plan?</li><li>What is bounded autonomy?</li><li>What does "open innovation" mean?</li></ul>

Where do you want to go from here?		
Control	**Creation**	**Conversion**
Mission (page 40)	Voice of the Customer (page 175)	Innovation Teams (page 310)
Culture (page 58)	Minds of Innovators (page 217)	Project Management (page 347)
Strategy (page 92)	Ideation (page 279)	For-Profit Metrics (page 389)
Portfolio Management (page 146)		Nonprofit Metrics (page 403)
Change Management (page 411)		

Or just turn the page to keep reading...

Cat Juggling (Portfolio Management)

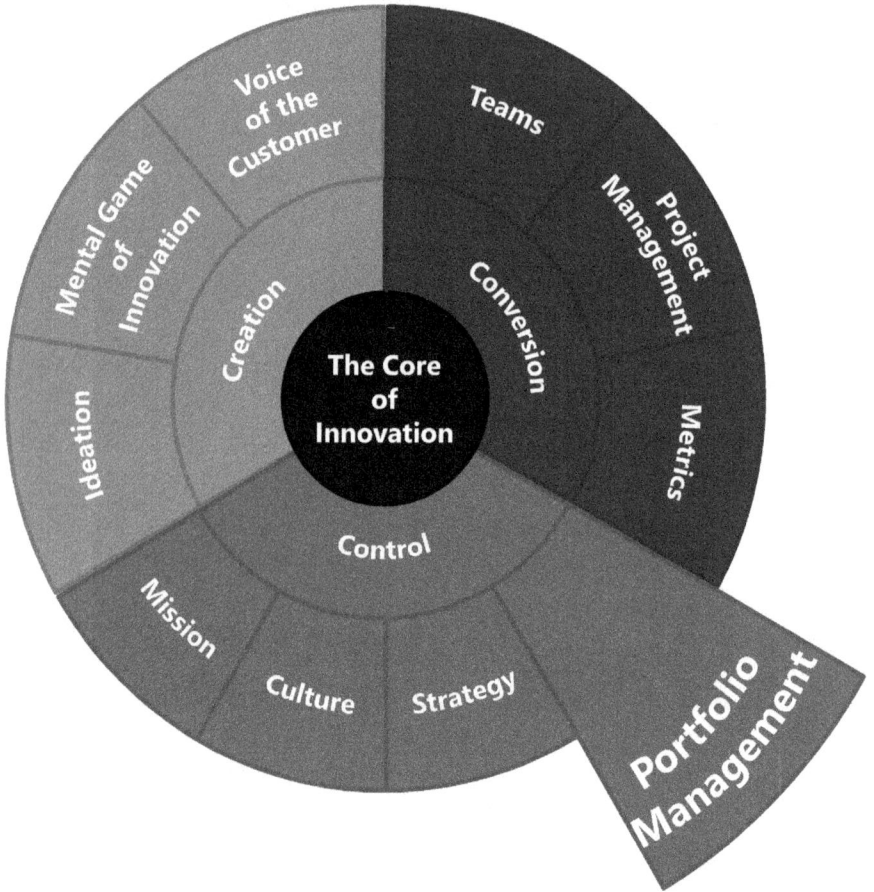

Simple Self-Assessment – Portfolio Management

Rate yourself on the following questions. To benchmark yourself against others, go to www.3point14Innovation.com and click the "Self-Assessments" menu.

- ***How well balanced is your innovation portfolio?***

  Like a dizzy toddler

  Like a Wallenda on a tightrope.

1	2	3	4	5	6	7	8	9	10

- ***Do you keep your portfolio of projects within your resource limitations?***

  Trying to do too much with too little

  Just right

1	2	3	4	5	6	7	8	9	10

- ***Is your organization willing to put pet projects to sleep?***

  We are a no-kill stray project shelter

  We prefer bullets

1	2	3	4	5	6	7	8	9	10

- ***Does your organization consider all the possibilities when assessing risk?***

  We don't bother calculating risk

  We evaluate all scenarios.

1	2	3	4	5	6	7	8	9	10

- ***Do you have strategic buckets defined for your organization?***

  It's on my bucket list to do

  Yes, and not all of our eggs are in just one

1	2	3	4	5	6	7	8	9	10

- ***Do you use formal evaluation tools to analyze your portfolio?***

  We just use a hammer.

  You should see the toolbox. It's huge!

1	2	3	4	5	6	7	8	9	10

- ***How flexible and adaptable is your portfolio process?***

  As rigid as concrete

  We can adjust like an elastic waistband on Thanksgiving.

1	2	3	4	5	6	7	8	9	10

Simple Summary – Portfolio Management

Key take-aways you should get out of this section:

- Balance is the key to good portfolio management. Balance needs to be sought over degree of innovation, time horizon, business unit, customer base, etc. Take multiple perspectives of your portfolio to determine the right balance for your organization, and your objectives.
- Live within your means. Resource constraints must always be considered. Focus on the important few rather than the trivial many. However, don't use resource constraints as an excuse not to innovate. Sometimes, resource constraints can actually encourage innovative thinking.
- The toughest choices are never between good and bad. The tough ones are between good and good. Between "this one is better" and "no, this one is better." The most critical personal characteristic for effective portfolio management is courage – having the guts to make a tough decision.
- Risk on a roulette wheel is easy to calculate. Risk for an innovation project is not. You need to evaluate multiple scenarios, estimate odds under conditions of uncertainty, and consider a variety of scenarios. And the element of risk that is most often forgotten is the risk from inaction. The status quo is not risk-free.
- Diversification of an innovation portfolio is as important as diversification of a financial portfolio. It is a way to mitigate risk, and all innovation efforts involve risk. Diversification should be considered along the dimensions of risk/reward, time horizon, and business area.
- Strategic "buckets" can be a helpful tool for portfolio allocations. These buckets are areas of investment, with resources assigned to each. Three possible buckets are for incremental, evolutionary, and radical innovation. A prospector strategy might allocate 10%, 30%, and 60% respectively, while a defender might allocate 75%, 20%, and 5% respectively. Having such resource buckets ensures at least some balance along critical dimensions for your organization.
- Four-quadrant portfolio evaluation tools are simple ways to gain insights on the balance and strategic impact of your portfolio. These tools deliver powerful information visually. Make sure that you use

multiple approaches, though, as no individual four-quadrant chart provides the one right point of view on the portfolio.

- Project scorecards are effective tools for evaluating projects against each other on criteria that the organization has identified as important. The specific calculations that the scorecard performs are not as important as the required thought processes and discussions among decision makers. The scorecard process can help weed out bad projects, and provide an objective means of comparing good projects against each other.

- Portfolio management is not a one-time event, but an ongoing process. Individual project decisions should be made in the context of the overall portfolio. And portfolio decisions should be re-evaluated as new information comes to light. The process needs to be flexible and adaptable to changing circumstances.

Walking and Chewing Gum Simultaneously

When people are trying to do many things at the same time, they often compare it to juggling.

"Hey, Pat, can we meet at 4:00?"
"No, I've got too many balls in the air right now."
"How about tomorrow?"
"I'll see if I can juggle my schedule around."
"Thanks...and can I borrow your red rubber nose and unicycle later?"

Portfolio management is another case of professional juggling. But instead of juggling balls or clubs, it's more like juggling cats.[280] Lots of screeching and hissing, hair flying all over the place, and blood almost certainly being drawn.

Okay, maybe it's not quite that bad. But projects and their champions will fight each other and you, the portfolio decision-maker, for the chance to survive. It won't always be pleasant.

Pleasant, no, but vitally important, yes. Good innovation portfolio management can make or break an organization's innovation efforts. It's quite possible that Texas Instruments is alive as an organization due to strong portfolio management.[281] TI was a successful high-volume/low-cost manufacturer of electronics. But when their markets began to demand a greater variety of specialized products with a diverse array of functionality, they suffered. They had to radically rethink their portfolio of products in development, as well as their manufacturing capabilities, just to survive.

It was not easy, but Texas Instruments now has a broad and differentiated set of products, and is one of the leaders in digital and analog technologies. They got where they are now because they successfully rebalanced the portfolio of product development projects they invested in.

---

[280] No animals were harmed in the writing of this book. Unlike making a Disney movie (for more on that, check out the footnotes on the bandwagon effect, page 231.

[281] Linda Kester, Erik Jan Hultink, and Abbie Griffin, "An Empirical Investigation of the Antecedents and Outcomes of NPD Portfolio Success," *Journal of Product Innovation Management*, November 2014.

Research has demonstrated that organizations looking to improve their innovation performance in the marketplace actually need to improve their innovation portfolio balance *before* they may be able to improve their market performance.[282] Yep. You may be doing a bunch of other stuff right, but if you get this wrong, it could all be for naught.

Portfolio management is where organizations get to strategically walk their strategic talk. Strategy is nothing – maybe less than nothing – if it exists in words but not in actions. Just as actions speak louder than words among individual people, so it is true with organizations. Drafting a strategic plan that says you'll do one thing, while the projects you actually work on do something else, is a waste of time and energy at best. Worse, it discredits the organization to employees and other stakeholders.

Portfolio management is also important, because innovation is a form of investment. Just like money managers investing in financial markets, innovation leaders need to manage their portfolio of investments in innovation projects. And just like financial investment management has some long-established guidelines for success, there are some well-established guidelines to help innovation leaders manage their innovation investment portfolios.

Balancing Act

A good diet is a balanced diet. What does that mean? It means you eat enough diverse foods to get the nutrients and calories you need to be healthy, while avoiding over-eating and unhealthy weight gain.

A good innovation portfolio is a balanced innovation portfolio. What does that mean? It means you do enough diverse projects to ensure the returns your organization needs to remain healthy, while avoiding committing to so many projects that your resources get strained beyond their ability to perform effectively.[283]

---

[282] Ibid.

[283] Note that when it comes to human resources and innovation, a little bit of slack time actually helps efficient performance. So keeping people occupied at 100% capacity will actually lead you to worse performance than at, say 95% capacity. If you want to be truly effective, build some slack into your planning. Anders Richtnér*, Pär Åhlström and Keith Goffin, "'Squeezing R&D': A Study of Organizational Slack and Knowledge Creation in NPD, Using the SECI Model," *Journal of Product Innovation Management*, November 2014.

In practice, a balanced portfolio is one that finds the happy medium between focus and diversification.

Focus requires a narrow view, with resources concentrated on a few critical points. Diversification requires a broad view, with resources spread across a number of investments to mitigate the overall risk.

Let's take a look at both of these competing points individually, and then bring them together again.

Green Eggs and Ham

Theodor Geisel was challenged by his editor, Bennett Cerf, to write a book using no more than fifty unique words. The author, better known to a generation of young readers in the US as "Dr. Seuss," took him up on the challenge.[284] The result was *Green Eggs and Ham*, such a popular and classic children's book that Jesse Jackson performed a reading from *The Book of Seuss* on Saturday Night Live.[285]

Essentially, what Cerf did was to set a budget for Geisel, not in terms of dollars, but in terms of words. Geisel, as an innovator, had to work within that budget.

No business, no matter how successful, has an unlimited budget. Resources will always be constrained. Budgeting limited resources against all the initiatives that an organization has is where strategy becomes reality.

Different organizations have different ways of creating budgets, from top-down approaches to bottom-up approaches to middle-out approaches to complicated iterative combinations of all of these. Inevitably, things become politicized, with all sorts of fun games to be played.

I'm always disappointed when I tell a particular story form my early career. At that time, I was sent on multiple unnecessary trips one December, because if my department didn't use our whole travel budget, we were likely to have the travel budget cut for the following year. Why am I disappointed when I tell that story? I'm disappointed, because I expect my audience to laugh at the incredible stupidity of that kind of thinking. I expect at least someone's jaw to drop and eyes to pop out of their heads, thinking that I must be making that

---

[284] Snopes verified. http://www.snopes.com/language/literary/greenegg.asp.

[285] Well worth watching: see it online at http://www.hulu.com/watch/279052.

up. Instead, it's generally received with blank stares and "yeah, so what, everyone does that." I don't get to earn any joke points.

Later in my career, I saw why this happens in so many places. While reviewing a multi-million-dollar budget proposal, which was put together with hundreds of person-hours of time to get justification down to the minutest detail (or so I thought), I was challenged by the CFO on the $500 "Office Supplies" line item. "You are only projected to spend $387 this year on office supplies, how do you justify $500 next year?" I didn't.

In my mind, the $387 could be rounded to the nearest $500, and for something like office supplies, what we did this year seemed like a decent estimate of what we'd do next year. It never occurred to me that a less-than-one-half-of-one-hundredth-of-one-percent portion of a budget would be questioned. But it was. And that led to a questioning of the believability of the rest of the budget justifications that I had prepared.

Admittedly, not every CFO is going to grill people over $113. But it helped me understand why people would game the system, spending money unnecessarily one year so as not to lose it the next. It wasn't about doing what was right for the organization; it was about avoiding personal pain.

People make decisions emotionally. The trick then, is to align their emotions with the rational outcomes that you want. If you want people to make decisions that are best for the organization, don't make it painful for them to do so. Robbing them of this year's travel budget, or office supplies budget, or whatever budget, because they didn't spend it all last year, makes it painful to do what is right. If they accomplished their objectives for less than what they originally thought they'd need, reward them, don't punish them.

I'm sure I'm preaching to the choir on that. Yet organizations continue to dole out the punishments.

While it's beyond the scope of this book to attempt to direct organizations in how to set their budgets, I will throw this recommendation out: use zero-based budgeting. Avoid the silly games described above. Not that it eliminates all the silly games, but it's better than the just-base-it-on-last-year method.

Regardless of the budgeting process, though, you will not likely be given all the resources you could ask for. The bad news that you already know (but I'll say it anyway) is that you won't be able to do everything you might want to do. The good news is that, just as Dr. Seuss demonstrated, resource constraints can actually drive innovation.[286]

In the business world, financial constraints have been found to lead to products that are more creative, generated using fewer inputs, and developed with less costly resources. And the more creative the people on the team, the greater the increase in novelty from resource constraints.[287]

Just in case you are a hyper-aggressive cost-cutter, don't take the previous paragraph as incentive to reduce innovation investment to zero in order to drive people's creativity to infinity. You can't make something out of nothing. Even MacGyver needed candlesticks, a microphone cord, and a rubber mat to make a defibrillator.[288]

The real point here is that you can't use limited resources as an excuse for failing to innovate. Invest resources in innovation, limit your portfolio of efforts to fit within the constraints, and then innovate like crazy to maximize the return on the resources invested.

Tough Choices

If there is just one thing that I can recommend to you for strategically managing your innovation portfolio, it's this: practice focused decision-making discipline.

The single biggest problem for organizations trying to manage their portfolio of projects is that they want to do everything. They don't make the difficult decisions to focus on doing activities they can actually get done well, and instead try to do anything and everything that seems to be interesting... Especially if some executive, board member, or key customer has it in their kennel of pet projects.

Hear this now – you can't do it all. I know you know that already. So stop trying.

---

[286] And don't forget the innovative problem-solving of the engineers in *Apollo 13* when their resources were absolutely constrained. I love a movie in which the engineers are the heroes! Check it out online at https://www.youtube.com/watch?v=Z3csfLkMJT4.

[287] Irene Scopelliti, Paola Cillo, Bruno Busacca and David Mazursky, "How Do Financial Constraints Affect Creativity?" *Journal of Product Innovation Management*, September 2014.

[288] Watch MacGyver save the day at https://www.youtube.com/watch?v=s4wqo_KyeTs.

It's not easy. You must make difficult decisions. And the most difficult decisions aren't going to be choosing between good and bad projects. That's easy – don't do the bad ones. Duh.

The difficult decisions come when you have to choose between multiple good projects. These choices can be so hard that some have compared it to – and this is not for the squeamish – shooting puppies.[289]

Before you call PETA on me for such a statement, understand what that means – all puppies are cute and adorable. But there is a limit to how many puppies you can take care of. Your choice is to either pick the few that you can properly care for, or try to take care of them all and fail. The former allows the few to grow into healthy, happy adults. The latter results in misery and slow starvation for all. Choosing between them isn't easy. You have to choose which ones you will care for...and that means also choosing the ones you will not care for.

Please note that no puppies were harmed in the writing of this book.

Figure 34: Effective portfolio management is not for the squeamish.

Here's the problem: just as people love their puppies, they love their pet projects. There is a reason that they are called "pet" projects, after all. The emotional attachment is the same.

I will actually argue that in many cases, the decision-making is harder than choosing between puppies. When the idea is your own, it's no longer just a puppy. It becomes your baby. Your creation. And no one wants to hear that

---

[289] I can't take credit for this powerful, if nauseating, analogy. I heard it in a presentation by Bob Cooper of Stage-Gate International. If you have a chance to see him speak, I recommend it. You won't forget it.

their baby is ugly. No one wants to see their child cut from the team tryouts. It's personal.

So again, I'll tell you that the single most important thing you can do to effectively manage a bunch of projects is to have the focused discipline to choose those you will do, and those you will not do. Better to do a few projects with excellence than too many projects with mediocrity (or worse).

Calculating Risk

One more point to make before moving on to portfolio decision-making. Warning...there is math ahead.

Don't worry, not much. And it is, as you must by now expect, simple.[290]

Let's start with an easy example, illustrated in Figure 35. You need to decide whether to make a $10,000 investment in an innovation project. You've determined that there is a 60% chance of the innovation being a success in the market, earning you $15,000. That means there is a 40% chance of failure, earning you $0.

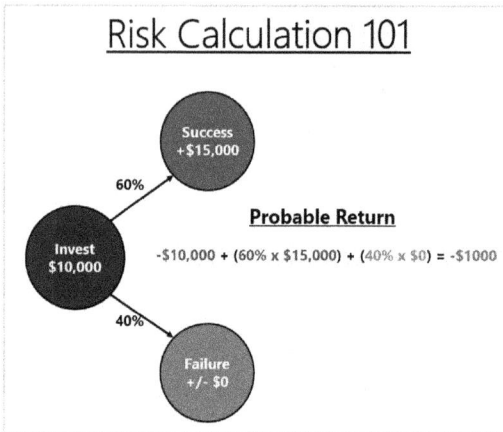

Risk Calculation 101

Success
+$15,000

60%

Probable Return

Invest
$10,000

-$10,000 + (60% x $15,000) + (40% x $0) = -$1000

40%

Failure
+/- $0

Figure 35: A simple example of using probabilities to determine the value of an investment.

Calculating the probable return on the investment is a matter of multiplying the probabilities of each outcome by their respective values, subtracting the cost of investment, and seeing where things total out. In this case, the probable value of this investment is a net loss of $1000.

So the right decision on this investment is don't do it.

Right?

Not so fast.

---

[290] To keep it simple, I've made probabilities and dollars exact amounts. Reality is never so neat, but this is a simplification to illustrate a point, so just go with it.

Such an assessment makes an unstated assumption. That assumption is this: that choosing not to invest has no adverse repercussions.

Is that assumption true for an innovation decision? Not necessarily.

If you choose not to innovate, you are taking the chance that no one else will, either. You take the risk that no one else will seek out, discover, and deliver new solutions that will steal customers away from your current solutions.

Let's expand the example a bit, illustrated in Figure 36. Let's consider what might happen if you don't invest. Let's say that there is a 60% chance that the status quo will continue, not gaining you anything, but not costing you anything, either. There is a 40% chance that your competitors will take away $10,000 worth of your business with their own innovation. In that case, the probable outcome for doing nothing is a net loss of $4000.

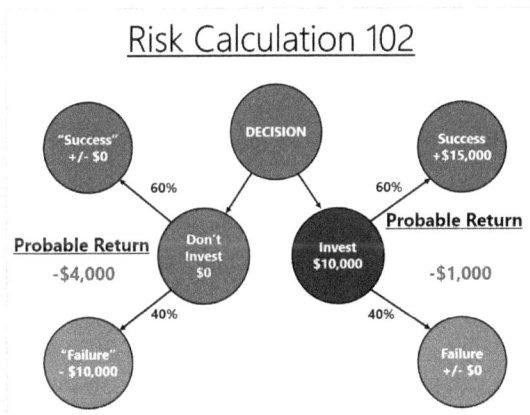

Figure 36: Expanding the risk reward calculation a bit.

In this scenario, if the world is moving forward, then trying to stand your ground gets you further behind than making at least a little effort to keep up.

Again, this is just a simplification to illustrate a point. The reality is much more complicated. Your decisions are never just "invest – yes or no?" You never have clear-cut probabilities and reliably accurate forecasts to do such clean calculations. Instead, you must use estimates based on assumptions, experience, historical data, and intuition. You must also choose among a wide array of uncertain possibilities.

The purpose here is to remind you that choosing to do nothing is still a choice. Choosing not to pursue an innovation must be evaluated for its costs and benefits, too. While it may prove to be the right choice, you have to conclude that consciously.

Math lesson over. There will not be a quiz. The exam will come when your thinking is tested on the job.

Strategic Egg Baskets

Diversification is usually thought of as a way to mitigate risk. While true, it also improves the financial value of innovations, reduces the likelihood of organizational failure, and may contribute more to firm performance than considerations of either value maximization or strategic fit.[291] Diversification also helps organizations to cope with change.[292]

So diversification is a good thing. But how do you do it, while maintaining focus?

Bob Cooper, Scott Edgett, and Elko Kleinschmidt advocate the use of "strategic buckets."[293] Since diversification is all about placing your eggs in multiple baskets, how about we call them "strategic egg baskets" instead? What? No? Too goofy even for this book? Okay fine. "Buckets" it is.

They compared the portfolio decision processes of strong innovation performers against those of poor innovation performers.[294] Their research demonstrated that direct linkage of the portfolio to the strategic plan was a common characteristic of the best innovation performers, and something that poor innovation performers rarely did.

Poor performers also tended to over-rely on financial measures to make portfolio selections. How could this be? Isn't financial performance the lifeblood of any organization, even if a nonprofit?

The problem lies in the difficulty of forecasting.[295] Forecasts are always wrong. Some are closer than others, sure, but if you rely too heavily on making decisions based on financial forecasts, which are in turn based on a heaping helping of assumptions with a large side of future uncertainty, you are bound to make some poor decisions.

---

[291] Regina C. McNally, Serdar S. Durmuşoğlu, and Roger J. Calantone, "New Product Portfolio Management Decisions: Antecedents and Consequences," *Journal of Product Innovation Management*, March 2013.

[292] Ithai Stern and Andrew D. Henderson, "Within-business diversification in technology-intensive industries," *Strategic Management Journal*, May 2004.

[293] Robert C. Cooper, Scott J. Edgett, and Elko J. Kleinschmidt, *Portfolio Management for New Products*, Second Edition, Basic Books, 2001.

[294] Which is the right way to conduct research that avoids the winners-wear-shoes fallacy mentioned in the "'Best Practices' and 'Innovation'" section, page 24.

[295] For more on the challenges of forecasting, go to the "Cloudy Crystal Ball" section, page 364.

So how do strategic buckets work?[296]

Based on your innovation strategy, you should be able to tell what areas you want to invest in. You should know the organization's risk profile, plans for the future, priorities for customer segments, etc. From this information, you can define a handful of strategic buckets. Keeping it to a handful, say 3-6,[297] keeps it simple.

These buckets can be defined in a few ways to secure good diversification. In addition to defining them by things like business units, customer, product line, etc., there are some other investment types that you should consider.

Diversify by Risk/Reward

One of the classic ways of diversification is by having a variety of risk/reward levels. In financial investing, investors look at the volatility of an asset to assess its level of risk. Highly volatile assets have to offer a higher rate of return, on average, than those that offer consistent returns. After all, if the rate of return on the risky one were just the same as for an investment that was practically guaranteed, then no one[298] would ever put a nickel into the higher risk "opportunity."

---

[296] Really? Not "egg baskets?" Darn.

[297] Cooper, Edgett, and Kleinschmidt actually say that typically, the number of strategic buckets ranges from four to twelve. Do what works for your organization, but remember, the more buckets you have, the more complexity to manage them. The more buckets you have to manage, the more directions you get pulled. The more directions you get pulled, the more multitasking you must do. And multitasking erodes performance. If you are in a large, complex organization, and you really need a dozen or more buckets, I recommend breaking them up into groups of 2-4. Rather than trying to manage a dozen strategic buckets at once, break it down into four groups of three buckets, or three groups of four buckets, or some other such combination. An executive level can manage the groups of buckets, while a managerial level below manages the individual buckets in their group. Break it down to keep it simpler to manage.

[298] This, of course, assumes that people behave rationally. We don't. At least not always. But for the sake of this discussion, we can continue to pretend that investors are rational, except when exuberant.

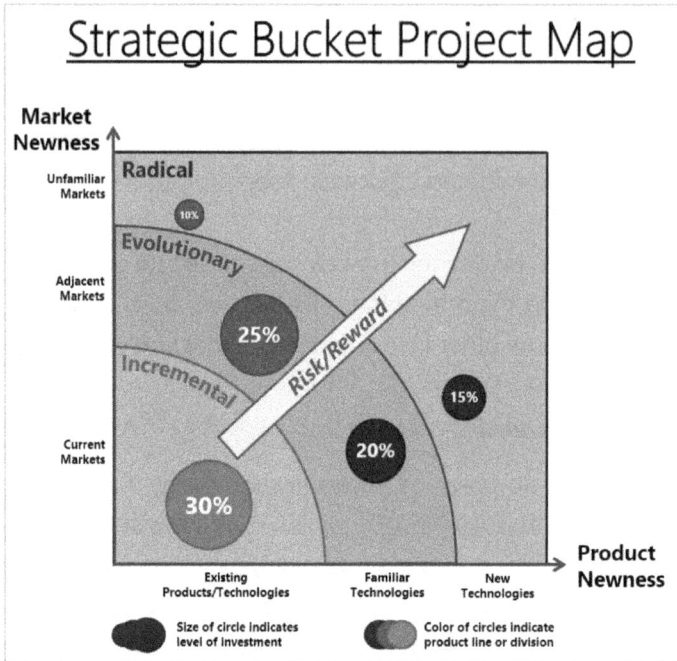

Figure 37: A risk/reward map for project types.

So, in general, low risk investments offer low returns, and high-risk investments offer high returns. The same should hold for innovation investments. You'll need to do your research to forecast the returns on those investments. Just remember to keep your forecasting simple.[299]

One simple way to define strategic buckets on a risk/reward basis is to use the classifications of incremental, evolutionary, and radical. Decide how much you want to invest in each type of innovation, and then support projects that fit within those buckets.

Figure 37 shows a tool for defining strategic buckets with a risk/reward component. It shows five strategic buckets, with percentages representing the amount of the total innovation investment allocated to each. I've triple checked to make sure the percentages add to 100%.

In such a chart, there is an amazing amount of information that can be captured in a simple visual. The colors of the circles could represent different business units, different product lines, or whatever other components of your

---

[299] For a simple and effective forecasting process, see the "Delphi Method" section, page 367.

strategic plan make sense. The size of the circles represents the relative magnitudes of the investments being made. And the location on the chart shows the technology and marketing newness that define the type of innovation being pursued.

This simple visual helps you to immediately grasp how diversified and balanced your strategic buckets are. If things look out-of-balance, it's easy to see the directions to consider in getting things re-balanced.

See? Not all of my tool recommendations involve four-quadrant charts.

Diversify by Time Horizon

Of course, risk/reward isn't the only consideration when determining how to diversify your focused set of strategic buckets.

A common theory of diversification in an investment portfolio has been that diversification over time is a way to reduce risk. Although some economists have challenged that belief when it comes to stocks and bonds,[300] the matter is pretty much settled for product development portfolios.

You must make sure your business is successful both today and tomorrow. Unless your organization is in an existential crisis,[301] you have to invest not only in what will bring returns in the present, but also in what will continue to deliver returns a few calendar pages down the road.

So diversify your buckets to include a range of time horizons. If you defined some innovation roadmaps,[302] then you already have a good view of your path to the future. Capture that in the buckets that you define.

---

[300] Zvi Bodie, Alex Kane, and Alan J. Marcus, *Investments, 10th Edition*, McGraw-Hill Education, 2013.

[301] Not an existential crisis like some Albert Camus novel. I'm talking about being in a situation where there is doubt about an organization's continuing as an ongoing concern. Then, understandably, you need to focus greater attention on the present. After all, there won't be a tomorrow if you don't survive today. However, even then, reserve a bit of your mind space for the future. Herculean efforts to survive the day are all for naught if you get hit by a bus tomorrow. It's a bit like having the organization in an Emergency Room. You must get the patient stabilized, but do so in a way that they will eventually be able to go home and live a long life.

[302] For more on innovation roadmapping, go to the "Innovation Roadmap" section, page 128.

Diversify by Business Area

What are "business areas?" I intentionally left that vague. It will depend on your organization. For larger organizations, these may be business units, geographies, or industries in which you compete. For smaller organizations, it might be customer segments, product lines, or even individuals responsible for different things. You define your "business areas." Then you invest across them consciously. Simple concept.

Impact of Strategy on Diversification

Just as financial advisors will recommend different portfolio choices for different demographic groups, you should have a different portfolio mix based on your strategic type. Remember the prospectors, analyzers, defenders, and reactors?[303] There is a good reason for understanding which one fits your organization. Your portfolio of projects should reflect your strategic type.

Prospectors should invest in a higher proportion of radical and evolutionary projects. Analyzers should have mostly evolutionary projects, with some radical and some incremental mixed in. Defenders should emphasize the incremental, stretching into evolutionary for some projects. Reactors? They need to...get a new strategy.

Portfolio Insight Tools

Well now, I've preached about the importance of balance, both from the focus side and from the diversification side. So it's time to open up the toolbox and unpack the simple portfolio tools.

Four-Quadrant Charts

I've said it before, and I'll say it again: I love four-quadrant charts. And I'm not ashamed to admit it.

While you do have to be careful not to let these charts sink from simple to simplistic, running your portfolio through a few of these can provide some good insights that will help to keep it balanced, and provide some direction

---

[303] For more on these strategic types, go to the "Types of Innovation Strategy" section, page 107.

on what to do with what you've got. Or what to go out and get if you ain't got it.[304]

Risk/Reward Map

Much like the Boston Consulting Group strategy matrix, the risk/reward map is a helpful tool for portfolio balancing. While similar, though, there is a critical difference. Instead of classifying things as dogs or cows, you get elephants and oysters. Yes, that's still two animals, but with a much wider range of size and species!

Perhaps the even more critical difference is that the BCG matrix provides strategic guidance on what to do with existing products, programs, and businesses, while

Figure 38: A Risk/Reward portfolio map, with better animals than the BCG matrix.

this map guides what to do with things aimed at the future.

Why is that such a critical difference? Because of uncertainty. Remember, forecasting is hard.[305] Forecasting is imprecise. With the BCG matrix, you can precisely know your market share. You can precisely know the current growth rate of the market (although that does not necessarily mean it will continue at that rate, but we'll let that slide for now). With the risk/reward matrix, you are making your best SWAG[306] as to what the risk and reward are going to be.

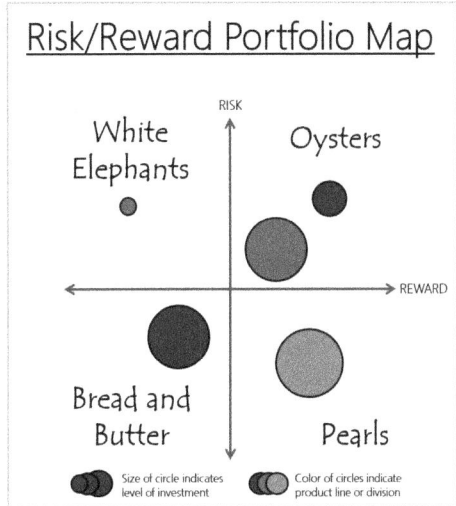

---

[304] For more information about going out and getting what you ain't got, see the "A Word (or a Thousand of Them) on Open Innovation" section, page 136.

[305] For more on simple approaches to the challenge of forecasting, go to the "Cloudy Crystal Ball" section, page 364.

[306] SWAG=Scientific Wild-A** Guess. More fun to say than "educated guess" or "best estimate." For more on forecasting under uncertainty, go to the "Cloudy Crystal Ball" section, page 364.

What that means is that you need to revisit your assessment as you learn in the process of development.

Project Types

If the classification by Incremental-Evolutionary-Revolutionary does not fit for you or your organization, another way to look at the same market/technology factors is with a four quadrat chart pitting market newness against technology newness, as in Figure 39.

Maintenance projects have neither great market newness nor great technological newness. These might be cost reductions or modest line extensions. Expansion projects take existing technologies into new markets, such as geographically expanding your parka business from North Dakota to the warmer climes of Antarctica, or expanding your ping pong ball business from sporting goods retailers to liquor stores.[307]   Taking   new technologies to an existing market would be an upgrade, like moving from the iPhone 17 to the iPhone 19cx gold.[308] And taking new technologies into new markets, well, that's as revolutionary as Elon Musk moving from electric cars to orbiting rocketry.

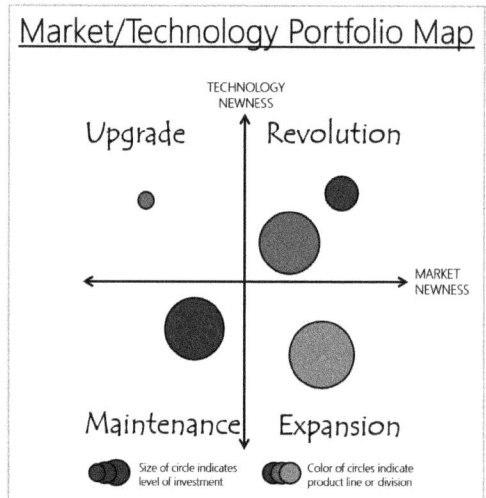

Figure 39: Another way to look at project types.

Place each project into the quadrant where you think it belongs, and look to see if you have a diverse range of projects in the pipeline. If you are up for

---

[307] Seriously. It's been done. http://abcnews.go.com/Business/story?id=3629340&page=1

[308] But definitely not like moving from Windows 7 to Windows 8 was. Ugh.

it, show each project with size and color coding to capture that information visually.

Time Horizon

Money in your pocket now is worth more than the same money put in your pocket later. That's why banks charge interest when you borrow from them, and why they have to offer interest to get you to deposit with them. Otherwise, you'd just stuff your mattress with cash.

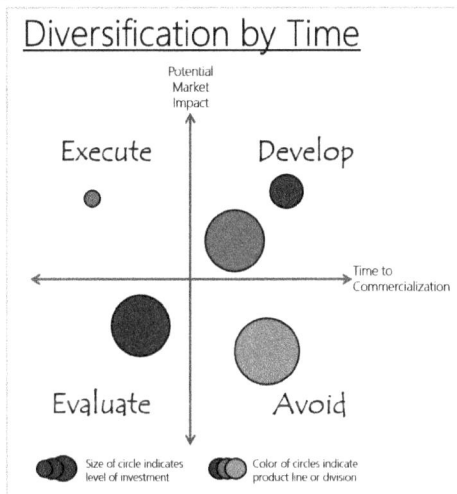

Figure 40: Ways to look at diversifying in time.

Projects that pay off today are more valuable than projects that pay off five years from now. That's why Wall Street investors demand quarterly returns (and unfortunately why those Wall Street demands trickle down through the organization to prioritize delivering short-term projects by arbitrary quarterly end dates).

So when you are looking at diversifying over time, you want those long term projects to have high potential for delivering a big impact on your mission. Avoid projects that have long horizons but minimal potential. Quickly execute those projects with high impact and short commercialization time. Evaluate those projects with low impact but short time horizon – are they worth the resources? As time goes along, keep re-evaluating the potential impact those projects can have, and move them to their new places on the chart. This is necessary to continually maintain a balanced portfolio.

Balancing Urgency

Choosing between projects is difficult.[309] Sometimes, a decision between two good projects will not be that one lives and one dies, but will rather be that one goes now, while the other waits its turn. If that's an option for you, here's a tool to help you decide which is which.

The Urgency Assessment map plots the level of uncertainty for a project against the opportunity cost of delaying the project. As we've discussed, uncertainty is an inherent part of innovation. Uncertainty can be reduced in a variety of ways, through concept reviews, prototyping, technology experiments, customer testing, test marketing, etc. Some of those methods are very costly. Others are cheap. So the horizontal line plots a continuum of uncertainty, ranging from low (or a low cost of reducing uncertainty) to high (with a high cost of reducing uncertainty).

That is plotted against the opportunity cost of delaying a project. That cost might be in the form of lost revenues from a new product, lost customers because a competitor beats you to market, losing leverage with suppliers, etc.

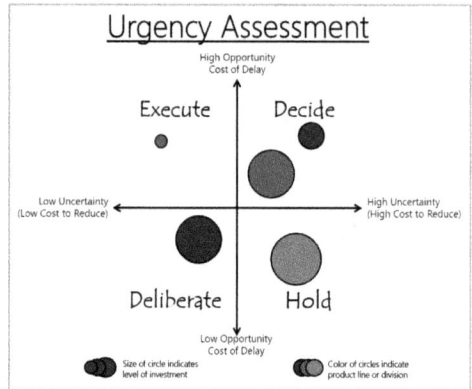

Figure 41: Assessing urgency based on uncertainty and opportunity cost.

Plot your projects on the chart when considering the options available to you. If there is not much cost to delay, and the uncertainty around the project is high, go ahead and put it on hold if you need to (with the ability to fast-follow if necessary). If both uncertainty is low and the cost of delay is low, make slow, deliberate decisions, holding if necessary, or proceeding if possible. If the cost of delay is high, but uncertainty is low (or can be reduced inexpensively), move the project forward immediately. If both uncertainty and cost of delay are high, then just make the best go/no go decision you can with the information available – but make a decision immediatley.

---

[309] Don't make me pull out the puppy analogy again. See page 155, if you dare.

Scorecards

Now, let's move away from the four-quadrant charts. Cooper, Edgett and Kleinschmidt demonstrate the value of strategic scorecards in their portfolio management research. These scorecards can and should be tailored to the needs of a particular organization, but in general, they will contain evaluations of Strategic Alignment, Competitive Advantage, Market Attractiveness (or what I call "Community Potential" for nonprofits), Core Competency Leverage, and Financial Investment.

Before getting into the mechanics of the scorecard, let's unpack those categories a bit.

Strategic alignment is what it sounds like. Does the project fit with overall mission of the organization and its innovation strategy? How important is the project as a component of the innovation strategy?

Competitive Advantage is all about whether a successfully completed project will do something different and better than other offerings that are out there (or that you anticipate to be out there by the time of launch). Does the product offer unique and perceivable benefits to the end user? Does the product meet primary customer needs better than other products? Is the product performance/benefit "ownable" (patent, trademark, trade secret, brand equity, etc.)? Will the Funder(s) of this product perceive it to be a good value?

That last question might have you scratching your head[310] and saying "huh?" Readers that are more articulate may even think, "What does he mean by 'funders?'"

In many businesses and most nonprofits, the source of funds that keep the organization going do not come from the people who actually benefit from the products and services. Donors give money to shelters to provide services to the homeless – the homeless do not pay for the services they use. Retailers give money to consumer goods manufacturers to produce products that their customers will want to buy – the customers don't give money directly to the manufacturer. Healthcare providers receive payment from individuals, insurance companies, and government agencies to provide care to patients in

---

[310] Or whatever else you like to scratch to express confusion.

a very complicated system of transactions – it's not typically just a direct payment from user to provider. The IT department does not have their paychecks signed by the employees whose computers they fix, but by the organizational leadership.

You can't just think of the beneficiary of your goods and services while innovating. Even if they are your primary concern, you *must* also think about who is paying for what you are doing, and make sure that they are satisfied with your work as well.

Market Attractiveness/Community Potential is all about what drives you to the market that you are looking to serve. For a business, this likely means that the market has big profit potential in an arena where the business has interest and capabilities. For a nonprofit, this likely means that the community they want to serve has a large and important need, and the nonprofit has the capabilities to address it.

Questions to ask yourself in this category include: How many primary customers will you be able to reach and help with this product? What are the production costs and financial potential? Is the need for your product growing, persistent, or declining?

Core Competency Leverage pertains to what you know how to do well. Can the product be efficiently distributed? Does the product lend itself to the skills and capabilities of the organization? Can the product be sourced/manufactured efficiently?

Investment Analysis pertains to the financial considerations of the business, and to the risks involved with moving forward on a project with an uncertain future. What is the probability of technical product development success (i.e., how likely are you to be able to make the valuable idea you have a reality)? What is the probability of marketplace success after launch (i.e., how likely is the market to embrace your product and pay for it)? What is the investment required for product development and launch? Does the expected return justify the required investment?

So, definitions now complete, it's time to move on to mechanics.

First, the simple version. See Figure 42 for the visual.

In this version, members of your portfolio evaluation team just rate each project being considered for development along the broad categories listed above. Rate them on whatever scale the team agrees on: 0-10, 0-100, 1-5, whatever. I don't recommend rating them from *e* to π, however, unless you are in the mathematics department of some school or another, and you think that would be fun.

Simple Innovation Scorecard

	Time 1	Time 2	Time 3	Time 4	Time 5
Strategic Alignment					
Competitive Advantage					
Market Attractiveness					
Competency Leverage					
Resource Requirements					
Totals					

Figure 42: The super simple version of an innovation scorecard.

Each person on the portfolio review team should do these ratings individually, just like you would do in the Delphi Method of forecasting.[311] Then bring your scorecards to a team discussion. Identify points of general agreement and disagreement. Where you agree, ask yourselves to confirm that you've thought of the situation from multiple perspectives, and you are not getting caught in a case of groupthink.[312] Where you disagree, discuss the

---

[311] For more on how the Delphi method works, go to the "Delphi Method" section, page 367.

[312] For more about the Bandwagon Effect that leads to groupthink and other cognitive biases, go to the "Cognitive Biases" section, page 224.

opposing points of view candidly, but respectfully (unless you are like me and my buddies, who use vulgar disrespect as an expression of affection).[313]

The portfolio decisions you make should never be made based on numbers alone. They should be based on the consensus of the group after thorough discussion (or on the discretion of the individual responsible[314] if consensus cannot be reached). The scorecard numbers are there to guide the discussion and identify worthy issues of debate. They are not to be wielded like puppy-shooting handguns.[315]

The still-simple-but-less-so versions can be found in Figure 43.

In these versions, the opportunity for capturing data in ways particular to your organization is much greater than in the super-simple version. That benefit comes at the cost of more detailed work to both complete the scorecard, and to design the scorecard in the first place. It's up to you to do the cost-benefit analysis of the level of detail appropriate for organization.

These scorecards include all of the questions previously listed for each of the different sections. You could add or subtract questions to tailor for your needs.

Each question is weighted as a percentage of importance within a section. If you think one question is more important than another, you could weight them 90:10, 80:20, 75:25, 66⅔:33⅓...you get the idea.

Each section can be weighted as a percentage of importance to the overall evaluation. If you keep all five sections, they could be 20:20:20:20:20 as shown above, or 30:10:35:15:10, or...no, I'm not going to do that again. You get the idea.

Once everyone has completed their individual ratings, then each project can be rolled up with average ratings and variability calculations, to identify the areas of agreement and disagreement, as well as how the ratings of each project compare to one another.

---

[313] I'd tell you some of the nicknames with which I've been labeled, but they are definitely NSFW.

[314] For more about effective decision-making and responsibilities, go to the "Negotiating the RAPIDs" section, page 334.

[315] Yeah, I went there.

Commercial Project Scorecard

	Member 1	Member 2	Member 3	Member 4	Member 5	Member 6	Member 7	Member 8	Member 9	Average Team Rating	Variance of Ratings	Weight	Total Points
Strategic Alignment												20%	0
Does the project *fit* with overall mission and innovation strategy?													
Is the project an *important* component of the innovation strategy?													
Competitive Advantage												20%	0
Does the product offer *unique* and *perceivable* benefits to the end user?													
Does the product meet *primary* and *secondary* customer needs better than other products?													
Does the end user perceive this product to be a good *value* for the price paid?													
Is the product performance/benefit "*ownable*" (patent, trademark, trade secret, etc.)?													
Market Attractiveness												20%	0
What are the *volume* projections?													
What are the production *costs* and *profit margins*?													
Is the market for this product *growing*?													
Core Competency Leverage												20%	0
Can the product be efficiently *distributed*?													
Does the product lend itself to the *skills* and *capabilities* of the organization?													
Can the product be *sourced/manufactured* efficiently?													
Investment Analysis												20%	0
What is the probability of *technical* product development success?													
What is the *investment* required for product development and launch?													
What is the probability of *commercial* success after launch?													
Does the expected *return* justify the required investment?													
										Total		100%	0

Nonprofit Project Scorecard

	Member 1	Member 2	Member 3	Member 4	Member 5	Member 6	Member 7	Member 8	Member 9	Average Team Rating	Variance of Ratings	Weight	Total Points
Strategic Alignment												20%	0
Does the project *fit* with overall mission and innovation strategy?													
Is the project an *important* component of the innovation strategy?													
Competitive Advantage												20%	0
Does the product offer *unique* and *perceivable* benefits to the end user?													
Does the product meet *primary* customer needs better than other products?													
Will the Funder(s) of this product perceive it to be a good *value*?													
Is the product performance/benefit "*ownable*" (patent, trademark, trade secret, etc.)?													
Community Potential												20%	0
How many primary customers will you be able to *reach* and help with this product?													
What are the production *costs* and *net revenues* (if any)?													
Is the need for this product *growing, persistent, or declining*?													
Core Competency Leverage												20%	0
Can the product be efficiently *distributed*?													
Does the product lend itself to the *skills* and *capabilities* of the organization?													
Can the product be *sourced/manufactured* efficiently?													
Investment Analysis												20%	0
What is the probability of *technical* product development success?													
What is the *investment* required for product development and launch?													
What is the probability of *community* success after launch?													
Does the expected *return* justify the required investment?													
										Total		100%	0

Figure 43: The still-simple-but-less-so versions of scorecards, for both nonprofit and commercial businesses.

Yes, less easy. But with the spreadsheet software doing the heavy lifting, it's still simple.

How you do it is up to you and the needs of your organization – particularly with regards to the demands of the culture. I've worked with organizations that had complicated product lines and business considerations, but who successfully use the super simple scorecard. They were comfortable with ambiguity and discussing projects in broad terms, with no problem handling healthy conflict when disagreements arose.

I've worked with small organizations that had simple product lines who preferred doing the still-simple-but-less-so ratings because they were very numbers and data oriented people, comfortable with completing longer surveys, but less comfortable with bringing up disagreement in a group setting. The spreadsheet forced the identification and discussion of points of disagreement in a healthy way that helped them move past long-standing issues of prioritization.

And yes, I've worked with groups in-between.

The scorecard is a great tool. Customize it for your situation, and it will work wonders for you. The decisions won't get any easier, but the process of making them will be less painful. Just as importantly, the decision clarity will help soothe any discontent for team members who see their preferred projects get weeded out.[316]

Portfolio Decision-Making

So what drives the ultimate decision on what stays and what goes? Balance. Your collection of innovation projects must be focused (limited) enough to be resourced adequately for excellent execution, while being diversified (broad) enough to mitigate the risks inherent in any individual project.

An organization needs to be more than the sum of its parts. What the organization does must be more than a jumble of individual, unconnected efforts. Making project resource decisions needs to be done with a view of how each individual project fits within the overall portfolio of the organization. And the portfolio needs to be managed with deep understanding of each individual project.

---

[316] Michael A. Roberto, "The Art of Critical Decision Making," *The Teaching Company,* 2009.

Organizations are like organisms.[317,318] To survive, all of the component organs have to work together as whole. So manage the portfolio, not just the projects.[319]

It ain't over 'til it's over

The last point to make about portfolio management is that it is a proverbial journey, not a proverbial destination.

Portfolio management is not something that is done once per time-period-of-your-choice and done. Decision-makers need to have some decision-making agility.[320] Again, the research in this area indicates that the most effective organizations are the ones that make quick but flexible decisions.[321] Flexible, but not fickle. They are able to update their assessments based on project learning and changing circumstances in the marketplace. They don't, however, arbitrarily change with the whims of pet project owners, and they don't follow every shiny new object they see.

---

[317] I bet that's why the words sound so much alike.

[318] Fortunately, organizations are like sea stars. You can cut off a limb, and a new one can grow back. Or so I've read. No sea stars were harmed in the writing of this book. Is that joke getting old yet?

[319] That doesn't mean you should neglect project management, though. Each part needs to be healthy for the whole to be healthy. See the chapter on Project Management, page 347.

[320] This is another reason that an organizational culture comfortable with I-don't-know-but-I'll-find-out is important for innovation success.

[321] Linda Kester, Erik Jan Hultink, and Abbie Griffin, "An Empirical Investigation of the Antecedents and Outcomes of NPD Portfolio Success," *Journal of Product Innovation Management*, November 2014.

Simple Study Guide – Portfolio Management

- What does it mean for a portfolio to be "balanced?"
- How do resource constraints impact innovation?
- Why is courage necessary when managing a project portfolio?
- How do you calculate risk for a project?
- What element of risk is often forgotten with innovation projects?
- On what dimensions should a project portfolio be diversified?
- What are "strategic buckets?"
- Describe some useful four-quadrant portfolio assessment charts?
- How do project scorecards work?
- How are project scorecards best used for portfolio decisions?

Where do you want to go from here?

Or just turn the page to keep reading...

THE CREATION SYSTEM

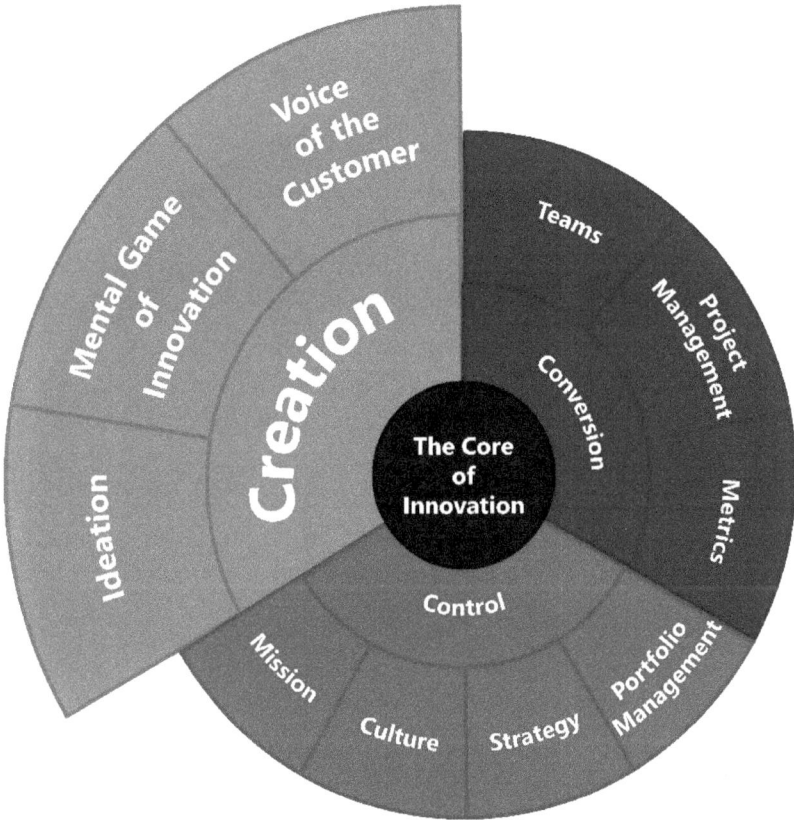

Solutions Need Problems (Voice of the Customer)

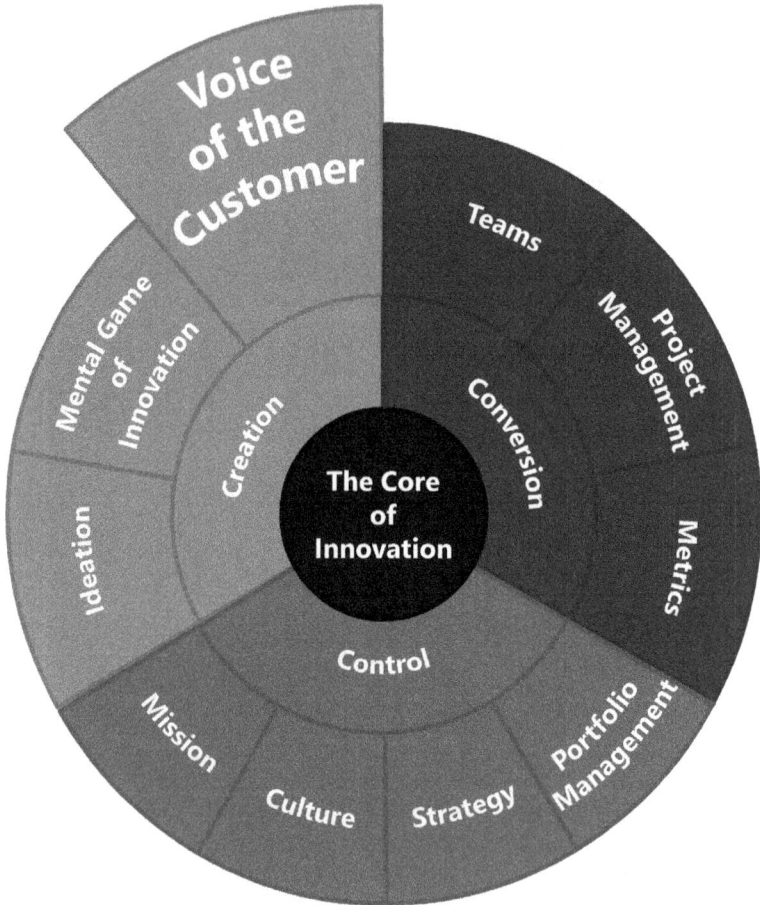

Simple Self-Assessment – Voice of the Customer

Rate yourself on the following questions. To benchmark yourself against others, go to www.3point14Innovation.com and click the "Self-Assessments" menu.

- ***Where do ideas for new products come from in your organization?***

  Online random idea generator

  Needs, problems, and pain points of potential customers

1	2	3	4	5	6	7	8	9	10

- ***How is design thinking incorporated into your organization?***

  We make pretty designs on notepads during meetings

  It's fundamental to the innovation process

1	2	3	4	5	6	7	8	9	10

- ***Do you have a clear understanding of the people you are innovating for?***

  As clear as lead.

  As clear as the waters of paradise.

1	2	3	4	5	6	7	8	9	10

- ***How are your empathic listening skills?***

  Huh? My what?

  I understand why you asked that

1	2	3	4	5	6	7	8	9	10

- ***Do you engage in customer visits and/or ethnography?***

  Ethanol-what-ography?

  As often as possible

1	2	3	4	5	6	7	8	9	10

- ***What do you do with data from your customers?***

  Store it in that warehouse from the end of *Raiders of the Lost Ark*.

  Sort it into a cohesive story that brings clarity to the chaos

1	2	3	4	5	6	7	8	9	10

- ***How do you capture and translate the Voice of your Customers?***

  With a long survey every decade or so

  We are QFD masters

1	2	3	4	5	6	7	8	9	10

- ***Do you involve your customers in the development process?***

  What do they know about their problems?

  As much as we can

1	2	3	4	5	6	7	8	9	10

Simple Summary –
Voice of the Customer

Key take-aways you should get out of this section:

- Innovation is about solving people's problems in a way that they value. Therefore, you have to start the approach to innovation with defining the problem that you are going to solve. Thinking that you will just have an idea that people will miraculously like will take, well, a miracle.

- Design thinking is an iterative approach to problem solving that involves uncovering and defining problems, creating solutions and evaluating them, and incorporating what is learned into a refined understanding of the problem. Repeat.

- Design thinking is most valuable at the front end of the innovation process, and should be incorporated throughout the process. Design should never be relegated to the back end as a way to make a new product pretty. Design is not just about aesthetics.

- Defining problems is hard work, with a mix of art and science to it. It starts with a thorough understanding of the customer, their needs, their challenges, and their objectives.

- "Voice of the Customer," or VoC, is not the same as "what the customer asks for." Probably because of the word "voice" in the name, VoC has been denigrated by many, who correctly point out that customers are bad at identifying and articulating solutions to their problems. VoC is actually about getting into the minds and hearts of customers to really, thoroughly understand their needs, what works well for them, what doesn't work so well, and where the pain points are in their lives. VoC requires not just listening to the words of customers, but understanding what those words mean, to that customer, in their minds.

- Thinking in terms of "jobs to be done" is an effective way to think about customer problems. What this means is that you don't focus on what your product does, but rather the result it delivers to the customer. An example would be a drill. Customers don't want a drill. They want a hole in something (or many holes in many things). If you think only about the drill, you will overly narrow the scope of the problem, and you will focus your attention on the wrong thing.

- Empathic listening is a critical part of the VoC process. By that, I mean listening carefully in order to understand. It means observing the customer with all of your senses, not just hearing their words.
- Two important means for understanding your customer are customer visits and ethnography. These methods help you to live the life of your customer, understand what is going on in their lives, and get personal perspectives on ways to solve their problems. They are the best ways to get beneath the words that customers will share with you in surveys and interviews. These methods enable you to know more fully what customers *mean* by what they *say*.
- Collecting VoC data can leave you with a huge jumble of quotes, observations, and other data. Once collected, it is critical to sort and organize that data into something that makes sense to you and to your organization. The data should become a story of sorts, telling you the highs and lows of life as your customer, and guiding you to problems and potential solutions.
- Quality Function Deployment (QFD) is a mouthful. Some people think of it as the "house of quality." It is an excellent tool for translating the stated needs of customers into technical guidelines for the development of innovative solutions. It can be made extremely detailed and complex, or (you know this is my preference), relatively simple and straightforward. In either case, the results can help you get through significant front-end challenges to the innovation process.
- Remember that perception is reality to your customers. You may have technical data showing that you have a superior and novel solution to your customers' problems, but if they don't perceive the superiority or novelty, guess what...you don't have a superior or novel solution.
- Involving customers in the solution process can be very rewarding. The ability to get rapid feedback and novel ideas from those you are trying to help will accelerate your solution process. Note: this is not the same as asking customers what they want. You will still have to go through the full creative process, and you will still have to do the real problem solving.
- Sometimes, the pursuit of perfection gets in the way of the delivery of good. Some organizations will forego collecting good data on customers because it isn't the "right" way to collect the data. But they can't afford the "right" way, so they don't do anything at all. That's silly. Get the best data you can with the resources available.
- Seek out novel ways to improve your data quality – dare I say, innovate the way you collect the data? Get the whole development

team involved, and not just in some PowerPoint debrief meeting. Get them among your customers so that they can have real experience with them. It will enhance the solutions that you get.

- Listen with appropriate caution to understand feedback on early prototypes. Some people will not be able to respond while thinking of the possibilities – they can only see the not-ready-for-prime-time thing before their eyes.

Spinning Wheels

Have you ever been a part of a meeting like this one that I was asked to observe?

A group of diverse, talented, and smart individuals met to generate ideas for a product innovation. They were working on a big, complex set of issues with great potential impact. Each participant was passionate and engaged in the topic. The discussions were energetic and positive.

For a while.

After about an hour, the faces of the participants had changed. They looked tired. A tone of agitation had crept into some voices. Folded arms communicated through body language that minds were closing.

Although my role was to be an outside observer, I decided to ask a question. "What is the problem that you are trying to solve?"

After a pause, one of the participants gave it a shot, but the blank looks on other faces indicated that it wasn't quite the problem that the others were working on.

I asked a follow-up. "Who is it that you are trying to solve a problem for?"

At that point, I was pulled aside by the leader who had arranged for this creative session. "That's a step we have planned for later. Right now, we are just coming up with ideas, figuring out what we can do."

That made the problem perfectly clear for me.

No, not the problem that they were trying to solve. But I had seen clearly why they were spending loads of intellectual energy and getting nowhere.

It doesn't matter how creative, talented, smart, and collaborative a group you have – if you don't define the problem, you can't create a solution. Lewis Carrol perfectly illustrated the problem 150 years ago in *Alice's Adventures in Wonderland*:[322]

"Would you tell me, please, which way I ought to go from here?"

"That depends a good deal on where you want to get to," said the Cat.

"I don't much care where–" said Alice.

"Then it doesn't matter which way you go," said the Cat.

---

[322] Happy sesquicentennial, Alice!

"—so long as I get SOMEWHERE," Alice added as an explanation.

"Oh, you're sure to do that," said the Cat, "if you only walk long enough."

That cracks me up every time I read it. It's not that it is so absurd. It's that it is so *real*. I've had that kind of conversation too many times.[323] Surely, we'll come up with a good idea, if we only talk long enough.

Like Alice, though, we aren't going to get where we want to go just by randomly going. To come up with great innovations, we have to start with the problems we are trying to solve, and the people for whom we are trying to solve them.

Design Thinking

When I think about "design," I don't think about iPhones, Dyson vacuum cleaners, or Anglepoise desk lamps.[324] I think of doors. Or, more specifically, door handles.

When I approach a door, the door communicates with me.[325] A horizontal bar or lever says "push." A vertical bar or handle says "pull." They say those things whether those words appear on the door or not.

Nothing drives me crazier[326] than when I pull on a vertical handle and discover that the door will only open with a push. Except, of course, when I push on a horizontal handle and find out that to open it, I have to pull. I feel like I'm a student at the Midvale School for the Gifted.[327]

Design is not something that you slap on at the end of a development process to make your product look pretty. That kind of approach to design is like putting lipstick on a pig. It won't make the pig a princess.

---

[323] I'm ashamed to admit that many of those times, I have been playing the role of Alice.

[324] You know the lamp that bounces on the ball in the Pixar movies? That's an Anglepoise lamp.

[325] No, it doesn't actually talk to me. And even if it did, I probably wouldn't hear it over all the other voices in my head.

[326] I should say that nothing drives me crazier in the world of door functionality. Plenty drives me crazier in the bigger world. Like people who stop to look around at the end of an escalator. Move along, folks. Move along.

[327] One of my all-time favorite cartoons from Gary Larson's *The Far Side*. Check it out online at http://www.2ndfirstlook.com/2012/09/gary-larson.html.

Design is not just about aesthetics, although that comes into play. The aesthetics are a means of communication, like the orientation of handles on a door. The aesthetics are just a part of the overall solution, telling people how the solution works in an easily understood, almost intuitive way.

Design thinking has become a trendy topic of discussion, but there is still a popular misconception of it as being confined to the art department. So if it isn't that, what is it?

Design is about solving problems for people and communicating solutions to them.

When someone is approaching a door, they have a problem – how does it open? The orientation of the door handle immediately communicates that. Amazingly, the orientation of the door handle communicates to the person even better than the words "push" or "pull." That is a simple example of design at work.

Deign is a non-linear, iterative process: first, you discover and define a problem, and then you create and evaluate solutions. Each rotation through the process gets you more learning, enabling you to further define the problem and refine the solution.

Michael Luchs lists six principles of design thinking that are critical to developing products that customers will value:[328]

1) **People-centered** – all too often, we focus on the product, be it a physical good or a service. What we need to focus on is the customer, and the customer's customer. They are the people who will be impacted by our products. What will their experience be throughout the life cycle of their interaction with the product? What will they think and feel in the whole process of learning about, acquiring, using, storing, and disposing of the product? What value can we create for the customer? The product is just a means to that end.

2) **Cross-disciplinary and collaborative** – design is not limited to the people with drafting tables in their offices. It includes the whole cross-functional project team. You want to take in multiple points of view.

---

[328] Michael I. Luchs, Scott Swan, Abbie Griffin (editors), *Design Thinking: New Product Development Essentials from the PDMA*, Wiley-Blackwell, 2015.

Even experienced designers in familiar markets can't necessarily predict what customers are going to want.[329] Incorporating the information, experience, and perspectives of a variety of team members will help get the team in touch with the customer faster.

3) **Holistic and integrative** – Products are not just sets of individual components hooked together, but they are systems intended to achieve an objective. Design thinking involves not only the details, but the overall system. In fact, it goes beyond just the product to consider how the product fits into the overall objectives of the customer.

4) **Flexibility and Comfort with Ambiguity** – Design thinking, like innovation, requires humility. You must be willing to take a risk in exploring one solution, only to find that it's the wrong direction to go. You have to be able to admit that, learn from it, and come up with a new direction, a new solution, or a new approach. And you have to do that in an environment filled with more questions than answers, and more uncertainty than certainty.

5) **Multimodal communication skills** – This is an academic way of saying that you find more ways to communicate than with just words. Pictures, models, hand gestures, sculptures, taped-together-paper-and-plastic-and-string-and-rubber-bands[330] – whatever gets the real understanding of the product to customers, teammates, executives, buyers, and whoever else will care about the product.

6) **Growth mindset** – the object of the game is learning how to solve the problem. Learning is growth, even if learning comes through failure. As said before, it takes humility.[331] It also takes courage, to get past

---

[329] Dan Zhang, "Industrial Designers: Are You Ready for Foreign Markets? Assessing Designer Confidence and Prediction Accuracy in a Transnational Marketing Context," *Creativity and Innovation Management*, September 2015.

[330] This describes one of the earliest prototypes, as translated from a white board sketch in my office, for a product that eventually made it to market – the Fellowes Laptop GoRiser, one of my all-time favorite projects that I got to work on. It may not be as world-changing a product as cheese in a spray can, but the process for creating and launching it was cool. Very cool.

[331] For more on how to fail well, go to the "Failure Tolerance" section of the chapter on Culture, page 58.

the fear of failure, and to get past the fear of looking foolish to your colleagues.

Design thinking is a key component of innovative thinking. It needs to be incorporated throughout the innovation process. The most unfortunate part of people relegating design to the tail end of the product development process – the final "make it pretty" phase – is that the greatest value of design thinking comes at the front end of the process. That's where you can do low-cost work to get feedback from customers, learn what's really important to them, and adjust the solution before making expensive development investments.

Defining a Problem is Hard

So we have to start with an understanding of the problems we are trying to solve, and the people for whom we are trying to solve them. If we are going to come up with valuable solutions, this point seems rather obvious. Yet so many organizations fail to do this.

How does such an obvious mistake happen so often? The problem (no pun intended...well, okay, maybe it's a little intended) is that defining problems is hard work. We tend to think solving them is the hard part, but how much harder is it to define the problem? Einstein is quoted as having said that if he had one hour to save the world he would spend fifty-five minutes defining the problem and only five minutes finding the solution[332] – so apparently he found it to be an 11-to-1 more difficult challenge.

Defining problems is an art, requiring insight and judgment, trial and error. It is difficult work, but it is one of the constraints that are paradoxically necessary for freeing creative thinking,

There are many approaches that people recommend for doing it. There is no single right way. Here are some tips, though, to get you started in the right direction.

1) **Define the people for whom you are solving the problem.** Some prefer to think of this as "who has an unmet desire or need?"

---

[332] Another quote that is probably just apocryphal. Curse you, internet memes! Still, it illustrates the point.

Understand those people. Consider also those who may be indirectly impacted by the problem.

2) **Research the problem space.** Gain a general understanding and share it with the team. Focus on understanding the causes of issues for the customer. What are their pain points? What contributes to the pain? How are they currently solving their problems? Why are those solutions insufficient?

3) **Explain why the problem is important to solve.** As Simon Sinek has eloquently communicated,[333] to inspire action, you must start with "why." Don't assume that the "why" is obvious. Everyone on the team should have a clear and common understanding. Be explicit about it.

4) **Play around with the scope of the problem.** The problem needs to be defined broadly enough to be worth solving, and narrowly enough to be solvable. Everlasting global peace among all people is probably too big, and deciding which sock to put on first is probably too small. Go for something in between.

5) **Phrase the problem in multiple ways.** Restating the problem in multiple ways can provide interesting insights, and ensures that the team members' varying perspectives and assumptions are all explicitly communicated.

Only after defining the problem – clearly, succinctly, and explicitly – should you begin looking for a solution.

But you don't just start by one day sitting in your favorite contemplation spot and saying to yourself, "I'm going to define a problem today." You start by looking where the problems exist – and that is where your customer lives.

Voice of the Customer – What it isn't

One of the most influential papers in the history of innovation research[334] is Abbie Griffin and John R. Hauser's "The Voice of the Customer,"

---

[333] See him do so in a TED Talk, online at
https://www.ted.com/talks/simon_sinek_how_great_leaders_inspire_action?language=en.

[334] Abbie Griffin and John R. Hauser, "The Voice of the Customer," *Marketing Science*, Winter, 1993. Winner of the John D.C. Little Best Paper Award for 1993 and named one of the top 20 articles published in the field of Marketing Science in the last 25 years by the INFORMS Society

(affectionately known to the innovation world as VoC). This paper laid the foundation for identifying, structuring, and prioritizing customer needs and perceptions of performance in the innovation process.

There is just one problem with this article. It used the word "voice" in the title. That has subsequently led many astray when they go out to identify customer needs. It has also led many otherwise insightful thought leaders to lambast "the voice of the customer" as useless.[335] So unfortunate. All because of one misunderstood word.

The "Voice of the Customer" is not – I repeat, NOT – about the spoken word. At least not about the spoken word alone.

Henry Ford is famous for many things, and one of them is the popular don't-listen-to-your-customers quote, "If I had asked customers what they wanted, they would have asked for a faster horse."[336] Steve Jobs, too, is often cited as someone who rejected listening to consumers. "People don't know what they want until you show it to them."[337]

So lots of people have created lots of internet memes and PowerPoint slides to prove that the "voice of the customer" is a fallacy you should ignore.

And you really should ignore it, if it means what they think it means. To them, though, I offer my best Inigo

Figure 44: "You keep using that word. I do not think it means what you think it means."

of Marketing Science. Abbie is my all-time favorite professor, so I may be biased regarding her work, but in this case, it's not just me.

[335] See an excellent retort to such arguments in Gerry Katz, "Hijacking the Voice of the Customer," *Visions*, January 2006.

[336] Nope. He never quite said that. Myth busted. Patrick Vlaskovits, "Henry Ford, Innovation, and That 'Faster Horse' Quote," *Harvard Business Review* blog post (with excellent sources cited at the end), August 29, 2011.

[337] Yep, he did actually say this, as quoted in *Business Week*, May 25, 1998. But that came after "We have a lot of customers, and we have a lot of research into our installed base. We also watch industry trends pretty carefully. But in the end, for something this complicated, it's really hard to design products by focus groups."

Montoya: "You keep using that word. I do not think it means what you think it means."

"Voice of the Customer" is not literally about listening to a customer's voice, telling you exactly what they need, and then you go out and make it for them. It is not about calling up a market research firm[338] and having them put together some focus groups with the expectation that the words "what I really need is..." will be followed by the perfect innovation idea for you to go forth and conquer. Nor is it about conducting a survey among target customers just asking them what they want.[339]

If people could articulate what they needed and how to satisfy that need, then innovation would be easy. But it doesn't work that way.

Customer needs are *not* solutions. A customer need is *not* "a faster horse." A customer need is "a means to travel long distances in a shorter period of time than currently possible." A customer need is not "a car." A customer need is "a means of getting from one place on land to another place on land, safely and comfortably, without expending personal physical energy to carry driver, passengers, and various items that need to be transported."

Your first job as an innovator is to have the insight about your customers that they can't necessarily articulate. It is *not* the job of a customer to tell you how to do your job.

Voice of the Customer – What it is

The "voice" of the customer is about going beyond getting inside the shoes of the people you want to serve and walking a mile in them. It's more like doing a Vulcan mind meld.[340] It is about getting inside their heads, experiencing life and all its pain points from their perspective.

---

[338] With all due respect to market research firms that really can give you insightful information.

[339] While I'd be more convinced of its authenticity if I could cite a credible source, I'll go ahead and throw out the rejection that Debbi Fields received before opening Mrs. Field's Cookies: "A cookie store is a bad idea. Besides, the market research reports say America likes crispy cookies, not soft and chewy cookies like you make."

[340] If you don't know what the Vulcan mind meld is, get online and see it here: https://www.youtube.com/watch?v=VEsrYaQYQSo. Rest in peace, Leonard Nimoy.

Remember Kelly Johnson, the lead engineer at the Lockheed Skunk Works, who first articulated the KISS principle?[341] That wasn't just his way of endorsing minimalist design principles. What drove the KISS principle for him was the voice of his customer. He knew that his team was designing tools of warfare, to be used by soldiers in battle conditions. The planes they were designing didn't just have to meet certain performance criteria in the air, but had to be maintained and repaired on the ground by people who were potential enemy targets.

So while those planes were still just sketches on paper, he showed his team a small pile of tools that would be available to the soldiers charged with maintenance and repair. Any plane they designed and built had to be maintainable with those existing tools. No need for the airfield staff to learn how to use yet another tool, no need for them to add still more weight to their equipment packs, and no need for them to have to keep track of more and more doohickeys when their minds needed to be focused on doing their jobs under extreme stress.

Did Johnson have those field technicians complete a survey of needs before initiating a fighter design project? Did he conduct focus groups with them, sitting behind a one-way mirror embedded into a field tent? Did he go through stacks of customer complaint letters? Doubtful. But he knew what life was like for all of his customers – from pilots to ground crew, from generals to airmen – and made darn sure that the entire development staff did, too. That deep understanding was built into everything they did. And, as a result, they created some of the most amazing military machines in history.

More recently, Steve Jobs has been credited with making some of the most amazing consumer machines in history. Since he is so often mentioned as the master innovator who ignored the voice of the customer, let's revisit his feelings on the topic:

> "You've got to start with the customer experience and work backwards to the technology...I've made this mistake probably more than anybody else in this room...As we have

---

[341] For more about the KISS principle and simplicity, go to the "Keeping Innovation Simple" section of the opening chapter, page 17.

tried to come up with a strategy and a vision for Apple, it started with 'What incredible benefits can we give to the customer? Where can we take the customer?'...I think that's the right path to take."[342]

That does not sound like someone who ignored their customer. That sounds like someone who put customers first, and demanded that his people deeply understand them, even if the customers couldn't necessarily tell you what they wanted. Innovation always starts with the customer in mind. And in heart.

So VoC is first and foremost about understanding your customer. It's about knowing what your customer is trying to do, and what they want to achieve. It's about knowing for whom they are doing what they are doing. It's about understanding what works well as they do what they do, and what is a pain in the cranium as they do what they do.

Jobs to be Done

Clay Christensen came up with a powerful way of framing customer needs, which he called "jobs to be done."[343] You need to think about what result the customer is looking for. That's not the same thing as thinking about the solution that you have.

The best way to illustrate the "job to be done" approach is to go through an example. A customer does not have a need for a more efficient drill, or a more powerful drill, or a lighter weight drill. Those are all potential solutions to the customer need. What the customer needs is a hole, or a bunch of holes. If the customer could get the required holes without a drill, they just might.

Or maybe they don't even need the holes. Maybe they are making the holes to solve a different problem. Maybe the holes are just their solution to a bigger job-to-be-done. Gaining insight on the bigger problem may be even more fertile ground for innovation.

---

[342] You can watch him say this on video in Drew Hansen's article, "Myth Busted: Steve Jobs Did Listen to Customers," *Forbes*, December 19, 2013.

[343] Clayton M. Christensen, Scott D. Anthony, Gerald Berstell and Denise Nitterhouse, "Finding the Right Job for Your Product," *Sloan Management Review*, Spring 2007.

When we think about making the existing solution better, rather than about better performing the customers' jobs-to-be-done, we lose out on opportunities to innovate. Getting those jobs done better is where you can *really* relieve your customers' pain points – curing the disease and not just treating the symptoms.

Those pain points may not be easy to see. I was talking to a friend the other day who suffered from chronic back pain for years. After finally undergoing successful back surgery, he said, "I never realized how much pain I was in. I just got used to it, and accepted it as part of life. It was my 'normal.' I didn't know how abnormal my normal was until after the surgery."[344]

Your innovation efforts need to be like his back surgery. You need to relieve pain that your customers aren't even aware that they have.

How to Listen to the Voice

Unfortunately, it is currently illegal in most countries to tranquilize and tag your customers in order to learn their behaviors in depth, the way biologists track wild animals.[345] Perhaps someday, a tag-and-release market research lobby will change that. In the meantime, we need to resort to the challenging tactic of... listening.

Stephen Covey's fifth habit[346] is "seek to understand, then to be understood." In delving into that habit, he describes two types of listening: listening to respond, and listening to understand. It's listening to understand, also known as empathic listening, that is the hallmark of an innovator. Unfortunately, not many people do that naturally.

We all tend to listen to respond. In the relationship world, that leads to misunderstandings, arguments, silent treatments, and the fall of civilization as we know it. In the innovation world, it leads to garbage products – goods and

---

[344] Okay, I didn't tape record the conversation. It was at a bar, and the music was loud enough that a recording would have sounded more like a classic rock mash-up than a journalistic interview, anyway. But I swear, he said something a lot like this.

[345] More brilliant reporting from the Onion: http://www.theonion.com/article/more-corporations-using-tag-and-release-programs-t-36271

[346] Stephen Covey, *The Seven Habits of Highly Successful People*, The Free Press, 1989.

services that no one really needs or wants.[347] And all the wasted resources spent developing them.

Empathic listening involves really trying to understand people. It means understanding the reality of people, not your preconceived notions or assumptions. It means questioning your understanding, and then testing it, by checking in with the people you are trying to understand. It means not only listening to the words, but also feeling the emotions behind them. It means watching the actions of the people to know what they really mean by their words.

Let's say that I did some customer research for this book, and heard that my target audience wants the book to be easy to read. I could jump on that, and publish it in 24-point Times New Roman, believing that it was now "easy to read." Then I get feedback that it is difficult to read because I obfuscate my sagacity through the supererogatory employment of erudite words and abstruse phraseology, or that I tend to run on and on and on and become repetitive and redundant, and I have too darn many distracting footnotes.[348]

Words like "easy to read," can have many meanings. You think you know what they mean, and then find out that the customer meant something very different. You must confirm and reconfirm your understanding to get it right.

That's the iterative nature of innovation in a nutshell. You observe and form a hypothesis about what you understand to be true. You test that hypothesis with the customer. You observe their response, revise your hypothesis, and do it all again, until you have something that really meets their needs.

My favorite story of understanding the reality behind the words comes from a colleague who was doing some laundry detergent research. They[349] had

---

[347] I think most of the needless stuff produced in the world get sold by – or at least printed in – the SkyMall catalog. If *Keep Innovation Simple* is half as humorous as the product listings to be found in airplane seat backs, I will consider myself successful. You just can't make up stuff like a watch that counts down the seconds you have left to live.

[348] To the charge of first degree footnote overuse, I plead "no contest." I throw myself on the mercy of the court.

[349] A key weakness of the English language is that there is no gender-neutral singular third-person pronoun. The attempt to rectify this with "s/he" stinks of political correctness, and I'd rather be a non-conformist. So if any of my English teachers are reading this and are tsk-tsk-ing

the opportunity to interact with consumers directly, and then observe their behaviors. One such consumer told them in the initial interview that they[350] never overfilled their washing machine. Then, while demonstrating how they actually did a load of laundry, they filled the machine with clothes to overflowing, *climbed on top of the load* to smash it all in there with their full body weight, climbed out, shut the lid, and started the machine. In their mind, if they could close the lid, it must not be overfilled.

So empathy isn't just hearing what people say and thinking you know what they mean.

Empathy is also not about thinking "well, if I was in that situation, here is what I would want." That's projection, not empathy. The crazy thing is, the people who are most naturally empathic are also the most likely to project their own desires onto the customers they try to serve.[351] Being naturally empathic to others' emotions can actually be dangerous when it comes to innovation. It may lead you to offer the solutions *you* would want in your customer's situation. That may not be what the actual customer wants.

This is why you must test for understanding. In Covey's fifth habit, that means checking with the person to whom you are listening by paraphrasing back to them what you think you heard. If they don't think you understood, you listen some more and try again.

In innovation efforts, checking involves a similar iterative effort to test your understanding. At first, you could do the same paraphrasing step through customer interviews. Then you could get feedback on written or visual concepts that you believe will solve the problems. Then it could involve testing prototypes with your customer, collecting their feedback, and applying what you learn to the next round of development. It could work all the way up to test marketing a new product to confirm your solution and your communication of it to your target customers.

---

me for using "they" as a singular pronoun, my apologies. Blame whoever came up with this language.

[350] Ditto. And ditto, ditto for the other theys in the paragraph.

[351] Scott Berinato, "Putting Yourself in the Customer's Shoes Doesn't Work: An Interview with Johannes Hattula," *Harvard Business Review*, March 2015.

Living with Your Customer

The best way to get insight into your customers' unmet and unarticulated (or unarticulatable) needs is through direct interaction. On-site, live-and-in-person, as they go about their business (or at least the business that you are interested in).[352] Two ways to do that are customer visits and ethnography.

Many organizations visit their customers. This is easier to do for B2B businesses, which tend to have fewer individual customers than B2C organizations. In the non-profit world, this is easier for organizations that represent industries rather than individuals for the same reason.

The value of visiting a customer is that you get to observe them in their natural habitat. When you visit, don't get locked in a conference room. Get out in their offices, on their manufacturing floor, in their field. See them with their customers if you can. This is how you can best listen with sensory organs besides your ears.

Ethnography takes the customer visit a step further. You become the Jane Goodall for your organization, observing, recording, hypothesizing about and evaluating the real behavior of your customers. Not that your customers are gorillas.[353]

Ethnography is a qualitative research process which goes beyond just observing events in the life of a customer. Ethnographers try to uncover *meaning* from what is observed. It's like trying to figure out how a computer operating system works by observing the inputs and outputs as it is being used. You are going beyond just "this happened then that happened," to getting at the whys and hows of the things that are happening.

Ethnography helps you, as an outsider, to gain an insider's perspective. Critical to this is not trying to impose your perspective on your observations. You need to let the meaning of events emerge from what you witness. This is not at all easy, given our predilection toward confirmation bias.[354] You need to

---

[352] Robert G. Cooper and Angelika Dreher, "Voice of the Customer Methods: What is the Best Source of New Product Ideas," *Marketing Management Magazine*, Winter 2010.

[353] You may feel that way, but it would be bad for sales to tell them so.

[354] For more about confirmation bias and other cognitive biases, go to the "Cognitive Biases" section of the chapter on The Mental Game of Innovation.

have the curiosity to see, hear, feel, taste, and smell all that is going on, unfiltered, and accept it for what it is.

Part of this is getting inside your customer's head, and understanding what they think and feel about their situation. Another part is getting outside their heads and seeing the situation from your own perspective. The first is relational, the second is observational.[355] The first helps you see things from a very attached, personal perspective, the second helps you see from a detached, impartial perspective.

Combine the two, and you have effective ethnography for innovation. You have the ability to see and solve problems in new ways, while having the connection to the customer that ensures you provide something that they want and will use.

Why doesn't everyone do ethnography? Well, it can be costly. Hiring professionally trained anthropologists to spend many hours in observations of many customers takes both time and money. Do-it-yourself ethnography can be less costly in financial terms, but it has high opportunity costs. It takes staff away from doing what they are best skilled at doing, to do something for which they lack extensive education, training, and experience.

Combining customer visits and/or ethnography with other quantitative research can be extremely valuable, though. Consider how you can best fit these methods into your VoC system. The laundry research example shows how rich the information you gather can be, and how much further ethnography goes than focus groups, surveys, and other long-standing traditions in market research. It's a deeper level of understanding.

If You Must

You will not always have the resources available to live with your customer for a bit of time. Surveys are still important sources of data for getting in the minds of your customers.

As much as I'd like to live a month or two with you, my personal and family obligations prevent me from doing so. As do many state laws against stalking.

---

[355] Anthropologists would call "relational" and "observational" the "emic" and "etic" perspective. I had never heard such words before learning about ethnography, though, so imposing my point of view on you, I assumed you wouldn't know those terms either. Score yourself two smartie-pants points if already you did.

So, at the end of this book, I have a survey. In my humble opinion, there are good ways and bad ways of conducting surveys. My less-than-surprising advice: keep it simple.

If you've flown with a major airline recently, you have almost certainly received an email after your flight, asking you to complete a survey about your experience. If you, like me, are among the half-percent or so of people who actually take the time to complete the survey, you have almost certainly experienced what I consider to be the bad way of doing a survey. And, you have almost certainly emerged with a stress headache.

These surveys have roughly the same number of questions as the number pi has decimal places (hint – neither ever ends). Did you use the restroom during the flight? Approximately how many minutes did you have to wait in line? Were you able to lock the door? Was the restroom clean? Was the toilet paper easy to find? Was there sufficient toilet paper? On a scale of 1 to 10, how was your flushing experience?

And then it's on to rating the overhead storage, the beverage service, and the voice quality of the flight attendants' "buh-bye." And, if you don't click every single check box that they demand of you, you get a red-letter error message "YOU SKIPPED QUESTION 834 PART A SUBSECTION III YOU IDIOT...COMPLETE IT NOW OR FACE THE WRATH OF... *ANOTHER SURVEY*!!!"

Seriously, these surveys are painful.

As a life-long product developer, I am filled with empathy for the people who put out surveys. I've been there. I thirst for data in order to make a better product. I need to know what potential customers might think. For some reason, though, those customers do not have my market research on the top of their priority list.

So I try to complete as many surveys as I can, knowing how hard it is to get the necessary data. But I will never, ever, do another airline survey. Did you hear that United, American, and Delta?!?

Remember that part of the experience that your customers have with you will be the survey that you beg them to complete. A long, painful survey with hundreds of "required" questions will only get completed by masochists. Everyone else will hate you for putting them through a modern circle of Dante's hell.

I understand why this happens. Product developers crave data that will help guide their work.

Figure 45: Taking some surveys is like an eternal punishment for the damned.

Unfortunately, such cravings cause them to prioritize their own needs over those of the customer. It drives them to think of the experience *they* want rather than that of the customer they want to serve.

I have made no secret of my preference for simplicity. I am an advocate of keeping your survey questions in the range of 2-5. Tops. I know that there are times and places for more extensive surveys, but those times and places are few and far between – *don't use them as your default!*

Examples of survey *styles* that are on the right track are the Net Promoter Score[356] and the Q3MA[357] surveys. I'm not advocating that these be used always and everywhere, of course, but they should give you the gist of what I'm talking about regarding keeping your surveys simple. Just a few questions, with quick quantitative check boxes and open-ended follow-ups, similar to Figure 46. It can be *slightly* expanded with a couple of other quick-click

---

[356] Originally expressed in Fred Reichheld, *The Ultimate Question: Driving Good Profits and True Growth*, Harvard Business School Press, 2006. Note that many of the claims made by Reichheld have been called into question by later academic research (for example, Douglas B. Grisaffe, "Questions about the Ultimate Question: Conceptual Considerations in Evaluating Reichheld's Net Promoter Score (NPS)," *Journal of Consumer Satisfaction, Dissatisfaction, and Complaining Behavior*, 2007. However, the challenges to Reichheld lie in the ability of his NPS to predict growth, and in the NPS being the one and only necessary measure for a business. I agree with those objections. As you will see in the chapter on metrics (page 389), there is no single metric that is right for everyone, all the time. Since I advocate neither of those aspects of this type of survey, I will stick to the recommendation to use such a simple means of conducting surveys.

[357] For more on this survey, get online and go to http://your-research-resource.com/q3ma-quick-market-test/

Simple Customer Survey

On A Scale of 0-10, How Much Did You Like Your Product Expereince?	Worst Experience Ever O O O O O O O O O O O Best Experience Ever 0 1 2 3 4 5 6 7 8 9 10
Why Do You Give That Rating?	Please provide whatever detail supports the reason for your rating above.

Figure 46: The simple two-question survey that no customer will fear, based on the NPS survey.

questions to help stimulate some thoughts for the customer or get helpful demographic information, but the whole survey should be able to be completed in a minute or so. Of course, if they choose to go longer, that's up to them, and the additional feedback would be gratefully welcomed.

The advantage to the customer is obvious: it's relatively painless. You can promise up front that it will be so. Think about the last time you were approached with a survey request. There is a good chance that your first thought was "oh no, how long is this gonna take?!?" With this simple survey style, you can tell your respondents up front that it won't eat up half of their day. That is so much more impactful than offering a chance to win a prize or even a small payment for their time.

The advantage to you, the surveyor, is that you will get information that is actually important. You ask them how they rate their experience and why thy rate it that way. In answering, their "why" comes from what is top-of-mind. You learn the stuff that was memorable about their experience, the stuff that was important to them. Good or bad. Quick, easy, simple, and powerful. Is it perfect? Heck no. But neither is a survey that irritates or annoys the people you are trying to make happy. And neither is a survey that gets selectively completed by only those with the pain tolerance of a Shaolin monk.[358]

Experts in market research might argue that you won't get at the information that you want to know. And they may be right about that. But think of it this way – if they are not talking about it, they may not value it anyway.[359] So let it go. Remember, you are looking to satisfy your customer, not yourself.

---

[358] For an incredible demonstration of this pain tolerance, get online and go to https://www.youtube.com/watch?v=iAXJue_IRsQ.

[359] This may not always be true. The recency bias (a cognitive bias not explored in this book) makes people remember more prominently things that occurred most recently. Some triggers

Are there things you might miss? Yes. I won't lie to you. But do you think the airline surveys I mentioned before really deliver that information? No! Because people don't respond to the surveys. If they hated the experience, they have little incentive to add to their suffering by answering questions about their preference for the color of the barf bags. The information you get back is biased, not coming from your full customer base, but from a few weirdos like me who complete the survey out of pity or a need for self-flagellation.

In all fairness to longer surveys, there is a place for them. The short, simple surveys are not the be-all and end-all of surveys. But they should be your first instinct. Don't let the 752-question survey requiring a complete medical history and list of all elementary school friends be your default.

If you do a survey, keep it simple. Keep it focused on your customer. Make it part of their experience with you, and part of your partnership in creating an experience they love.

Sorting the Laundry - Structuring Your Understanding

In the information age, few people are suffering from an insufficient volume of data. Anyone living with too little information is probably being held captive in the tallest tower in the castle by an evil dragon, and requires immediate rescue.

We are pummeled with information on so many topics in so many ways that we can't possibly digest it all. You used to be able to go into a restaurant and get a cup of coffee for a buck. If they offered variety at all, it was small, medium, or large. Now you have to choose from seventeen sizes, full-caf/half-caf/decaf, brewed or pressed, foam or no foam, skim milk/low fat milk/whole milk/half-and-half/cream, hot or iced, and with or without flavor shots – and if it's with, then how many, and which of 39 different flavors do you want? The cups have to be labeled with a list of contents long enough to be bedtime reading material, except for the fact that waking up is the reason you ordered the coffee in the first place.

Everywhere you go there are options and requests, news flashes and phone calls, meetings and water cooler talk, podcasts and broadcasts. Phones

---

may be helpful to get the most valuable information, especially for early parts of the product experience. Just keep it simple, and customer-focused.

vibrate twice for a text, three times for an email, and some sort of Morse code message if you actually get a phone call. "Hang on a second, my phone is buzzing...either the Titanic is sinking, or my mom is calling me..."

You can't stop the flow of data. The days of the data dump have been taken over by the days of the data deluge. The only way to manage it is to filter it for relevance, and structure it for meaning. Transforming the chaos of data flow into something that provides usable information is a critical skill of an innovator,[360] and a key to simplicity.

What a good innovator will do is to put the chaos of data into a form that has meaning. A good innovator filters out the irrelevant, and structures the relevant into a meaningful whole.

Emerging from your VoC research, you will have a long laundry list of information, including qualitative comments and observations, and quantitative trends and behaviors. To make sense of it, you have to sort it.

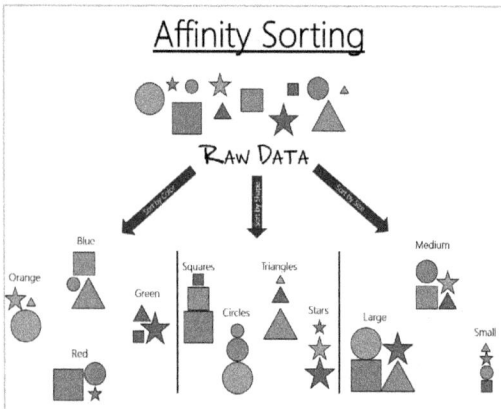

Figure 47: Affinity Sorting - putting your data together in ways that make sense, to make insights easier to see.

Affinity diagrams are a great way to get a pile of disparate information into an understandable whole.[361] It's a little like taking a jumbled pile of playing cards and sorting them into their respective suits.

This is one of those exercises that make innovators famous for their use of sticky notes.[362] But

---

[360] For more on the skills of innovators, see the "Thinking of Innovators" section of the Mental Game of Innovation chapter, page 250.

[361] For more in-depth guidance on affinity diagrams, and the whole VoC collection and selection process, check out Gary Burchill and Christina Hepner Brodie, *Voices into Choices*, Joiner Associates Inc., 1997.

[362] Or infamous.

such notes make the exercise easy.[363]

Write a bit[364] of VoC information on a sticky note. It could be a recorded observation, a quote from an interview, a piece of trend data, whatever. Just make sure it is one unit of thought. Then stick it on a big wall. Repeat until all of the potentially relevant data is on the wall, or until you need to find a bigger wall.

Now start sorting, putting bits together that fall into common categories. This will be a little less obvious than with the playing cards, and can generate some lively discussion. With playing cards, you have a fairly definitive way of sorting the cards meaningfully. With customer data, however, you will be finding ways to group them as you go. Not everyone will have the same idea of what the categories ought to be.

Imagine the data as a bunch of shapes in different colors and sizes, as in Figure 47. Some people will find it "obvious" to sort by color, others by shape, and others by size. Who is right? Whoever has the perspective of the customer in mind.

When stuck trying to figure out the best way to sort your data, default to what the customer will find to be the most relevant. It will be easier, unfortunately, to think in terms of relevance to your organization. Force yourself into the mind of your customer, or involve the customer in the process. It's their point of view that counts.

You may find that there are multiple layers of groupings that occur. That's fine. Whatever will enhance your ability to understand your customer will work.

Evolving Expectations

One means of structuring the customer data that can be extremely valuable is by Kano attribute types. The Kano model[365] defines three different kinds of product characteristics – basic attributes, performance attributes, and excitement attributes – and then shows what happens to those attributes over time.

---

[363] Thank you for the Post-It notes, Spencer Silver and Art Fry!

[364] Or would it be a byte? I know it's not a bite.

[365] This simple but insightful model was created in the early 1980's by Japanese professor Noriaki Kano.

Basic attributes are minimal expectations for a product. A car should have wheels. Food should be safely edible. A dry cleaner should accept shirts and pants. You can't win with basic attributes. Huge improvements in the performance of a basic attribute yield little impact on customer satisfaction.

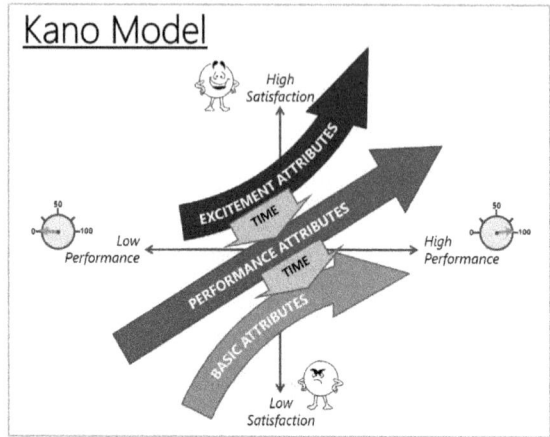

Figure 48: The Kano Model -Focusing on different kinds of attributes has very different impact on customer satisfaction; and time changes what kind of attributes you are competing with.

Basic attributes are entirely expected by the customer, and they will barely notice that you even offer those attributes. However, you better believe that they'll notice if you don't have them. They will not be pleased.

Performance attributes allow for some differentiation. A car has an ability to accelerate. Food has flavor, color, texture, temperature. A dry cleaner has an ability to remove common stains without damaging materials. With these kinds of attributes, some products will have higher performance, others lower performance, and consumers will have a preference for the higher. You can win by being better than your competitors on these attributes. But it's not easy. Your competitors are working hard to beat you on those same factors, too.

Excitement attributes are those that catch the consumer by surprise, and make them really take notice of a product. A car that does not require a driver, food "cooked" with liquid nitrogen, and a dry cleaner that cleans clothes by teleporting them back in time to the moment before the stain occurred then directly back to the owner's present-time closet are all excitement attributes.

Differentiating these three types of attributes was insightful enough. But Kano did not stop there. He also showed what happens to an attribute over time. Excitement attributes become performance attributes, as everyone in the market starts to offer their own versions of them. Performance attributes become basic attributes as customers become used to having them. They become mere expectations.

Air conditioning, radios, power windows, and air bags were all once "wow!" excitement attributes in cars. Over time, they have all become performance or basic attributes. In order to compete, you simply have to innovate. At the very least, you need to constantly improve on your performance attributes, just to keep up with customer expectations. If, however, you really want to get ahead, you need to innovate by creating new excitement attributes that make people say "hallelujah!"

Building the House-Translating the Data

Understanding your customers is just step one. Ensuring a common understanding of your customers in the organization is step two. This is more than sitting in a dark room illuminated by a presentation about the customer. Truly having a common understanding involves translating what you know into everyone's language.

Customers will have their own language, which is important to know and understand as you listen to and communicate with them. That language may not be the same as what your marketing team speaks. Which is not the same as what your engineering team speaks. Which is not the same as what your sourcing team speaks. Which is not the same as what your operations team speaks. Which is not the same as what your sales team speaks. And so on, and so on...

Translation is not always easy, and there is not easy agreement on how to do translations. Take the *Odyssey* of Homer, for example. Wikipedia lists over a hundred English language translations of the work, with an average of one new translation every two years in the 21st century. If translation was easy and universally agreeable, it would have been done only once.

The simple tool to help with VoC translation is Quality Functional Deployment (or QFD). You may be more familiar with the "House of Quality," a key concept of QFD.

Now, I must admit that I hesitate to call QFD "simple." I've been in too many training sessions in which QFD is explained, and the majority of the audience leaves with the understanding, "huh?"

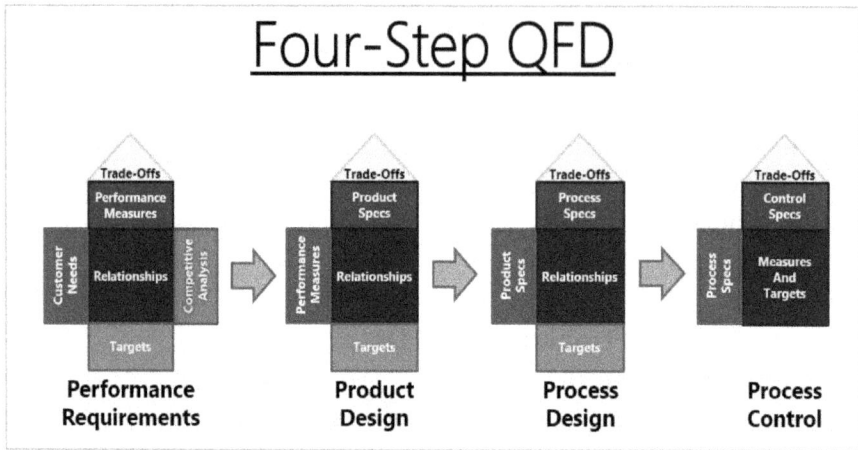

Figure 49: The whole darn full-blown QFD process

The idea behind QFD is simple, though. In a four-step process, you translate customer needs into product attributes, product attributes into organizational action items, action items into implementation decisions, and implementation decisions into production plans. The "houses" that are created are the tools that translate one thing into another.

It is way beyond the scope of this work to go into details on the whole process.[366] Here, I'll just introduce a simplified first step – the HoQ for translating customer needs into product design attributes.

The structure of the HoQ is presented in Figure 50. To fill it out, follow these steps:

1) **Define your objective**. It always helps to have a link to your mission and strategy explicitly listed on everything that you do.

2) **List customer needs**. Start with the needs stated in their language, such as "Easy to read." Step 2 1/2, is to rewrite the customer needs based on your language and interpretation of what they have said. Instead of "easy to read," you write "conversational language, fun, concise, illustrated." List these needs in the boxes on the left.

---

[366] To do so, there are many good, deep reads. One I'd suggest is Joseph P. Ficalora and Louis Cohen, *Quality Function Deployment and Six Sigma, Second Edition: A QFD Handbook*, Prentice Hall, 2009.

3) **Assess current performance against needs.** Evaluate how you and your competitors are addressing these needs currently. Identify strengths, weaknesses, and areas of opportunity. Capture this performance in the boxes on the right.

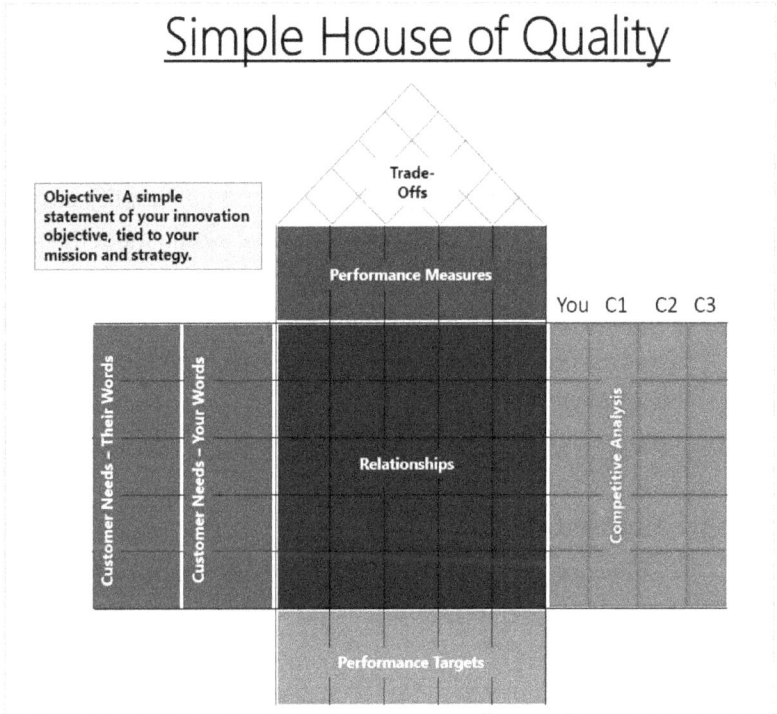

Figure 50: A Simple House of Quality for translating customer needs into measurable performance targets.

4) **List measurable attributes.** List the measurable and controllable attributes of your product that address the customer needs. Don't list attributes beyond your control. There's nothing that you can do about them anyway. Measures can be qualitative, but quantitative will be more manageable. Capture these in the "Performance Measures" on the top.

5) **Consider how attributes impact needs.** Think about how changing the performance measures will impact the customer needs. Does

increasing the attribute meet the need or make it worse? Is there an attribute optimum or does it have a linear relationship to the need?

6) **Evaluate attribute interactions.** Think about how the attributes interact with each other. Does changing one attribute automatically change another? For example, consider a car. One attribute might be traction, and another might be fuel economy. Traction will improve with increasing car weight, but fuel economy will be reduced with increasing car weight. Capture such interactions in the "roof" at the top of the diagram.

7) **Determine target values**. For each attribute, identify targets for how the attribute is measured, based on what would meet the needs of the customer.

8) **Prioritize the attributes.** Determine which are most important to the customer, and which you are able to affect the most. You may not be able to meet the targets for them all, so you should focus on the most important.

Example Exposed Again

To avoid leaving you with that "huh?" feeling, here is an example – one done for this very book you are reading.[367] Another opportunity to expose myself to public scrutiny.[368]

Starting with the objective, based on the organizational mission exposed earlier, the intent of this effort is to help people get their innovation engines[369] running more smoothly, by creating a comprehensive book on innovation that they will actually read and use.

Next, I input customer needs. In speaking with other innovation practitioners seeking help with doing innovation better (my target customer), common themes around books were comprehensiveness (covering all topics

---

[367] Okay, I admit this is not a full and detailed HoQ. It is just an example to help you understand how it all works. For more detailed examples, check out the books referenced earlier.

[368] The earlier exposure came in the "Exposing Myself" section of the Mission chapter. This is the only kind of exposing myself that I do. No need to call the police.

[369] For more about the innovation engine, what it is, and how it works, see "The Innovation Engine" section of the opening chapter, page 29.

in the field of innovation, or at least the key ones), believability (coming from a source they find credible, and supported with valid reasons to believe, like case studies, examples, research, etc.), relevance (applying to their field of work, up-to-date, and not isolated to a particular industry or professional function), ease of reading (not mired in overly technical language, not dull, concise, to-the-point, understandable without extensive contemplation, etc.), and providing tools (information and processes that they can use on their jobs without a major corporate undertaking).

Note that for the sake of simplicity, I'm listing the customer needs as I understand them, without using customer language. I don't recommend doing that in practice...knowing the real language of the customer is critically important. Imagine negotiating a peace treaty with the Klingons without Uhura there to translate what they are actually saying.[370] That would be bad.

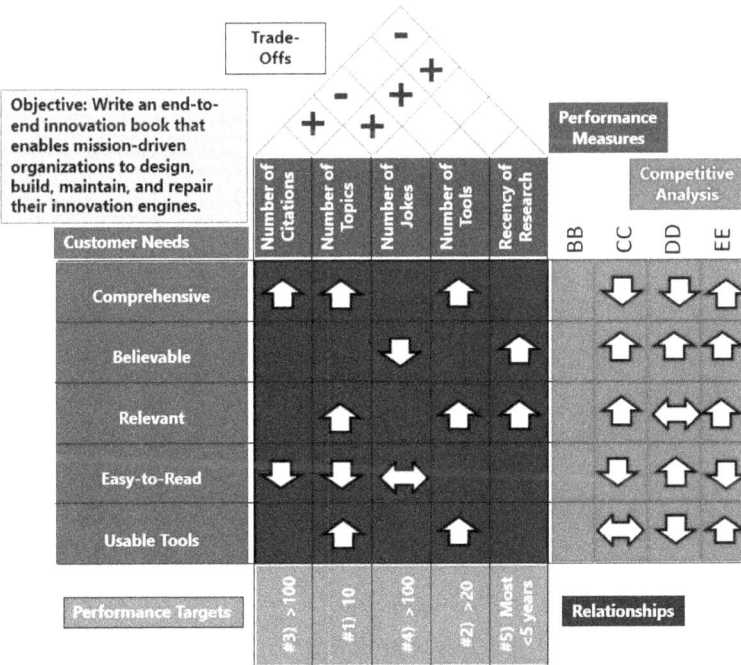

Figure 51: The House of Quality created for this very book. Please don't laugh.

---

[370] Trekkie nerdiness. Just go with it.

Next, I do a little assessment of some other innovation books out there. Up arrows represent that they deliver on a customer need well, a down arrow not so much, and a side-to-side double arrow representing an "uncertain/it depends" kind of feeling. These ratings are qualitative customer input from conversations I've had. That was sufficient for my purposes, but you may want to get more serious and quantitative, depending on your resources and needs.

"BB" is me...this is my first book, and without feedback yet, I'm not going to fill in how I did (although I'm hoping for all up arrows, of course). The others are cleverly named CC, DD, and EE to avoid offending any highly respected authors (and even the disrespected ones), but they are real writers in the field of innovation.

Next, I start contemplating what attributes of the book I should use. These are all aspects of the book that I can control and measure. Again, for simplicity, I chose just five for this example. When you are doing this, make sure you clearly understand what you are measuring. For example, "number of jokes" may seem straight forward, but that really depends on the definition of "joke."[371] Notice also that this makes no quality measure for these jokes. A quality measure would be wise, but in this case, excessively difficult to assess with any precision or validity, so I'll gloss over that.[372] My bad jokes will just have to count as much as my good ones.

I then look at the relationships between the measurable attributes I've listed and the customer needs. Up arrows represent an attribute that delivers more against the customer need the more of it I offer. Down arrows represent attributes that adversely impact the customer need the more of it I have. And, again, side-to-side arrows represent those unknown, maybe good/maybe bad sorts of attributes. Does the number of jokes make the book easier to read by being more entertaining, or does it make it harder to read because there are so many hilarious jokes that the reader can't even see the valuable content through their tears of joy? That's an opportunity for future customer research.

Then I need to consider how the attributes impact each other. Sometimes increasing one will tend to increase another: the more topics I cover, for

---

[371] Some mean people may tell me that the entire book is one big joke, but they would be using a different definition of the word in that case. And they are stupid.

[372] And my ego is too fragile to hear that you don't like my jokes.

example, the more citations I'll probably have. Those are indicated by a plus sign. Sometimes, increasing one will tend to decrease another: for example, the more citations I have may decrease the number of jokes I have, because I'm thinking "I just did a footnote, there's no need to do another."

You put these interactions in the "roof of the house" in order to prepare for the trade-offs you will likely have to make in developing your product.[373]

Now, for determining target values. This is a tough point for me. I have never written a book before. I have never gotten feedback on a book I've written. How many citations is enough? How many jokes are too many? That's why there are iterations in the development process. First, a concept was put out there with some feedback. Then an "alpha" sample, with further feedback. Then a full-length beta prototype, with much more feedback.

Finally, I prioritize the attributes, with topics first, tools second, citations third, jokes fourth, and recency of research fifth. I'm still working to deliver on all of them, but if push comes to shove, I know which puppies will have to go back to the shelter.[374]

Prioritizing Your Understanding

Like the Project Scorecard,[375] you can add levels of complexity to adjust to your needs and capabilities. Customer needs can be broken down into primary/strategic needs, secondary/tactical needs, and tertiary/operational needs. Griffin and Hauser describe 5-10 primary needs, each with 3-10 secondary needs, each with 0-3 tertiary needs.

In the example provided, only a handful of primary needs were shown (with some secondary needs listed in the paragraph describing the process).

That can mean starting with hundreds of customer needs to consider. If you can manage that, go for it. This may not only make sense, but may be necessary for large organizations with big project teams working on complex

---

[373] Unless you are a TRIZ master, in which case you eliminate trade-offs with your contradiction matrix the way Green Lantern overcomes super villains with his power ring. For an all-too-brief introduction to TRIZ, go to the TRIZ section, page 299.

[374] That's better than shooting them, right?

[375] For more on the project scorecard and how it works, see the "Scorecards" section of the Portfolio Management chapter, page 167.

products – a car company comes to mind.[376] It may be completely out of the realm of necessity or possibility for a smaller organization working on simpler projects – like a guy writing a book. You will have to tailor the tool to your own needs.

Perception is Reality

What your customers believe to be important in performance *is* what is important in performance. Their ability to perceive differences in performance factors is also important. If they can't perceive a difference, then there is no difference.

Take, for example, a development effort to create a product that has superior performance to the current market leader.[377] You spend a great deal of time, money, and mental energy in development, and your technology folks finally come up with something that they can measurably demonstrate is superior.

Figure 52: It's bad enough that we have cognitive biases that make us lie to ourselves, but then we go and trick ourselves with bad stat analysis. Oy. These two charts represent the same data – the one on the left makes it look like there is a big difference; the one on the right, not so much. Which is correct? The one that correlates with how your customer feels about that attribute.

---

[376] Griffin and Hauser mention Toyota going way beyond just three levels, to eight – coming up with such detailed needs as transporting rotten apples in a pickup without rusting the truck bed. For Toyota, that may be fine, but to me, that is going *way* beyond the call of duty (and beyond usability of the tool). That's no longer simple.

[377] This scenario is based on an actual product development project that I worked on.

Then you take it to your customers, and they try the new product. Their response? Meh.

Why?

In this case, two things could be going on.

First, when comparing products on a chosen performance metric,[378] you can get so focused on the numbers that you forget how they correlate with what the customer actually perceives. In Figure 52, the left side chart says "look at us, we beat them!" The scaling of the data exaggerates the difference.

The right side chart says "Really? Looks like a tie to me." Unfortunately, in the real-life case on which this scenario is based, the right side correlated with the customer perception better than the left side. What looked great on a technical graph did not translate to anything the consumer could actually notice.[379]

Only by really understanding your customer can you know what to believe.

Second, you might be falling into the time trap in the Kano Model. You may be trying to compete on an attribute that once excited consumers, but over time has become a mere expectation. You may be just beating the competition at faster rotary phone dialing while the market has moved onto voice recognition on their smart phones.

Only by understanding your customer can you know the relevant attributes to address and measure.

Hot Line to the Voice of the Customer

You can get the Voice of the Customer built directly into your innovation process by involving the customer, co-creating the solutions to their problems.[380]

No, I'm not reversing course form my earlier statement that it's not the customers' job to solve their problems. That's still your job. Letting them help, though, can be quite valuable.

---

[378] For more on innovation metrics, go to the sections on "Innovation for Fun and Profit" (page 389) and "Innovation for Fun and Not-for-Profit" (page 403).

[379] As they say, "There are three kinds of lies: lies, damned lies, and statistics." And if you think that is a Mark Twain quote, you can add "quote attributions" as another form of lies.

[380] For more on co-creation and other open innovation efforts, see the section "A Word (or a Thousand of Them) on Open Innovation" in the Strategy chapter, page 136.

Conducting co-development efforts with customers has been shown to have great potential in generating more and higher quality ideas.[381] Users can help generate more novel and beneficial ideas than can problem-solvers on their own. On the other hand, user ideas are often less feasible than those of the solution providers.

What this adds up to is that involving customers in both the solution process and the needs discovery process may be able to push you to create more novel and high value solutions than you'd come up with on your own. No, this doesn't replace the need for developers in your organization – they are the ones who will make the product ideas a reality, and not just a customer fantasy. Having customers and staff work together collaboratively is the trick.

Don't Let Perfect Get in the Way of Good

You find yourself trapped in a big, dark basement. Not just dark, but pitch black. You know there has to be a way up and out of there, but you have no idea which way to go. You've screamed and shouted for a while, hoping someone would hear you and help you out, but now you are just hoarse. And starting to get hungry.

Judging by the echoes of your earlier screams, this basement must be pretty darn big, and you are not close to a wall. You try to explore around, but you quickly get tired of bumping your head on low-hanging ductwork, and you just tripped and fell over who-knows what laying on the ground.

Then you remember that you have matches in your pocket. They will only illuminate a small area around you, and they will only last for a brief time. You'd much rather find a light switch that will make finding your way out easier, illuminating the whole basement in glorious soft-white fluorescent bulb light.

So what do you do?

A) Start lighting matches, using them as best you can to find your way out;

---

[381] Marion K. Poetz and Martin Schreier, "The Value of Crowdsourcing: Can Users Really Compete with Professionals in Generating New Product Ideas?" *Journal of Product Innovation Management*, March 2012.

B) Keep exploring around in the dark until you find the light switch, and save the matches for lighting candles on a cake (assuming you get out of the basement before your next birthday);

C) Say, "Hey, I'm reading this book for innovation help, not for a poor imitation of Stephen King stories."

Okay, except for those impatient ones who answered "C," my guess is that most, if not all of you answered "A." Let's face it, it seems pretty obvious.

Yet I've had innumerable arguments about customer research with people who answer the VoC equivalent of "B."

Resource constraints will often prevent organizations from doing the same kind of consumer research done by the likes of Procter & Gamble, Pepsico and political parties in an election year.[382] That doesn't mean you shouldn't do what you can.

If you can't afford an army of Ph.D. anthropologists to do ethnography for you, get out and do some yourself. Will it be dissertation-worthy? Probably not, but it's better than not doing it at all. And the value of experiencing the research, versus just reading about it or seeing it presented in a PowerPoint deck, will add value in itself.

If you can't hire an expert in QFD to walk your team through a week-long review of eight-level VoC data (including how rotting apples might affect your product), you can still work your way through a House-of-Quality exercise with primary and even secondary needs, to structure the information and drive better choices in your ideas.

If you can't afford to produce near-manufacturing quality prototypes to test in the entire Kansas City market over a three-month period, you can still produce concept drawings or makeshift samples made out of LEGOs to share with the customers you know to have good imaginations.

The important thing is to get the best quality and volume of information about your customer and their problems that you can collect and manage. Then have the creativity and courage to try out potential solutions with them, and iterate your way to successful innovation.

---

[382] Others do an intense level of consumer research, too, but I liked the P alliteration.

Frankenstein's Monster vs. the Villagers

One clarification – or perhaps a point of emphasis – when it comes to testing prototypes with customers. I mentioned just a couple of paragraphs ago to share crude prototypes *with the customers you know to have good imaginations*. This can be a very important point.

Prototypes can be like Frankenstein's monster.[383] They can be ugly, even scary. They don't work right. They have too many features, not enough features, or the wrong features. If you test it with the common villagers, you may have to deal with a violent reaction against them.

The challenge is that you may be able to see what it *could be*, while they are looking at what it *is*. You end up with a conversation like this:

You: "So, what do you think of our prototype of the Widgetenator 9000?"

Customer X: "I don't like the color."

You: "Okay, great. What color would you like better?"

Customer X: "I don't like brown."

You: "Okay, got it. Is there another color besides brown that would work for you?"

Customer X: "I prefer purple."

You: "Okay, great. Imagine, then, that it comes in purple. What would you think about a purple Widgetenator 9000?"

Customer X: "But it's brown."

You: [sigh] "Yes, but if it was purple..."

Customer X: "But it isn't."

You: "Is there someone else that I could talk to?"

This is another critical skill in listening to customer feedback, especially when it comes to early prototypes. Some customers will see the possibilities that you see, or even some that you don't. Others will be so fixated on what is immediately before their eyes that they won't be able to see anything else. Listen accordingly.

---

[383] Comically captured by Mel Brooks in *Young Frankenstein*: get online and catch a scene at https://www.youtube.com/watch?v=4yznraw9AqM

That does not mean ignoring criticism. It means listening to it and considering where it is coming from.

I have seen some very successful product launches have near-death experiences in their prototype stages. The villagers attacked and nearly killed the monster[384] before it could be taught to dance and sing.[385]

For a real-life example of this, look no further than *Toy Story*, the first-ever feature-length computer animated film. The movie broke even on its $30 million production budget in its opening weekend, and ultimately took in over $360 million dollars at the box office. Yet it almost died an untimely death in an early schematic stage, when Disney execs didn't like what they saw.[386] The Pixar team managed to negotiate two weeks to make some changes...and the rest is very happy history.

The point is to listen carefully throughout the innovation process, but especially in the early prototype stages. Accept the feedback for what it is, consider where it is coming from, and why it is coming. Seek to deeply understand, not just to hear the words.

---

[384] Watch the villagers attack at https://www.youtube.com/watch?v=qLvGnro4Cgw.

[385] Watch doctor Frankenstein and his creation putting on the ritz at https://www.youtube.com/watch?v=w1FLZPFI3jc.

[386] John Lassiter describes the disappointment and frantic comeback from the brink in a twentieth anniversary documentary at http://www.hulu.com/toy-story-at-20-to-infinity-and-beyond.

Simple Study Guide - VoC

- What steps do you take to define a problem?
- What is design thinking?
- When is design thinking most valuable in the innovation process?
- What is "Voice of the Customer?"
- What is *not* "Voice of the Customer?"
- What is "empathic listening?"
- Why are customer visits and ethnography of value?
- How do you make sense of all the customer data that you collect?
- What is Quality Function Deployment (QFD)?
- How does customer perception impact the development process?
- How can customers be involved in the development process?
- What methods can you employ to gather customer data?
- How should you listen to feedback on your "Frankenstein" prototypes?

Where do you want to go from here?

Control	Creation	Conversion
Mission (page 40)	Voice of the Customer (page 175)	Innovation Teams (page 310)
Culture (page 58)	Minds of Innovators (page 217)	Project Management (page 347)
Strategy (page 92)	Ideation (page 279)	For-Profit Metrics (page 389)
Portfolio Management (page 146)		Nonprofit Metrics (page 403)
Change Management (page 411)		

Or just turn the page to keep reading...

The Shortest Distance to Innovation is Not a Straight Line (The Mental Game of Innovation)

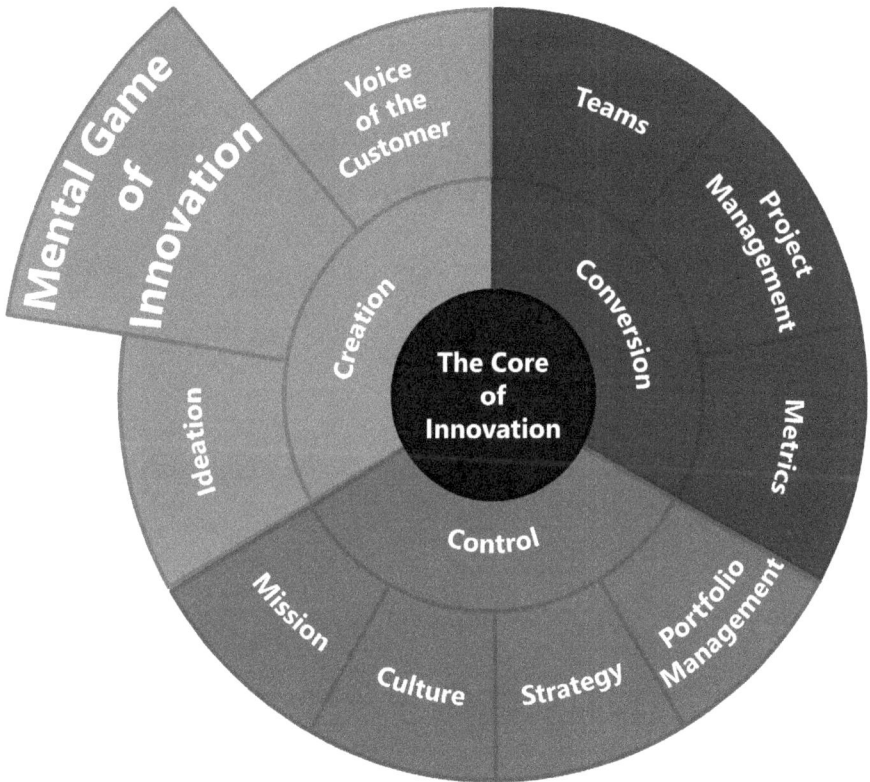

Simple Self-Assessment – The Mental Game of Innovation

Rate yourself on the following questions. To benchmark yourself against others, go to www.3point14Innovation.com and click the "Self-Assessments" menu.

- ***How simple are the decision-making processes in your organization?***

  Like walking a
  labyrinth blindfolded   Like ABC and 123

1	2	3	4	5	6	7	8	9	10

- ***How familiar are you with "cognitive biases"?***

  I'm more familiar with ancient
  Etruscan mathematics   I'm Daniel Kahneman

1	2	3	4	5	6	7	8	9	10

- ***Do you have any cognitive biases?***

  No, I'm a Vulcan.   Of course, we all do.

1	2	3	4	5	6	7	8	9	10

- ***Have you ever used Edward DeBono's Six Thinking Hats?***

  No, but I wore a   I have a full set of all six
  dunce cap once.   colors in my desk drawer.

1	2	3	4	5	6	7	8	9	10

- ***How good are you at multitasking?***

  I'm the best—squirrel!   I focus on one
  –the best at it.   thing at a time

1	2	3	4	5	6	7	8	9	10

- ***Are you willing to accept the personal risk of failure?***

  I prefer my sterile   Failure is the surest
  bubble of safety   route to success

1	2	3	4	5	6	7	8	9	10

- ***Are you willing to take the shots from people who like the status quo?***

  Actually, I like the
  status quo   Bring 'em on!

1	2	3	4	5	6	7	8	9	10

- **Do you practice mindfulness?**

No way, I don't do
that hippie dippie stuff!

Like Yo Yo Ma
practices the cello

1	2	3	4	5	6	7	8	9	10

- **How often do you experience the state of "flow"?**

Whenever I go
river rafting

Whenever I have
creative work to do

1	2	3	4	5	6	7	8	9	10

Simple Summary – The Mental Game of Innovation

Key take-aways you should get out of this section:

- Although most people don't believe it, and it doesn't "feel" right, simple decision rules outperform complex algorithms. Don't waste time, money, and energy over-calculating and detail-diving to create precise answers that will turn out to be just as wrong, or worse, than simply-derived estimates and close-enough answers.

- Humans have evolved a set of quick-thinking processes for managing the complexity in our world. Most of the time, these processes serve us well. We simply don't have the time or the mental processing speed to rationally consider *everything* around us all the time. So mental shortcuts can be incredibly helpful.

- Sometimes, however, those mental shortcuts lead us astray. These "cognitive biases" can lead us to bad decisions, unnecessary conflict, and irrational behaviors.

- Although we can never fully overcome our irrational biases, simply being aware of them, in ourselves and in our teammates, can help to overcome their downsides.

- Also, being aware of these biases can help us to work more effectively. Leveraging the "in-group bias," for example, can be used to help teams work together more effectively.

- DeBono's Six Thinking Hats serve as an important tool to guide effective thinking, overcome cognitive biases, and drive strong decisions. These hats are of six different colors, that represent six different modes of thought: process thinking, factual thinking, optimistic thinking, pessimistic thinking, emotional thinking, and creative thinking. Employing the right sort of thinking at the right time is an important skill for team leaders.

- Multitasking doesn't work. No, it doesn't. Many think they can do it well, but it turns out that those people are actually the worst at it. Multitasking has costs, by creating inefficiencies, reducing quality of thought, and hampering memory. Eliminate multitasking as much as possible, for you and your teams.

- Innovators have an attitude. They want to serve the needs of others, and they believe that they can do it. They have "respectful irreverence" for the past. They know it well, and respect the thought that has come before them. But they don't revere it to the point of being unable to do anything differently. They like to change the status quo, even if they respect how it came to be.

- Serial innovators – those who can work within organizations to create major innovations repeatedly – have "pi-shaped" minds. They have broad, but shallow knowledge in many areas, and deep knowledge in both business and technology (not just in the digital IT sense, but in other domains of expertise). The broad knowledge enables making connections between disparate information, while the two deep areas of expertise enable them to execute their ideas for an organization.
- Innovators need thick skin, and thick skulls. In the innovation process, they need thick skin to listen to and accept criticism of their ideas and solutions. They can't be afraid to fail – or they at least need the courage to overcome that fear. They need thick skulls to handle the metaphorical blows to the head that they will take from those who don't want the status quo changed.
- Innovators are able to handle ambiguity and uncertainty. They live by the mantra, "love chaos, hate confusion." They love to make sense of the ever-changing, chaotic world, and relieve the confusion that it can cause. Confusion breaks teams down. Bringing order to the chaos so that it makes sense and has meaning is the sign of a strong innovator.
- Innovators are not afraid to leverage their intuition. Intuition is not some mystical knowledge from the great beyond. It is a rapid, unconscious mental processing of a situation based on a lifetime of collected knowledge and experience. While innovators may challenge their gut feeling to make sure it is not leading them astray, they will still give that gut feeling the attention it deserves.
- There is a mind-altering drug that all innovators should take regularly. It does not come in a pill, you can't drink it, and you don't inhale it. It's mindfulness meditation. The mental benefits to mindfulness are only just recently getting scientific attention, but the list is growing rapidly. All of the benefits are directly relatable to innovative thinking.
- Create an environment in which you and your team can, to the extent possible, get into the mental state of "flow." Some people call it being "in the zone." It's the mental state in which you are the most creative, the most engaged in the problem you are trying to solve, and the most effective at solving it.

Mind Games

I am not a Clinical Psychologist. I do not even play one on TV. But innovation is fundamentally a mental game, so I've become fascinated by the role of psychology in the process of innovating. I've learned just enough to be dangerous. But then I believe that the best innovators are a bit dangerous, so I'm okay with that.

After all the talk about process and strategy, it's time to get all touchy-feely. If you are an accountant, mathematician, engineer, coder, lab rat, or Vulcan, you may now be experiencing discomfort at that thought. I was once an engineer, and I've worked with enough Star Trek fans[387] to know that I might lose some readers here.

But this stuff is not just for sales people, marketers, and Tony Robbins.

Like it or not, innovation is a fundamentally human endeavor. Humans are not robots or androids. Heck, we are not really even rational beings. No matter how Spock-like you think you are, you can be quite illogical in reality. Our minds are a messy mix of emotions and lizard-brain reactions only moderately tempered with intellect and rationality.

Good innovators use this to their advantage.

Simple Decision-Making

When trying to simplify – make the complex clear – it can help to do something that sounds irrational and ripe for producing error: ignore some information, *even when that information has relevance* to the decision.

But wait...isn't more information better? Don't organizations run the risk of missing something important if they go around ignoring relevant information?

This is another opportunity for you and your organization to simplify. More information and more complex analyses, don't lead to better outcomes, and "simple decision rules relying on small subsets of the available information can,

---

[387] Myself among them. I watch the entire unveiling sequence of the updated Starship Enterprise in *Star Trek: The Motion Picture* without even thinking of the fast forward button on my remote. I'll stay up late to watch the *TOS* episode "Spock's Brain," although I'll never be able to stomach the TNG episode "Shades of Gray." *Trek* beats *Wars* in the *Star* sci-fi battle, hands down.

depending on the environment in which they are used, achieve high payoffs."[388]

So what kind of environments are best suited for simple decision-making approaches? Those that are characterized by uncertainty of outcome and redundancy of input.[389] Guess what? Those are the characteristics of an innovation environment. You are working toward an unpredictable future. That's uncertainty. You go through a customer discovery process to find trends, consistencies, and correlations among unmet needs and pain points. That's redundancy.

So simplifying your decision-making process with simple rules can help make better innovation decisions than complex, expensive, and, yes, rational decision-making processes.

It's not only that the simple approach works well. It's that the environment for innovation does not hold to the conditions required for hyper-rational approaches to work.

When innovating, much of the relevant information is unknown, based on assumptions and estimates. Rigorous mathematical treatment of such situations means that the answers you get are only as good as the assumptions you put in. Garbage in, garbage out.

There are obvious uncertainties over things you can't control. You don't know how a competitor will respond to your plans. You don't know what the competitor's initiatives are going to be. You don't know how economic conditions are going to change. You don't know what the wheat crop yield in Argentina is going to be.

There are even uncertainties about things over which you do have at least some level of control. You don't know if your organization is going to make it through the year with the original budget, or if you will have to make adjustments along the way. Personally, I can't remember a year of corporate life that did not have at least one revised budget along the way.

---

[388] Nathan Berga and Ulrich Hoffrage, "Rational ignoring with unbounded cognitive capacity," *Journal of Economic Psychology*, December 2008.

[389] Gerd Gigerenzer and Wolfgang Gaissmaier, "Heuristic Decision Making," *The Annual Review of Psychology*, 2011.

You don't know if you'll have the same staff working on a project that you started with. Someone could win the lottery and quit, while another falls ill and misses time at a critical point in a project. Someone could get transferred, go back to school, or pursue their dream to herd sheep in New Zealand. You just never know.

There is a cost-benefit trade-off with complicated decision analyses. Is it worth the effort and resources to generate the results that you get? In the great big world of innovation, the answer is "nope."

Unfortunately, many find comfort in the rigor of the inputs and the precision of the outputs. They feel confident when they see a forecast of 3,763 units shipped by October 16th at 3:47PM, rather than hearing someone say "I think we are likely to ship around 3,500 units, give or take 500, by sometime in the fall." The former sounds scientific. The latter sounds like the words of a BSer.

Then the results come in. Due to some last-minute wheeling-and-dealing, the sales team was able to negotiate shipping a total 3,600 units by the last Friday in October. The rigorous forecast was precise, but precisely wrong. Fans of the rigorous model will say, "Look how great the system worked, with less than 4.5% error! And only two weeks late!" Meanwhile, the simple estimate was even closer, and cost much less to generate.

While that was a made-up scenario, it has been shown to be a pretty good reflection of reality under conditions of uncertainty. Rigor in the name of precision can be a waste of resources. Simple decision-making processes can perform as well or better, without the costs.

However, simple rules can have their drawbacks as well. It is important to be aware of the ways simple thinking can derail us. Awareness can help reduce the chances of bad thinking, and improve the chances of good thinking.

Cognitive Biases

Psychologists and Behavioral Economists have uncovered a host of ways that our brains deviate from rationality. That goes for everyone, everywhere. We have evolved systematic ways of thinking and acting irrationally. For the most part, those irrationalities have helped us as a species to survive. But, occasionally, they make us stupid.

My favorite example of the latter is the "Rhyme as Reason" bias: we tend to believe statements to be more truthful if they contain a rhyme. Seriously. They'll believe you every time, if you can just make it rhyme.[390]

Could anything be less rational? If you think of something less rational that doesn't involve teenagers or romantic relationships, please let me know.

But actually, there is a reason for these biases. More often than not, they are good for us. We cannot be purely rational with every decision we make in life. We would go insane. The simplest decision, like what to have for breakfast, would take so long to analyze that we would starve to death. Having a "gut decision" (pun intended) to rely on is going to be better for us than having to rationally evaluate everything.

Still, we need to be able to override the gut when necessary. "Damn, that box of doughnuts looks good...breakfast, baby! Oh wait, Last night I ate half of that birthday cake. With ice cream. And whipped cream. And sprinkles. With a milkshake. Fine, I'll eat these leftover Brussels sprouts instead of doughnuts."[391]

In addition to overriding our biased guts to avoid overindulgent eating, we need to overcome these cognitive biases while innovating.[392]

There are dozens of identified biases that we all have. There are way too many cognitive biases to go through all of them here. That would be a book in itself.[393] Some of these biases, though, are particularly damaging to innovation efforts. I've narrowed them down to a single "Dirty Dozen" of anti-innovation biases. Are these the right dozen? Well they are if you agree with my biases.

Bias #1: Confirmation bias and the backfire effect. This is the one that most people have heard of. Unfortunately, even those who have heard of it think everyone else does it, while they themselves remain perfectly objective.

---

[390] See? You believe that statement more than if I had written, "People really will believe you more often if you state your proposition with words having a correspondence of sound." Gotcha!

[391] I'd rather eat the doughnuts and run an extra couple of miles a day for the next month, but I tip my hat to you Brussels sprout lovers if you can stomach them for breakfast. Or at all.

[392] Jeanne Liedtka, "Perspective: Linking Design Thinking with Innovation Outcomes through Cognitive Bias Reduction," *Journal of Product Innovation Management*, November 2015.

[393] In fact, it is a book. Check out Daniel Kahneman's *Thinking, Fast and Slow* for a fascinating read on many of them, and the neurobiology behind them.

Confirmation bias occurs when we tend to accept data that matches our preconceived opinions, while rejecting data that contradicts those opinions. As my dad has often told me, "people use information the way a drunk uses a streetlight – for support rather than illumination."[394]

We succumb to this bias while believing that we are acting in a perfectly rational manner. Let's say that I'm not a believer in confirmation bias. I'll cite one paper published in the *Journal of Science that is Possibly True but Probably Not* that reports some data that failed to support the existence of the bias. Then, when much smarter

Figure 53: Confirmation bias - we will tend to hold on to one piece of information that confirms what we already believe, rather than a fistful of contradictory information.

people present two-hundred papers from the *Annals of Rigorously Peer-Reviewed Science* that do demonstrate the effect, I'll simply call into question the validity of the methodologies, the motives of the experimenters, and biases of the journal editors.

In fact, it is often worse than just dismissing contradictory data. The "backfire effect" frequently comes into play, in which people presented with data that contradict their opinions, far from questioning the validity of their opinions, actually become *even more* convinced that their opinions are correct.

For an example, go no farther than the story of Ignaz Semmelweis.[395] Never heard of him? In the mid-1800's, he figured out that having doctors

---

[394] He's got a million of 'em. I could have written a book called *Sh*# My Dad Says*, but somebody beat me to it.

[395] The backfire effect has even been dubbed the "Semelweiss Reflex" due to his experience. In his book, *The Game of Life*, Timothy Leary defined the Semmelweis reflex eloquently as "mob behavior found among primates and larval hominids on undeveloped planets, in which a discovery of important scientific fact is punished." Then he went and shared some psychedelic drugs with the Beatles. Not that I condone such behavior.

sanitize their hands between patients dramatically reduced disease transmission and mortality rates. But, because the conventional wisdom of doctors at the time was based on the theories of Theodoric of York, the medical community completely rejected his hand-washing suggestions, focusing instead on advancing the science of blood-letting. Poor Ignaz went insane and died at an early age, while thousands of people, primarily infants and mothers, continued to lose their lives unnecessarily for another half century.[396]

Bias #2: Self-serving bias. In general, we like to be right. We like to feel intelligent and insightful. We like to be sure of ourselves. So when we think about how the world works, we adjust our thinking to feed such feelings.

If something went well, we serve ourselves by taking credit – the good results were because of excellent planning and execution, keen insights no one else could see, hard work, and high skill.

And if something goes wrong? Well, that's always due to outside forces beyond anyone's control or ability to foresee.[397]

If you want to see an example of this, just read corporate annual reports. With

Figure 54: Self-Serving Bias - We tend to take credit and deflect blame.

few exceptions,[398] annual reports are nothing but self-serving. "Our exceptional results in region X were due to our unique insights on the market and superior strategic execution that allowed us to outpace our competitors. However, the poor performance in region Y was hindered by an El Niño that

---

[396] Rebecca Davis, "The Doctor Who Championed Hand-Washing and Briefly Saved Lives," *National Public Radio Morning Edition*, January 12, 2015.

[397] Miller, Dale T., and Michael Ross (1975), "Self-Serving Biases in the Attribution of Causality: Fact or Fiction?" *Psychological Bulletin*, March 1975.

[398] The Berkshire Hathaway annual report is definitely an exception to the rule. If you want refreshingly candid reports on a company, check these out. Warren Buffet delivers.

lasted longer than expected, sunspot activity that fouled up GPS satellites, and a political coup in Aardvarkovia that caused ant farm prices to skyrocket." This will often be followed by a comment like "In fact, things would have been much worse if not for our excellent planning and execution, keen insights no one else could see, hard work, and high skill."[399]

But so what? How does this impact innovation? My primary concern here is with the ability to learn, which is critical to improving innovation efforts over time. Without an honest assessment of what was done well and what was not, you're likely to repeat mistakes and miss out on growth opportunities. Taking the annual report example above, it is possible that region X had a horribly flawed strategy, but the competition did so much worse that the company succeeded in spite of themselves. With their self-serving blinders on, they'll never know the difference, and repeat the flawed strategy until it kills them.

Bias #3: Choice blindness. People will tend to defend their decisions, with seemingly rational explanations – even when asked about choices they didn't make. No really. People will explain why they made decisions that they did not, in fact, ever make. Experiments done at Lund University in Sweden[400] have shown how most people will explain away the decisions they make, even when they aren't the actual decisions that they made. Whether picking flavors of jam and tea,[401] laptop computers,[402] or pension plans,[403] most people not only

---

[399] This bias is predominant in the Western world, but is not universal. In many global cultures, the opposite is true – people will accept responsibility for things beyond their control, while denying credit for their achievements. And even in the Western world, people who tend toward depression exhibit the opposite of self-serving behavior. Still, the important lesson here is to be aware that these biases may exist, making it critical to challenge yourself to be as objective as possible in determining cause and effect of successes and failures. If you want to do the heavy reading, check out Julian B. Rotter, "Generalized Expectancies for Internal Versus External Control of Reinforcement," *Psychological Monographs, Generalized and Applied*, 1966.

[400] These experiments are fascinating to watch. Go online and watch at https://www.youtube.com/watch?v=wRqyw-EwgTk.

[401] Lars Hall and Petter Johansson, "Using choice blindness to study decision-making and introspection," unpublished paper.

[402] Schanzer, Jessica, "Choice Blindness in Consumer Decision-Making" (2013). Psychology Honors Papers. Paper 31. http://digitalcommons.conncoll.edu/psychhp/31.

[403] Owen McLaughlin and Jason Somerville, "Choice blindness in financial decision making," *Judgment and Decision Making*, Vol. 8, No. 5, September 2013.

don't realize that their choices were switched, they will continue to defend those false choices.

Figure 55: Choice Blindness - Sometimes, we really believe that we have rational reasons for our choices, but we are actually blind to our real motives. We can even justify a choice for something we never even chose.

But so what? This makes for a funny parlor trick and all, but why does it impact innovation? Well, because we ask people about their motivations all the time in the process of making products for them. We have focus groups and customer visits. In our sincere efforts to understand them, we ask them to explain themselves. *And we take what they say as true*. There is no doubt that they are being sincere. But there is a darn good chance that they are telling you what they believe to be true, but not what is *actually* true. They tell you they like the car for its gas mileage and acceleration, but what they really like, deep down, is the way the headlights remind them of their dog's eyes.

Bias #4: Zero–risk bias. Given a choice between the two, people tend to prefer, to reduce a small risk to zero, rather than making a larger reduction to a bigger risk. For example, someone may prefer to reduce a 1% chance of losing $100 to 0%, rather than reducing a 50% chance of losing $1000 to 25%, even if the cost of the risk reduction is the same. The expected return of the first reduction is only $1, while the expected return on the second is $250. But we are naturally risk averse, so making something a sure thing, even for a trivial return, seems better.

Hopefully, it is obvious why this can be a problem for innovation. Developing new products and services is a risky investment. Managing risks wisely is important to maximizing investment return. You should do so as rationally as possible.

Figure 56: Zero-Risk Bias - We will often prefer to reduce a small risk to zero, rather than making a much larger reduction to a bigger risk.

Consumers are subject to this as well.[404] Knowing this can help you communicate your benefits in a way that is influential for them. Depending on the price of your new product, money back guarantees may work better for introducing it the market than, say volume discounts, even if the volume discounts are more valuable. As with most new things, there will be resistance to change – even if the change makes people better off. Understanding and leveraging these biases, working with the way people naturally think, can help to overcome such resistance.

Bias #5: The Bandwagon effect. Wanna prank someone? All you need is an elevator, a hidden camera, and a group of friends who can keep a straight face better than Harvey Korman.[405] Then see what you can make innocent people do by leveraging the power of their instinct to conform.[406]

---

[404] W. K. Viscusi, "An Investigation of the Rationality of Consumer Valuations of Multiple Health Risks," *Rand Journal of Economics*, Winter 1987.

[405] The brilliant straight man of the Carol Burnett Show of the 1970's, who could not always keep a straight face. Especially around Tim Conway – watch at https://www.youtube.com/watch?v=3qqE_WmagjY

[406] Watch the elevator fun in action at https://www.youtube.com/watch?v=BgRoiTWkBHU. Yes, it's an advertisement for Prudential, but no, that doesn't mean I'm endorsing them. Their ad had the right *Candid Camera* footage, and their message resonates with mine. But that's just a coincidence (unless, of course, you are from Prudential's marketing department, in which case you owe me endorsement money).

While we may not literally follow each other over a cliff, we humans can be lemmings.[407] We will think an idea is good, just because the majority around us think it is good. Even as we are about to plummet to our doom, we will go along with the crowd.

Figure 57: The Bandwagon Effect - We will often follow the crowd rather than our own judgement, even when we believe we are right.

The famous (at least in psychology circles) Asch line judgement tests are a great example.[408] Test subjects are placed in a room with what they believe are other test subjects, but who are really co-conspirators with the experimenters. The test is to pick a pair of line segments that match in length. The co-conspirators lie, picking two clearly different line segments and saying they match. At first, the test subject may resist and pick the line segments that really do match in length. But, eventually, they begin to conform. Most will start picking the same way everyone else does, even when they know they are

---

[407] According to the Alaska Department of Fish and Game, the whole lemmings-committing-mass-suicide thing is just a myth, perpetuated by a Disney – *Disney!* – documentary, *White Wilderness* from 1958. Apparently the filmmakers thought it perfectly acceptable to stage a fake mass cliff-dive of the cute little rodents for the sake of their movie. If only they would have done that with some of the creators of the inane shows my kids want to watch on the Disney Channel. If you want to delve further into the horrifying lengths to which Disney documentarians went to produce quality family programming, read this: http://www.adfg.alaska.gov/index.cfm?adfg=wildlifenews.view_article&articles_id=56.

[408] Solomon E. Asch, "Studies of independence and conformity: I. A minority of one against a unanimous majority," *Psychological Monographs: General and Applied*, 1956. To watch such an experiment in progress, complete with the beauty of 1970's fashion, check out the video at https://www.youtube.com/watch?v=TYIh4MkcfJA. For a more up-to-date version of the experiments, watch the video at https://www.youtube.com/watch?v=VgDx5g9ql1g. In either case, you may be shocked at the behaviors you observe.

wrong. The effect is even stronger in cultures that are more "collectivist" than others.[409]

For innovators, there are two dangers here. One is inside the team. Often an idea will excite people. One person says "Look what a great idea this is!" The next says "Hey, you're right, this really is a great idea," and pretty soon the whole team is dancing a jig on the conference room table, singing praises for the idea. Even people who initially thought "Well, I don't like that idea" get swept up in the wave of excitement, either afraid to look stupid to their peers, or overwhelmed by their compatriots' euphoria.

Then, down the road, when the idea turns out to have been a bad one, the team says, "Why didn't anyone say anything?"

The second danger is from outside the team, in terms of customer input and feedback. Focus groups notoriously get dominated by a few loud voices, and other participants just go along.[410] In such cases, it takes a good moderator and good listeners to ensure that the data collected is legitimate, and not just groupthink.

Bias #6: Endowment effect. This is a strange, irrational effect in which people will demand much more to give up an object once they have it in their possession than they would be willing to pay for exactly the same object when they don't possess it. The most prominent example in academic research is that of Kahneman, Knetsch and Thaler.[411] In addition to their academic evidence, they offer a great anecdote that illustrates the point perfectly:

> "A wine-loving economist[412] we know purchased some
> nice Bordeaux wines years ago at low prices. The wines have
> greatly appreciated in value, so that a bottle that cost only $10

---

[409] Rod Bond and Peter B. Smith, "Culture and Conformity: A Meta-Analysis of Studies Using Asch's (1952b, 1956) Line Judgment Task," *Psychological Bulletin*, January 1996.

[410] One of many reasons not to over-rely on focus groups for your Voice of the Customer research (for more on the Voice of the Customer, see the chapter of the same name, page 176).

[411] Daniel Kahneman, Jack L. Knetsch and Richard H. Thaler, "Experimental Tests of the Endowment Effect and the Coase Theorem," *Journal of Political Economy*, December 1990.

[412] Yes, an economist. Probably one that models people as if they behave rationally. Oh, the irony!

when purchased would now fetch $200 at auction. This economist now drinks some of this wine occasionally, but would neither be willing to sell the wine at the auction price nor buy an additional bottle at that price."

Make sure you get this point: this wine enthusiast places a different value on exactly the same bottle of wine, depending on whether or not he owns it. If he owns it, he values it way above the $200 auction price, or else (in rational economic theory, at least) he would sell it for that price. However, he values the wine he doesn't own way below the $200 auction price (remember, this is exactly the same bottle of wine), or else he would buy it for that price. The only difference between the bottles of wine is his ownership, yet the amount of value he places on them are dramatically different.

How does this play out in innovation? Well, a couple of ways. One is with feature creep. It's hard to give up features that you put into a product once they are there. Don't expect that if you have a prototype tested with your customers, and 99 out of 100 say they don't need a feature, that you'll be able to eliminate it easily. Once you "possess" that feature, the "cost" of

Figure 58: Endowment Effect - We will tend to value what we have more than what we don't.

eliminating that feature goes up. It will be higher than the cost of adding the feature in the first place.

Your customers may react the same way to the elimination of a feature from an existing product. Even if all of your research says you can get rid of it, it's unnecessary, no one uses it, etc. you'll hear nothing but disappointment after the elimination. It will feel like you took a pacifier out of a cranky baby's mouth. People will hate losing the feature a heck of a lot more than they liked adding it.

And beware of this bias in your internal processes. A key reason to *Keep Innovation Simple* is that, contrary to Ronald Reagan's assertion that nothing is more permanent than a temporary government program, the persistence of corporate processes may, in fact, be at least as permanent. Officially add a sign-off here and there, and soon you'll have a bureaucracy that rivals that of the Federal National Bureau Department of Redundancy and Repetition. When you go to streamline the system later, you'll find it hard to eliminate even the most unnecessary of steps. The feared cost of eliminating a step will exceed the value that people expected when it was first added.

Bias #7: The Sunk Cost Fallacy, or "irrational escalation" as it is known in psychology circles. This is the classic case of throwing good money after bad. The classic example is the Concorde supersonic transport.[413] The bias is even known as "the Concorde fallacy" to some.

Through both development and commercial operation, the Concorde was plagued by cost overruns and huge financial losses. But because so much time, money, and human effort had already been sunk into it, the British and French governments, along with the British Airways-Air France investors, kept it going on and on.

Figure 59: The Sunk Cost Fallacy - better known as throwing good money after bad.

In 1977, journalist Peter Gillman described it as a "supersonic bust," saying,

> "Faster than the speed of sound comes the plane of the future. It has cost at least fifteen times the original estimates. It is described as a "commercial disaster" by a review committee of one of the countries that built it. It is besieged by the environmentalists. The Concorde is the benighted offspring of Anglo-French diplomacy and once-and-future

---

[413] Peter Gillman, "Supersonic Bust: The Story of the Concorde," *The Atlantic Monthly;* January 1977.

dreams of glory in the skies. Now its builders are trying to keep it from crashing in a sea of red ink..."

But it wasn't until the actual crash of a Concorde outside of Paris in 2000, combined with the general downturn in the aviation industry after September 11, 2001, that the "commercial disaster" was finally scuttled – after over three decades of committing the sunk cost fallacy error.

When getting caught in this bias, the attitude is one of "we've come too far to stop now...If we quit now, all out efforts will have been in vain...If we don't keep going, we'll never recover our investment..."

The problem gets worse the bigger the investment, too. As crazy as it sounds, the more that has been sunk into a losing venture, the more we are willing to keep sinking into it.

For innovation, the challenge here is investing in projects that are doomed to failure, and continuing to do so, taking resources away from better projects with a higher chance of success. When there is emotional attachment to pet projects, the challenge is even greater. That's why courage to make tough decisions is so important for effective portfolio management.[414]

Bias #8: Projection Bias and the Shared Information Bias. Projection bias happens when we unconsciously assume that others share the same knowledge we have, think the way we do, and value what we value. We project onto others our own set of thoughts and feelings, as if we are in some sort of Vulcan mind meld with them. [415]

Here's an easy demo. Find somebody willing to play a guessing game with you. You select a common song that you are confident the other person would know if they heard it. Now, without unconsciously humming the tune, tap out the song with your fingers or knuckles on a table for them to hear. See if they

---

[414] For more on the difficulty of decisions in portfolio management, go to the "Tough Choices" section of the Portfolio Management chapter, page 154.

[415] Colin Camerer, George Loewenstein, and Mark Weber, "The curse of knowledge in economic settings: An experimental analysis," *Journal of Political Economy*, October 1989. Please note that researchers did not test any actual Vulcans.

Figure 60: The Projection Bias – we tend to proceed as if everyone shares our knowledge and perspectives. We get frustrated when they don't.

can guess what you are tapping. The vast majority of the time, they will have no idea what song it is, even if you do something as common (at least in the US) as "Mary Had a Little Lamb" or "Happy Birthday to You."

The tapper thinks they've made the song perfectly clear for anyone to hear. Tappers will actually hear the song playing in their heads, and then assume that the guessers ought to be able to hear it, too. Unfortunately for the listeners, they aren't telepathically linked to the tapper. They can't hear the melody in their heads. They have no clue what the heck the tapper is tapping.

This happens in much of our communication. The person trying to convey a message (like the tapper in the game) has information firing amongst their neurons that the receiver (the listener in the game) simply doesn't – and can't – possess. It can be incredibly frustrating for both parties.

This can be a big challenge in Voice of the Customer efforts.[416] Both the customer and the developer will tend to project onto each other. Customers will have a level of knowledge in their activities that the developers can't come close to. Customers won't even realize how much knowledge is within them, so they won't even think to tell developers about most of it. They project their tacit knowledge onto the developers. This is why it is so critical for developers to observe and dig and observe and dig until they can hear the music inside their customers' heads.

Developers will tend to project their own preferences onto their customers as well. In the process of solving problems, they may proceed with solutions that they would want if they were in the customers' situation. That may not be the solution that the actual customer wants. This is not a matter of arrogance,

[416] For more about how to hear the Voice of the Customer better than the listener in the song-tapping game can hear the tapper's music, go to the "Voice of the Customer" chapter, page 176.

as if the developer is consciously telling the customer "you should want something different...my way is better." It's unconscious projection. That is why ongoing customer feedback and empathic listening skills are so important.

The impact is not just on VoC, either. Innovation is a team sport, and team members can project onto each other. The resulting miscommunication can cause delays and rework in the process. But that's not all...[417]

There's a corollary of sorts with the curse of knowledge, called the "shared information bias." That's the tendency for members of a group to focus their discussions *on information with which all members are already familiar*! So rather than spending time uncovering all of the important information hidden within individuals' minds, teams will tend to spend their energy rehashing the same data, facts, and figures that they all already know. And the frustration level rises because nothing new emerges to help make progress.

So here we are with some very dangerous biases that threaten good teamwork. One makes people think that everyone knows (or should know) what they have buried deep in their brains, and the other makes people not share the information that they have buried deep in their brains, even when the team can benefit from that knowledge.

I swear, when I read about these biases, I often wonder how we ever survived as a species.

Bias #9: Overconfidence Bias and the Curse of Knowledge. This is a blend of biases, based on the same theme – believing that things will turn out better than a truly objective assessment would suggest. The overconfidence bias leads us to underestimate the impact of external forces on what we are doing, and to overestimate what we are capable of achieving.

One of the most common forms of overconfidence emerges when we lay out plans for work. We tend to believe that we can accomplish more with the

---

[417] I feel like I'm doing a late-night infomercial when I say that. "But wait...there's more!" as in this infomercial: https://www.youtube.com/watch?v=piFaTt4VXgg. I'm considering offering plastic geese with the next edition.

time available than is actually possible. This can lead us to overpromise and underdeliver – not from lack of effort, but from unconscious overconfidence.[418]

Figure 61: Overconfidence Bias - We can become unrealistic with our expectations for our innovations. That can lead us to bad investment decisions.

The curse of knowledge is an insidious form of overconfidence, in which people who know less about a subject are actually *more* confident in their perspectives than are experts with more knowledge on the topic. In nerdy engineer speak,[419] our confidence is inversely proportional to our expertise.[420] For experts, it's a case of "the more you know, the more you know you don't know." For non-experts, it's a case of "ignorance is bliss."

The real danger here is that confidence sells.[421] It sells us internally, so that when we feel confident, we stop looking at alternatives. It sells us externally, so that when someone tells us something with confidence, we don't stop to question or challenge.

---

[418] I have been SO guilty of that in the writing of this book. Every aspect of its production took significantly longer than I thought it would. If I had a book sale for every time I told my friends and family "I'm almost done with the book," *Keep Innovation Simple* would be a NYT Bestseller.

[419] Yes, I am proud to be a nerdy engineer.

[420] Justin Kruger and David Dunning, "Unskilled," *Journal of Personality and Social Psychology*, December 1999. I guess this explains why I thought I could write a book.

[421] Speaking of confidence, notice how this book is written. In general, I state my points like "This is the way it is," or "Here's what you must do." While I really am confident that the evidence supports everything I'm writing, let's face it, no one really knows anything with absolute certainty. We are learning all the time, and discovering that what we once knew, just ain't true. But no one is going to read a book that constantly says "This might be true, and the evidence suggests that it is, but it may not, in fact, be true, even though I think it probably is." And I want people to read this, because I am just arrogant enough to think there is some valuable stuff somewhere in these pages. So read on with a combination of confidence and skepticism. Believe it, practice it, but always with a hint of doubt that there may be even greater wisdom if we look for it. If I'm wrong, let me know so I can overcome my inherent self-delusions and correct the mistake. That's how we will all learn and improve. I think.

There is indeed a con in confidence.[422] For example, my last name is Barbera (go ahead and check the front cover if you need to). Fans of Scooby Doo, the Flintstones, and the Jetsons will inevitably ask me if I have any relation to the guy from the Hanna-Barbera cartoons. I always answer, "Yes! In fact, my dad was the voice of Yogi Bear." I say it with unwavering confidence, and no one ever doubts it.[423] At least no one did before. Now that you know there really is no relation, you can call me out when you hear me say it.

It's one thing to deceive someone else with confidence in your voice, but we actually deceive *ourselves* with overconfidence all the time. What difference does that make for innovation? Well, research has shown that the frequent overconfidence of decision makers in estimating the success of new products leads to elevated product pricing, lower than expected sales, and poor budgeting.[424]

Because confidence sells, it can mask poor performance, even when overconfidence is what leads to bad decision-making.[425] To combat this, you must nurture a culture of challenge, in which it is encouraged to question assumptions and conclusions, no matter how confidently presented. Seek out those people that may not be as certain as others. Get their perspectives. Quite possibly, they are your best and brightest.

Bias #10: Identifiable victim bias. Joseph Stalin is supposed to have said, "The death of a single Russian soldier is a tragedy. A million deaths is a statistic."[426] That effectively describes the identifiable victim bias.

---

[422] Remember that "Rhyme as Reason" bias I mentioned earlier? I just used a form of that on you. Bwahahahaha!

[423] Don't worry, I always 'fess up. It's worth a good laugh.

[424] Dmitri G. Markovitch, Joel H. Steckel, Anne Michaut, Deepu Philip, and William M. Tracy, "Behavioral Reasons for New Product Failure: Does Overconfidence Induce Overforecasts?" *The Journal of Product Innovation Management*, December 2014.

[425] Brad M. Barber and Terrrence Odean, "Boys will be boys: gender, overconfidence, and common stock investment," *Quarterly Journal of Economics*, 2001, 116: 261–292. No, I am not one of the article's authors. I am Brad Barbera, not Brad Barber. No need to check the book jacket cover.

[426] As referenced in Richard E. Nisbett and Lee Ross, *Human Inference: Strategies and Shortcomings of Social Judgment*, Englewood Cliffs, NJ: Prentice-Hal, 1980. Certainly one of the more nauseating quotes from one of the more nauseating people in human history.

People tend to focus on the anecdotal but highly emotional rather than on a rational evaluation of the whole. The classic example comes from nonprofit marketing. Solicitations for donations almost always include a photo of one suffering person, front and center. Statistics, pie charts, and Venn diagrams are relegated to the footnotes of support materials. Even pictures of thousands of suffering people are not as effective at capturing our attention as that one lone sufferer. That's because we are so much more sensitive to one identifiable victim than we are to the general masses.

People make decisions emotionally. Even decisions that would seem to be purely rational, like which toilet bowl cleaner to buy, are made emotionally.

A photo of a weeping child suffering from hunger will drive decisions far more effectively than a list of statistics – even such gloomy numbers as 795 million people in the world do not have enough food to lead a

Figure 62: Identifiable Victim Bias - We are prone to focus on an individual example that we can see, especially when that example is emotionally moving, rather than on a long list of rational, objective data.

healthy active life,[427] or 3.1 million children under five die each year from being under nourished,[428] etc.

On one hand, innovators can't let themselves get caught up in the bias. It will lead them toward greasing the squeaky wheel rather than effectively lubricating the whole car. Or, without the metaphor, the innovator can't let themselves get distracted by the narrow needs of one visible customer and

[427] *The State of Food Insecurity in the World 2015 - Meeting the 2015 international hunger targets: taking stock of uneven progress*, Food and Agriculture Organization of the United Nations, Rome, 2015.

[428] Maternal and Child Nutrition Study Group (Group members: Robert E Blackemail, Harold Alderman, Zulfiqar A Bhutta, Stuart Gillespie, Lawrence Haddad, Susan Horton, Anna Lartey, Venkatesh Mannar, Marie Ruel, Cesar G Victora, Susan P Walker, and Patrick Webb), "Maternal and child nutrition: building momentum for impact," *The Lancet Online*, 06 June 2013.

forget to address the higher-priority and broader needs of the whole group of potential customers. You can't listen exclusively to the loud mouth in the focus group room, nor to the fist-waving complainer bellowing in your face. Of course, you don't want to dismiss them entirely, either. You want to make sure that you have a realistic, and holistic, view of the situation.

On the other hand, innovators can leverage this bias to be even more effective. Customer segmentation that uses identifiable people who exemplify the segments helps to provide innovators with an understanding of and motivation for particular groups. Seeing individuals experiencing the need being addressed can help innovators to connect emotionally and empathically with the customer they are trying to serve.

The bias can also be leveraged when communicating innovative solutions to customers. Showing customers someone experiencing the need for the solution, then benefiting from the innovation, can help them to relate and understand. Telling a compelling human story with your product will be more influential than any set of statistics, no matter how impressive. Customers will buy a story that gets them in the heart. This is not just true for consumer goods. It is true for B2B and non-profit organizations as well. All transactions are fundamentally between humans, so communication on a human level is required.

Does that mean that you should hire soap opera directors to create the sales materials for your asphalt paving business? No. Well, not necessarily. Just don't rely on claims that your new asphalt contains 3.7% less organosulfur compounds to make the sale. Produce goods and services that truly deliver on relevant and important performance measures, but be able to communicate them to your customers with a compelling personal story.

Bias 11: The In-group/Out-group bias. Humans have evolved as a tribal social species. The past couple of decades of increasing globalization have not yet altered our brains from millennia of isolated, local living. Few people have a view of the world as a single tribe of humanity. Instead, we approach the world as if we are parts of small clans. And we think that those in our clan are good, and those in other clans are bad. Even people who have been most socialized to cooperate with other people exhibit this bias.[429]

This tribal mentality causes us to frame people either as being part of our in-group or as part of some out-group. Racism, sexism, and a bunch of other -isms are the truly ugly side of this mentality. We are perpetually in a state of us-versus-them.

Wanna know why political election time is filled with negative attack ads? The campaigners are playing on our tribalism. Those ads don't bother to rally support for the candidate in your in-group, because you will naturally identify with them anyway. Instead, by maximizing the distance felt toward the candidate in the out-group, you experience the "call to arms" needed to get you in the voting booth to defeat the bad guys.

Figure 63: In-Group Out-Group Bias - We can be biased against those that are not in our "tribe," even when the reasons for being in the "tribe" are as trivial as cheering for different shirts.

This is not just true in life-or-death matters. It's true in every trivial thing we do as well. Sports rivalries are a prime example. Packers or Bears? Red Sox or Yankees? Canadiens or Maple Leafs? Celtics or Lakers? Brazil or Argentina? Cork or Galway?[430] Even though, as Jerry Seinfeld points out, these rivalries essentially boil down to cheering for different shirts,[431] they frequently result in violent crimes between otherwise reasonable people.[432]

---

[429] Bradley J. Ruffle and Richard Sosis, "Cooperation and the in-group-out-group bias: A field test on Israeli kibbutz members and city residents," *Journal of Economic Behavior & Organization*, June 2005.

[430] A reference to the sport of camogie. Someday, I gotta take in a game, so I can understand my own references. It looks like it's fun to watch!
https://www.youtube.com/watch?v=7oePVvm1tU4

[431] Get online and watch his stand-up commentary on this at
https://www.youtube.com/watch?v=we-L7w1K5Zo.

[432] For scores of examples, check out the fan violence section of the Wikipedia entry, "Violence in Sports." Yes, I used the word "scores" for its pun value. Got a problem with that? Huh?!? Do ya?!?

There is a bright side to this potentially sinister bias, though. Our perception of in-groups and out groups is surprisingly malleable. By reframing how we perceive the defined "group" to which we belong, people we initially place in an "outgroup" can suddenly become part of our "in-group."[433]

Put a Michigan Wolverines fan and an Ohio State Buckeyes fan in the same room on the final week of the Big Ten football season, and the animosity in the room will be palpable. Add a couple of non-sports fans telling the two of them that football is stupid, however, and they will suddenly unite as allies in the war for football fandom.

Truly, the enemy of my enemy is my friend.

Deep inside, we recognize ourselves as being part of many circles. When our circle of identity intersects with others, we have an in-group. When the circles don't intersect, we have an out-group. If we consciously reframe our circle of identity, we can make almost anyone part of our in-group.[434]

Specific to innovation efforts, the biggest impact of this bias comes in the form of managing innovation teams. Innovation is a team sport. If your team is just a collection of out-groups in the form of functional silos, they are not going to play well together. If your team is a single in-group, focused on a common cause, your results are going to be dramatically better.

If you work in an organization dominated by functional silos, the trick is going to be getting the team to self-identify as an in-group, aligned against a common cause, at least during the time that they are working together on the project.

Bias #12: Bias Blindness and Naïve Realism. I suppose that this could be considered the grand-daddy of all cognitive biases. Bias blindness/naïve realism means that we tend to see ourselves as unbiased, while seeing

---

[433] Samuel L. Gaertner, John F. Dovidio, Jason A. Nier, Brenda S. Banker, Christine M. Ward, Melissa Houlette, and Stephanie Loux, "The Common Ingroup Identity Model for reducing intergroup bias: Progress and challenges," *Social identity processes: Trends in theory and research*, edited by Dora Capozza and Rupert Brown, Sage Publications Ltd, 2000.

[434] Irene V. Blair, "The Malleability of Automatic Stereotypes and Prejudice," *Personality and Social Psychology Review*, August 2002.

everyone around us as biased. Well, guess what? We can't all be right on that point.

We tend to believe that we have a firm, objective grasp on reality as it really is. We think that our reality is fundamentally true and unalterable, plain for all to see if they just choose to look. Because we have such a firm and objective grasp, we believe that those who don't see reality in the same way are either ignorant, uninformed, biased, or clinically insane.

We then believe that the logical solution to any conflict in perception is to merely provide the missing information that will properly adjust the other's world view. If that doesn't work, then you can just dismiss them as lunatics.

Some of you may be nodding your head to this, saying to yourself, "yes, that's right. I'm constantly surprised at how many lunatics there are in this world." If you are one of these people, then you need to pay special attention to overcoming your bias blindness.

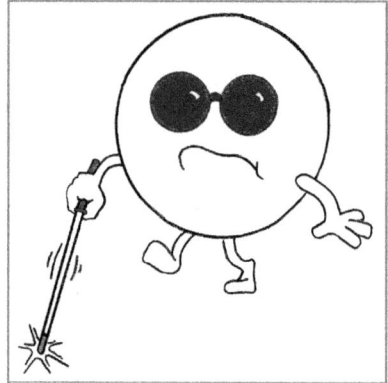

Figure 64: Bias Blindness - We tend to be unaware of our own biases, while acutely aware of others' biases. Except for your author, who is totally objective.

Unless you are a bodhisattva,[435] you are as limited in objective knowledge as anyone else. The impact on innovation is obvious. If you fail to take into account multiple perspectives, you will make poorer decisions, address suboptimal problems, and deliver suboptimal solutions. Before engaging with others, swallow a spoonful of humility, remove your sunglasses, and recognize that you are just as biased as anyone else around you.

The Route to Rationality

So how does a good innovator overcome the inherent irrationality of humans, while still keeping things simple? What are we to do about all the

---

[435] One of my favorite words, concepts, and Steely Dan songs. A bodhisattva is essentially someone who has achieved enlightenment, and commits themselves to teach the rest of us how to get there, too.

mental forces that lead us astray, without overindulging in excessive and unproductive rational rigor?

First, the bad news: There is no way to overcome the cognitive biases. The best we can hope to do is to mitigate their adverse effects.

Now the good news: The treatment is simple! That should be obvious, or it wouldn't fit the theme of this book. The way to mitigate the damage of cognitive biases is to be consciously aware of them. That's it. This awareness alone can help us avoid the worst of the damage.

Recognize that you are as biased as anyone else is. Challenge yourself to think from an objective perspective. Get comfortable with being wrong. Create an environment where "wrong" is okay, where failure *is* an option.

Recognize that others (teammates, managers, executives, customers, suppliers, consultants, partners, regulators, and everyone else) doubt their own biases, and they all think you are as biased as they come. Disarm them by expressing your awareness of this bias, even laughing about it, and try to get everyone to lay their own potential biases out on the table for all to see.

Share your knowledge of cognitive biases with everyone you meet. Okay, maybe not everyone. That crabby guy on the subway may not be interested. But at least share with your colleagues and coworkers. As a team, work to overcome these biases by challenging each other. You may not be able to eliminate these biases, but as a group looking out for one another, and driving for a common goal, you can drive much greater rationality. Go ahead and leverage the bandwagon effect on that.

In a team setting, you can challenge your collective biases by defining "proof" in advance of testing. For example, if you find yourself expecting a certain result to happen, figure out what proof you would need to convince yourself that you are wrong. Then, if the data comes out to be the proof you defined in advance, you will be ready to accept it (or at least a little readier for it).

Thinking Caps

Another way to force your way out of cognitive biases is to have the team put on their thinking caps. Edward DeBono's thinking hats,[436] to be specific.

---

[436] Edward de Bono, *Six Thinking Hats, 2nd edition*, Back Bay Books, 1999.

De Bono devised the thinking hats to represent different points of view when approaching a problem. By taking the time to consciously approach the problem from these specific points of view, teams can break free of groupthink, overconfidence, confirmation bias, and all the others that can get in the way of good, innovative decision-making.

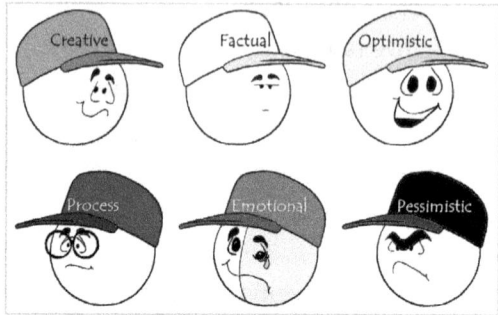

Figure 65: DeBono's Six Thinking Hats - ensuring that you are approaching any problem from a variety of perspectives while looking fashionable at the same time.

The six hats are six different colors, each representing a different way of thinking:

- **Blue Hat**: **Process Thinking** – monitors how the team is working together and ensures that all thinking styles are being used appropriately.
- **White Hat**: **Factual Thinking** – focuses on the objective data, in terms of both what is already known and what is needed to be learned. The data is neutral. "The facts, ma'am, just the facts."[437]
- **Yellow Hat: Optimistic Thinking** – explores the positive aspect of an idea, looking for the potential benefits and value that it could deliver.
- **Black Hat**: **Pessimistic Thinking** – DeBono actually calls this "judgement," but that seems too final to me. This hat identifies the potential flaws in an idea, the reasons it won't work, and points out where things can go wrong. Playing the role of "devil's advocate' can actually be the most powerful role in the thinking hats process, but as gentle Uncle Ben told Peter Parker,[438] "with great power comes great

---

[437] I was so disappointed to learn that Jack Webb's Sergeant Joe Friday never actually said that. It really is a curse to be such a stickler for quote accuracy.

[438] See this wisdom being handed down to Spiderman's alter ego here: https://www.youtube.com/watch?v=-o308cW0hKl

responsibility." If this thinking gets overused, it can derail the whole process.

- **Red Hat**: **Emotional Thinking** – gets out the feelings and emotions of the team as they work through the decision, and opens the door for gut feeling, hunches, and intuition. In my experience, this is the hat teams like to use the least. It can be uncomfortable sharing emotions with a group, particularly in a professional setting. But like it or not, emotions are essential to effective decision-making.[439]

- **Green Hat**: **Creative Thinking** – searches for possibilities, potential alternatives, and different directions. This is classic divergent thinking that frames questions in terms of "could" instead of "should."

The process of using the different hats is simple.[440] Direct the team to put on the various thinking hats throughout the development process. This is usually done figuratively, but sometimes, it helps to do so literally. Encourage team members to break out of their natural inclinations and see things from alternative perspectives. Force the person who always throws out new ideas to put on a black hat, and start questioning implementation. Force the Eeyore[441] of group to put on the yellow hat and start thinking of the positives of the project.

An ideally balanced team[442] may do this naturally, but even if the team is balanced, they can get carried away with one mode of thought at times. This approach provides structure to the thinking of the team, and is especially helpful if the natural balance of thought isn't there.

The team leader should be skilled with the blue hat thinking, able to engage their "observing ego" – that way of thinking about what's going on as if you were a separate, impartial, dispassionate observer. Wearing the blue hat means acting as a facilitator for a moment, not judging, but guiding the

---

[439] Antoine Bechara, Hanna Damasio, and Antonio R. Damasio, "Emotion, Decision Making, and the Orbitofrontal Cortex," *Cerebral Cortex*, March 2000. Seriously fascinating reading.

[440] Or else it wouldn't be brought up in this book.

[441] If you don't know Eeyore, he's the pessimist of the *Winnie the Pooh* cast of characters. See him in lethargic action at https://www.youtube.com/watch?v=LBRCWAn4QKU.

[442] For more about balancing team roles, see the "Putting Together the Skill Set Puzzle" section of the Team chapter, page 317.

process. And guiding the process does not mean toward the decision that you want, but simply ensuring that all the right perspectives are being used.

When emotions get high, the blue hat cools things down with "okay, I think our red hats have caught on fire. Let's take a break, and then come back with some white hat thinking..."

When the team is getting irrationally exuberant about all the things the new Widgetinator 2.0 will do in the market, the blue hat says, "yes, the possibilities are impressive, but to ensure that we can achieve all this potential, let's put on our black hats and start thinking about what might get in the way of execution..."

Don't underestimate the power of this tool. It may sound quirky, even juvenile, but it works. And works well.

Mind Juggling

A master juggler can keep three running chain saws in the air simultaneously without losing a limb (or an audience member). Ask them to recite the Gettysburg Address while calculating the square root of 7 and posting cat memes on Facebook, though, and they can't do it.

The conscious human mind does not multitask well. Worse yet, those who believe that they multitask well are actually likely to be the worst multitaskers. And, unfortunately, they are also the most likely to engage in multitasking activities.[443]

In public speaking presentations, I demonstrate this by asking participants to copy three lists: one of random words, one of random six- and seven-digit numbers, and one of colors. The first time they do it, one list is exposed for five seconds, then another list for five seconds, then another, and so on. By the end of this one-minute exercise, each list has been exposed to the audience four times, for a total of twenty seconds each.

Then I repeat the exercise, but this time with each list exposed once for the full twenty seconds. Typically, the audience is able to copy 25% or so more in

---

[443] David M. Sanbonmatsu, David L. Strayer, Nathan Medeiros-Ward, and Jason M. Watson, "Who Multi-Tasks and Why? Multi-Tasking Ability, Perceived Multi-Tasking Ability, Impulsivity, and Sensation Seeking," *PLOS ONE*, January 23, 2013.

that exercise than in the first. The same number of words/letters/digits/colors are involved, so why is the first exercise so much less efficient?

The brain cannot switch instantly between tasks. Once attention is focused on a particular task, the brain wants to keep doing that. It gets in a rhythm, and starts doing the task efficiently. When it has to stop and change direction, it takes time to shut down the first thinking process and start-up the next thinking process.

In manufacturing, this is called changeover time. It's downtime that the equipment isn't productive. Efficiency-minded managers plan around this, minimizing the number of changeovers required.

We apparently haven't figured out that it applies to thinking jobs, too. Most information-age jobs involve multitasking on a non-stop basis. Job descriptions go out saying "must be able to multitask efficiently." How ironic that the research shows that those who think they multitask well are actually the worst at it.[444] They are not actually good at multitasking. What they are good at is getting distracted. So such job descriptions end up attracting the worst performers.

But we keep making people do it. And we seek out and invest in tools to help them do it better. But we should not be investing in making people more efficient at what they should not be doing in the first place.[445]

Innovation is ultimately a thinking game. The better innovators are able to think, the better the innovations that will result. The less time innovators have to spend switching between tasks, and the fewer distractions they have from the task of innovation, the more innovation output they will produce.

How often do you find yourself thinking, "I didn't have time to do X, Y, or Z today?" What if you could do 25% more with the time you have? What if you could focus on A until it was done, then B until it was done, then C...maybe then you'd have time for X, Y, and Z, too.

Okay, I get that the simple list-copying demo doesn't correlate exactly to the work environment, so the 25% mentioned may not be the actual

---

[444] Ibid.

[445] Peter Drucker, as usual, was more eloquent: "There is nothing so useless as doing efficiently that which should not be done at all." Connie Robertson, *The Wordsworth Dictionary of Quotations*, Wordsworth Editions, 1998.

productivity increase you would experience. But it's going to be an improvement.

Look for ways to organize your days so that you can work on one thing for a solid block of time. Turn off your email notifications and the ringer on your phone. Move to a quiet conference room away from your desk. Go to your public library and work in a quiet cubicle. Only switch tasks when you must.

If you are a manager of others, enable them by simplifying their workflows. Eliminate or postpone TPS reports and other distractions that don't ultimately deliver value to your customer, and earn value from them in return. That means keeping the work relevant and focused on the mission and strategy. Manage project portfolios so that you and your team are not working beyond capacity, having the courage to deal with your surplus puppies.[446]

Perhaps the best thing you can do as a manager of innovators is to be a relevancy filter. A common cliché I hear in organizations is "stuff flows downhill."[447] That comment is trotted out when a manager assigns a subordinate to do a task that an executive assigned to the manager. If that "stuff" is relevant to the work that needs to be done, great. No problem. But if it distracts from the actual value-producing work at hand, the courageous manager[448] will filter it out.

Multitasking cannot be eliminated completely in a complex world. The most effective people are the ones who filter out the irrelevant. Focusing only on those things relevant to the goal dramatically reduces the adverse impact of multitasking. Doing less at one time, you accomplish more over time.[449]

The Thinking of Innovators

So now that we've spent a bunch of time talking about how *not to* think, let's delve into how *to* think when it comes to innovation.

---

[446] If you don't yet get the puppy analogy, go to the "Tough Choices" section of the Portfolio Management chapter, page 154. Be warned...it's not for the faint of heart.

[447] Except no one says "stuff." They use another word beginning with an "S." Followed by an "h." I'm just trying not to earn an NSFW rating for this book. Get it? Got it. Good.

[448] See the Whack-a-Mole reference (page 256) for the obligatory warning statement regarding such behavior.

[449] Eyal Ophir, Clifford Nass, and Anthony D. Wagner, "Cognitive control in media multitaskers," *Proceedings of the National Academy of Sciences of the United States of America*, August 24, 2009.

Of course, not all innovators are created equal. If there is anything that all innovators have universally in common, it's that they are all unique. They have their individual personalities – some introverted, and some extroverted; some impulsive, and some patient; some even-tempered, and some unpredictable. At different times they will be under different levels of external stress, different levels of physical health, different levels of mental exhaustion, and different levels of caffeine stimulation. They will all respond differently to problems, have differing short- and long-term memories, and have different cognitive approaches to the particular circumstances they are facing.[450]

The attitude of the best innovators[451] is what I like to call "respectful irreverence." It's a paradoxical way of thinking, in which the innovator has tremendous respect for what has come before, while not revering it in a way that prevents them from looking for a different and better solution. They want to know how things have been done and why they have been done that way, while simultaneously ignoring anyone who says, "That's the way we've always done it, so that's the way we'll always do it."

Having respect for the past enables understanding of both the customer and the organization addressing their problems. That same understanding and demonstration of respect for the past can lower resistance to the adoption of new ideas.

Irreverence enables novelty and creative problem solving. It enables heretical questions that would otherwise never be asked for fear of offending worshipers of the sacred cows. It enables the courage to challenge the status quo.

---

[450] William Revelle and Debra A. Loftus, "Individual differences and arousal: Implications for the study of mood and memory," *Cognition and Emotion*, September 1990. To my knowledge, Dr. Loftus has not relation to the novelty toy manufacturer Loftus International, but I am grateful to her for helping me with my writing style, and with my understanding of the state of psychological research today – although any errors in that department are mine, and not due to a lack of her trying to educate me.

[451] Okay, so the attitude of innovators is not based on a research study in which the innovators of the world were given a validated attitude survey instrument, and the result was that "respectful irreverence" differentiated the best from the rest. That's just how I describe what I've observed in my experience combined with what I've read in the literature. Take it for what it's worth.

So, to paraphrase F. Scott Fitzgerald,[452] the sign of a first-rate innovator is the ability to hold these two opposing attitudes in their head simultaneously. If, however, you can't hold them both, then I'd suggest you hold onto the latter if you want to innovate.

But attitude alone won't get you there. What else is there about the minds of innovators? How do they think?

In addition to the cultural characteristics described in the chapter on a culture of innovation (which apply equally well to innovative individuals), here are some characteristics of the innovative mind...

Pi-Shaped Minds

How can something as nebulous a concept as a "mind" have shape? Well, you have to use your imagination.

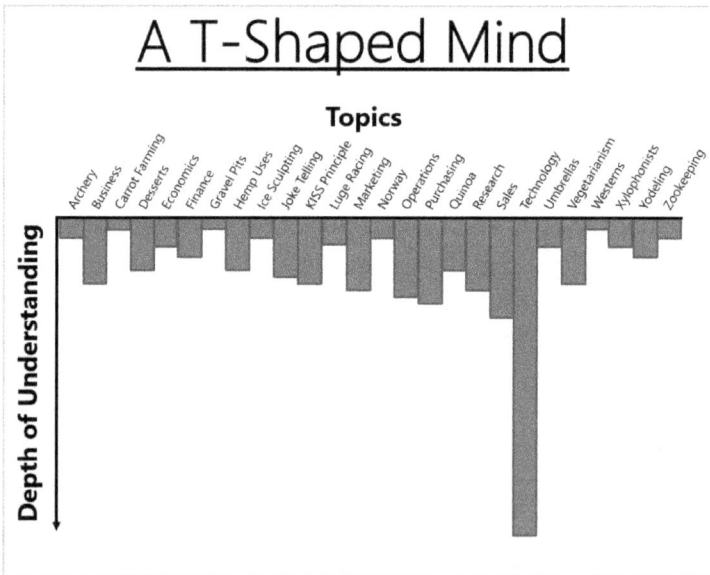

Figure 66: Diagram of a T-Shaped mind. Shallow understanding in many different topics, and deep understanding in an area of particular expertise.

---

[452] What he actually said was "The test of a first-rate intelligence is the ability to hold two opposing ideas in mind at the same time and still retain the ability to function."

Imagine the shape of a mind being represented by the depth of knowledge in various topics. A flat mind would have shallow knowledge in a variety of topics, but no deep knowledge in any one of them.

Most people have deep knowledge in a particular subject of some sort, though. That makes them T-Shaped. For example, Figure 66 shows someone who has broad but shallow knowledge in a variety of topics, with deep knowledge and expertise in a relevant technology.

Research on serial innovators identified another shape of mind that correlated with the ability to be a serial innovator. These people, who repeatedly come up with great innovations, not as entrepreneurs, but as innovators within larger organizations,[453] have minds that can be described as "Pi-shaped."

The Pi-shaped person continues to have broad and shallow knowledge in a variety of topics, and the deep knowledge in some technology area. In addition, their knowledge goes deep in the area of business. They know their

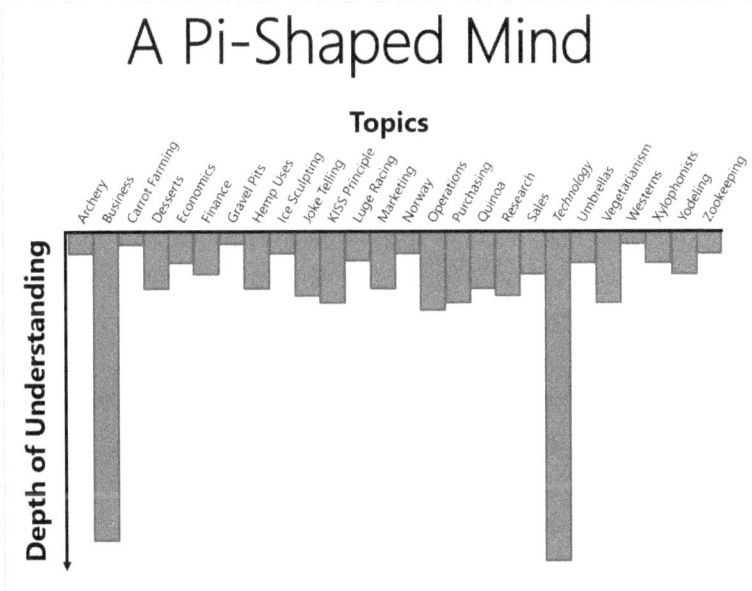

Figure 67: The pi-shaped mind of a serial innovator. Not only is there deep functional knowledge, but also deep business knowledge that drives them to solve problems in a way people both inside and outside of the organization will value.

---

[453] Abbie Griffin, Raymond Price, and Bruce Vojak, *Serial Innovators: How Individuals Create and Deliver Breakthrough Innovations in Mature Firms*, Stanford Business Books, 2012.

customer, and have the curiosity to understand them even better. They know how an organization functions, and what is important to help the organization thrive. They know what drives profits and losses. They understand sourcing and distribution challenges, as well as sales and marketing challenges. They may not have deep functional expertise in all of these areas, but they do have a sound holistic understanding of them all.

The combination of deep technical and business knowledge, with a broad array of shallow knowledge in other subjects, enables a serial innovator to a) make connections in novel ways, b) turn those connections into solutions, c) ensure the solutions have value for both the organization and for the customer, and d) make those novel and valuable solutions into real goods and services through effective execution.

Problem-Solving Framing

Innovations are possibilities turned into realities. To identify possibilities, an innovator not only defines the problem clearly, but considers solutions in terms of "could" versus "should."

All too often, when we are faced with a problem, we immediately jump into thinking about what we "should" do. The problem with "should" is that it takes us too quickly into a particular solution, and starts us down the path of needing to defend that solution. When we instead start with "could," we open our minds to many options. Some may not go anywhere, but starting with "could" allows us to take multiple perspectives, find superior alternatives, and possibly combine alternatives in a way that the original "should" would not.

Here's a simple example. Let's say the problem is finding two numbers that add up to 100. If you start with a "should," such as "one of the numbers should be 13 because my dog's birthday is August 13," then there is just one answer (13+87, if you hadn't already guessed).

However, if you start with "it *could* be 13+87," you still keep your mind open to the infinite number of other possibilities that might just be better for some reason or another. Personally, I like 53+47, because they are the only two prime numbers that add up to 100, but that's just nerdy me.

The innovator knows to start with "could." That is not, however, where the solution thinking ends. "Could" represents divergent thinking. That's just a fancy term for allowing thinking paths to go in many directions. After doing sufficient divergence, though, the thinking must change over to convergent – bringing the multiple paths back together to a single solution.

That's where "should" comes in. All of the data collected about the customer gives you a set of "shoulds" that will help guide the final decision process.

The innovation process is a series of diverge-converge-diverge-converge thinking phases. Select your framing wisely, using "could" when you need to generate multiple options, and "should" when you need to work it back to just a few, or just one.

Thick Skin

Innovators need to be able to hear feedback and accept it for what it is. Sometimes, that feedback is harsh, even personal.

On more than one occasion, I've sat behind the one-way mirror observing focus groups, and had my ideas laughed at and called stupid. After one particularly grueling deep dive into customer data, I thought I discovered the unique insight that was going to make customers stand-up and offer a champagne toast in my honor. Instead, the loudest of the panelists said, "What idiot thought of that?!?"

Oh well.

You move on. You take the feedback and learn from it. You make adjustments and start driving forward again.

Be careful, though. I hear inspirational stories all the time, about successful entrepreneurs who prove their naysayers wrong. They go through rejection after rejection, critic after critic, hater after hater. But they persevere, and win in the end. The moral of these stories is always "so ignore the critics and follow your dreams."

That's a nice sentiment, but it's stupid.

If someone tells you that your innovation stinks, you ought to give it a sniff. They may be wrong, and you can ignore them and move on. Or they may be right, and you can load it up with deodorizer.

The way to overcome criticism is *not* to just ignore it. The way to overcome criticism is to accept it as a data point. Data is neutral. It just is. How you interpret that data, though, is what can be good or bad. If the data is not what you hoped for, understand why, and decide what to do from there.

It takes thick skin to be an effective innovator.

Whack-a-Mole

And perhaps it takes a thick skull as well.

Resilience. Grit. Courage. Fortitude. Whatever you want to call it, innovators need it.

The philosopher Arthur Schopenhauer issued a warning to innovators[454] when he said, "Every truth passes through three stages. First, it is ridiculed. Second, it is violently opposed. Third, it is accepted as being self-evident."

The innovator is on a search for a new truth. The old truth is the way things are. Dissatisfied with that truth, the innovator seeks out a new way of doing things that is better. This involves risk. And not just the kind of risk that the organization takes on with any project. This risk is particularly personal.

The innovator is often in the role of being the rodent that pokes its head out of the hole, only to face having it whacked back down. As Schopenhauer points out, the first risk faced is that of being ridiculed, shamed, or embarrassed. Then comes the violent opposition. For

Figure 68: The mole that sticks its head out of the hole risks getting it whacked.

innovators, this typically does not take the form of physical violence. Rather, it takes the form of coworker complaints to management, poor performance appraisals, lost wages, or even termination.[455]

Even the best serial innovators face the challenge of getting whacked. In the book *Serial Innovators*, some of those who successfully drove *billion-dollar*

---

[454] I don't think he was actually warning innovators per se, but he may as well have been.

[455] Gina Colarelli O'Connor and Mark P. Rice, "New Market Creation for Breakthrough Innovations: Enabling and Constraining Mechanisms," *Journal of Product Innovation Management*, March 2013.

innovations were almost fired before they had a chance to make their impact.[456]

Innovation involves change and disruption (if I may use that term outside of the specific Clay Christenson context). Those things are not comfortable for most people. And that leads to violent reaction from the corporate antibodies. An attitude of irreverence, even when buffered with a healthy dose of respect, can be interpreted as a challenge to authority. And many in positions of authority don't appreciate being challenged. Asking questions for the sake of learning and growth, or challenging the status quo purely for the sake of challenging the status quo, are interpreted as insubordination.

Being an innovator can make you a PITA[457] to many people in an organization. Many people, if not most, actually like the comfort of the status quo. Innovators make them uncomfortable. Innovators must be prepared to deal with the reactions that they will receive. Those reactions will often be something other than cheers and pats on the back for their heroic efforts.

I tell you this not to discourage you. I tell you this to set your expectations appropriately. No overconfidence bias allowed.

Here's the bright side. If you survive a few hits from the mole whacker, you can make a huge difference to your organization, and to your customers. You are on a modern equivalent of Shackleton's quest for the South Pole.[458]

> "Difference makers wanted for hazardous innovation quest. Small wages, long months of complete darkness, constant danger of getting whacked in the head. Safe return doubtful. Honor and recognition in case of success."[459]

---

[456] Tom Osborn's story in the beginning of the book tells of his nearly getting the axe from Procter & Gamble three times before he almost single-handedly created Always Ultra, generating huge profits for the company, and radically changing the feminine hygiene market. Ultimately, he was inducted into the Victor Mills Society, the highest honor for R&D leadership and creativity at P&G. Yet he was almost an unemployment statistic.

[457] "**P**ain **I**n **T**he **A**ssets." Or something like that.

[458] For more about the Shackleton example of mission, go to the "Mission Statement How To" section of the Mission chapter, page 48.

[459] Okay, the wages need not be small. They can actually be quite rewarding. The long months of complete darkness and the head whacking dangers are quite real, though. The honor and recognition may or may not actually present themselves, depending on the culture of your

Perhaps I've been whacked in the head too many times in my career, but *that* is an adventure that I want to do. And it doesn't even mention the intrinsic reward of making others' lives better with the innovations we create.

Note: the cause-and-effect road here is a one-way street. Being an innovator means that you are very likely to be a PITA to some folks in your organization. Maybe even to most folks. But the same is not true in reverse. Being a PITA does not automatically make you are an innovator. Some PITAs are just PITAs.

Love Chaos, Hate Confusion

Here is a chaotic exercise for you. If you really want to make this a powerful example, time yourself. Look at Figure 69, and find the numbers that are missing in the series. Ready, go!

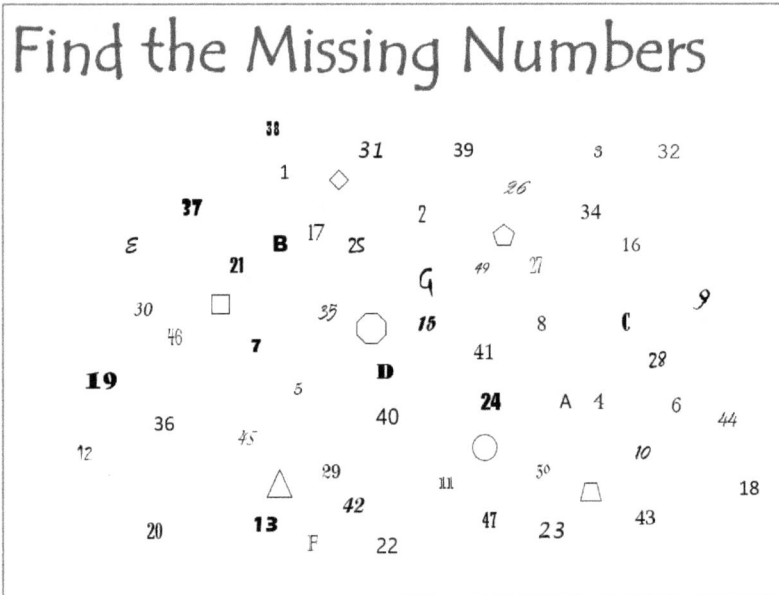

Figure 69: See how long it takes you to find the missing numbers in the series.

organization (see the story of my experience with rituals and ceremonies in the "Cultural Change" section of the chapter on innovation culture, page 82). The point here is that if you are getting in the innovation game purely based on extrinsic motives, you are likely to fail. It's the intrinsic reward, the passion for solving problems and helping others, that separates the great innovators from the mediocrities. The other rewards follow, they don't lead.

So how long did it take? Was it easy? Which numbers do you think were missing?

The numbers in the exercise are like the chaotic data that confronts us all the time. We get a bit here, a bit there, and we can see that there are some connections, but we aren't necessarily sure how things go together. Even when we look through all the data, we have to ask ourselves if we missed anything, if we misinterpreted anything (was that a 4 or a 9?), or if we counted anything twice.

Chaos can lead to confusion. Innovators love the chaos, but hate the confusion.

Most people prefer order to chaos, at least when they get past their teenage years. This is especially true in organizations, when people need to work together to achieve a common goal.

Innovators, however, must be comfortable with ambiguity. They are dealing with an unpredictable future, after all.

I've often heard the phrase "the best way to predict the future is to create it." That's a nice, inspiring sentiment, but it's unrealistic. The future isn't something that any individual or organization can create. There are over seven billion people on the earth making individual decisions that collectively create that future, and those decisions are not predictable. Heck, I don't even know what I'm going to be craving for lunch today.

What we can do is respond to the information we have. We can make predictions about the future, and create plans for what we foresee. Better yet, we can predict multiple scenarios and create contingency plans for each. We can think in terms of probabilities, with our eyes and ears open for new information that impacts those probabilities.

An innovator doesn't fight the chaos, but embraces it. An innovator doesn't try to impose order on the chaos, but recognizes the order that emerges from it, and works with it. It's like intellectual judo.[460] An innovator

---

[460] One of the philosophies of judo as a martial art is that resisting a more powerful opponent head-on will result in your defeat, whereas adjusting to your opponent's attack and using their force to your advantage will enable you to defeat even stronger enemies. I don't care if your name is Kal-El and you came here from the planet Krypton, you are still weaker than the inherent chaos of the world and unpredictability of the future. You are better off going with it and adjusting to it than wasting energy fighting it.

recognizes that the problem isn't with the chaos, but rather with the confusion that we all-too-often allow to be our response to it.

Chaos results from there being irrelevant information mixed in with relevant information, and from the relevant information coming from a near-infinite variety of directions. An innovator must do two things to manage that: filter out the irrelevant, and sort the relevant into a form from which they can derive meaning.

Let's do that number-finding exercise again – but this time with a relevancy filter and a little re-organization of the relevant. Now see how long it takes to find the same missing numbers in the series in Figure 70...

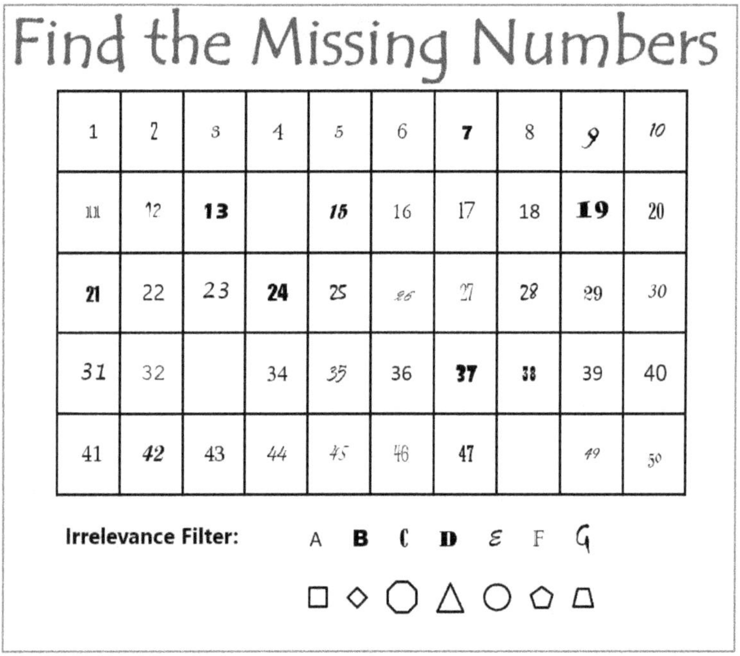

Find the Missing Numbers

1	2	3	4	5	6	7	8	9	10
11	12	13		15	16	17	18	19	20
21	22	23	24	25	26	27	28	29	30
31	32		34	35	36	37	38	39	40
41	42	43	44	45	46	47		49	50

Irrelevance Filter: A   **B**   **C**   **D** ε F   G

□ ◇ ○ △ ○ ⬠ ◲

Figure 70: The same data as before, just filtered and sorted.

How long does it take to find the missing numbers in the series now?

A simple example, but hopefully a powerful one.

That's how innovators find the solutions to unresolved problems. It takes work to filter and sort, but the result is worth the effort.

Think this might be just a crazy example made up by an only-partially sane author? How about the real-life example of Dmitri Mendeleev, who took a hodge-podge of chemistry data, and turned it into the periodic table. Not only did he use it to correct previous mistakes others had made regarding the properties of several discovered elements, but he used it to predict the properties of many elements that had not even been discovered yet. Structuring data *works*.

Intuition

Intuition is an important part of decision-making.[461] No, that doesn't mean waiting for mystical inspiration from ghosts, fairy godmothers, or genies living in brass oil lamps.

Remember that before I launched into a long list of cognitive biases that can lead us astray, I mentioned that those biases evolved in us for good reason. They helped us survive as a species. While those quick reactions can sometimes lead us into irrational thinking, which can be bad, they can also lead us to good, nonrational thinking.

What's the difference between irrational and nonrational? Irrational implies that the thinking is, frankly, stupid. Finding a statement to be more believable just because it rhymes is irrational. Nonrational means that the thinking does not involve rational, logical, slow, deliberate thought. It's a reaction. Quick thinking. A good choice, but made without putting a host of if-then-else thinking together first.

An example of nonrational thinking would be the reaction of a firefighter who, while battling a blaze, senses that something is different. They can't quite say exactly what it is, but they choose a course of action based on their gut feeling for the situation. When they would normally open a door, their gut tells them to leave it closed instead. Later, they find out that had they opened the door, they would have fed oxygen to fuel in a way that would have made the situation dramatically worse, possibly injuring themselves and others in the process. They didn't know that rationally at the time, but their nonrational decision-making was spot on.

---

[461] Katrin Eling, Abbie Griffin and Fred Langerak, "Using Intuition in Fuzzy Front-End Decision-Making: A Conceptual Framework," *Journal of Product Innovation Management*, September 2014.

This intuition comes from knowledge and experience wired into our brains in a way that we don't even notice. That knowledge and experience helps us to make judgements when we don't have the time or resources available to think it through. It's the fast, unconscious thinking that gets us through most of our daily choices, rather than the slow, conscious thinking that we use for more difficult and complicated decisions.[462]

Intuition can be powerful, both as ally and foe. Good innovators listen to their guts, but are not slaves to them. They listen, because they know that their intuition might be making connections for them that they can't (or don't) reach logically. They are not slaves to them, though, because they know that those common cognitive biases might be at work, leading them astray.

When it comes to intuition, what to heed and what to ignore will depend on the time and resources available for decision-making. If resources are available to resolve an issue with sound reasoning, then by all means, look for that kind of resolution. If resources are not available, then make the best decision you can with the information you have, including your intuitive feel.

Intuition does not just work on the individual level, either. Team intuition also has an impact on innovation success.[463] Team intuition comes from the phenomenon of "collective memory," in which a group shares a set of common experiences, and holds a common understanding of who on the team knows what.

Both managers and team members should do all they can to help their team develop a collective memory. This can be done by ensuring that every team member understands the expertise that other team members possess. Team members should share a common understanding of what the team as a whole knows, and participate in the building, sharing, and reinforcing of that collective understanding.[464]

---

[462] Daniel Kahneman, *Thinking, Fast and Slow*, Farrar, Straus and Giroux, 2011. Kahneman calls the fast unconscious thinking "System 1" and the slow, conscious thinking, "System 2."

[463] Mumin Dayan and Said Elbanna, "Antecedents of Team Intuition and Its Impact on the Success of New Product Development Projects," *Journal of Product Innovation Management*, November 2011.

[464] David P. Brandon and Andrea B. Hollingshead, "Transactive Memory Systems in Organizations: Matching Tasks, Expertise, and People," *Organizational Science*, December 2004.

To prevent over-reliance on team intuition, managers should strive for two things: sufficient relevant experience to allow intuition to be of value, and the presence of a few less experienced team members. Why? Partly to give them a chance to learn and grow, but just as importantly, to challenge the experienced members to think with the curiosity of a beginner.[465] Beginners can operate with naïve "permission" to ask the stupid questions that the experienced won't allow themselves to ask. And sometimes, those questions turn out to be not-so-stupid.

Connecting

Connecting disparate information is a critical skill for the would-be innovator.[466] One of the ways to identify serial innovators is that they expect themselves to be able connect dots between things, when others don't even see the dots being on the same metaphorical page.[467]

Having a little bit of knowledge in many different fields is one of the ways effective innovators make connections. They have the imagination to believe that connections may exist in places that others never consider. If, for example, they are working on color cosmetics, they may think, "I wonder if the application of paint to a car would offer any insights that would be interesting?" They may not know much about paint application in the automotive industry, but they know enough to know where to look for more information, and they know who to contact for getting greater expertise.

They are willing to look foolish in their exploration. They are willing to be wrong, and acknowledge that the path they explored went nowhere. But they may go just a little further down the path, beyond where others would have given up, and discover that the path led to fertile grounds after all.

---

[465] For more on putting together effective teams, see the "Putting Together the Skill Set Puzzle" section of the Team chapter, page 317.

[466] Marion Poetz, Nikolaus Franke, and Martin Schreier, "Sometimes the Best Ideas Come from Outside Your Industry," *Harvard Business Review*, November 2014.

[467] Abbie Griffin, Raymond Price, and Bruce Vojak, *Serial Innovators: How Individuals Create and Deliver Breakthrough Innovations in Mature Firms*, Stanford Business Books, 2012.

The One Drug I Recommend for Would-Be Innovators

If you could take a drug that would make you a better innovator, would you consider it? What would you think if you read the following about such a discovery?

> "Suppose you read about a pill that you could take once a day to reduce anxiety and increase your contentment. Would you take it? Suppose further that the pill has a great variety of side effects, all of them good: increased self-esteem, empathy, and trust; it even improves memory. Suppose, finally, that the pill is all natural and costs [almost] nothing. Now would you take it? The pill exists..."[468]

It exists, and it's completely legal. Just don't do it while driving.

Actually, it doesn't come in the form of a pill. Nor is it injected through a needle. Nope, it's not something you drink. We're talking about...

Mindfulness meditation.

Yes, mindfulness. That thing that trendy companies like Google are encouraging (or pushing, if you are not a believer) to their employees. That thing practiced for centuries in eastern cultures. That thing that may look like lazy sitting around, but is actually challenging work.

I bring this topic up, not because it's trendy, but because it has real value. If you are already a believer in mindfulness, skip the next couple of paragraphs, lest you lose faith in me.

If you are not a believer, I get it. Completely. I was an engineer a long time ago (in this galaxy, not one far, far, away). I am a real numbers and science guy. I didn't buy into the hippy-dippy thing in college. I never attempted to follow-

---

[468] Jonathan Haidt, *The Happiness Hypothesis: Finding Modern Truth in Ancient Wisdom*, Basic Books, 2006. I added the "almost" because everything, even mindfulness, has an opportunity cost. The twenty minutes you spend meditating is twenty minutes of watching *The Real housewives of Walla Walla Washington* that is forever lost to you. A small price to pay, but a price nonetheless.

the Steve Jobs mind-expansion-through-LSD path.[469] I tried yoga, but only because Tony Horton told me to.[470]

I never tried mindfulness meditation until I started seeing the science coming out, demonstrating all of its positive effects on the brain. Mindfulness meditation:

- Reduces stress,[471] a key inhibitor of creativity, intelligence, learning and memory, and team performance;[472, 473, 474, 475]
- Reduces cognitive rigidity;[476]
- Improves visuo-spatial processing, working memory, executive functioning, and ability to sustain attention;[477]
- Decreases reactivity and increases response flexibility;[478]

---

[469] Although I have occasionally awoken with the gnawing feeling in my gut that I had come up with several brilliant ideas at the bar the night before, but I couldn't remember them, and I had no idea what I was trying to write on the cocktail napkin.

[470] If you've ever viewed any of the P90X exercise videos, you know that Tony is no contemplative monk.

[471] Paul Grossmana, Ludger Niemann, Stefan Schmidt, Harald Walach, "Mindfulness-based stress reduction and health benefits: A meta-analysis," *Journal of Psychosomatic Research,* July 2004.

[472] Reg Talbot, Cary Cooper and Steve Barrow, "Creativity and Stress," *Creativity and Innovation Management,* December 1992.

[473] Marie D. Sauro, Randall S. Jorgensena, and C. Teal Pedlowa, "Stress, Glucocorticoids, and Memory: A Meta-analytic Review," *The International Journal on the Biology of Stress,* December, 2003.

[474] Yuncai Chen, Céline M. Dubé, Courtney J. Rice, and Tallie Z. Baram, "Rapid Loss of Dendritic Spines after Stress Involves Derangement of Spine Dynamics by Corticotropin-Releasing Hormone," *The Journal of Neuroscience,* March 2008.

[475] Aleksander P. J. Ellis, "System Breakdown: The Role of Mental Models and Transactive Memory in the Relationship between Acute Stress and Team Performance," *Academy of Management Journal,* June 2006.

[476] Jonathan Greenberg, Keren Reiner and Nachshon Meiran, "Mind the Trap: Mindfulness Practice Reduces Cognitive Rigidity," *PLoS ONE,* May 15, 2012.

[477] Fadel Zeidan, Susan K. Johnson, Bruce J. Diamondc, Zhanna David, and Paula Goolkasian, "Mindfulness meditation improves cognition: Evidence of brief mental training," *Consciousness and Cognition,* June 2010.

[478] Daphne M. Davis and Jeffrey A. Hayes, "What are the benefits of mindfulness? A practice review of psychotherapy-related research," *Psychotherapy,* June 2011.

- Increases cognitive processing speed;[479]
- Improves emotional intelligence and alleviates negative mental health issues;[480]
- Improves team effectiveness and problem-solving efficiency;[481]
- Enhances capacity for strategic forecasting and futuring;[482]
- Increase capacity for perspective-taking and empathic concern.[483]

From an innovation standpoint, perhaps the most important effect is on your attention to what actually is, without your imagination getting in the way. You can be in the moment and fully attentive with your customers; you can experience your product or service as it is, not as you believe it ought to be. You can assess the reality of a situation with all the clarity of corrective lenses without the rosy filter of biased sunglasses. Mindfulness skills are effective innovation skills. And that's science for all you skeptics out there.

Okay, believers in mindfulness, you may rejoin us now.

Mindfulness can help break down cognitive biases, and focus on the reality of the present. Our expectations often get in the way of our experiences, creating filters that alter the experience before we have even had the chance to actually experience it. It can help us make connections by clarifying what really is possible, rather than being limited by mental constructs that post "road closed" signs to our otherwise free thinking.

So if mindfulness meditation is so powerfully positive, why doesn't everyone do it?

---

[479] Adam Moore and Peter Malinowski, "Meditation, mindfulness and cognitive flexibility," *Consciousness and Cognition*, January 2009.

[480] Li-Chuan Chu, "The benefits of meditation vis-à-vis emotional intelligence, perceived stress and negative mental health," *Stress and Health*, April 2010.

[481] Herbert S. Kindler, "The Influence of a Meditation Relaxation Technique on Group Problem-Solving Effectiveness," *The Journal of Applied Behavioral Science*, October 1979.

[482] Henning Breuer and Annette Gebauer, "Mindfulness for Innovation. Future Scenarios and High Reliability Organizing, Preparing for the Unforeseeable," *SKM Conference for Competence-based Strategic Management*, 2011, Linz, Austria.

[483] Jennifer Block-Lerner, Carrie Adair, Jennifer C. Plumb, Deborah L. Rhatigan and Susan M. Orsillo, "The case for mindfulness-based approaches in the cultivation of empathy: Does nonjudgmental, present-moment awareness increase capacity for perspective-taking and empathic concern?" *The Journal of Marital and Family Therapy*, October 2007.

We could just as easily ask why people don't quit smoking, why people don't eat a balanced diet, why people don't get enough exercise, why people drink too much even after experiencing the throbbing headache and room-spinning nausea of a wicked hangover, yada yada yada...

But let's continue to focus on mindfulness. In the US, at least, part of the problem has been a stigma associated with it. It's mystical, magical, new age hippie nonsense. People who wear blue suits, white shirts, and red ties do not put on tie-dyed tank tops, light up some incense, and chant "ooooooohhhhhhhmmmmmmm...."

Even those who are aware of and believe in the scientific evidence have to overcome the inertia of life habits that don't include meditation. It's hard enough to take thirty seconds to floss my teeth in the morning, let alone to set aside twenty minutes or more to just sit still and breathe.

We are a society that loves drive-through fast-food so that we can eat in our cars and throw away the paper bags, not "wasting" time on sitting at a table and getting dinnerware dirty, even if we have washing machines to clean it all. It's hurry, hurry, hurry, gotta get more done (at least until the next episode of *Breaking Bad*, *Game of Thrones*, or *Keeping Up with the Kardashians* comes on).

Or maybe we have legitimate fears about what it may do to us. What if this mindfulness stuff stifles my innovativeness? After all, part of it is accepting life as it is, in the moment. As an innovator, I want to change the world for the better in the future! If I become all calm and accepting of things as they are, won't that kill my drive to make things better?

Or what if we get so focused inwardly that we forget the very real troubles of the outside world? What if we forget our customers by becoming obsessive about our internal mind space? Isn't it selfish to be getting all wrapped up in ourselves when so many others need help?

Let's address these issues.

The Age of Aquarius Concern

Guess what? It is no longer 1973. Mindfulness, as of 2015, is mainstream in the Western World. Or at least well on the way to becoming so.

First came the scientific interest. When brain-scanning technology became a validated means of observing how the brain functions, and the dramatic differences in structure between a typical US citizen's brain and that of a Buddhist monk were seen, the research exploded. How could the way we think change our neurobiology in a physical way?

Exploring that question led to a host of other explorations. Thousands of studies have been done by seemingly every university for every application, from psychotherapy to heart health. Fortune 500 companies are establishing the practice officially in their wellness programs. Professional athletes and federal officials practice it.

It's not just for hippies anymore.

Not Enough Time in the Day

Efficiency and time-management guru Hyrum Smith[484] had a great response to those who would say they didn't have time for something. He'd say something like, "Brad, if you asked me to meet with you, and I said, 'Gosh Brad, I would really like to sit down and talk with you, but I don't have the time,' I would be lying to you. The truth of the matter is not that I don't have time, but that I value some other way to spend my time more than I value meeting with you."

Ouch.

There are 1440 minutes in every day. Even if you take out for things that are physically required for survival, like eating, drinking (water, that is), unmentionable bodily functions,[485] and sleeping, there are at least 840 minutes available. You have the time available. You can't honestly say that you don't have time. You can only say that you'd prefer to spend your time doing other things, like checking your *Words with Friends* app and wondering if "ZYQIX" is a real word. It would earn some killer points if it was.

---

[484] Creator of the *Franklin Day Planner*, back in the days when calendars were kept on paper.

[485] Does that count as mentioning the unmentionable?

Don't feel like you have to start right off the bat at twenty minutes. Even 3-5 minutes of informal mindfulness techniques have been shown to help.[486]

Look, I understand that other things are important. Work, childcare, relationships with loved ones, exercise, hygiene, recreation. It's not that nothing else is important. But if you made meditation a priority, you would find that there is time to meditate.[487]

And mindfulness meditation can create its own time, by improving your productivity. Recall how much multitasking inhibits our ability to function effectively. That's largely a result of an inability to focus on a task at hand. Mindfulness meditation improves focus.

Focus has been linked to improved productivity in a variety of ways,[488] including the ability to stick with solving problems longer, working effectively with other people, avoiding adverse emotional reactions, and...wait for it...being more innovative.[489] Professionals trained in mindfulness meditation have been shown to be better at staying on task and engaging in less switching between tasks.[490]

So you either have the time already, or you'll free the time up. No excuses.

Innovating Abilities

How about for innovation specifically? That is what this book is supposed to be about, after all. Well one study showed that mindfulness reduces cognitive rigidity,[491] which is the inability to consider alternatives to the current

---

[486] Shauna L. Shapiro, Doug Oman, Carl E. Thoresen, Thomas G. Plante and Tim Flinders, "Cultivating Mindfulness: Effects on Well-Being," *Journal of Clinical Psychology*, July 2008.

[487] Yes, I realize that applies to taking thirty seconds to floss my teeth, too. Stop using my own arguments against me. I hate that.

[488] Daniel Goleman, *Focus: The Hidden Driver of Excellence*, HarperCollins Publishers, 2013.

[489] I don't know if Goleman defines innovation with three circles, but if I see him, I'll ask.

[490] David M. Levy, Jacob O. Wobbrock, Alfred W. Kaszniak, and Marilyn Ostergren, "The Effects of Mindfulness Meditation Training on Multitasking in a High-Stress Information Environment," *Graphics Interface Conference*, Toronto, Ontario, 2012.

[491] Jonathan Greenberg, Keren Reiner, and Nachshon Meiran, "Mind the Trap": Mindfulness Practice Reduces Cognitive Rigidity," *PLoS One*, May 15, 2012.

situation, to take alternative viewpoints, or to creatively solve problems. Yeah, I think an innovator would like to reduce that.

Another study showed that mindfulness training improved insightful problem-solving,[492] with increased ability to identify contradictions, to break out of cognitive rigidity, to reframe problems, to improve attention, and to activate areas of the brain associated with learning. Nothing there that an innovator wouldn't want.

Lost in Self-Absorption

Although mindfulness meditation turns attention inward, it does not turn us into narcissists. In fact, quite the opposite is true. Mindfulness actually helps people to be more attuned to others.

Would it be helpful in your innovation efforts to be more attuned to customers? Uh, yeah.

Amazingly, the impact is not just in our ethereal thoughts, but in our very brain structures. The brain tissue in areas of the brain associated with learning and memory, regulating emotions, empathy, and the ability to take someone else's perspective, all become denser with mindfulness training.[493]

Going with the Flow

A phenomenon related to mindfulness is what psychologists call a state of "flow." Athletes will call it "being in the zone." Bill Russell, my all-time favorite basketball player, described the feeling like this:

> "Every so often a Celtics game would heat up so that it became more than a physical or even mental game, and would be magical...When it happened, I could feel my play rise to a new level. It came rarely, and would last anywhere from five minutes to a whole quarter, or more...At that special level, all

---

[492] Xiaoqian Ding, Yi-Yuan Tang, Chen Cao, Yuqin Deng, Yan Wang, Xiu Xin and Michael I. Posner, "Short-term meditation modulates brain activity of insight evoked with solution cue," *Social Cognitive & Affective Neuroscience*, January 2015.

[493] Britta K. Hölzel, James Carmody, Mark Vangel, Christina Congleton, Sita M. Yerramsetti, Tim Gard, and Sara W. Lazar, "Mindfulness practice leads to increases in regional brain gray matter density," *Psychiatry Research*, January 2011.

sorts of odd things happened: The game would be in the white heat of competition, and yet somehow I wouldn't feel competitive, which is a miracle in itself. I'd be putting out the maximum effort, straining, coughing up parts of my lungs as we ran, and yet I never felt the pain. The game would move so quickly that every fake, cut, and pass would be surprising, and yet nothing could surprise me. It was almost as if we were playing in slow motion. During those spells, I could almost sense how the next play would develop and where the next shot would be taken...My premonitions would be consistently correct, and I always felt then that I not only knew all the Celtics by heart, but also all the opposing players, and that they all knew me. There have been many times in my career when I felt moved or joyful, but these were the moments when I had chills pulsing up and down my spine."[494]

Ever had your innovation work cause chills to pulse up and down your spine? There is evidence that mindfulness increases an individual's ability to perform in a state of flow, and thereby have overall better performance.[495]

Flow is an essential component of the kind of creative problem solving that leads to innovation.[496] When innovators get into deep problem-solving mode, they have intense focus on their objective. The challenge they face is difficult, pushing the skills that they have to their limit. They enter a mental state in which their actions and their awareness are simultaneously focused on the task at hand; no daydreaming about how it's Taco Tuesday, or that latest episode of *Dance Moms*.

Time has no meaning when in a state of flow. Hours go by like minutes. Focus is so intense that external distractions go unseen and unheard. You

[494] William F. Russell and Taylor Branch, *Second Wind: The Memoirs of an Opinionated Man*, Random House, New York, NY, 1979.

[495] Ying Hwa Kee and C.K. John Wang, "Relationships between mindfulness, flow dispositions and mental skills adoption: A cluster analytic approach," *Psychology of Sport and Exercise*, July 2008.

[496] Mihaly Csikszentmihalyi, *Creativity: Flow and the Psychology of Discovery and Invention*, HarperCollins, 1997.

forget that you are hungry or thirsty. You forget the external world altogether...it's just your mind against the goal. The creative act itself becomes self-rewarding. It's not a means to an end, but an end in itself.

I love to research and write. Producing this book has involved me getting into intense states of flow at times. Four-, five-, and even six-hour stints, often late into the night and early hours of the morning, searching through available research, forming ideas, organizing thoughts, forming connections, typing furiously at my keyboard, deleting and rewriting, cutting and pasting, creating graphics to illustrate key points, and searching YouTube for classic TV videos. I'll emerge from such sessions both mentally and physically drained, similar to having gone on a long run.[497]

The point of all this quasi-mystical psychological story-telling is this: to maximize your innovative potential, and to maximize your team's innovative potential, you need to create the conditions for flow to take place.

It's not something that you can force. You can't tell everyone "hey team, I'm going to get into flow now...talk to you later!" You can't schedule a meeting with flow on your calendar.[498] But you can help to create the four conditions that allow flow to happen.[499]

First, clarify the objectives. The task needs to be clearly understood, with any necessary background information, both to help reinforce understanding, and to identify open questions for exploration. The task should have meaning, linked to the existing motivations of the team – in other words, linked to the mission that they support.[500]

Next, create an environment for immediate feedback. The flow state is engrossing, so the feedback needs to be a part of it. This is different than creating a prototype, sending it out to customers, and awaiting their response.

---

[497] Running is another activity that gets me into flow, but I'll save that for another book.

[498] You could, however, schedule time with either Tramar Lacel Dillard, the obnoxious waitress at Mel's Diner or the Progressive Insurance representative, but they are all "Flo." I'm talking about "flow," which is different.

[499] Mihaly Csikszentmihalyi, Sami Abuhamdeh, and Jeanne Nakamura, "Flow," *Handbook of Competence and Motivation*, edited by Andrew J. Elliot and Carol S. Dweck, Guilford Publications, 2005.

[500] For more about mission, see the chapter on "Mission," page 40

This is in-the-moment, providing real-time information needed for adjustments and course corrections.

In Bill Russel's case, he knew immediately if his shots went in, if he was positioned correctly for a rebound, or if he was able to block an opponent's shot without fouling. That's in-the-moment feedback, very different from the kind he would get from coach Red Auerbach the next day in practice.

In the creative process, the feedback is somewhat more challenging. You don't have a customer standing over your shoulder saying "wow!" and "ugh!" with every action you take or thought you express.

Creative flow requires innovators to be so immersed in the customer and business needs that they are capable of "internalizing the field's criteria of judgement to the extent that they can give feedback to themselves" in the moment, while in the state of flow.[501] That's not a substitute for later feedback from the business and customer, any more than Bill Russel's game-time feedback was a substitute for coaching and practice. They build on each other.

The third condition is matching the challenge to your capabilities. The challenge needs to be both difficult and meaningful (mission-oriented), while the skills and capabilities need to be up to the task. Figure 71 shows the balance required between the challenge and the skills. If the challenge is way beyond the capabilities to handle it, stress and anxiety occur. If the capabilities drastically exceed challenge, boredom, frustration and annoyance result.

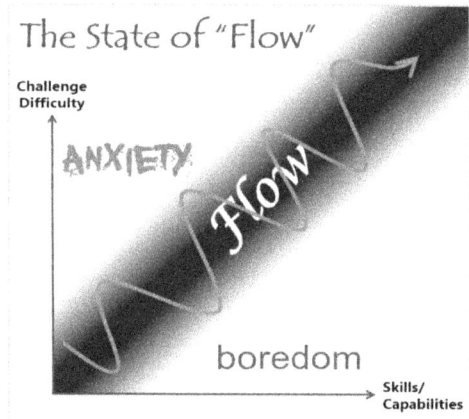

Figure 71: The state of flow comes when the difficulty of a challenge is roughly equal to the skills and capabilities of the individual. Creative growth follows a path that alternates between a little more stress and a little more relaxation, as skills grow to exceed challenges.

Growth in skills, abilities, and accomplishment occur in the space where challenge and abilities are similar. As the challenge is pushed just a little

---

[501] Mihaly Csikszentmihalyi, *Creativity: Flow and the Psychology of Discovery and Invention*, HarperCollins, 1997.

beyond the current capabilities, the innovator seeks out new knowledge and skills to compensate. As they become more adept with those skills, the challenge becomes easier. When the challenge is too easy, they pursue the next level of challenge, repeating the back-and-forth cycle.

The cycle roughly follows the four-stage learning model, a.k.a. the four stages of competence[502] (see Figure 72). At first, you don't know what you will need to know. Once you know what you don't know, you work at acquiring the knowledge you need. With practice, you learn to apply that knowledge and become adept at it, and with further practice, you get so good at it that you no longer have to even think about it.

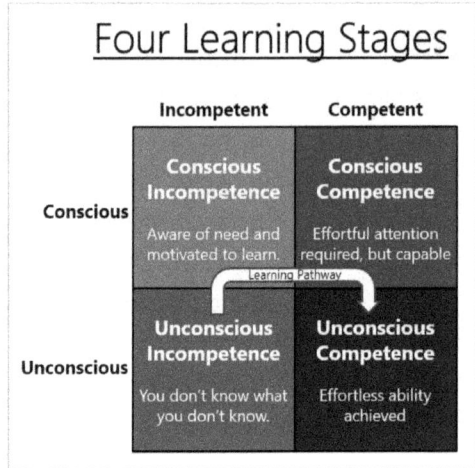

Figure 72: Four stages of learning, or four stages of competence. I wish I could credit the originator of this, but that is a known unknown.

The fourth condition for flow is the environment, which needs to have two opposing characteristics: one for stimulating novelty, and the other for undisturbed immersion in concentrated activity.

In most organizations, the former is much easier to get than the latter. Stimulation is all around us. Data is everywhere. The problem usually isn't insufficient stimulation as much as it is filtering the stimuli for relevance and meaning. The trick for having a stimulating environment is to have the right kind of stimulations...those that may lead to creative connections. Seek diversity. Meet new and interesting people. Go to museums, art events, movies, concerts. Read books outside of your normal area of interest. Get out of your office and work in a coffee shop, near a busy urban square, or at a park – wherever there is a variety of activity going on. Don't allow yourself to get in a mental rut.

---

[502] There are several claims to the original authorship of the four stages of competence model. If you invented it earlier than the late 1960's or early 1970's, please go to the Wikipedia page with proof and put an end to the debate.

The need for an immersive environment tends to be more of a challenge. Finding the physical space and time to separate yourself or your team from all the other obligations of life, whether personal or professional, is darn difficult. It is also darn valuable to creative problem-solving. It can happen anywhere,[503] but you need to have the opportunity to get into and sustain a state of flow for an extended period.

Organizations looking to raise their innovation capability should consider creating these opportunities, or at least allow their innovators to create them for themselves. Block off chunks of time devoted to solving creative problems, alone or in small teams. Schedule a long meeting with yourself so that the Microsoft Outlook calendar shows you as unavailable. Get yourself to a good thinking and action space (like Bill Russel on a basketball court or a surgeon in the OR, flow takes place while doing, not just thinking).

Earlier, I mentioned that I frequently got into flow while writing this book. There were also at least as many hours spent pushing to make progress without ever getting into flow. Times when every movement outside my window – squirrel![504] – would distract me. Times when contemplating items for the grocery list would occupy my mind, and the craving to binge watch episodes of *The Flash* felt like some mind-control super-villain drawing me toward the TV. By far the worst days were those when I had a series of conference calls or meetings dispersed throughout the day. I could never get into a rhythm, writing for an hour, talking on the phone for two, writing for 45 minutes, getting in the car to catch a train (and try to write for half an hour on the ride) to get downtown to meet with someone, then do the reverse to get back to writing.

Those were the least productive days of writing, by far.

---

[503] I once had a "eureka!" moment on how to solve the balancing-nails-on-a-single-nail-head problem (see it online at http://science.wonderhowto.com/how-to/do-you-balance-14-nails-single-nailhead-find-out-with-diy-gravity-puzzle-0138858/) while driving alone down a long stretch of highway, observing the shapes of telephone poles. I did not, however, figure out how to set the world record. Alexander Bendikov apparently has way too much time on his hands. And too many nails.

[504] If you have not seen the animated feature film *Up!*, you may be wondering why the heck the word "squirrel" suddenly appears in the middle of the text. It is the best illustration of silly distraction that I know. See it online at https://www.youtube.com/watch?v=xrAIGLkSMls.

The times I got into flow were those when I was able to balance stimulation and immersion. I have a "thinking chair" where I can sit, with all of my innovation resources (books, journals, magazines galore) within arm's reach. There, I found that I was able to get totally absorbed in the task, creating for hours until my mental gas tank ran empty. When the chair wasn't working, I became indebted to several public libraries, coffee shops, and restaurants for letting me sit in their chairs and occupy a portion of their WiFi bandwidth.

Those days, the words seemed to simply appear on my laptop screen. Pictures and captions came together. One journal article would lead to several other journal articles, all with relevance and insight that were connected and impactful on the text.

I learned to use the busy-with-other-things days for stimulation. Talking with other innovators, working with organizations on their innovation systems, networking with people in fields I didn't know existed (I knew there were dating services, and I knew there was relationship counseling, but I didn't realize there were relationship discovery coaches), reading books and magazines unrelated to innovation and product development. Running, stair climbing, and exercising.[505]

Keeping innovation teams in the "flow zone"[506] helps them to not only solve problems creatively now, but to build the capacity to solve bigger problems in the future. This is why having experienced people on a team drives faster and more effective innovation outcomes.[507] They simply get better at it. Give them the four things they need – clear goals, deep grounding in market needs to enable self-feedback, matching of task to capabilities, and a balanced stimulation/immersion environment – and watch them innovate better and faster.

---

[505] Please exercise. It's a great way to get your brain fit. Carl W. Cotman, Nicole C. Berchtold, and Lori-Ann Christie, "Exercise builds brain health: key roles of growth factor cascades and inflammation," Trends in Neurosciences, September 2007.

[506] No, the earth does not have a flow-zone layer with a formerly-growing-but-now-shrinking hole in it over Antarctica. That's different.

[507] Nagaraj Sivasubramaniam, S. Jay Liebowitz and Conway L. Lackman, "Determinants of New Product Development Team Performance: A Meta-analytic Review," Journal of Product Innovation Management, September 2012.

Nothing Worthwhile Comes Easy

So, is it worth twenty minutes a day for these benefits – real, tangible, professional benefits? Just 2% of your waking hours? Less time than a single episode of *Innovations with Ed Begley, Jr.*?

Yes, it is.

But there is still one reason that you may not want to do it.

It is not easy.

Our minds are like a muddy river, with tons of thought-silt floating and churning within the chaotic flow of our thoughts. When I first started meditating, I thought "What? Count my breaths? How hard can that be?" It took me a long time to make it to ten breaths without some thought or another distracting me.

"I need to make sure that I add yogurt to my grocery list."

"Oh jeez, I forgot to call Pat back."

"My toes are cold."

"Squirrel!"

Sometimes I'd count to ten, and realize that I was counting, but not actually paying any attention to my breathing. I'd make it to 27 and realize that I hadn't actually tied a number to any breath I had taken since number two.

And then I'd get mad at myself. Frustrated with myself. And that defeated the purpose of the meditation.

I may be more easily distractible than most, but I don't think so. This story seems to be a common experience for many beginners. I'm still a beginner, and the story still rings true. Sticking with something that is difficult and frustrating takes commitment, perseverance, support, and a firm belief in the ultimate benefits.

But if people can do that with the game of golf, they can do it with mindfulness. Give it a go. You won't regret it.

Simple Study Guide – The Mental Game of Innovation

- How can you simplify your decision-making?
- What are "cognitive biases"?
- Which cognitive biases are the most likely to hurt innovation efforts?
- How can you overcome cognitive biases?
- How do DeBono's Six Thinking Hats work?
- What is wrong with multitasking?
- What is an attitude of an innovator?
- What does it mean to be "pi-shaped?"
- What social dangers do innovators need to be able to handle?
- What are the benefits of mindfulness?
- What is "flow" and why should you want to be in it?

Where do you want to go from here?

Control	Creation	Conversion
Mission (page 40)	Voice of the Customer (page 175)	Innovation Teams (page 310)
Culture (page 58)	Minds of Innovators (page 217)	Project Management (page 347)
Strategy (page 92)	Ideation (page 279)	For-Profit Metrics (page 389)
Portfolio Management (page 146)		Nonprofit Metrics (page 403)
Change Management (page 411)		

Or just turn the page to keep reading...

The Ugly Truth of the Miracle of Birth (Ideation)

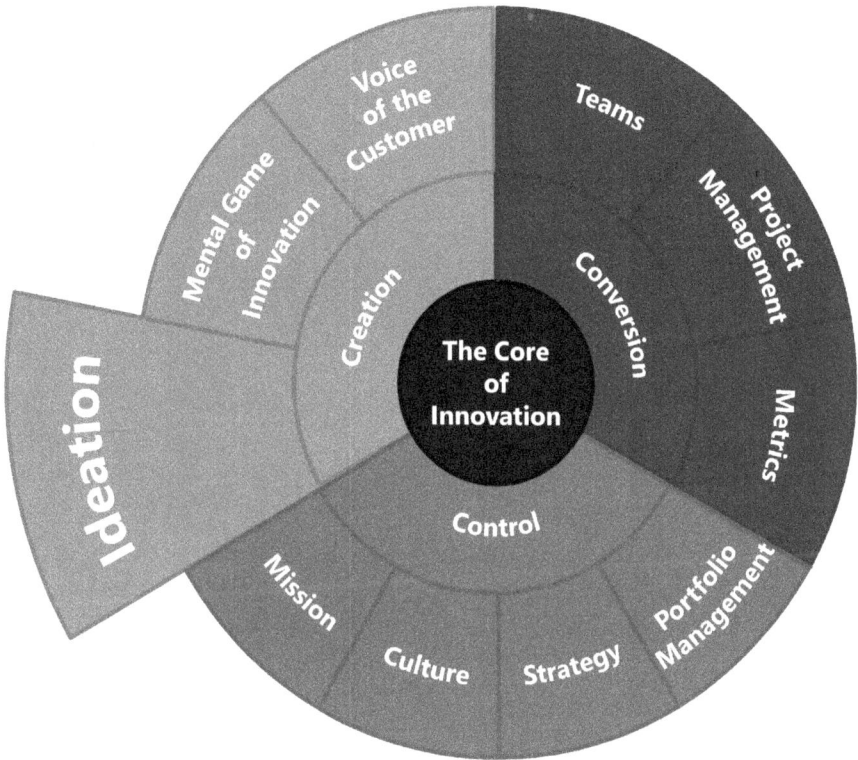

Simple Self-Assessment - Ideation

Rate yourself on the following questions. To benchmark yourself against others, go to www.3point14Innovation.com and click the "Self-Assessments" menu.

- ### How much ownership do people in your organization feel for innovation?

  That's somebody else's problem   Like proud parents

1	2	3	4	5	6	7	8	9	10

- ### How willing are people in your organization to accept hard feedback?

  Everyone wears ear plugs   Like brave soldiers under fire

1	2	3	4	5	6	7	8	9	10

- ### How often do "pet" projects linger in the organization?

  We could run a pet adoption agency   "No pets allowed" sign at the door

1	2	3	4	5	6	7	8	9	10

- ### Do you do much brainstorming in your organization?

  Only when we need great ideas   No, it's useless

1	2	3	4	5	6	7	8	9	10

- ### How does your organization treat features on products?

  The more the merrier!   Keep 'em focused and few

1	2	3	4	5	6	7	8	9	10

- ### Do you seek unique ideas with people outside of your immediate field?

  What do they know?   Sure, they have a unique perspective

1	2	3	4	5	6	7	8	9	10

- ### Do you have a formal process for selecting the ideas you generate?

  We throw darts at them   A structured group process

1	2	3	4	5	6	7	8	9	10

- ***How much do you think through a product's value proposition?***

A value what?

We consider all
the costs and benefits

1	2	3	4	5	6	7	8	9	10

- ***Do you create concept statements to communicate and test your ideas?***

We don't need
to test our ideas

We do it all the time

1	2	3	4	5	6	7	8	9	10

Simple Summary – Ideation

Key take-aways you should get out of this section:

- Many people, if not most, feel a high level of ownership for their ideas. That can be good, because they are devoted to making the ideas work. Unfortunately, it also tends to make them resistant to feedback, change, and outside efforts to improve the ideas.
- One of the things that will make any idea ugly is feature creep. That occurs when features are added and added to the product until it looks like an absurd Swiss army knife. Adding features complicates the product, and can actually make it *less* usable, not more. Better to keep it simple and focused.
- Bringing in outside viewpoints during the ideation process can be very valuable. Outsiders should have some related knowledge, but not necessarily specific knowledge in your field.
- When thinking of ideas, start with customer problems. Focus all the attention on solving problems for the customer, not on the products you currently produce.
- Classic brainstorming – putting a bunch of people in a room to vocalize ideas – has been repeatedly proven to be a lousy way to generate ideas. Individuals generate more and higher quality ideas than groups. Use ideation methods that leverage the thinking of individuals, like brainwriting. If you want to take advantage of people building on each other's ideas, adapt the technique to let the idea building take place individually. The group environment inevitably shuts off the flow of good ideas.
- For generating wilder ideas, use the heuristic ideation technique. It's guaranteed to push the creative limits of ideas. The SCAMPER technique can also jog some creative thoughts that may not come out in typical problem-solving ideation.
- TRIZ, or the theory of inventive problem solving, presents a promising set of tools for generating inventive solutions to problems. The contradiction matrix and the patterns of technical evolution are particularly powerful tools.
- Creating a formal value proposition helps to think through all of the end-to-end benefits and costs that a customer would experience with your product. In so doing, it can help identify areas in which you can increase the overall value to the customer, either

through reducing the costs they experience or through increasing the benefits they receive.

- A concept statement is a simple way to capture the essence of a product idea, and communicate it to customers for their feedback. The feedback received can then be incorporated into further development and refinement of the idea.

Barbed-Wire Babies

I was born in that strange era where doctors believed that women didn't know how to properly give birth. Even though they had been doing it just fine for thousands of years, there was this short period of a couple of decades, where medicine's conventional wisdom was that women were, apparently, doing it all wrong.

When I was born, my mom was knocked out cold with anesthesia. My dad sat in a waiting room with a handful of cigars to pass out once the birthing procedures were all over. There was no shared experience in the miracle of birth between mother, father, and child. There were no controlled breathing exercises. No tears of pain turned to tears of joy when the baby was laid in its mother's arms.

Instead, there was a nurse who came out to the waiting room. "Mr. Barbera, you have a son."

My dad went to the window, expecting to see this beautiful thing that he and his beloved bride had wanted for so long.

Instead, he saw newborn me.

As he is fond of telling me, I was not pretty. My face was contorted and wrinkly. My head was bald. My skin was a blotchy mix of red and blueish white. "You looked like you had been beaten with barbed wire," he tells me on any occasion that seems appropriate – like my birthday, or when I bring a girlfriend over to meet the folks.

And that is what newborn innovations are like.

Innovation, like comedy, is not pretty.[508]

That may sound funny, but it is important to understand. We must recognize that newborn innovations are unfinished lumps of clay, not finished works of art.

Why is that so important to emphasize? Two reasons. First, by the time we see new innovations reach the marketplace, what we see are the finished, polished, buffed-with-a-fine-chamois versions. The versions that have been designed, tested, refined, retested, and re-refined.

---

[508] An important lesson from comedian Steve Martin, the original wild and crazy guy.

We rarely see or even hear rumors about the number of trees sacrificed to wadded-up pieces of graph paper covered with ugly pencil sketches. No one speaks of the arguments, frustrations, fears, and stupidities experienced by the creators in the process of creating. We don't hear about the disdainful mockery thrown at prototypes when they are first offered to test users for feedback.

I will never forget the words of feedback I read when a customer evaluated a packaging change that I helped to execute: "What kitchen-ignorant idiot of an engineer thought that this was a good idea?!?"

And that's just for changing the lid on a mayonnaise jar. Imagine if it was something really important.

It's not just kitchen-ignorant idiot engineers who go through the ugly process of innovation. It's everyone. Even the most consistently successful geniuses in their business go through it.

Take Pixar, for example. They have never failed to produce a hit when they've released a feature film. Yet Ed Catmull, President of Pixar, says that "early on, all of our movies suck. That's a blunt assessment, I know, but I choose that phrasing because saying it in a softer way fails to convey how bad the first versions really are. I'm not trying to be modest or self-effacing. Pixar films are not good at first, and our job is to make them so—to go, as I say, 'from suck to not-suck.'"[509]

This is a natural part of the creative process. As I first wrote this book, I thought I was typing out some good stuff. Then I went through the review and editing process. I can't count the number of times I stopped and said "that sucks." My baby was ugly. Even after rewriting, and re-editing, I found errors, typos, poorly stated ideas, and even outright blunders. I could relate to the feeling expressed by James Michener: "I'm not a very good writer, but I'm an excellent rewriter."[510] Well, at least I can relate to the first half of it.

---

[509] Ed Catmull, (2014) *Creativity, Inc.*, as quoted in *Fast Company*, April 2014.

[510] Two things: that's an internet quote that I could not verify, so take that for what it's worth. Second, if you are thinking to yourself "Brad, you aren't even a good rewriter," well, I'll take that under advisement, then do my Stuart Smalley affirmations to recover. Maybe this isn't the best writing, but that's...okay. See Stuart perform his success affirmations with Michael Jordan online at https://screen.yahoo.com/daily-affirmation-michael-jordan-000000862.html.

When you try to innovate, your innovation baby is going to go through a beaten-with-barbed–wire stage, too. Don't take it personally; it's just part of the process. You need to be aware that all innovation babies are ugly, because when that baby is yours, there is a good chance that you won't be able to see that it is ugly.

All parents think that their baby's face belongs in a Gerber ad. Part of our mental wiring is devoted to blinding us to seeing anything but the most precious, adorable, lovable thing that ever existed. Had evolution not built that in, sleep deprivation alone would lead parents to throw their babies in a box stamped "Return: Defective." That would not be good for the survival of our species.

Your innovations can become your babies. If you take the slightest pride in your work, the littlest bit of ownership in

Figure 73: Me, after I stopped looking quite so barbed-wire beaten. I'm the one without the big yellow ears.

what you produce, you will become attached to your creation. You will see all the potential good that it will bring to the world, and imagine the future accolades it will receive.

It will be hard to hear the actual feedback that you will inevitably get.

Be ready for it.

Don't let that worry you too much, though. Eventually, even I stopped looking like I had received the barbed wire beat down, and became your typical baby cute enough not to be placed in a box. My parents no longer had to tie a pork chop around my neck to get the dog to play with me. Your innovation eventually won't need the pork chop, either.

What Makes Your Baby Ugly

Newborn innovations are ugly because they are not fully formed. They are all possibility with no reality. They are like a Mr. Potato Head with disjointed parts in a pile next to a brown lumpy potato.

Pretty soon,[511] arms are poking out where the eyes were meant to be, shoes are being worn on the ears, and I can't bring myself to say where the lips have been placed. It's a hot mess. But your kid is laughing to the point of tears over it, so you let it go. After they go to sleep, you can pretty it up all you want.

Your innovation is going to experience much that will turn it into the equivalent of the shoe-eared potato. It will take time, experimentation, creative problem solving, and feedback listening skills to get it presentable to anyone outside the family.

Here are three things that can be particularly detrimental to your baby's cuteness. Watch out for them.

Making Pet Rocks

With all due respect to Gary Ross Dahl,[512] in the world of innovation, pet rocks are ugly.

Recall that pet rocks are those things that have novelty, can be executed effectively, but are either useless, or their cost is so out of proportion with their value that no one who could pass a sobriety test would ever want one.

Pet rocks make me sad. These are frequently the inventions of people who can't see that their baby is ugly. I've had to inform many such people in my career that such is the case with their babies. It's never fun.

One inventor in particular stands out in my mind. He had an invention that he felt would fit within a product line my company sold. It didn't.

The invention provided a modest consumer benefit, but not one that couldn't be provided in a number of other ways. But that wasn't why the baby was ugly. In order for someone to use it, he expected them to drill half a dozen holes in their family room furniture to install it.

---

[511] Especially if you have that creative kind of kid that doesn't like to follow directions or make the toy look like the picture on the box. By the way, those are the kids that grow up to be innovators.

[512] Creator of the pet rock fad in the 1970's. May he rest in peace.

Now, even if people felt okay with holes in their furniture (they generally don't), it was going to be a DIY assembly challenge beyond the skills of even the most adept IKEA customer.

When gently provided that feedback, with suggestions on further development possibilities to overcome those challenges, the inventor replied with, "no, I've considered that, and it works better my way."

That was many years ago. The product, to my knowledge, has never seen the marketplace. The ugly baby never grew up.

Chasing Unicorns

In the fantasy world, unicorns are beautiful. In the innovation world, they are not.

Unicorns, those novel ideas that would have great value, if only they could be executed in reality. As a sales friend of mine once told me (an engineer), "if you could make half the stuff I've sold, we'd be rich!"

Usually, unicorns do not come in the form of requiring time travel devices or anti-gravity engines. They are not that obviously impossible. Rather, they come in the form of over-promised benefits that end up being under-delivered. Let's say you are making a hair tonic to regrow hair on a bald head. You have discovered a chemical that causes a thousand hair follicles to suddenly sprout thin little hairs on an average head. That's an incredible achievement, and technically, you can say that your product regrows hair on a bald head.[513] But you won't sell much of it when customers start looking like they have a fungus on their heads instead of hair.

Products don't just need to meet technical requirements. They need to satisfy customer requirements. Remember, perception is reality.[514] If you can't deliver the perception, it's just a unicorn.

---

[513] At least you could if you got the FDA to agree to it.

[514] For more about customer perceptions, go to the "Perception is Reality" section of the Voice of the Customer chapter, page 176.

The Creep from the Black Lagoon

Here's one more thing that makes your innovation baby ugly: feature creep. No, that's not the monster of a 1950's B-movie horror classic. It means adding unnecessary features and benefits to the point that the innovation becomes a pain in the keester.

For example, I have a friend whose house was apparently owned by a light switch aficionado before she moved in.[515] There is a switch for every light bulb. Not just for every room, but for practically every last bulb in the room. And I swear, almost every switch in the house is different.

One is just a plain, flat, metallic pad that is touch-sensitive, so it doesn't actually depress when you push it. In one bedroom, the switch has four separate buttons. In the bedroom next door, there are three.

Some of the switches look like miniature versions of a *Star Trek* transporter control panel. There is a sliding bar on one side for brightness level, a toggle switch for on and off at the bottom, and a set of seven LED lights to tell you how bright or dim the lights connected to that switch should be (in case you can't tell by how bright or dim the lights actually are). I'm afraid I'm going to get beamed into the Romulan neutral zone if I touch anything on these things.

Some switches have dimmer sliders split in half, with one side operating the lights of one room, and the other side operating the lights of a different room. Some switches even have – and I could not possibly make this up on my own – a switch for the switch. Yep. There is a little switch that turns on or off the bigger switch that turns on or off the lights. How is it that I, as a five-decade light switch user, have never experienced the need for a switch to my light switch? Ever?!?

Every one of those switches ultimately "works," in the sense that they give you a dizzying level of control over which lightbulb will glow at what brightness level and for how long. But that's not what I want. I just want to be able to walk into a room and see.

House lighting, like innovation, ought to be simple.

---

[515] Thank you, Lisa Coughlin, for providing this example...and for the non-stop support you provided as I wrote this book!

We are all prone to feature creep. We say to ourselves, "Hey wouldn't it be cool if we could do that, too?" We end up with office chairs that require a licensed technician to adjust in 473 different ways, when all we want is to be able to sit comfortably while we work. We end up with television remote controls that have 46 buttons on them, and they still can't control the DVD player (which has its own remote control with 45 buttons). All I want to do is watch the annual Puppy Bowl on Animal Planet, and I have to press more buttons than I'd need to gain entry to the highest-security wing of CIA headquarters.[516]

I'm reminded of what my friend once said to me when I was wearing some old and outdated pants. Sure they were old, but I figured that if they still fit, they'd look okay. "Hey, I can still fit in these," I said.

"Brad," he said, "just because you *can*, doesn't mean you *should*."

The same is true for your innovations. Just because you can do something, doesn't mean you should do it. Focus. Focus on delivering what the customer wants in the way that they want it. And that's it.

"Keep innovation simple" applies not only to how you do it, but to what you do. Use design thinking[517] to solve problems in simple, human-centered ways, that don't require adding new features. "Perfection," as Antoine de Saint Exupéry so eloquently put it,[518] "is not achieved when there is nothing more to add, but rather when there is nothing left to take away."

Helping Baby Grow Up to Be Pretty

It may be possible to modify pet rocks to have real value for someone. It takes thick skin,[519] but if you can accept the early criticism, without taking it

---

[516] Note to any agents of the CIA, FBI, NSA, A.R.G.U.S. or S.H.I.E.L.D. – that was just a colorful metaphor. I don't actually know how many buttons I'd need to push to gain access to the highest security wing of Langley. Please don't raid my home looking for national security documents.

[517] For more on design thinking, go to the "Design Thinking" section of the Voice of the Customer chapter, page 182.

[518] Except he put it in French.

[519] For more about thick skin, thick skulls, and other necessary anatomical characteristics of innovators, see the "Thinking of Innovators" section of the Mental Game of Innovation chapter, page 250.

personally, and without rejecting it out of hand, the baby has a chance to grow up to be pretty.

It may be possible to bring unicorns into the real world, like the Wright brothers making "impossible" heavier-than-air flight possible. Technical hurdles can be overcome, new technologies developed, organizational capabilities advanced.

Feature creep can be overcome, with relentless focus on the customer problem to be solved, and with the discipline to do what you should, and don't do what you can, but shouldn't.

The successful innovator will remember that the parenting role for an innovation is not to make cute babies, but rather to help ugly babies grow up to be healthy and productive citizens of the organization and its market space.

It Takes a Village

There are two conflicting myths that different people believe about who should be involved in generating ideas.

One follows the saying, "Experience is the mother of wisdom" (or, as P.J. O'Rourke put it in a book title, "age and guile beat youth, innocence, and a bad haircut"). The belief is that you should have people who are thoroughly familiar with the customer and their needs, pain points and objectives. Such experts are best able to create solutions because they best understand the problems. If you want to solve an advanced calculus problem, you ask a mathematician. If you are struggling to write a good bridge for your latest song, you seek out another musician. Developers of the internet were digital computing experts, not Al Gore.

The other says the opposite. This group follows the advice of Robert Heinlein: "Always listen to experts. They'll tell you what can't be done and why. Then do it." The best ideas come from people who are not mired in the status quo. Experts are too close to the trees to see the forest. If you ask an expert, you'll just get your problem solved the same way it's always been solved. You won't get real innovation. Experts are too mired in the way things are to be able to see the way things could be. Just look at the Wright Brothers, a couple of bicycle repair boys, who beat the well-funded expert, Samuel Pierpont Langley, to heavier-than-air flight.

Both views are myths. And, both have some truth to them.

To solve a problem, you have to understand the problem. And some level of expertise is required to understand the problem. Random ideas are never the precursors to innovations.

A level of expertise is necessary to deliver the solution, too. Product delivery doesn't just happen. It requires planning and coordination.

But habits are hard to break, and when a particular type of problem has been approached in a particular way for a long time, it can become entrenched as the "right" way to solve it. As the old saying goes, when you have a hammer, every problem looks like a nail.

Outsiders, though, can indeed have a fresh perspective. By coming at it from different directions, wildly new solutions may come up. Experts in the field will either smack themselves in the head and say "why didn't I think of that?" or worse – they will sometimes continue to fight against the new solution. Remember Theodoric of York?[520] When you believe in an imbalance of the humors, you're going to keep prescribing a lot of bleedings.

But outsiders can also give you two things that are of little value – dumb looks and bad ideas. Because they lack expertise, frequently they may greet your questions with that look you get when someone is rapidly speaking a language that you don't understand. You're afraid to even nod your head, for fear of discovering that you just agreed to sit through one of those time share presentations for a hotel in a country you're not sure even existed when you were in school studying those kinds of things.

And contrary to popular belief, there are bad ideas in brainstorming. Lots of 'em. And when the people doing the brainstorming don't understand the topic at hand, you get even more of 'em. Expecting someone with no knowledge in your field to give you the breakthrough idea you've been looking for is like expecting a three-year old to solve the problem of interstellar space flight.

The trick is to reject, and embrace, both myths. How? By bringing experts together with outsiders from related, similar fields. How you define "related" or "similar" is up to you, and open to interpretation, but make sure there is

---

[520] If you don't, he was first discussed on page 62. Check out the footnotes there to find where you can see him online.

some sort of relatedness. The more distant relations, the more radical the ideas you may get, but the greater the risk of getting nothing of value.

Research on safety equipment, for example, had carpenters, roofers, and in-line skaters generating ideas for improving the safety and comfort of each other's equipment. Each group was better at coming up with novel solutions for the other two groups than for their own products. And the bigger the dissimilarity, the more novel the solutions – for example, the in-line skaters came up with more novel solutions for carpenters than the roofers did.[521]

Now, "more novel" may or may not mean "better." That's where the experts in the field come in. These experts must be open-minded enough to consider even the most novel solutions, but must also be competent enough in their domain to recognize good solutions.

The best guide is to "never become so much of an expert that you stop gaining expertise. View life as a continuous learning experience. You must continue to gain expertise, but avoid thinking like an expert."[522]

Forget Brainstorming – Generate Good Ideas Instead

To be successful in selecting your innovation efforts, you need to be able to get the organization thinking in two opposite directions: divergent and convergent. Divergent thinking allows you to explore a wide variety of potential options, while convergent thinking allows you to select and focus on the most valuable ideas that you can actually get done.

You've probably been involved in a brainstorming session. That's when you lock a group of people in a room, tell them there are no bad ideas, and then start writing down whatever they say. Or at least the stuff that is fit to print.

An hour later, you leave the room with a half dozen bad ideas, file them appropriately in the nearest shredder, then go back to doing what you were doing before the brainstorming interruption.

The only thing accomplished in this stereotypical form of brainstorming is that all participants were distracted from any chance of achieving a state of

---

[521] Marion Poetz, Nikolaus Franke, and Martin Schreier, "Sometimes the Best Ideas Come from Outside Your Industry," *Harvard Business Review*, November 2014.

[522] Attributed to Denis Waitly, author of *The Psychology of Winning*, Penguin Group Incorporated, 1995.

flow, productivity was reduced for the day, and the innovation team ended up frustrated by the dearth of ideas to work on next. And you probably ate a doughnut or cookie that would require an extra 2000 steps to be recorded on your Fitbit.

Traditional brainstorming does not work.[523] It hasn't ever worked.[524]

Individuals generate more and better ideas than groups. Social dynamics in groups conspire to prevent innovative ideas from emerging. This is one area in which the evidence is unequivocal. I may not label anything a "best practice," but I think traditional brainstorming can officially be labeled a "worst practice."

One researcher concluded, "The evidence from science suggests that business people must be insane to use brainstorming groups." But people continue to do it, perhaps because they don't know of other ways. Or maybe they actually are insane.

So now, no more excuses. Stop the madness. Here are some better ways to generate innovation ideas.

Brainwriting

Brainwriting takes advantage of being an individual idea generating technique, while also taking advantage of the one potential positive of group ideation: the ability for people to build on each other's ideas.[525]

A group will start with each individual having a grid to complete. The grid lists the problem to be solved[526] at the top, with boxes for entering individual ideas for solutions beneath.

---

[523] Gary R. Schirr, "Flawed Tools: The Efficacy of Group Research Methods to Generate Customer Ideas," *Journal of Product Innovation Management*, May 2012.

[524] Ibid. Brainstorming was first proposed in 1957, with the claim that more and higher-quality ideas could be generated by a brainstorming group than by individuals. By 1958, that was already demonstrated to be false. But the guy who came up with brainstorming was an advertising exec, and was better at getting his ideas into mainstream heads than were the researchers who proved him wrong. And over a half-century later, we are still suffering the ill effects.

[525] Note that this is only a potential advantage – when done in an open group discussion format, it still tends to squash both the quantity and quality of ideas. The actual idea generation, recording, and evaluation should always be done individually.

[526] For more on defining problems effectively, see the "Defining a Problem is Hard" section of the Voice of the Customer chapter, page 185.

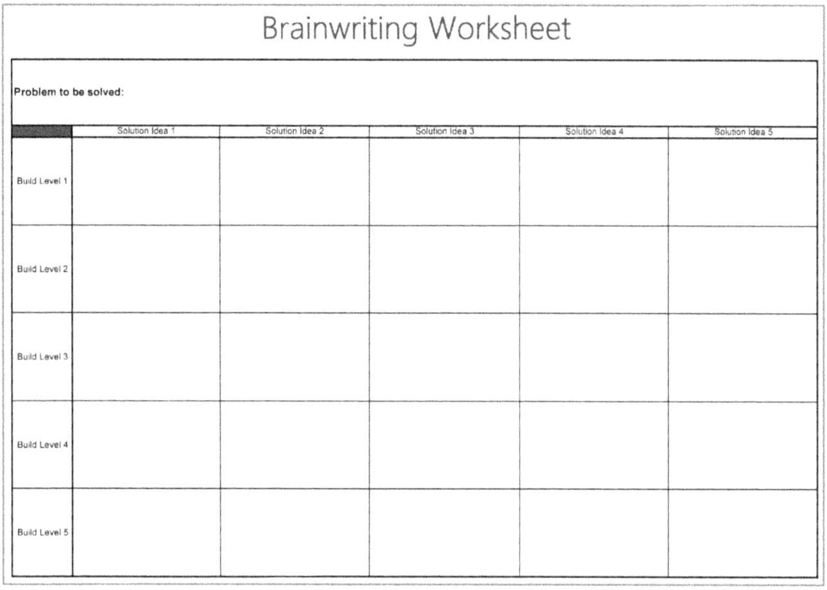

Figure 74: The brainwriting grid used at Pi Innovation. Other formats are possible. But I like this one.

Participants are given a set amount of time, say five minutes, to generate and record whatever ideas they can to solve the problem.

At the end of the allotted time, they pass their grid to the next person, and receive someone else's grid. They then can either add their own new ideas, or build on previous ideas from an earlier person. The process continues for a few rounds, between four and eight, depending on the number of people trying to generate ideas.

If you are doing this kind of session on paper, it's probably most efficient to have everyone in one room. If that's the case, make sure to keep everyone quiet. It's the talking part that makes groups bad at coming up with good ideas.

You can also do this remotely, with the grids electronically passed from one person to another. This may take some training, coordination, and discipline for the team to stick to time limits, send the grids to each other in proper sequence, etc. But at least you don't have to worry about group conversations.

Heuristic Ideation Technique (HIT)

No, the acronym does not indicate that violence is involved. This technique is just a fancy way of saying that ideas are generated by referencing random attributes, then coming up with solutions that have those attributes. It probably sounds harder than it actually is. Trust me, it's simple. And it can be

HIT Idea Stimulator

Problem to be solved:

	Thing 1:				
Characteristics	1)	2)	3)	4)	5)
1)					
2)					
3)					
4)					
5)					

(left axis: Thing 2:)

Figure 75: the HIT format used at Pi Innovation. Note that "Thing 1" and "Thing 2" are not the characters from Dr. Seuss' *The Cat in the Hat*.

fun. And it can really push the bounds of novelty in the solutions that are generated.

Perhaps this can best be explained with an example.

Starting with a clear problem statement, a moderator will guide the group through a quick set-up. First, they name two things. Random things. No need to be related to the company, the industry, the market, or anything else. It's probably best to get away from those things for the sake of novelty, anyway.

Then the group identifies 4-5 attributes for the first thing, whatever it may be. Let's say, "tree." Attributes of a tree might include "hard," "light-sensitive," "green," "burnable," "deciduous."[527] Repeat for the second thing, let's say "Dog." Attributes of a dog might be "furry," "playful," "fast," "cuddly," "distractible."[528]

Each of the attributes is listed out, across the top for thing 1, and down the side for thing 2. Now, each square in the grid is the intersection of two attributes. For example, one square would be at the intersection of deciduous and distractible. The moderator then challenges individuals to look for solutions to the problem that would have both of those attributes.

If I was doing this exercise for this book, with those two attributes, I could come up with the idea of a book loaded with distracting footnotes and updated annually with all of the latest research and customer feedback/input included. Hey, that just might work...

Not all of the boxes will prove productive. I can't come up with anything for my book in the "furry and green" category. That's okay. If you can't think of anything, just move on. When the whole grid dries up, start over with a new problem, new things, new attributes. Continue until tired, bored, frustrated, hungry, or called by nature out of the room.

I will admit, that I used to do this exercise as a group technique. But the research is just too clear to continue that way. Each individual should have their own grid, and generate ideas within it. If there is time for exchanging and building, as in the brainwriting method, give it a try. But have the ideas generated, recorded, and evaluated individually.

SCAMPER

This technique can help to stimulate ideas based on attributes of an existing product. Again, start with a statement of the problem to be solved. Next, outline the various parts of the goods or services that you want to change or improve.

---

[527] I was writing this section as I looked out at the changing colors of autumn, which made me reach deep back into the biology class vocabulary compartment of my mind for the "deciduous" attribute.

[528] Squirrel! (https://www.youtube.com/watch?v=xrAIGLkSMls)

SCAMPER Ideation Worksheet

Problem to be solved:

Parts of Existing Product or Service:
(Could be people, order of events, materials, components, features, processes, etc.)

	Solution Idea Format	Solution Idea 1	Solution Idea 2	Solution Idea 3
Substitute	If we substitute *[new part]* for *[existing part]*, we could deliver *[valuable benefit]* for *[beneficiary]*			
Combine	If we combine *[existing part]* with *[existing part]*, we could deliver *[valuable benefit]* for *[beneficiary]*			
Adapt	If we adapt *[existing part]* to do *[different or additional function]*, we could deliver *[valuable benefit]* for *[beneficiary]*			

Figure 76: A SCAMPER technique worksheet. Only the top half is shown, but I think you can figure out how the bottom looks.

Let the SCAMPER acronym stimulate thoughts about how the physical product or service could be changed. The "M" and the "R" both stand for two things each. In the past, I've seen this presented as the SCAMMPERR technique. That may be more memorable, but it just seems so inelegant. I'll stick with SCAMPER.

S is for "Substitute." What could be substituted for some part of the product? Let's say you are Amazon, and you are thinking of your delivery system. You go through this technique, and you say "hey, I bet we could substitute drones for US Postal Workers!" Sorry, USPS folks. I don't think they meant it personally.

C is for "Combine." What parts might be combined into one, while still serving the functions required for the customer? My favorite example: the spork. No explanation required.

A is for "Adapt." Ask yourself what existing part could be adapted to do some other function, or what ideas from other places could be adapted to your situation. Henry Ford adapted the Chicago slaughterhouse processes to building cars by assembly line.

M is for either "Modify" or "Magnify" and "Minify." Personally, I like leaving it at just modify, but some find it helpful to think in terms of size changes. The Big Bertha golf driver dramatically increased the size of the club head to improve distance and accuracy. The Motorola Razr dramatically reduced the thickness of cell phones.

P is for "Purpose." Can some part of the product serve a new or different purpose? The exteriors of public transportation buses and trains have been repurposed as mobile billboards, decorated with a variety of advertising.

E is for "Eliminate." What part of your product can you completely get rid of? Automated Teller Machines (ATMs) eliminated the need for customers to fill out forms and visit a teller to withdraw funds from their accounts.

R is for either "Reverse or Rearrange." Could you do things in a different order, rearranging the parts? Typically, a restaurant has their customers sit, order, get food, eat, pay. McDonalds rearranged the process, having people order, pay, get food, sit, eat. The original Volkswagen Beetle rearranged the engine by locating it in the rear of the car, providing good traction and acceleration while keeping the overall weight to a minimum.

TRIZ

It is unfair to the topic of TRIZ to treat it as a tool or technique, on par with brainwriting, HIT, and SCAMPER. To all TRIZ aficionados and devotees, I profusely apologize. It's not due to lack of respect for the topic.

Quite the opposite. TRIZ is such an enormous topic, that I really can't devote much attention to it in a keep-it-in-the-shallow-end overview of innovation. But it is definitely something worth further study.

What is TRIZ you ask? TRIZ is an acronym that stands for the Theory of Inventive Problem Solving. "Wait a minute," you are thinking, "shouldn't that be TIPS?" Well, TRIZ originated in Russia, so it's a Russian acronym.

The letters aren't important. What is important is the concept. Maybe a little history will help. Genrich Altshuller devised TRIZ by observing how inventions came about. As a patent clerk, he had access to information on all sorts of new inventions, and he observed patterns in them. He observed that the most impactful inventions were the ones that resolved contradictions.

A contradiction arises when the needs of a product to do one thing conflict with the needs of the same product to do the opposite. My favorite example, because it's so simple: a speaker giving a presentation wants to point at words and pictures and data and whatever else on a screen or board that the audience sees. The speaker wants the pointer to be long, so that it can reach words high on the screen. At the same time, the speaker wants it to fit in a pocket, so that it can be easily transported from presentation to presentation. That is a contradiction. It needs to be both long and short.

Such situations are usually handled as trade-offs. Instead of making it either long or short, it's made some mid-length that is long enough for most situations, and could be considered somewhat portable in a big enough briefcase. But it never fully satisfies either need.

TRIZ identifies a wide variety of ways that inventors have historically found to resolve contradictions. In this case, behold! The telescoping pointer. It extends to be long enough to point to the top of the screen when needed to point, and then collapses down to fit in a pocket when needed to travel. No need for making an unsatisfying trade-off, when you can eliminate the contradiction altogether.

Altshuller identified thirty-nine engineering features and forty inventive principles for resolving contradictions, and created a matrix to identify which inventive principles would help to resolve which contradictions. In the case of the pointer, you look on the matrix at the intersection of shape and length (you can't do length and length on that matrix). The idea is that if I make the shape right for portability, the length is wrong for functionality; and if I make the length right for functionality, the shape is wrong for portability.

Anyway, you look in that cell of the contradiction matrix, and it offers four inventive principles. One of those is "nested doll," which is essentially what the telescoping pointer is: one part fitting inside another, fitting inside another, fitting inside another, just like a nested doll.

The matrix is huge, 39x39, with each of the engineering features plotted against each of the others. Then each cell with a contradiction that has been resolved in the past contains a list of the principles that have been used to resolve that contradiction.

Once you see which of the forty principles might work for you, you can focus your thinking on how they might be applied to your specific situation. Perhaps that is why I find TRIZ so appealing. It is much like the philosophy that I have expressed about innovation. There are fundamental principles about how innovation happens. Applying those principles to your specifics will help guide you, whatever you do, to be more successful with your innovation efforts.

TRIZ also offers a way to look into the future, with a list of eight patterns that have been observed regarding how things tend to evolve.

Let's go back to the pointer example. One pattern seen in many products is the increased use of fields – if you are not a techie type, think about the magnetic field you could "see" with some iron filings in your grade school science class. There is a tendency for big solid objects to be broken down into smaller pieces, then eventually replaced with energy. That's exactly what happened with the pointer. The long stick was broken down into the multi-piece telescoping pointer, then later evolved into the laser pointer that uses energy to do the job of pointing.

My favorite evolutionary trend is, of course, the trend toward increased complexity, followed by – you guessed it – simplification.

That is an all-too-brief and all-too-shallow overview of TRIZ. I believe it to be a high potential tool, but it is not one easily reducible to the kind of simplicity discussed here. I invite you to do some further digging into the subject. You may find it to be of value in guiding innovative solutions. It has been applied to services and other human interactions, so it's not just limited to physical products that require physical engineering.[529]

---

[529] A good primer on TRIZ is Ellen Domb and Kalevi Rantanen, *Simplified TRIZ: New Problem Solving Applications for Engineers and Manufacturing Professionals, Second Edition,* Auerbach Publications, 2007. You can also find out more online at www.triz-journal.com.

Selecting Ideas to Pursue Further

Linus Pauling's statement "if you want to have good ideas, you must have many ideas," is often quoted in innovation circles. The evidence would suggest that this indeed is the case.[530] Having more ideas goes hand in hand with having better quality ideas.

Pauling's comments about ideas did not end there, though. He went on to say about those many ideas, "most of them will be wrong, and what you have to learn is which ones to throw away." Indeed, that *is* the trick.

This can be an area in which it is difficult to find balance. You want to avoid excessively complex decision-processes. You also want to make sure that the pursuit of simplicity does not cross the line into simplisticicity. Yes, I just invented a new word there.[531]

Simplistic would be having one person, even in a role of decision-making authority, choose what they like best.[532] Over-complication would be a full portfolio management scorecard review done by a large team on every idea generated. Simple falls in between.

Get a small group of people well-versed in the VoC work that you have done. Make sure that they bring a diverse set of viewpoints. Review the ideas with them, and then let the gang vote on 'em.

So how do you do the voting? There are dozens, maybe hundreds of ways to do the voting. Here's one that I am certain you will find to be beneficial, called **cumulative voting**.

Each person on the evaluation team is given a number of votes, (let's say ten). They can then assign their votes however they want across the ideas being evaluated. They could put one each on ten different ideas they like, all ten votes on one idea they really, really like, or any distribution in between.

Prior to voting, ground the participants in the criteria for the decision. A simple approach to decision criteria is to use the five broad categories from

---

[530] Karan Girotra, Christian Terwiesch and Karl T. Ulrich, "Idea Generation and the Quality of the Best Idea," *Management Science*, April 2010.

[531] If it has as much value to you as it does to me, then by golly, I'm declaring my new word an innovation. A very, *very*, VERY small one.

[532] I've seen WAY too many organizations choose this route, including some that should clearly know better. The arrogance of such decision-makers astounds me.

the portfolio management scorecard.[533] An even simpler approach is to base it on two questions:

- Should we do it? That is, will it deliver value to both customer and organization?
- Can we do it? That is, is it feasible? Does our organization have the ability to execute against such an idea?

Intuition plays an important role in selecting ideas. Immediately following idea generation, the uncertainty for all of the ideas is at a peak. There is little, if any, customer input yet, forecasting is virtually impossible, and resource requirements are only vague notions.

That is the time when relying on the collective intuition of the team is best.[534]

Just as it is true for generating ideas, the initial voting is best done individually, not in groups. One process for collective voting is to let people record their votes publicly on a wall chart with sticky dots, colored markers, etc. This provides a great visual of what ideas get the most votes. The problem, though, is that the visual impact can influence people during the process itself – the bandwagon effect rears its ugly head. Someone who would have voted for idea X sees that no one else has voted for it, but idea Y has a dozen votes already, so they place their votes on idea Y instead.

Public voting like this can also allow participants to game the system. Say someone initially thinks that they should allocate their votes across four or five ideas. However, when they see the voting publicly, they notice that a couple of ideas they would have voted for already have a large number of votes. Rather than go with their initial distribution, then, they take the votes that would have gone to those already popular ideas and instead, cast them for a less popular idea to get it over the threshold for consideration.

Any public display of the voting process can and will impact how votes are cast. It's best to do the voting independently. Follow the lead of the news

---

[533] See more about scorecards in the aptly-named section "Scorecards," page 167.

[534] For more about team intuition, go to the "Intuition" section of the Mental Game of Innovation chapter, page 261.

broadcasts during an election year, and don't release vote totals until the polls have closed.

Once the votes are cast, the ideas are sorted and discussed, similar to the Delphi method.[535] It should not be a matter of drawing a line under the ideas that got votes, and saying "go!" The portfolio management process[536] is critical to overall innovation success. The decisions made about the initial ideas to pursue in the Fuzzy Front End have direct impact on the portfolio that will exist down the road, and the organization's ability to innovate successfully.[537]

Keeping portfolio needs and strategic considerations in mind, the responsible decision-maker must select the best ideas for further development.

Should you include customers in the evaluation of ideas? The answer is an unequivocal maybe.

There can be great value in having people who will use your product tell you up front whether or not they like your ideas. If they are never going to use your product, better to find out early and not waste the resources developing something they don't value. On the other hand, the customers will only be evaluating the idea based on what they would like to have. They won't be thinking about whether or not you can actually execute the idea.

That wouldn't be so bad, as you could always screen out the ideas that you can't do, except for one thing. Customers will expect that you execute the ideas they choose, and may reward you with discontent that hurts your efforts to serve them.[538]

My rule of thumb: if you can get customer input, in a simple and cost-effective way, without making public promises (explicit or implied), go for it.

---

[535] For more about this method, see the "Delphi Method" section of the Project Management chapter, page 367.

[536] For more about portfolio management, see the "Portfolio Management" chapter, page 146.

[537] Alexander Kock, Wilderich Heising, and Hans Georg Gemünden, "How Ideation Portfolio Management Influences Front-End Success," *Journal of Product Innovation Management*, July 2015.

[538] Paul M. di Gangi, Molly M. Wasko, and Robert E. Hooker, "Getting customers' ideas to work for you: Learning from Dell how to succeed with online," *MIS Quarterly Executive*, December 2010.

Should the people involved in executing projects be involved? Yes, if possible. Being involved in the decision-making process helps to build commitment to the outcome.[539] They will also have the best insight on project feasibility, and can help design the solution for executability.

Value Propositions

The next step for the raw ideas is to have them worked up into more detailed and refined value propositions. This is an important part of developing the business case that will justify expending resources on further development.

From the opening definition of innovation,[540] I've talked about value. An innovation must create value for someone, somewhere, somehow. Thinking through a formal value proposition is a critical exercise to ensure that you are going to do just that.

Figure 77 shows a template for thinking through what value you are promising to deliver to your customer.[541] It's not just about all the good things you and your product will do for them. It's not a sound bite advertisement.

The question you are trying to answer is this: how does the total *experience* with your product measure up, once you've taken *all* of the costs and benefits, as perceived by the consumer, into account. Notice the emphasis on "all" in that statement. It' not just a handful of performance measures directly related to the product. And notice the emphasis on the word "experience." It's not just about the physical actions that happen, but about the full mental, emotional, and physical journey that your customer goes through in learning about your product, making decisions about your product, acquiring your product, using your product, storing your product, and disposing of your product at the end of the experience.

---

[539] Thomas W. Malone, Robert Laubacher, and Chrysanthos Dellarocas, "Harnessing Crowds: Mapping the Genome of Collective Intelligence," *MIT Sloan School Working Papers*, March 19, 2010.

[540] If you missed the definition of innovation according to the Pi Picture Dictionary, go to the "What the #&%! Is Innovation, Anyway?" section, page 4.

[541] It's based on Dr. Mohan Sawhney's "teeter-totter" model Value Proposition Framework (you can see him discuss this model at https://www.youtube.com/watch?v=xP9zqcUn6jQ). The template offered in this book doesn't give you the excellent imagery of costs and benefits balanced on a customer fulcrum, but, hey, it's easier to write on.

Value Proposition Development Template

Customer Benefits   Customer Expenditures

Promise(s)	Differentiator(s)	Support(s)	Total Lifecycle Cost	Effort of Use	Risk
What benefits are provided to customers? What jobs are customers enabled to accomplish? What problem does the product or service solve?	What makes the offering better than alternative ways to get similar benefits?	Why should a customer believe your claims about the product or service you are offering?	What are the total costs for the customer, including: • Price • Operating costs • Maintenance costs • Repair costs • Storage Costs • Psychological Costs • Disposal costs	What is required of the customer to make the offering useful? • Needed Inputs • Preparation for use • Physical effort • Mental effort • Psychological effort • End-of-use	What could go wrong for the customer? • FMEA • Missed expectations

Customer Context

What customers does the offering serve best?
Under what scenarios does the offering best operate?
In what environments will the offering operate, and how does that impact the costs and benefits?

Figure 77: A value proposition template, used to think holistically about how your product fits the needs and capabilities of your customer.

On the benefits side, you need to consider what functional benefits the customer will experience, how the product is different from the status quo and any substitute solutions, and the support that you offer to make your promise believable. On the cost side, you need to consider not just the financial price that the customer will need to pay, but also the time and effort they must expend on your product, and any risks they incur in the experience.

Finally, you need to consider this all from the perspective of your target customer. This is where all of the Voice of the Customer[542] research you have done will come into play. Remember that the value you create is the value that the customer perceives, regardless of how you think they should value it. Customer perception is your reality.

Concept Development

In developing ideas, it is easy to get focused on the product and what you need to do to it. It cannot be emphasized too much that you need to be sure to keep focused on the customer in all that you do.

---

[542] For more about the Voice of the Customer, refer to the "Voice of the Customer" chapter, page 176.

Developing a strong product concept is a critical step in the process, precisely because it focuses your attention on how the product idea is going to impact the target customer, all in terms that the customer will understand.

The concept needs to capture the essence of the idea in simple, customer-relevant language. Basically, it is a simplified statement of the value proposition work that you have already thought through in detail.

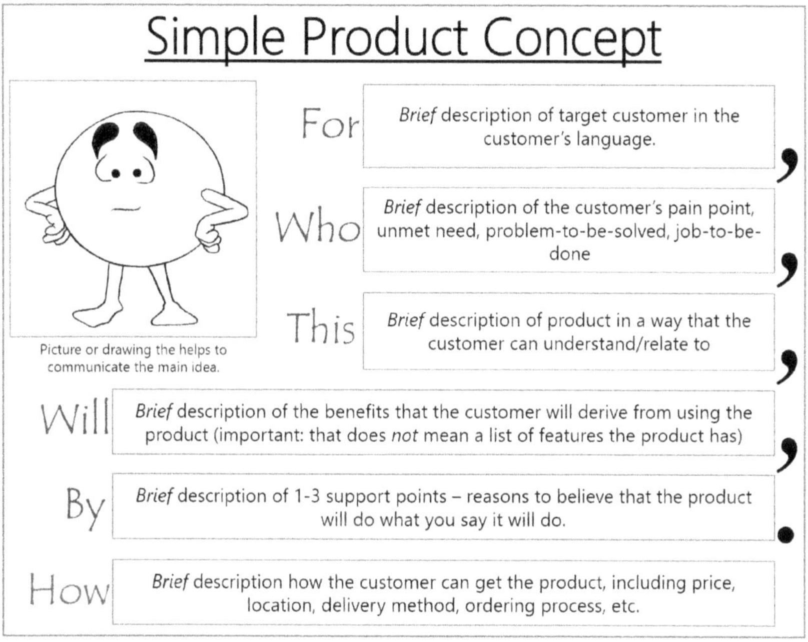

Figure 78: Template for drafting a customer-oriented product concept.

Elements of the product concept should include:
1) Who the intended target customer is;
2) The customer problem you are solving;
3) The essence of the product idea;
4) Key rational and emotional benefits (*not features*) of the product;
5) Support reasons to believe the product will deliver value;
6) What the costs of the product will be to the customer.

When you have a clear understanding of those elements, you can assemble the concept into something that can be shared with customers for feedback. That, in turn, provides you with early guidance on what will be critical for execution of the idea. And *that* will help your baby grow up to be pretty.

Simple Study Guide - Ideation

- Why do people have trouble accepting feedback on and input to their ideas?
- What is a pet project?
- How does customer perception impact "unicorn" ideas?
- What is feature creep?
- How can outsiders effectively contribute to new ideas?
- Is brainstorming an effective means of generating good product ideas?
- What is brainwriting?
- What is the Heuristic Ideation Technique?
- What is the SCAMPER technique?
- What is a TRIZ contradiction matrix and how does it work?
- What are the elements of a good value proposition?
- What makes for an effective concept statement, and how can it be used?

Where do you want to go from here?

Control	Creation	Conversion
Mission (page 40)	**Voice of the Customer** (page 175)	**Innovation Teams** (page 310)
Culture (page 58)	**Minds of Innovators** (page 217)	**Project Management** (page 347)
Strategy (page 92)	**Ideation** (page 279)	**For-Profit Metrics** (page 389)
Portfolio Management (page 146)		**Nonprofit Metrics** (page 403)
Change Management (page 411)		

Or just turn the page to keep reading...

THE CONVERSION SYSTEM

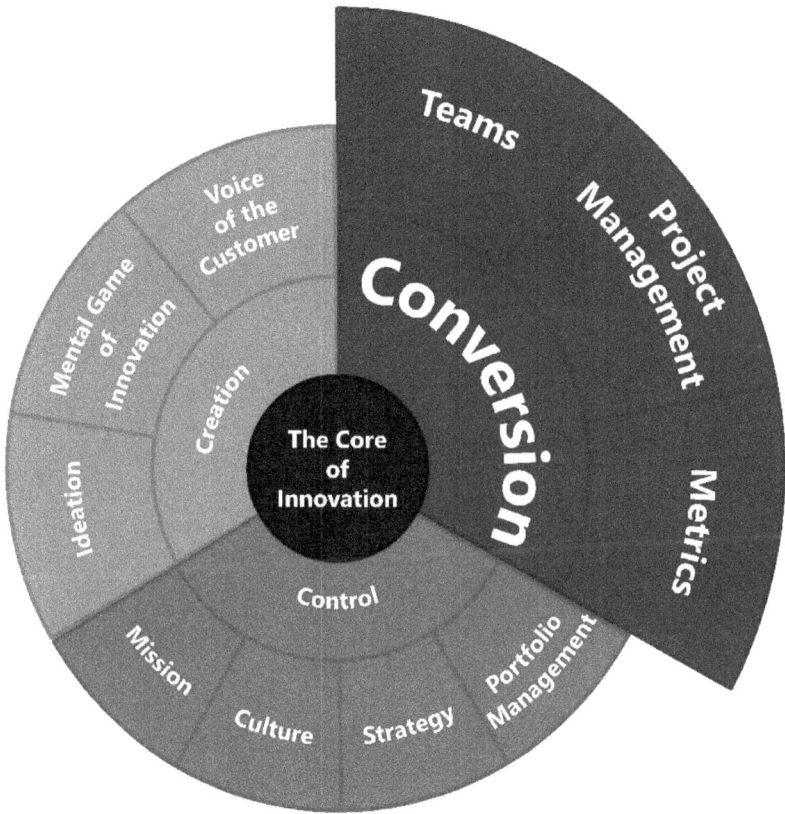

Octopi (Teams)

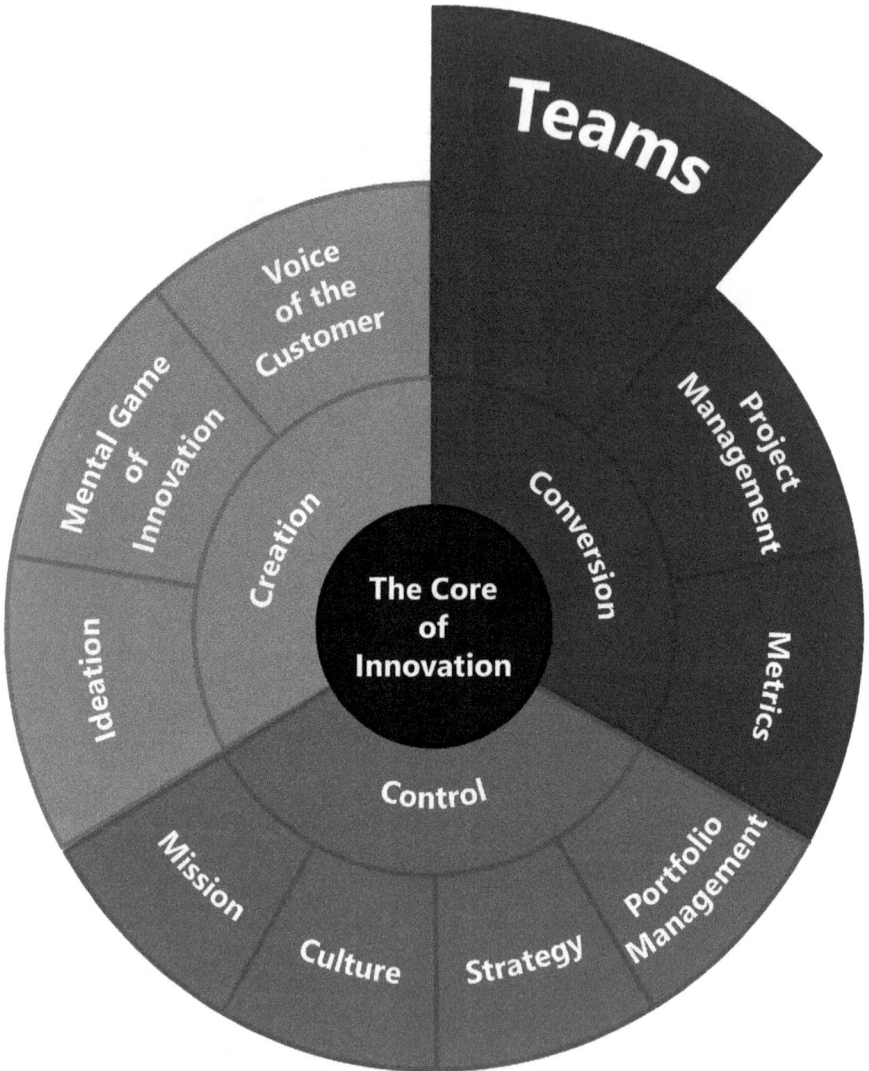

Simple Self-Assessment - Teams

Rate yourself on the following questions. To benchmark yourself against others, go to www.3point14Innovation.com and click the "Self-Assessments" menu.

- ***Is innovation a team sport in your organization?***

  Is there an "I" in team? · · · · · · · · · · We even have a mascot

1	2	3	4	5	6	7	8	9	10

- ***Do your team members have the right mix of professional and team skills?***

  Like oil and water · · · · · · · · · · We cover all the bases

1	2	3	4	5	6	7	8	9	10

- ***Do you have chameleons/bridgers/diplomats that bind your teams together?***

  Sounds like characters in a horror movie · · · · · · · · · · We seek them out and train them

1	2	3	4	5	6	7	8	9	10

- ***Is your team octopi shaped?***

  What's up with the freaky creatures? · · · · · · · · · · Go team Kraken!

1	2	3	4	5	6	7	8	9	10

- ***Do you actively build perceivable team identity, even with dispersed teams?***

  Do drivers' licenses count? · · · · · · · · · · Team Kraken shirts, mugs, handshake...

1	2	3	4	5	6	7	8	9	10

- ***How clearly does your organization communicate?***

  Clear as chocolate pudding · · · · · · · · · · Clear as cold spring water

1	2	3	4	5	6	7	8	9	10

- ***Do your teams have clearly defined and understood roles and responsibilities?***

  Maybe. I think. I dunno. · · · · · · · · · · Like Webster's dictionary

1	2	3	4	5	6	7	8	9	10

- **Does your team have a transformational leader?**

  Wait, who's turn   One we'll follow
  is it to lead?   through Hades and back

1	2	3	4	5	6	7	8	9	10

- **Does your team have a healthy level of conflict?**

  We're not on   Perfect
  speaking terms   creative tension

1	2	3	4	5	6	7	8	9	10

Simple Summary - Teams

Key take-aways you should get out of this section:

- Innovation is a team sport. The best innovation teams are cross-functional, meaning that they involve people from different parts of the organization that are involved in the creation and execution of new products. Functions could include marketing, R&D, engineering, operations, sales, market research, supply chain, packaging, communication, geographic business units, etc.
- Teams operate at different performance levels. On the low end of the spectrum, a working group is a silo-separated cluster of individuals who do their work then throw it over the wall to the next person. On the high end of the spectrum, members of a high-performance team share a common purpose and objectives, operate in a coordinated fashion, and are committed to each other's performance and personal growth. The latter gets far more done, far more efficiently, and for more creatively.
- Teams need to have a complete set of skills to be successful. Not only do teams need to have the full professional skill set, but they also need to have the full teamwork skillset. A simple three-role team model will suffice: adapters (who make things happen and execute effectively), explorers (the conceptual, big-picture, change-agents), and bridgers (the ones in-between who help adapters and explorers to get along, stay aligned, and keep coordinated).
- Teams need to ensure that they are communicating effectively. That doesn't just mean writing eloquent emails and speaking respectfully. It means being candid and open, sharing information freely, and creating a safe and trusting work environment that encourages sharing.
- An octopi-shaped team is one in which at least one member has deep professional skills and knowledge in every necessary function, and broad shared knowledge with each other across a variety of topics, including each other's area of expertise. Knowing who to go to for what information is critical to team success. Sharing broad knowledge even outside of professional capacity builds relationships and trust.
- With geographically dispersed groups, the keys to developing a high-performance team are promoting shared identity and effective, frequent communication. Even when people are not located in the same area, inclusively developing the mission and strategy, sharing

common rituals, and finding real-time communication opportunities will help to unify the team, which will help them to function more effectively.

- Effective communication can be promoted by following a CLEAR model. This model covers how the message is connected to the work people do, the specific things being requested, a description of what success looks like, what resources are available, and what benefits the receiver of the message can expect.

- Clearly defining roles and responsibilities supports team cohesion, particularly when decision-making is required. The RAPID model for decision-making defines who recommends, who needs to agree, who needs to perform, who provides information, and who is actually accountable for the decision. Thinking through those roles in the decision-making process will help ensure strong decisions and team buy-in.

- Research in the field of marital counseling can actually be applied to building effective teams. Teaching team members about effective work relationship behavior, particularly in the area of managing conflict, can rapidly help build more effective teams.

- Team leadership is an important contributor to team performance. Having a transformational leader significantly improves the results delivered by teams. Characteristics of a transformational leader include charisma, inspirational motivation, intellectual stimulation, and individualized consideration.

The Myth of the Lone Innovator

You may have noticed by now that I am a bit of a nerd. And I've come to terms with that. I may be the only one in a room who will laugh out loud at a math joke. Or I may be the only one who will laugh at a grammar joke.

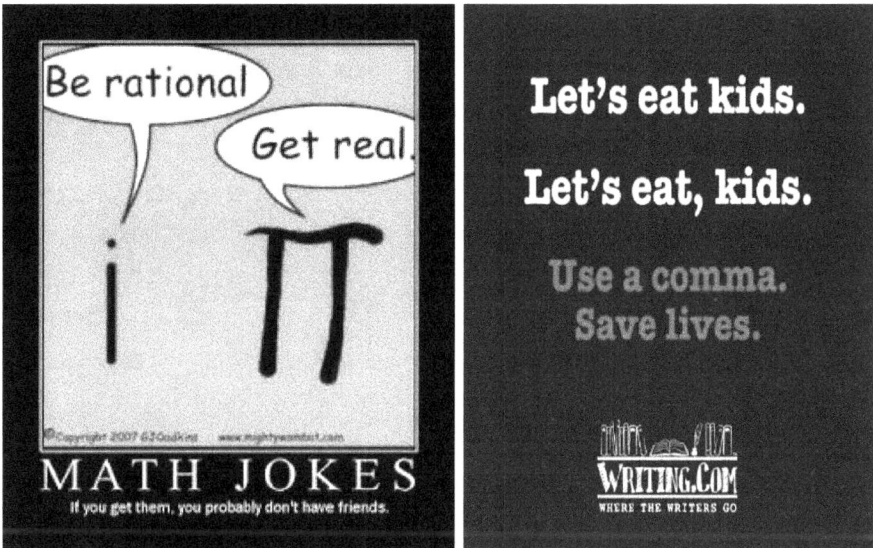

What does that have to do with innovation?

I'll get to that in a moment. But first, let's talk about a famous innovator.

Steve Jobs is often cited as the great innovator of our time, who single-handedly took Apple from near bankruptcy to become the most valuable company in the world.

Without taking anything away from his achievements, he didn't do it by himself. Apple employs nearly 100,000 people, and that does not include the hundreds of thousands who create apps for Apple operating systems. As Rick Tetzeli, co-author of *Becoming Steve Jobs*, says, "The resurrection of Apple was a team effort, a fact that gets overlooked to the detriment of everyone, including Steve."[543]

Research into what drives creative team performance confirms that having individuals with high creativity is not sufficient for developing highly creative

---

[543] Rick Tetzeli, "The Real Legacy of Steve Jobs," *Fast Company*, April 2015.

products.[544] Teams need to be involved, and they need to be managed, at least to some extent, along all three dimensions of interpersonal effectiveness, coordination, and control. Missing any one of those dimensions in team management can hinder innovative outcomes. In fact, recent trends in how teams are organized and managed along these lines have significantly contributed to increased economic productivity.[545]

Teams that solve problems collaboratively, sharing the problem-solving duties, are better at learning, and faster at developing new products. Those teams emerge from safe, supportive, challenging, and engaging environments.[546]

Innovation is a team sport. Like all team sports, there are stars and there are role players. There are Hall-of-Famers and there are draft busts. But no HOFer ever played alone. Michael Jordan did not play 1-on-5. Johnny Unitas did not throw the football to himself. Pele was not much of a goalkeeper, and Eileen Duffy-O'Mahoney wouldn't have won so many titles without Sophie Brack and Kathleen Mills-Hill on her team. That last one is for all you camogie fans out there.[547]

Remember that innovation consists of three components: creativity, significance, and execution. Few individuals are good at, or even capable of, all three. So the trick is to assemble the right team of people, who have the right set of combined skills, and then get them to collaborate effectively.

Getting Your Teams to Another Level

Teams work together and perform at different levels. One model of growth with teams goes through the four stages of forming, storming, norming, and

---

[544] Rita Bissola, Barbara Imperatori and Renata Trinca Colonel, "Enhancing the Creative Performance of New Product Teams: An Organizational Configurational Approach," *Journal of Product Innovation Management*, March 2014.

[545] Sandra E. Black and Lisa M. Lynch, "What's driving the new economy? The benefits of workplace innovation," *The Economic Journal*, February 2004.

[546] Ludwig Bstieler and Martin Hemmert, "Increasing Learning and Time Efficiency in Interorganizational New Product Development Teams," *Journal of Product Innovation Management*, July 2010.

[547] Admittedly, I know virtually nothing about the sport of camogie, but from what I do know, it seems pretty cool. Watch online at https://www.youtube.com/watch?v=70ePVvm1tU4.

performing. At the risk of promoting such a model just because it rhymes (and is therefore more believable),[548] I'll instead turn to a model based on how the team members interact.[549]

The lowest level team is just a **working group** – a collection of individuals that do their own work individually. They finish whatever they are supposed to do, throw it over the wall, and let someone else deal with it. They are not expected or encouraged to work collaboratively.

The next level is the **pseudo-team** – although they have a need to work in an integrated way, they don't. Organizations that complain about an excessive "silo mentality" are seeing the effects of pseudo-teams.

The next level is the **potential team** – they are at least trying to work together, and making an effort at improving how they do so.

All the way at the fourth level, at last, is the **real team** – this is a group of people playing different roles but doing so with common purpose, approach, goals, objectives, and accountability.

And finally, the highest level is the **high-performance team** – not only do members share the elements of a real team and execute well, but they are also committed to each other's professional (and even personal) growth. At this point, the team might be better described in terms of family than as a mere team.[550] Listen to interviews of people who played on some of the great teams in sports history, and almost all will talk about the feeling of family that those teams possessed.

We all want high-performance innovation teams. So how do we get them?

Putting Together the Skill Set Puzzle

You know your organization, and what you are trying to do (particularly now that you have clearly stated your mission for all to understand [551]). You

---

[548] For more about the "Rhyme as Reason" fallacy and other cognitive biases, go to the "Cognitive Biases" section of the Mental Game of Innovation chapter, page 224.

[549] Jon R. Katzenbach and Douglas K. Smith, "The Discipline of Teams," *Harvard Business Review*, March-April 1993.

[550] Stephen K. Markham and Hyunjung Lee, "Marriage and Family Therapy in NPD Teams: Effects of We-ness on Knowledge Sharing and Product Performance," *Journal of Product Innovation Management*, November 2014.

[551] For more on how to create a mission, refer to the "Mission" chapter, page 40.

are in the best position to identify the particular combination of skills that your team needs. Note that you don't need one person for each skill. Even organizations large enough to be able to provide such specialists will have overlap between teammates, and that's a good thing. It means the team can benefit from multiple perspectives.

You will obviously need a complete set of professional skills (Marketing, Sales, Engineering, Supply chain, Distribution, Packaging, Information Technology, Service Delivery, and the like). These are the roles most managers think of.

An innovation leader also needs to think of the team dynamics, and look for people to fill roles that enable a team to be effective. These roles are based more on thinking style and personality than in functional responsibility.

There are a variety of team theories out there, with various degrees of evidence for their impact on innovation. For example, the Belbin theory[552] defines nine roles for a team. The Team Management System of Margerison and McCann[553] has eight distinct roles and one shared role. *The Ten Faces of Innovation* by Kelley and Littman define ten roles for a strong innovation team.[554] And research indicates that the more roles a team can play, the better the results of their innovation efforts.[555]

So, clearly, an innovation leader must always have a full complement of all the necessary functional roles and all the variety of team roles, resulting in a development team roughly the size of a major university football team. Plus the marching band.

Ha! Just kidding. Had you going there for a minute, though.

---

[552] Aitor Aritzeta, Stephen Swailes and Barbara Senior, "Belbin's Team Role Model: Development, Validity and Applications for Team Building." *Journal of Management Studies,* January 2007.

[553] Dick McCann and Charles Margerison, "Team Management Profiles: Their use in Managerial Development," *Journal of Management Development,* Vol 4, No 2, 1985.

[554] Tom Kelley and Jonathan Littman, *The Ten Faces of Innovation: IDEO's Strategies for Defeating the Devil's Advocate and Driving Creativity Throughout Your Organization,* Currency/Doubleday, 2005.

[555] Miha Prebil and Mateja Drnovšek, "Effects of Team Structure on Innovation Performance: An Empirical Study," *Chinese Business Review,* August 2013.

Obviously, huge teams are not the answer. Research shows that teams should have no more members than minimally necessary.[556] In fact, further research suggests that smaller-than-optimal teams perform better than larger-than optimal.[557] Bigger teams can actually be detrimental to outcomes.

Apparently, the cliché is true: too many cooks spoil the broth. Avoid the trap of thinking that if one woman can have a baby in nine months, maybe nine women can have a baby in one month. Not only is throwing more people at a problem not going to help, it can often hurt.

So what's an innovation leader to do?

The roles defined in the team theories mentioned above are good to consider and keep in mind when forming a team, but it is unrealistic to expect that every team is going to have all of the functional skills and be able to play all of the team roles.

So go for balance and simplicity. Rather than worry about 8, 9, or 10 types of roles, let's focus on three. And, you guessed it...this is grounded in research.[558]

On one end of the spectrum, get people who are good at "doing things better." These are people who like to solve problems, using tried and true ways. They are detail-oriented and grounded in reality. We'll call them "Adapters."

On the other end of the spectrum, there are the people with a knack for "doing things differently." These are the folks that search for problems, and approach solutions from unusual angles. They tend to be conceptual, big-picture thinkers, with little reverence for the status quo, confidently generating new ideas. Let's call them "Explorers."[559]

---

[556] J. Richard Hackman, "The design of work teams," *Handbook of Organizational Behavior*, 1987. Of course, only you can determine what's "minimally necessary?"

[557] Allan W. Wicker, Sandra L. Kirmeyer, Lois Hanson, and Dean Alexander, "Effects of Manning Levels on Subjective Experiences, Performance, and Verbal Interaction in Groups," *Organizational Behavior and Human Performance*, December 1976.

[558] Michael Kirton, "Adaptors and innovators: A description and measure," *Journal of Applied Psychology*, October 1976.

[559] The original theorist, in this case Dr. Michael Kirton, chose to use the term "innovator" for this end of the spectrum. So as not to cause confusion with "innovator" as I am using the term, I took the liberty of changing the name to "explorer." Please don't sue me, Dr. Kirton. I respect your work.

And now for a warning.

These two types drive each other nuts. An extreme adaptor would describe an extreme explorer as an impractical, confusing, out-of-touch with reality, and abrasive quack. An extreme explorer would describe an extreme adaptor as a dogmatic, timid, can't-see-the-forest-for-the-trees conformist. They each think the other is flat wrong.

That makes them both wrong, because they are actually both right. Got that?

You need both perspectives to innovate. You need both the reality side and the novelty side. But if these folks are like oil and water, how do you get them to work together effectively?

That's where the third type comes in. The chameleon. The diplomat. The bridger. Bridgers are for teams what diplomats are for organizational cultures.[560]

These chameleons are the in-between group on the continuum between adapters and explorers. They can relate to both sides, and help each understand the perspective of the other. Bridgers are the emulsifier for the Adaptor's oil and the Explorer's water. They are the eggs that make the team mayonnaise.[561]

Required Team Roles

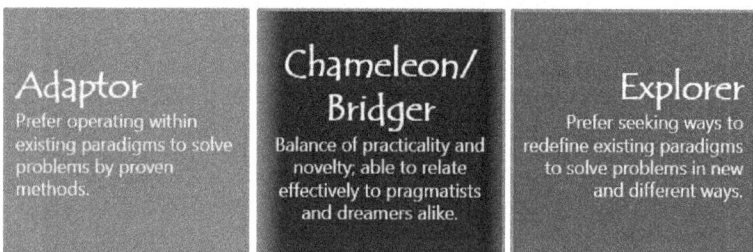

Adaptor	Chameleon/ Bridger	Explorer
Prefer operating within existing paradigms to solve problems by proven methods.	Balance of practicality and novelty; able to relate effectively to pragmatists and dreamers alike.	Prefer seeking ways to redefine existing paradigms to solve problems in new and different ways.

Figure 79: The simplified required roles for an innovation team.

---

[560] For more about the diplomat role in a culture, refer to the "Subcultures" section of the Culture chapter, page 87.

[561] Sorry, I couldn't resist that metaphor. I was a mayonnaise engineer at one point in my career. Mayonnaise is basically all vegetable oil and vinegar, with a dash of spice and a pinch of salt. Oh, and egg yolks. They are the magic ingredient that enable the water in the vinegar to stay

It's tempting to think that a full team of chameleons would be best, so that everyone understands both Adapter and Explorer points of view. That's not really how it works, though. As "in-betweens," bridgers won't be as detail-oriented and grounded as true Adapters, nor will they be as visionary and challenging of the status-quo as Explorers.

To have a successful innovation team, you need a balance of Adaptors, Explorers, and Bridgers. These three roles are easier to identify than the sometimes-subtle differences between the roles defined in other systems, and they are easier to keep track of.

So, when setting up an innovation team, you should (when possible):

- Make up your innovation team with the functional expertise required to get the product to market;
- From the pool of people available with the functional expertise, select a team that has a balance of Adapters, Bridgers, and Explorers;
- Appoint a strong project leader (preferably a bridger by nature);
- Make sure that the whole team will be recognized and rewarded equitably.

In short, create a balance of individual strengths on the team, both technical and psychological.

Note that I said above, "when possible."

What do you do when it's not possible to have the choice of a functionally diverse team with a balance of Adapters, Bridgers, and Explorers?

Say you have a small organization, and the ability to select from a big pool of resources simply isn't there. Or you're from a larger organization, and the resources that are available don't match the resources you'd prefer. What happens from there?

Get out your thinking caps. DeBono's six thinking hats.[562]

Running a team through the various modes of thinking in a structured way will help balance the range of thinking that you need to make good decisions.

---

together with the oil. I made thousands and thousands of pounds of the stuff in my early career. I still have nightmares sometimes, but I'll save those stories for another book.

[562] For more on DeBono's six thinking hats, refer to the "Thinking Caps" section of the Mental Game of Innovation Chapter, page 245.

It's not perfect. People who are natural-born Adapters will find it hard to put on a green hat, and extreme Explorers will find it hard to put on a black hat. Both may want to put on their red hats and yell at the other that regardless of what color hat they are wearing, they are staining it brown (if you know what I mean).

No, it's not perfect, and it takes practice. But it is an excellent tool to ensure both that effective thinking is taking place, and that teammates are building mutual understanding. It's like the proverbial walking in the other's shoes, only with hats.

Innovation is a Team Sport

Philosopher Arnold J. Toynbee said, "Society is the total network of relations between human beings. The components of society are thus not human beings but relations between them." For innovation, the team is its own little society. It is not just the set of individuals on the team, but the relationships between them that count.

Successful product development teams are cross-functional in nature. Organizations that operate in independent silos will find it hard to be successful.[563] However you are organized, make sure that the different parts of the organization chart are represented on a product development team.

Effective teams will have a broad team intelligence, meaning a) that at least one person will have the specific functional knowledge required for every aspect of the development process, and b) team members will be aware of each other's knowledge. As a team member, I don't have to know everything myself, but I do have to be willing to share what I know openly. I also have to know who to go to for information that I don't have.

There are some aspects of knowledge that every team member should possess. Each member should have a good general understanding of the types of products being developed, the market and customer for which the products are being developed, and the process by which the products will be developed.

---

[563] Robert G. Cooper, "Third-Generation New Product Processes," *Journal of Product Innovation Management*, January 1994.

This common base of knowledge will help the team to integrate each individuals' specialty knowledge, and to find successful solutions quickly.[564]

So which functions should be represented? As many as possible.

The more functions represented on a development team, the better.[565] With more functions available on a team, the better able they are to solve problems, adapt to change, learn, and apply the knowledge that they acquire.

This translates to better team performance. New product success rates are better when teams operate with more effective team intelligence, and speed-to-market is enhanced.[566]

The ability to operate with such a "collective mind" is going to depend on the ability of team members to overcome the curse of knowledge and tendency to share what people already know.[567] To do this, the team needs to operate as an Octopi.

The Pi Pi Pi Pi Shaped Team

And now for the grammar-math joke you've all been waiting for...Figure 80!

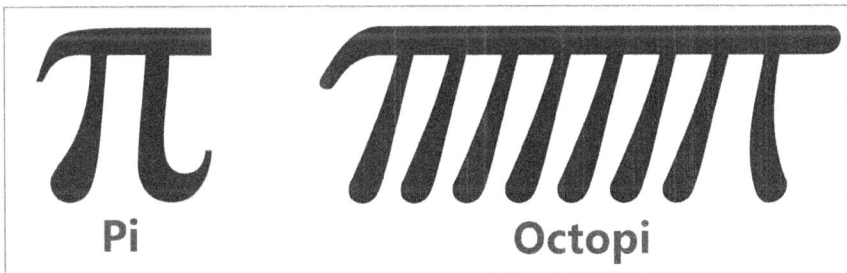

Figure 80: Is it a grammar joke? Is it a math joke? It's two jokes in one!

---

[564] Ali E. Akgün, Mumin Dayan, Anthony Di Benedetto, "New Product Development Team Intelligence: Antecedents and Consequences," *Information & Management*, February 2008.

[565] Ibid.

[566] Kuang-Ting Zheng, T.C. Lin, Jack Shih-Chieh Hsu, and Neeraj Parolia, "Understanding the Impact of Transactive Memory Systems on Project Team Performance: The Mediating Role of Knowledge Intergration and Collective Mind," *Proceedings of the Southern Association for Information Systems Conference*, March, 2010.

[567] For more on these and other cognitive biases, see the "Cognitive Biases" section of the Mental Game of Innovation chapter.

Hey, I didn't say it was a funny joke. I just said that it was a joke.

You see, there's this grammar debate about whether the proper English plural of octopus is octopuses or octopi (it's octopuses), and you take the Greek letter pi and put it together so it has eight legs, and it becomes octopi, and...

Never mind. If I have to explain it, it bombed. Don't worry, I won't be making stand-up comedy my profession.

But I needed to share that not-so-funny joke to set this up...

As discussed earlier, the best serial innovators have pi-shaped minds,[568] with deep business knowledge and deep technical knowledge. For teams to be effective, they need to have a "collective mind" that is octopi-shaped.

Figure 67 showed what a pi-shaped individual mind might look like. Figure 81 shows what an octopi-shaped *team* might look like. Imagine that each person on the team is represented by a different color on the chart. Their individual depths of understanding in various categories adds up to knowledge that looks like the octopi joke, with depth in multiple technical areas, and

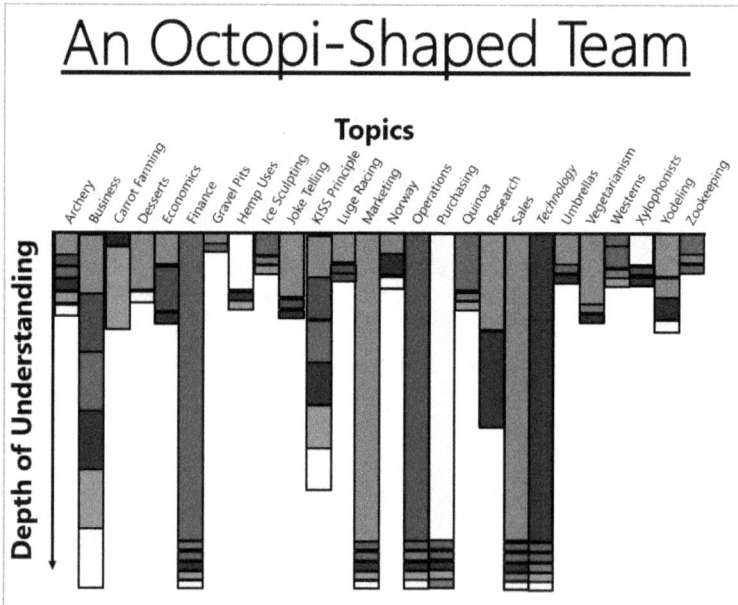

Figure 81: The octopi shaped team collective mind.

---

[568] For more on what a Pi-Shaped mind is, see the "Pi-Shaped Minds" section in the Mental Game of Innovation chapter, 252.

breadth in a wide variety of other topics. Each team member knows a little bit about the areas of expertise of all the other team members, so that collectively, they can share and leverage their combined knowledge effectively.

To have an effective knowledge sharing system, teams need to be able to integrate their individual knowledge through strong social interactions, and to be able to recognize the contributions and behaviors of each team member.[569] Such integration and observation is inhibited by silo walls in organization charts.

If you've got an organizational culture that embraces cross-functional interaction already, you may have an environment that will naturally grow octopi-shaped teams.

If you aren't so lucky, what can you do to help teams be more effective? Try to create a subculture for the team that will support the life of the octopi.[570]

To help them integrate their knowledge, help them to do two things: understand the nature of each other's' roles, and build the shared breadth of knowledge among them.

Understanding each other's roles is more than just having a bit of knowledge about the function and how it works, although that is obviously important. It also includes understanding the specifics of the individual's situation in their role – what their workload is like, the demands of their management, their biggest challenges, their strengths and weaknesses, etc.

The shared breadth of the team comes from connecting outside of the boundaries of the innovation work. Team members need to find common interests and share common experiences. That comes from time spent outside conference meeting rooms and email exchanges.

Team-building exercises have earned their share of criticism, for being ineffective, for being silly, and for being wasted expenses. They don't have to be like that.

---

[569] Kuang-Ting Zheng, T.C. Lin, Jack Shih-Chieh Hsu, and Neeraj Parolia, "Understanding the Impact of Transactive Memory Systems on Project Team Performance: The Mediating Role of Knowledge Intergration and Collective Mind," *Proceedings of the Southern Association for Information Systems Conference*, March, 2010.

[570] For more on cultures and subcultures, refer to the "Culture" chapter, page 58.

One of the most effective team-building environments I have experienced came in the form of Friday-morning doughnut hour. The group gathered in a manager's office every Friday morning, informally bringing in cheap snacks to eat. There was no set agenda, and no formal time constraint. The team was just hanging out, shooting the breeze, and connecting. Sometimes, we discussed work, but usually we talked about other random topics. It made working together infinitely easier. And more enjoyable.

When you think team-building, don't think that it has to be a holiday party, an obstacle course complete with a trust fall, or trying to walk with all of your feet strapped to two-by-fours. Simple is better. Simple works.

Perception is Reality in Teamwork, Too

Recent research on geographically dispersed teams has altered the thinking of what constitutes "proximity" among team members. Earlier research emphasized physical proximity as a crucial factor in team performance, with even short distances of separation being shown to inhibit effective collaboration.

That understanding is being refined, though, as the increased dispersion of teams has risen in the past few decades. Increased mobility, the introduction of new means of communication, and virtual collaboration tools have enabled more and more people to work together in different spaces. And they are becoming more effective at doing so.

It seems that the change has to do with our perception of what it is to be close to one another. Physical distance is not as important as *perceived* distance. It is possible to have close physical proximity but high perceived distance, and it is possible to have close perceived proximity even when separated by large physical distances.

These paradoxes are possible because perceived distance is emotional, not physical. Physical distance can contribute to perceived distance, but only in an indirect way. Perceived distance is a matter of communication and group identity.[571]

---

[571] Michael Boyer O'Leary, Jeanne M. Wilson and Anca Metiu, "Beyond Being There: The Symbolic Role of Communication and Identification in the Emergence of Perceived Proximity in Geographically Dispersed Work," *MIS Quarterly*, December 2014.

Teams located in the same physical space are not more likely to have better relationships just because members have to look each other in the eye more often. Rather, it's because they are more likely to bump into each other in the hallways, by the watercooler, or at the vending machines for an afternoon pack of Famous Amos cookies. These chance meetings are opportunities to have relationship-building conversations, or maybe to see identity-reinforcing team logo shirts.

Such things, as trivial as they may seem, can support the in-group identity[572] that bonds people together unconsciously. So what can be done for physically dispersed teams to help them build such an identity?

First, do the foundational things that help to create authentic meaning and identity for the team – define the mission, support a common team culture, establish behavioral norms, build the strategy – and do so inclusively. Stimulate a sense of team ownership from the start. Don't try to build your house on a weak foundation.

Things like team shirts, hats, satchels, and Lucite paperweights won't serve as a foundation. Those things are window dressing. They don't have meaning on their own, but derive their meaning from the foundational work. They are symbols of team identity, and can help to sustain it, but they will never create it. The reason such baubles get ridiculed is that all-too-often, managers try to use them to produce meaning, which they just can't do.[573]

Establish the foundation, then – and only then – give people symbols of the foundation that they will already value. The uniform doesn't make the team. The team makes the uniform.

---

[572] For more on the in-group/out-group bias, refer to the "Cognitive Biases" section of the Mental Game of Innovation chapter, page 224.

[573] My favorite example of this comes from the days in the 1990's when "Total Quality Management," the precursor to six sigma, lean, and similar programs today, was all the rage. I was trained to be a "Total Quality Facilitator" in my company's TQM initiative. The common complaint among the trainees was that in spite of lip service to the program, there was no real support for it. That truth was forever etched into my mind when the training was over, and we received our symbolic bauble of our TQM training, a black canvas satchel embroidered with giant letters saying "TGM Facilitator." The irony was the most eloquent expression of how much the organization *really* valued quality...or should I say "quality?"

Second, establish means of frequent, high-quality communication between team members. Failure to communicate has dangerous consequences. Even if everyone works within ten meters[574] of each other, don't expect that to ensure, by itself, strong communication links. And don't expect that having lots of meetings will result in lots of good communication, either. Effective communication is less about volume and more about quality. High quality communication involves clarity,

Figure 82: Failing to communicate has unfortunate consequences, as demonstrated so memorably in *Cool Hand Luke*. See a clip at https://www.youtube.com/watch?v=Oik6dXm-0l0

trust, and respect. Make such characteristics part of the team's required behavioral norms.

There is still no substitute for face-to-face interaction, where all the nuances of communication in terms of body language, facial expressions, and direct eye contact can help people understand each other fully. Especially in the early stages of team formation, create opportunities for face-to-face interaction.

Reality of work life, though, means that such forms of communication are not always feasible. To whatever extent possible, then, give teams the ability to communicate in real time. Phone calls and video conferencing have been found to be particularly important forms of communication for geographically dispersed teams.[575] Texts, emails, and social media connections should also be leveraged. The caution here is that it is difficult to distinguish tone in such formats, so be careful to think about how a message could be interpreted before hitting the send button (especially if you are emotional while writing).

And don't be afraid to open yourself a bit personally. Remember that those shallow-depth common interests that form the body of the octopi are critical

---

[574] Seriously, why can't the US adopt the metric system already? It's so much easier. For those that don't know meters, ten of 'em are about 33 feet.

[575] Michael Boyer O'Leary, Jeanne M. Wilson and Anca Metiu, "Beyond Being There: The Symbolic Role of Communication and Identification in the Emergence of Perceived Proximity in Geographically Dispersed Work," *MIS Quarterly*, December 2014.

to holding the team together. I'm not saying that you confess your secret super-hero identity the first time you meet someone. You can keep your Clark Kent glasses on, but still be willing to discuss your stamp-collecting hobby with a fellow philatelist on the team.

I learned the value of relationship-building while working on international projects with Japanese and German colleagues.[576] Finding opportunities to meet and have personal time over dinners and all-night karaoke singing was exhausting, but always led to leaps forward on projects. We were more efficient and effective in communicating and decision-making after singing off-key duets of Frank Sinatra songs together.

Identity and communication. The lifeblood of an octopi team.

CLEAR Communication

Regarding effective communication in a professional environment, Bill Jensen offers a great model to follow.[577] He calls it CLEAR communication.

Yes, CLEAR is an acronym, and, with all due respect to Mr. Jensen, it's a bit forced in order to have the acronym not only be a word, but to be the specific word "clear." But let's cut him some slack there, because it really is a valuable mnemonic.

Whenever you are communicating with your innovation team, include these five elements in what you are saying:

C is for Connected – what you are telling people should be connected to what they are doing. Sometimes, this will be obvious, but other times, not so much. How many times have you received an email and thought "why am I included on this?" Had the sender made that explicit, you wouldn't have to ask.

L is for List – as in a list of things that you want the receiver of your communication to do. Don't just throw something at someone and expect them to figure out what they are supposed to do with it. That doesn't mean that you are issuing a command (especially if you are sending the message to your CEO). You can accomplish this point with "could you please," if that's more

---

[576] I am forever indebted to my friends and colleagues from Kao Corporation. Particular shout – outs go to Keith Pings and Haruya Kato (Kato-san), who are the best professional mentors I could have asked for.

[577] Bill Jensen, *Simplicity: Working Smarter in a World of Infinite Choices*, Basic Books, 2001.

appropriate, but you still offer a clearly defined set of next steps that you'd like to see.

E is for Expectations – which means helping them understand what success looks like. You should provide them a clear description, with metrics,[578] of what the outcome of their actions should be.

A is for Ability – meaning the resources they have at their disposal to do what you are asking. Such resources could include time, money, people, tools, or whatever else you have in mind. It could even be your own effort offered in assistance.

R is for Return – meaning what they will get out of successfully achieving what you are asking them to do. You need to answer their WIIFM question... "What's in it for me?" Keep in mind that when you ask somebody to do something, they are most likely not sitting at a desk, staring at their phone, awaiting your instructions for personal fulfillment. They are busy doing things that are important to them. Help them understand why your request is not only important to you, but important for them as well.

Here's a made-up example of the model. Imagine that I could reach you by email, and I wanted you to read my book.[579] I could send you a CLEAR message:

> Hello potential reader!
>
> Since you are an innovator looking to get more out of your innovation efforts, *[connected]* I'd like for you to read my new book, *Keep Innovation Simple [list]*. Just go to my website to access it *[list]*. You will enjoy reading it, learn about how to make the entire innovation process work together, and discover simple tools that you can use in your innovation work here and now *[return]*. Or maybe I should say there and now,

---

[578] For more on innovation metrics, go to the sections on "Innovation for Fun and Profit" (page 389) and "Innovation for Fun and Not-for-Profit" (page 403).

[579] I do, but if you are reading this now, then you are already reading my book, so it's kind of a moot point to ask you to read it. You can still leave me your email, if you'd like, by connecting at the Pi Innovation website. I'd love to keep the conversation going. And make it less one-way.

since we aren't in the same room *[superfluous joke – not part of the CLEAR model]*.

Anyway, if you have a pdf reader (and if not, you can download one for free), you can download and read the book *[ability]*. Please let me know what you think by going to the world's easiest survey at the end *[list]*. That will help me to help you by making future editions of the book even more valuable for you *[return]*. Or you can tell me to leave you alone (but I hope not) *[return mixed with superfluous joke]*.

You will have my eternal gratitude for reading and giving me feedback! *[return]*

Best regards,

Brad Barbera

Notice that the five elements don't have to go in order, they just need to be in there.

The one point of communication for which this will be most critical is in the communication of project objectives – having crystal clarity around the goal is one of the critical factors for team success.[580]

Give this model of communication a try. Not every single thought needs to fit the model, but the more you do it, the clearer and more effective your team communications will be.

Muddy Communication

So if identity and communication make octopi possible, what are the threats to the health of octopi? Well, anything that unsettles identity or inhibits communication.

In a chaotic world, the thing that gets in the way of common identity and effective communication is a lack of clarity. And what leads to a lack of clarity is living too much by assumptions.

---

[580] Nagaraj Sivasubramaniam, S. Jay Liebowitz and Conway L. Lackman, "Determinants of New Product Development Team Performance: A Meta-analytic Review," *Journal of Product Innovation Management*, September 2012.

In a classic *Odd Couple* episode, Phelix Unger demonstrates what happens when we assume. [Spoiler alert! Don't read the whole footnote if you'd rather see the online video.][581]

Figure 83: In the eBook, you could click here to find out what happens "When you 'assume'..."

We live in a world of assumptions. It's actually a good thing, most of the time. If we had to make every little thing in life explicit, we'd go insane. Imagine what would happen to the simple request "Could you go get some milk?"

It would become "Because I am planning on serving you a bowl of cereal in the morning for breakfast, and because I believe that you are going to want cereal because it is what you have had every day for the last seventeen months, and because I believe that my time is currently better spent cleaning the bathrooms so that the green stuff I see in the shower does not spread disease to us all, I hereby request that you get in the car on the left side of the garage (as you face it from the outside of the house, not from the inside), open the garage door by depressing the button on the remote opener attached to the driver's-side sun visor, start the car by inserting the key into the ignition slot and turning it clockwise, shift the car into reverse, back out of the driveway without bumping the car into any other cars or pedestrians or the dogs that they may be walking, close the garage door by depressing the button on the remote control again (the same one that is attached to the driver's side visor), then, once in the street, shift the car into drive, proceed to the nearest grocery store by turning right on Elm Street, left on Washington Drive, then right on Second Avenue, parking in the store parking lot in a space demarcated by yellow lines as being appropriate for parking a car but not currently occupied by another vehicle, walking through the entry door, proceeding to aisle seven, grasping a gallon-sized bottle of milk with 2% milkfat and marked with an expiration date at least eight days from today, carrying it to a checkout lane

---

[581] To see this classic scene from a classic sitcom, get online and go to https://www.youtube.com/watch?v=LfvTwv5o1Qs. If you don't feel like doing all the work of typing that into your search bar, I'll just let you know that Phelix ends the scene with "When you assume, you make an ASS out of U and ME."

staffed by a clerk employed by the grocery store, exchanging the required quantity of money with that check-out clerk, re-acquiring the gallon of milk from the clerk, returning to the car by exiting walking through the door marked "exit"... if you don't get the gist by now, you aren't going to.

Anyway, most of the time, assumptions are a good thing, much like most of the time, our cognitive biases[582] are good things. But not all the time.

When communicating in a team, err on the side of being too explicit. Maybe not as explicit as the previous directions for acquiring milk, but explicit enough to avoid confusion.

Have you ever taken a stats class? Do you remember any of it? Remember that there are two types of errors in hypothesis testing? Well there are two types of errors with assumption testing, too. Type 1 error: not explicitly confirming assumptions between team members, and discovering that your assumptions are not well-aligned. Type 2 error: explicitly confirming assumptions that are well-aligned, and coming across as intelligence-insulting. Both types of errors can annoy the Brussels sprouts out of people.

This is a situation in which team members need to be tolerant of each other.

In the first case, we all need to recognize the fact that we live in a world of assumptions. That is our reality. Occasionally, confusion, misunderstandings, and frustrations are going to occur. I'll assume that you know what I'm thinking, and you'll assume that I know what you're thinking, but we will both be thinking that the other is thinking something that the other ain't thinking. When that occasionally happens, laugh it off and learn from it. As sender of a message, state your assumptions. As receiver of a message, ask to clarify the assumptions. As either, forgive and learn (not forget) to get better clarity in the future.

In the second case, accept that when others are being excruciatingly clear, it's not because they think that you are an idiot. It's just a means of ensuring that the communication is understood and effective. No need to roll your eyes like a teenager on the receiving end of a parental lecture. If you are consistently

---

[582] For more on cognitive biases, go to the "Cognitive Biases" section of the "Mind of Innovation" chapter, page 224. I would assume that you could guess that by now, but I don't want to make an ass out of either of us.

getting too much clarification on how to buy a gallon of milk, just let the other know with respectful feedback. Since they will have read this book, too, they will accept it graciously. And if they haven't read this book, you'll send them the link (in a CLEAR email, of course).

Remember that innovation is best done with thick skin. That includes normal everyday communication, as well as it includes specific feedback on your work. Innovation is also pretty darn fun, so laugh about stuff more. Life is too short to get upset about little things. And being upset is bad for your ability to innovate.[583]

Negotiating the RAPIDs

One area where clarity is critical is decision-making. When the responsibilities for a decision are not clearly understood by all parties, bad decisions can be made, decisions can be delayed, and execution can fall short.

To make decision-making clear, a project manager should follow a RAPID model of decision-making responsibility.

Yes, another acronym.

In the RAPID model,[584] the idea is to map out who has what responsibility involved in a decision. Although one person[585] should have the specific decision-making authority (the one who will be held accountable for the results of the decision), a variety of stakeholders should be considered as well.

Note that some of the boxes will consist of more than one person, and some of the people may fit in more than one box. That's okay. Just make sure that you think about all of the boxes.

---

[583] For more about the mental side of innovation, check out the "Mental Game of Innovation" chapter, page 217.

[584] The RAPID model was created by Bain and Company to clarify decision accountability. Also see Paul Rogers and Marcia Blenko, "Who Has the D? How Clear Decision Roles Enhance Organizational Performance," *Harvard Business Review*, January 2006.

[585] If more than one person must be responsible for a decision, then be VERY careful not to diffuse decision-making responsibility too much: when everyone is responsible for something, then no one is. See, for example, Steven J. Karau and Kipling D. Williams, "Social loafing: A meta-analytic review and theoretical integration," *Journal of Personality and Social Psychology*, October 1993.

THE CONVERSION SYSTEM: TEAMS

R is for Recommend – This is the person (or people) who will bring a recommendation to the decider. This is often a role played by the deciders themselves.

A is for Agree – This is the person (or people) who need to agree to the recommendation. They recommender(s) must work with them to ensure that they are aligned. If differences cannot be sorted out, both parties present their case to the decider.

P is for Perform – This is the person (or people) who will have to do the work

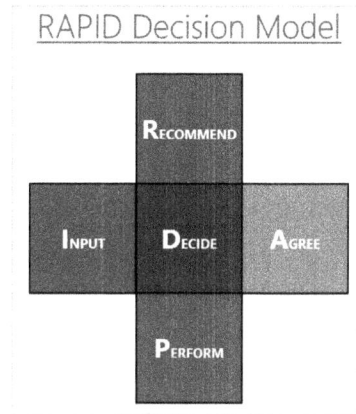

Figure 84: RAPID decision model map. Make sure you consider the points of view of all stakeholders.

after the decision is made. The recommender(s) should consult with the performer(s) for two purposes – to gain insights into the feasibility of any recommendations, and to build the support required for strong execution.

I is for Inform – This is a person (or people) who have data that will help drive the decision. They may not have responsibilities beyond data collection and communication, but they have critical knowledge that must be leveraged.

D is for Decide – The person (or people) who must make the decision and will be held accountable for the results of that decision. The decider is not only responsible for the decision, but for ensuring that the RAPID model is effectively followed.

Laying out these five roles among the team will help ensure the quality of both the decisions and the follow-ups from them. Use this formal model to ensure completeness and clarity, especially with the most important decisions. Even informally, this model can help a decision-maker to get the full set of information and perspective required for making a high-quality judgement.

Marriage Counseling

John Gottman's research on marriage has made him one of the most recognizable and influential people in the field of psychology. He's uncovered some unique and powerful insights into what makes marriages work, what makes marriages fail, and behaviors that people can adopt to have healthier relationships.

His work need not be limited to marriage, though.

Yep, you and your innovation teams can learn much from Gottman's research.[586]

Building group cohesiveness helps to make teams more creative[587] and drives successful innovation team performance.[588] Caring behavior between team members supports both team learning and faster product development.[589] Elements of team dynamics, like "social cohesion" "psychological safety," and "superordinate identity" (a fancy way of saying that members feel a common group identity) have been directly linked to the value that products deliver to their customers.[590]

Like it or not, the soft, warm-fuzzy side of management is a necessity.

The most effective innovation teams have a sense of "we-ness." Note that this "we-ness" is very different from Chandler Bing's WENUS. It's a matter going beyond just making equitable transactions (you scratch my back and I'll scratch yours) between team members. It's a matter of team members investing in something they are building together – a collective "we," a team.

[586] Stephen K. Markham and Hyunjung Lee, "Marriage and Family Therapy in NPD Teams: Effects of We-ness on Knowledge Sharing and Product Performance," *Journal of Product Innovation Management*, November 2014.

[587] Rita Bissola, Barbara Imperatori and Renata Trinca Colonel, "Enhancing the Creative Performance of New Product Teams: An Organizational Configurational Approach," *Journal of Product Innovation Management*, March 2014.

[588] Nagaraj Sivasubramaniam, S. Jay Liebowitz and Conway L. Lackman, "Determinants of New Product Development Team Performance: A Meta-analytic Review," *Journal of Product Innovation Management*, September 2012.

[589] Ludwig Bstieler and Martin Hemmert, "Increasing Learning and Time Efficiency in Interorganizational New Product Development Teams," *Journal of Product Innovation Management*, July 2010.

[590] Subin Im, Mitzi M. Montoya, and John P. Workman Jr., "Antecedents and Consequences of Creativity in Product Innovation Teams," *Journal of Product Innovation Management*, January 2013.

It's the classic example of the whole being greater than the sum of its parts. Elements of such "we-ness" include:[591]

- Security
- Empathy
- Respect
- Acceptance
- Humor and pleasure (this is why I emphasize lightening up and having fun on the job, and in reading this book, I hope)
- Shared Meaning and Vision (are you starting to see why the mission is emphasized throughout this book?)

So how can a team build "we-ness?" I've covered shared mission and humor already. Let's look at how to build the other four. Gottman offers several suggestions, centered on his concept of "the bid."

Our days are filled with making and receiving "bids" for connecting with others. Simply saying "hello" to someone is an example of such a bid. Let's call the person who first says "hello" the "bidder," and the one to whom the greeting is directed the "biddee."

When a bidder makes a bid, the biddee has three options: to turn toward the bid, to turn away from the bid, and to turn against the bid.

If someone says "hello" to you, and you say "hey, how ya doin'?" you have turned toward the bid. You have responded positively to it, and engaged with them. Your "how ya doin'" is even making a bid of your own back to them.

If someone says "hello" to you, and you just keep walking away without any acknowledgement, you have turned away from their bid. You have chosen to avoid engagement completely.

If someone says "hello" to you, and you say "What's it to *you*, cretin?!?" you have turned against their bid. You've engaged, but with hostility.

So guess which responses build relationships? Very good. Turning towards the bids.

Guess which responses damage relationships. Very good again. Turning away from the bids and turning against the bids.

---

[591] Jefferson Singer, "Positive Couple Therapy: 7 Elements of We-ness (SERAPHS)," *Psychology Today Online*, May 28, 2014.

Now, guess which response damages relationships *the most*? If you guessed turning against, well, surprise! Not so much. It turns out that turning away is the most damaging. In relationships, the opposite of love is not hate; it is cold indifference.

So, in building team relationships, one of the keys is to make bids to others, and respond to others' bids effectively. Buying doughnuts for the team on the way into the office is a bid. Saying thank you to the person who brought the doughnuts is a turn-towards. Asking how team member's weekend went is a bid. Actually listening to their reply is a turn-towards.

In addition to understanding this bidding process, another key to healthy relationships is understanding, respecting, accepting, and tolerating differences. There are an uncountable number of possible differences people have: values,[592] working styles,[593] emotional command systems,[594] learning styles,[595] coping styles,[596] life experiences,[597] etc.

I once worked for a CEO[598] who believed strongly that a cluttered desk was the sign of a cluttered mind.[599] The executive team would actually do office inspections to see that people were keeping their offices tidy.

---

[592] Charles A. O'Reilly III, Jennifer Chatman and David F. Caldwell, "People and Organizational Culture: A Profile Comparison Approach to Assessing Person-Organization Fit," *Academy of Management Journal*, September 1991. Note that Charles A. O'Reilly III should not be confused with Charles Nelson Riley. https://www.youtube.com/watch?v=rPYxkQfbBc8

[593] Carson Tate, "Differing Work Styles Can Help Team Performance," *Harvard Business Review*, April 2015.

[594] Jaak Panksepp, "Affective consciousness: Core emotional feelings in animals and humans," *Consciousness and Cognition*, March 2005.

[595] Richard M. Felder and Joni Spurlin, "Applications, reliability and validity of the index of learning styles," *International Journal of Engineering Education*, January 2005.

[596] Caroline M. Coppens*, Sietse F. de Boer and Jaap M. Koolhaas, "Coping styles and behavioural flexibility: towards underlying mechanisms," *Philosophical Transactions of the Royal Society B*, October, 2010.

[597] Citation needed. Unless you are willing to just believe me that our past experiences are all different.

[598] Who was a truly smart and wonderful person...apart from this OCD tendency.

[599] For those of you expecting an Einstein quote here, it turns out he probably never said, "If a cluttered desk is the sign of a cluttered mind, what then is an empty desk the sign of?" All those posters lie.

My office must have horrified them. I am a pile maker. Ask me for something, and I know to go about a third of the way down in the second pile from the right to find it. If, however, I am forced to file it properly in a manila folder, then place that folder into a green hanging file, in a labeled desk drawer, it will take me hours to find it again later. That's just not how my brain works.[600] So if I knew an inspection was coming, before going home, I'd take the piles off my desk, shove them somewhere out of sight for the night, then pull them out in the morning and put them right back where they were.

Think about the waste in that. C-suite executives spending their time walking around the offices doing neatness inspections. Middle managers spending time and energy pretending to conform to their organizational neatness expectations. Both could have been more efficient and focused on delivering real value to customers (and to the firm) by simply accepting that different people have different ways to keep themselves organized.

The same thing happens within teams. The structured, detail-oriented person on the team thinks that the creative concept person is flighty and out-of-touch with reality. The idea person thinks that the execution-oriented person lacks vision and brings up petty objections just to get in the way of progress. The business suit person thinks that the t-shirt and jeans person is sloppy and careless, while the t-shirt person thinks the suit is uptight and out-of-date. The hard-driver thinks that their accommodating teammate is weak and can't get things done, while the accommodator thinks the driver is an arrogant bull-in-a-china-shop breaking the team apart. The person who operates on Lombardi time [601] thinks the one who is always late to meetings is inconsiderate and disorganized, while the stressed-out late comer scrambling from meeting to meeting thinks that the early bird needs to lighten up and focus on more important things than the minute hand on the office clock.

---

[600] With full admission to confirmation bias, I present this from an online organization advisor: "There are filers and there are pilers. Too often pilers try to turn themselves into filers, and they shouldn't." So there.

[601] If you have twenty-five free minutes, it's worth spending them watching this sales training film featuring Vince Lombardi training Ron the Salesman in business and life lessons. It's over fifty years old, so please forgive the sexist references to manhood. http://www.historicfilms.com/tapes/15514

We are biased[602] to believe that we are right and that those who think differently are wrong. We must overcome that bias, and accept that people are simply different. Even when those differences drive us crazy, we need to be able to respect and tolerate them. In doing so, we will have better, stronger, and more productive working relationships.

And Gottman's last suggestion is to build shared meaning. When goals are clearly communicated, and the mission[603] is commonly understood and supported by all, the shared meaning will follow. A way to reinforce the shared meaning is to develop rituals that bond everyone together.[604] Things like the fifteen-minute stand-up meeting can be a ritual.[605] Monday morning doughnuts, Wednesday pizza lunches, or Friday afternoon happy hours can be rituals. Team shirts or hats can be symbols akin to rituals. Let such things follow and support the shared meaning that you create.

Follow the Leader

Even the best performing and close-knit teams benefit from leadership, and innovation teams are no exception. One of the demonstrated drivers of product development team success is the presence of a transformational leader.[606]

Now, you may be asking "what is a transformational leader?" I'm glad you asked.

---

[602] There we go again...more about "Cognitive Biases" in the Mental Game of Innovation chapter, page 224.

[603] And there we go again...more about strong missions in the "Mission" chapter.

[604] More about effective rituals can be found in the "Cultural Change" section of the chapter on Culture, page 82.

[605] More about simple and effective meetings can be found in the "Simple Meetings" section of the Project Management chapter, page 377.

[606] Nagaraj Sivasubramaniam, S. Jay Liebowitz and Conway L. Lackman, "Determinants of New Product Development Team Performance: A Meta-analytic Review," *Journal of Product Innovation Management*, September 2012.

Transformational leadership has four dimensions: charisma, inspirational motivation, intellectual stimulation, and individualized consideration.[607] That's a lot to throw out all at once, so let's break it down a bit.

Charisma is not just about having that magical air about you that people can't help but be attracted to. It's not something you are born with. Rather, it's about how you behave. Charisma is behaving in ways that followers admire. Such behaviors make people want to identify with you, and be associated with you. Such behaviors are rooted in principles, allowing the leader to take stands on issues, and act with conviction. These behaviors allow followers to form an emotional tie to the leader.

Remember all the talk about mission? That's also part of being a transformational leader. **Inspirational motivation** is the way in which a leader is able to create and communicate a vision and mission that is appealing and inspiring to followers. By challenging people to perform at their best and giving them a sense of meaning to their work, transformational leaders inspire high levels of achievement.

Transformational leaders do not stop at rah-rah cheerleading, though. Such leaders provide **intellectual stimulation** to their teams, encouraging them to calculate the risks involved in various courses of action, challenging their assumptions and directions of thought, and stimulating creative thinking. They solicit and share ideas. They challenge their team members, and appreciate being challenged by them in return.

Finally, the **individualized consideration** that a transformational leader provides to each person helps them to grow to their full potential. They pay attention to each person, understand their particular needs, and serve as their mentor. The transformational leader is as devoted to maximizing the potential of individuals as they are to maximizing the performance of the team.

Finding transformational leaders for every project may be challenging, but developing your skills in this area, and developing others to have these skills, will have great benefits for your organization, and particularly for your innovation efforts.

---

[607] Timothy A. Judge and Ronald F. Piccolo, "Transformational and Transactional Leadership: A Meta-Analytic Test of Their Relative Validity," *Journal of Applied Psychology*, October 2004.

Healthy Conflict

In a mechanical device, to operate as a cohesive system generally means that there are no conflicts between components. Innovation teams are not mechanical devices, however.[608]

One of the most important findings of Gottman's (and others') research is that conflict is normal.[609] Conflict is not a sign of dysfunction on the team. Rather, it's just a sign of natural differences in perspective. Dysfunction arises not from having conflict, but from how we manage it.[610]

Of all the teams I've been on, whether in business or athletics, the ones that have performed the best were always the ones with regular, healthy conflict. My best professional partners have always been those that have contradictory perspectives to mine and a willingness to express those perspectives candidly. The evidence suggests that I'm not alone in this experience. Teams that perform best, and produce the most innovative outcomes, are those that have dissent, and high levels of participation in decision-making.[611]

Leveraging the six thinking hats[612] can help to drive healthy dissent by forcing contrarian thinking in a safe environment. If you don't want to get quite so formal, just remind yourself to raise objections, even to your own ideas,[613] if everyone jumps on the "great idea" bandwagon.

---

[608] Ron Ashkenas and Markus Spiegel, "Your Innovation Team Shouldn't Run Like a Well-Oiled Machine," *Harvard Business Review Online*, October 28, 2015.

[609] John M. Gottman and Joan DeClaire, *The Relationship Cure; A 5 Step guide to Strengthening Your Marriage, Family, and Friendships*, Three Rivers Press, 2001.

[610] Karen A Jehn and Jennifer A. Chatman, "The influence of proportional and perceptual conflict composition on team performance," *International Journal of Conflict Management*, January 2000.

[611] Carsten K. W. De Dreu and Michael A. West, "Minority dissent and team innovation: The importance of participation in decision making," *Journal of Applied Psychology*, Dec 2001.

[612] More on Edward DeBono's six thinking hats can be found in the "Thinking Caps" section of the Mental Game of Innovation chapter, page 245.

[613] Be prepared for people to look at you funny if you are the only one to challenge your own ideas. I've questioned my own ideas when there was initial consensus on several occasions, and each time I've received some form of the question, "wait a minute, didn't *you* just suggest that?!?"

Managing Emotional Conflict

What to Do	How you do it
Pay Attention to Yourself	When you sense that you are in conflict, check how you are responding, and consciously choose to make that response effective.
Avoid Judgement	Give the benefit of the doubt to the person with whom you are in conflict. Do not judge them or condemn their behavior.
Understand First	Find the understandable part of their point of view. Use paraphrasing back to them to ensure your understanding, and that they know you understand.
Reflect on Your Reaction	Consider what might be driving your own upset. Understanding what is driving your emotions can help you keep them under control.
Offer Assurance	Assure the person with whom you are in conflict that you want to find a mutually acceptable solution to the problem. Demonstrate that you want them to be satisfied, as well as pursuing your own satisfaction.
Work Together	Ask the other party to work with you, collaboratively, to find that mutually satisfactory solution. Mutual compromise is okay, but overcoming the conflict entirely is even better.

Figure 85: When work conflict gets emotionally charged, follow these steps to diffuse the bomb, make the conflict healthy, and drive to positive progress (in both the work and the working relationships)

How do you keep conflict healthy? Figure 85 offers a quick guide.[614] Remember, in conflict, the only things that you can control are your own responses. The good thing is that your effective responses can help the other person to react effectively, even if they don't have all the brilliant conflict training that you are about to absorb.

First, be mindful of the situation. When you sense conflict, activate the "Yellow Alert" in your brain.[615] It's not time to go to battle stations yet, but you need to heighten your awareness of the situation. Determine that you are going to respond as effectively as possible, to keep the conflict healthy.

---

[614] Adapted from Brent J. Atkinson, *Developing Habits for Relationship Success: A Workbook*, W.W. Norton and Company, 2006.

[615] If you need a reference to a good "yellow alert," get online and go to https://www.youtube.com/watch?v=cZDDuxRh7Bw.

Second, give the other person the benefit of the doubt. In my humble opinion, one of the biggest problems with political discourse today is that opposing parties demonize one another. It's not that some people simply have a different perspective on an issue than others do. It's that they are evil, self-righteous misanthropes, and they must be crushed like the bugs that they are. Gee, I wonder why that doesn't lead to more effective outcomes?

Third, genuinely listen to the opposing point of view. Hear them out. Look for the understandable part of their perspective. Often, you will find that there is more in agreement than there first appeared to be.

Fourth, pay attention to your emotions. They will impact your behavior. Simply observing them, though, can help to keep them from escalating out of control. If you find yourself getting upset, understand what is driving that. Do you feel like you have been publicly insulted? Are you afraid that you will suffer consequences due to poor project execution? Does their tone-of-voice remind you of the way that manipulative ex who broke your heart used to talk to you?

Crazy as that may sound, getting a grip on why you are feeling upset will also help diffuse the potential emotional bomb building inside you.

Fifth, offer your opponents assurance that you are on their team, and that you want to work toward a common objective. Then, finally, ask them to work with you toward that goal. It's not you *versus* them, but you *and* them seeking a mutually acceptable solution – a "win/win" scenario. Share your point of view in that spirit, not in a tone of "Here's why you are wrong and I am right."

Be willing to take a time out. Get away from the topic. If necessary, get away from each other. Then come back and revisit the issue at a more productive time. Don't hold grudges. Heck, if you can, laugh about it. Remember, fun is a key part of a productive team. No need to make a big deal, demand apologies, and that sort of thing. Focus on resolving the issue for the good of the team and the common goal.

I know all of this is easier said than done. Practice it, and it will get easier. Post these rules on the wall for the team to see at every meeting if you need to. Whatever it takes to keep conflict healthy.

Reaching Out-of-Bounds

One final factor for team success actually has nothing to do with the internal workings of the team. It has to do instead with the ability of the team to extend outside of its boundaries, to communicate effectively with other teams, and other organizations.[616]

This may seem counterintuitive at first. How do teams become more successful by communicating to the outside world? Well, the team must be able to gather information that will help them in their work, whether it be in working process, technology, or market awareness. Strong two-way communication outside the team brings information in that will help to drive their success.

Keeping executives well-informed of progress will help to ensure the support required for the project. Keeping suppliers informed will help to ensure that you will have their insights and capabilities working for you. Keeping customers aware can help to ensure that they remain committed to you, and to secure stronger and more frequent feedback throughout the development process.

Simple Study Guide - Teams

- What is meant by "innovation is a team sport?"
- What are the different levels of team performance?
- What are three roles recommended for strong team performance?
- What are characteristics of good team communication?
- What is an octopi-shaped team, and how does it function?
- How can geographically dispersed teams still develop strong team cohesion?
- What is the CLEAR model of communication?
- What is the RAPID model for decision-making?
- How can relationship research be applied to building effective teams?
- What is a transformational leader?
- Why do teams need to effectively communicate outside of the team?

---

[616] Nagaraj Sivasubramaniam, S. Jay Liebowitz and Conway L. Lackman, "Determinants of New Product Development Team Performance: A Meta-analytic Review," *Journal of Product Innovation Management*, September 2012.

Where do you want to go from here?

Control	Creation	Conversion
Mission (page 40)	Voice of the Customer (page 175)	Innovation Teams (page 310)
Culture (page 58)	Minds of Innovators (page 217)	Project Management (page 347)
Strategy (page 92)	Ideation (page 279)	For-Profit Metrics (page 389)
Portfolio Management (page 146)		Nonprofit Metrics (page 403)
Change Management (page 411)		

Or just turn the page to keep reading...

Trampling Wildflowers (Project Management)

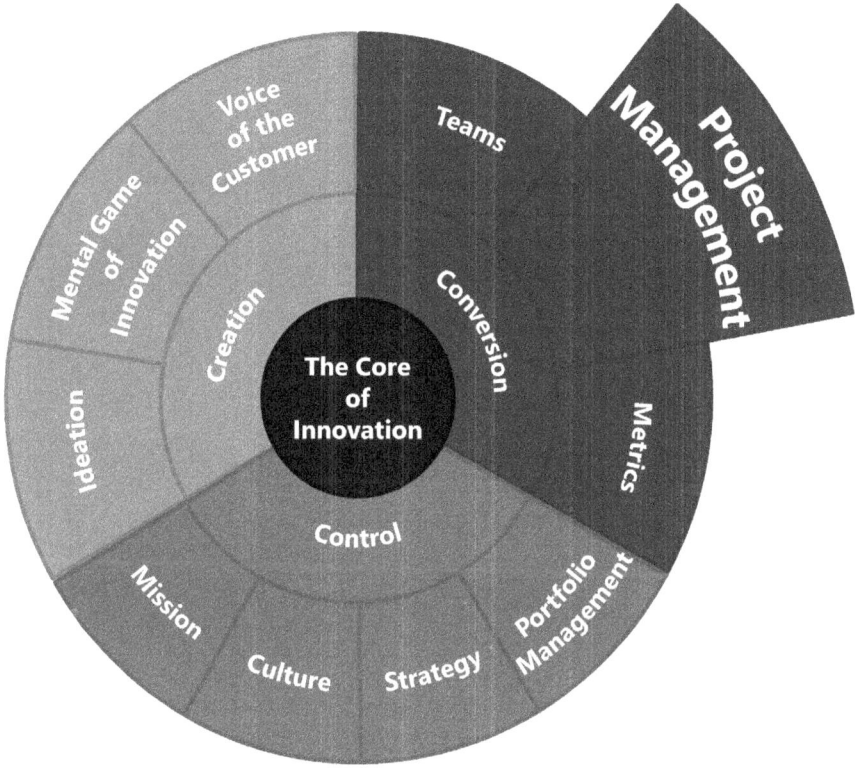

Simple Self-Assessment – Project Management

Rate yourself on the following questions. To benchmark yourself against others, go to www.3point14Innovation.com and click the "Self-Assessments" menu.

- ### Do you follow a structured project management approach?

We prefer winging it | | | | | | | | It's all under control

1	2	3	4	5	6	7	8	9	10

- ### Do you build flexibility into your management process?

Structure *and* flexibility? Huh? | | | | | | We can bend the rules when necessary

1	2	3	4	5	6	7	8	9	10

- ### Do you use project charters for guiding all of your projects?

We chartered a boat once | | | | | | Yes, for every one of them

1	2	3	4	5	6	7	8	9	10

- ### Does your organization push for faster execution on all projects?

All the time. Or is it never? | | | | | | Only when appropriate

1	2	3	4	5	6	7	8	9	10

- ### How well does your organization forecast innovation initiatives?

Random number generator | | | | | | Like the oracle of Delphi

1	2	3	4	5	6	7	8	9	10

- ### Has your organization ever performed a pre-mortem?

Is that a heavy metal band? | | | | | It helps our contingency planning

1	2	3	4	5	6	7	8	9	10

- ### How much time do you spend in meetings?

Is there any other way to work? | | | | | Meetings are quick and efficient

1	2	3	4	5	6	7	8	9	10

- ### Does your organization follow through on After Action Reviews?

Too busy doing the next thing | | | | | | Regularly and effectively

1	2	3	4	5	6	7	8	9	10

Simple Summary – Project Management

Key take-aways you should get out of this section:

- Innovation is an investment, but there is a key difference between investing in innovation and investing in financial assets: coordination and control. That control comes in the form of project management. It's like investing with insider information, only legal.
- For managing new product development projects, there are vocal advocates for both a phased gate approach and a lean/agile approach. No clear research is available that says one is always better than the other. The key is to make sure that you are managing the process consciously and systematically.
- No matter how you do it, effective project management requires making tough decisions.
- Regardless of the project management approach, innovation is not a linear process. Flexibility requires maintaining a constant focus on the ultimate goal, making adjustments to the plans as new information is gained, and making decisions in the context of the overall portfolio.
- If you use only one tool to manage an innovation project, make it the Project Charter. It is the single most important tool for guiding and managing the project.
- Going faster does not always equate with greater success. Speed is one component of doing a project right, but not the only component. If it adversely impacts customer satisfaction, excessively drives up development costs, or inhibits execution with excellence, it may not be worth it. The more radical the innovation, the less critical is speed to market.
- Forecasting is hard. Complex forecasting models do not help, and can even hurt. Keep forecasting simple. The Delphi Method is a simple and effective process.
- The pre-mortem is a way to identify potential project-killers and plan contingencies for them in advance.
- An "oobeya room" can be a great physical tool for organizing and managing projects. Find a single spot to collect and post information, plans, and artifacts of the project. Oobeya rooms make great places to hold team meetings as well.

- Almost everyone has too many meetings that are too long and too unproductive. Simplify your meetings with the conflict/coordination meeting and the working meeting.
- Always, always, always do an After Action Review for a project. Do it for phases within a project. It is a valuable learning tool, and helps reinforce meaning for the project teams.

Project Cartography

As the devil is always in the details, it's the specifics of the plan that make things hellish. That's when you must keep in mind what Eisenhower said about plans and planning: "plans are useless, but planning is indispensable."[617]

Note that he did not mean that after preparing detailed plans you should then spend your afternoon running them through a shredder for stress relief. Having a plan is critical for execution, especially with more complex efforts. You don't wake up one day and build a watch without planning out all the parts you'll need and how to assemble them properly.

But battle planning and innovation are different than watch-making. The plan for making the watch is more-or-less certain. If you have all the pieces and follow all the assembly instructions properly, you're virtually assured of producing a functional watch.

However, when you plan an undertaking that involves uncertainty, the plan itself is not as important as the planning process, in which you consider scenarios, alternatives, and possibilities. Innovation is not as predictable as watch assembly. As Eisenhower went on to say, "There is a very great distinction [between planning and the plan], because when you are planning for an emergency, you must start with this one thing: the very definition of 'emergency' is that it is unexpected; therefore, it is not going to happen the way you are planning."

The plan assumes that everything goes according to, well, the plan. Innovation never goes exactly according to plan. The more radical the innovation, the more likely that it won't go according to plan.

Good planning is about learning and preparation. It's about anticipating difficulties and planning contingencies. It's about learning and building a storehouse of information that you can apply when the project train runs off the Gantt chart track.

I have repeatedly emphasized that innovation is an investment. I have used analogies with retirement planning to illustrate several points about wise investing. But now is the time to unveil the key difference between investing

---

[617] For more on innovation planning, refer to the "Creating and Innovation Plan" section of the Strategy chapter, page 129.

money in stocks and bonds, versus investing in your organization's innovation efforts.

Coordination and control.

When you buy stock in a company, you have no control over that company's behavior.[618] When you invest in your organization's innovation efforts, you have that control. You coordinate the resources. You still can't predict the future with any accuracy, but you can choose how you respond to the future as it unfolds.

Innovation project management is one way to choose your responses. Your projects will not go as planned. They will never go exactly the way you believed that they would on day one. To execute an innovation project effectively takes flexibility, adaptability, systems thinking, focus on the end objective, and, yes, a little bit of luck.

Applying project management control to innovation is important. It helps to guide decision-making, align and coordinate resources, and ensure strategic resource allocation. Unfortunately, organizations across all sectors have focused too much on the trees of managerial control and lost sight of the innovation forest.[619] The plan and the adherence to the defined process have taken priority over achieving the objectives of innovation and securing a return on the investment. The resulting common project management controls inhibit learning, innovation and creativity.[620]

For that reason, among others, I have seen variations on

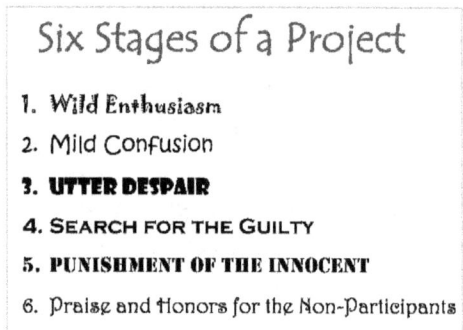

Six Stages of a Project

1. Wild Enthusiasm
2. Mild Confusion
3. **UTTER DESPAIR**
4. SEARCH FOR THE GUILTY
5. PUNISHMENT OF THE INNOCENT
6. Praise and Honors for the Non-Participants

Figure 86: A sign I've seen in one form or another in every organization. And even if the sign isn't there, everyone can relate.

---

[618] Unless maybe you are T. Boone Pickens, but that's not the level of investment that most of us could ever dream of.

[619] Anne Keegan and J. Rodney Turner, "The Management of Innovation in Project-Based Firms," *Long Range Planning*, August 2002.

[620] Thomas Gillier, Sophie Hooge, and Gérald Piat, "Collaborative Design of Value in Creative Projects: An Expansive Value Management Model," *i3 First Interdisciplinary Innovation Conference*, December 2013.

Figure 86 posted in cubicles or on office walls in almost every organization I've ever visited.

When managing innovation projects, we have to realize that the conditions are different than for other projects, and adjust the principles of project management to the particulars of innovation.

Gated Community or Lean 'n' Mean?

So what kind of project plan should you have? There are two general types of approaches for new product development projects: phase-gate/waterfall or lean/agile. Each has its adherents. Each can (and should) be tailored to the specific needs of an organization.

The phase-gate/waterfall approach generally consists of a series of work "phases" with decision-making "gates" between them. The approach was codified by Robert Cooper and Scott Edgett, and you may be more familiar with their trademarked approach called Stage-Gate.® [621] Whether you call

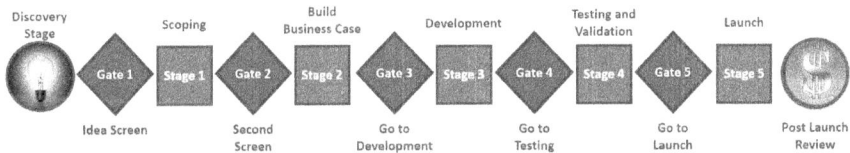

Figure 87: A generic Stage-Gate process depiction. Source: Stage-Gate International.

them phases or stages, the concept is the same. "Waterfall" is the software industry version of the approach. The phase work is performed by the project teams, while the gate decisions are generally made by higher levels of executive management.

The intent here is to do a defined set of activities in each phase. The results of those activities feed into a decision as to whether or not to invest in the development activities of the next phase. Each decision gate authorizes a higher level of investment. Ideally, bad projects get killed early, before the more significant money gets spent.

---

[621] For Stage-Gate info straight from the creator's mouth (or pen, or keyboard, whatever), read Robert G. Cooper, "Formula for Success in New Product Development," *Marketing Management Magazine*, March/April 2006.

The gates should be more than just giant deck presentations to executives. They need to have muscle. They need to have teeth. Real decisions need to be made. Tough decisions. Real resources need to be allocated to work on the next stage, or projects need to be killed. The decisions need to be clear, and communicated effectively.

One group I encountered had created their own phase-gate approach. Or so they thought. It consisted of 26 phases with 26 gate meetings scheduled every two weeks. In other words, it was a one-year idea-to-market plan with 26 bi-weekly executive updates. That is *not* what a phase-gate approach is all about.

I've seen other organizations say that they are going to have five stages and five gates because that's what is in the book and by golly, they are going to do what the book says. They apparently missed the part in the book that says that five is a guideline that works for many organizations, but you really ought to adjust to the needs of your own.

Bigger, more complex projects on long time lines may require more stages and gates. Smaller, incremental projects on tight time schedules may need fewer (maybe only one or two). Some organizations use multiple processes with different numbers of stages, depending on the type of project. That's okay, but be careful not to go over the edge into excessive complexity.

The Lean/Agile approach is quite different. Without getting bogged down in too much terminology (such as scrums, Kanban, sprints, stories, MVPs, and my personal favorite, "code smell"), the approach is generally to go through a series of development efforts aimed at creating a prototype, testing it with customers, learning from the results, and incorporating

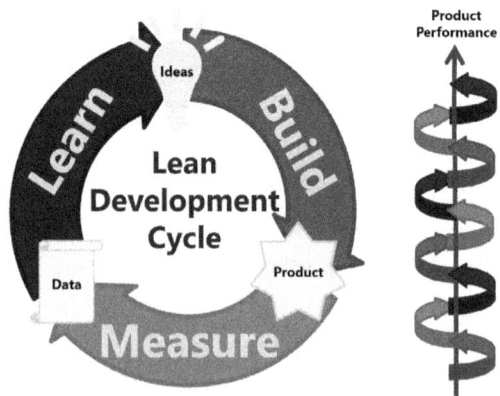

Figure 88: Overview of a lean development cycle. With each cycle, the additional learning improves product performance as perceived by the target customer.

what is learned into the next round of development.[622]

The idea here is to learn quickly what works and what doesn't with a series of experiments. Developers have an idea to solve the customer problem; they build a prototype to test with customers; they collect data from the customer's experience with the prototype; they learn from the experiment; they repeat the cycle with more ideas. Only this time the ideas come from a smarter place, based on data from the customer.

Regardless of what kind of process you choose, when implementing a new process, I suggest following the teen-driver philosophy. Start by erring on the side of obeying the rules, even to a fault. When you give a teen driver the keys to a car, you teach them that they must obey the rules of the road to the letter. They have to come to a full and complete stop at a stop sign. They must drive not even 1 mph over the speed limit. They must signal their lane changes even if no other car is in sight. You stay on top of them until these rules become instinctual in their developing brains.

Only after much experience at the wheel and a good driving record do you let the rules get a little fuzzier. Only with experience do you start to say "I've got to get my pregnant wife to the hospital a little faster than the speed limit says because her contractions are getting awfully close together, and I just had the car detailed."

Please note that I am not advocating anarchy here. [Note to the NSA, FBI, and IRS: please don't come knocking on my door now that I mentioned anarchy.][623]

The point here is that when you really know the rules, when you know why they are there, and when you have a good track record of following them, only then should you start making rational, sensible decisions about bending the rules on occasion. Only then should you evolve the rules to build more flexibility into your process.

---

[622] It's much more than that, but hopefully that gives you the gist. For more on Agile, check out Dan Olsen, *The Lean Product Playbook: How to Innovate with Minimum Viable Products and Rapid Customer Feedback*, John Wiley and Sons, 2015.

[623] Oops, I said "anarchy again." Doh!

In fact, the best innovators do exactly that. The PDMA CPAS study data[624] show that organizations with the best outcomes are more likely to be flexible in their processes, using conditional decisions, skipping stages, and parallel processing. They did not start that way, but evolved to those points as they gained experience over time.

Those examples are being done by organizations that started by defining and obeying the rules of the road. If you start with a process that does not actively promote and enforce the rules, you will find that no one follows a process at all. And that is what the worst of the worst do.

Phase-Gate or Agile? I've witnessed some seriously heated debates on the topic. I've read the blogs, articles and books on the topic. I've searched for real research into the topic. To date, I haven't found anything that says definitively one is better than the other in all situations. So you'll have to choose what works best for you.

One critically important note to make about the difference – or perhaps the similarity – between the two. There is a serious misunderstanding, even among those who ought to know better, that the Stage-Gate approach represents an attempt to make the inherently non-linear nature of innovation conform to a linear process. While some people and organizations may misuse the process in that way, it really isn't meant to be like that.

It's not the fault of the process if someone misuses it, any more than it's the fault of the cinnamon tree for Darwin Award nominees doing the cinnamon challenge.[625]

The way it is depicted in Figure 87, the process certainly looks linear. But in the words of Bob Cooper, the one who originally defined the stage-gate process, "new market creation is the result of managing a set of events and activities that appear linear, but are not."[626] Maybe Figure 89 is a more accurate way to depict it.

---

[624] Stephen K. Markham and Hyunjung Lee, "Product Development and Management Association's 2012 Comparative Performance Assessment Study," *Journal of Product Innovation Management*, May 2013.

[625] What's the cinnamon challenge, you ask? Serious stupidity. http://abcnews.go.com/blogs/health/2012/03/09/cinnamon-challenge-sparks-health-concerns/

[626] Robert G. Cooper, "Third-Generation New Product Processes," *Journal of Product Innovation Management*, January 1994.

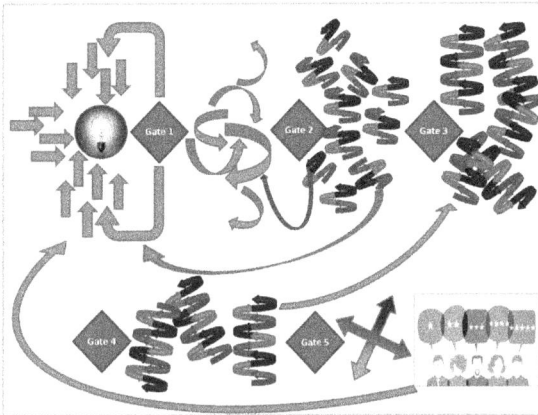

Figure 89: The reality of Stage-Gate is that there is still a great deal of chaos, churn, change of direction, rethinking, etc. At least if it's done right. It is NOT to be an excuse to force through ideas from beginning to end on a perfectly linear path.

Within each stage, there is a great deal of chaos to make sense of. You probe in one direction, learn, and adjust. What you learn on one project impacts what you do on another. New information comes into play that changes your original plan.

If you are using a Stage-Gate process to force projects straight through, unchanged from the original idea, with gates being just pass/fail decision points devoid of flexibility, then stop it. Stop it now. You're hindering your own ability to innovate, and you are giving a perfectly good process a bum rap. Yes, you need to make sense of the chaos, but that doesn't mean putting on blinders that keep you from seeing the chaos.

This should not scare you off, though, if you are looking for the simple route to innovation. Remember, simple is not about making things easy. That's simplistic. Simple is rather about making the complex clear. The processes involved in doing that are intended to help create clarity out of the chaos, not to force linearity where it can't be forced. And that's okay...it's even a good thing. Exploration, experimentation, learning, and improving is what will make innovation successful.[627]

Kicking-Off

So where do you start when managing an innovation project? That depends, in part, on how you define project management.

---

[627] Gina Colarelli O'Connor and Mark P. Rice, "New Market Creation for Breakthrough Innovations: Enabling and Constraining Mechanisms," *Journal of Product Innovation Management*, March 2013.

The Fuzzy Front End – that part of the process in which customer needs are being explored, technologies are being researched, and ideas are being generated, needs to be managed. In the generic stage-gate process, it's front and center.[628] However, that's not where I'm going to start, because the fuzziness of the front end renders many of the typical project management tools inoperable.

If I can liken a project to running a race, the fuzzy front end is like pre-race training, and the project like the actual race. There is a great deal of planning and management required in that front end, but the execution is just plain different.

So I'm going to start with the Project Charter. This is the point where a project gets initially defined sufficiently to be managed as a project. The ideas have been screened and selected, the objectives clarified, and the resources allocated.

At least, that has all happened enough to get started. Things will most assuredly change along the path of execution.

The project charter is the single most important document for project execution. It provides clarity for the team on all the who, what, when, where, why, and how questions needed to proceed.

Because the charter is so important, it is that much more important to keep it simple. Keep it something that people will use as a guide throughout the process. Figure 90 shows a simple project charter. One page. I strongly recommend doing what you can, short of using 2 point fonts, to keep the charter to just one page.

"But Brad," you ask, "there is so much relevant information the team needs! How can that be placed on one page without resorting to 2 point (or smaller) fonts?"

The charter should not contain *all* of the information relevant to the entire project. Those details can be captured and referenced elsewhere when needed. The project charter should only contain the critical points, the ultimate

---

[628] Actually, it's on the far left, but you know what I mean.

guidelines, the keys to success. Not every detail. Keeping it simple will be challenging,[629] but the work will pay off in value.

The charter should have some critical topline information, such as who is on the team, who is championing the effort, the target date for launch, etc.

Project Charter Template

Project Name:	
Charter version:	
Project Executive Sponsor:	
Project Leader:	
Project Team:	
Portfolio placement(s):	
Target launch date:	

Brief Description of Solution/Idea/Concept:	Link to Strategy/Mission:
Target Customers:	Expected Resources Required: Human – Financial – Time –
Customers' Job-to-be-done:	Metrics for Success: Year 1 – Year 2 – Year 3 –
Competing Solutions:	Critical Assumptions:
Why Solution Delivers Unique and Superior Value:	Identifiable Risks:

Figure 90: The Project Charter - the key to getting your projects started off on the right foot, and not dancing with two left feet.

That should be followed with other essentials, such as:

---

[629] Remember, simple does not mean easy.

- Brief Description of the Solution/Idea/Concept:
- Link to Strategy/Mission (How does this project deliver against them?)
- Target Customers (who are they and what are their key needs)
- Expected Resources Required (Human, Financial, and Time)
- Customers' Job-to-be-done[630] (critical for framing the innovation effort)
- Metrics[631] for Success (from multiple perspectives, and over multiple time frames)
- Competing Solutions (how are customers currently getting their job-to-be-done, done?)
- Critical Assumptions (The things you'll have to prove along the way to be successful)
- Why the Solution Delivers Unique and Superior Value (what is it about this concept that will deliver a customer-perceivable difference over other solutions)
- Identifiable Risks (the known unknowns that could impact the success of the project).

These elements will serve as the focus of the team throughout the project.

Some people will recommend that the project charter be chiseled into stone tablets and bronzed, never changing. They use other documents for the inevitable changes along the way.

That's a fine approach, but not one that I prefer to follow. Personally, I like the idea of the project charter being a living document, updated as the project moves along. With proper version control,[632] this approach keeps the single living document as the ultimate rule book for the project innovation game.

The main objective of the innovation management process is to learn, and apply what was learned to the execution of a new product. You start with a bunch of assumptions, and then test those assumptions along the way, until

---

[630] For more about jobs-to-be-done and other aspects of understanding customers, go to the "Voice of the Customer" chapter, page 176.

[631] For more on innovation metrics, go to the sections on "Innovation for Fun and Profit" (page 389) and "Innovation for Fun and Not-for-Profit" (page 403).

[632] "Version control" means more than just changing the file name descriptively. It means ensuring buy-in from stakeholders on all changes, communicating any updates in a timely and effective manner, and ensuring that people are always referencing the latest version.

the assumptions are minimized and the conclusive data maximized. Sometimes, the things that are learned along the way show that the original idea requires significant modification. In such cases, updating the charter with the new information (and any new questions that information generates), is quick and efficient.

The team must always be able to reference the same document to know where they stand and where they need to go. Updates should not occur so frequently that there is confusion about which to reference. Only when significant changes have occurred should the charter be updated.

Leverage the power of a structured project charter, keeping it simple to maximize its usefulness.

The Need for Speed

In the product development world, especially in highly competitive markets, there is a demand for speed. Speed to market.

So we must ask the question – is speed critical to success?

Well, let's look at the National Football League for an analogy.[633]

The league likes its metrics. Every year before the annual draft, an event called the NFL Combine measures athletes interested in breaking into the league on a variety of metrics, from height and weight to vertical jumping ability to repetitive bench-pressing that defies ordinary concepts of "strong."

But the highlight of the event is arguably the 40-yard dash. That's the one that makes the highlight reels on ESPN. Everyone wants to know how fast their favorite players were. Some coaches won't draft someone who doesn't impress in the forty. Some owners will draft anyone who does impress.

In the fifteen years since electronic timing has been used, the six fastest times in "The Forty" have been recorded by eleven players.[634] Of those eleven, only one has had an NFL career of any real noteworthiness. The others ranged from above average to thoroughly unremarkable.

---

[633] In an effort to avoid gender and national bias, I attempted to find a similar analogy in the sport of camogie, but they apparently don't have a combine event like the NFL does.

[634] Matt Reevy, "11 Fastest 40-Yard Dashes in NFL History," *Sports Cheat Sheet*, October 24, 2015.

On the flip side of the coin, you have Jerry Rice, possibly the greatest receiver of all time. His "forty" time was described as "pedestrian" by his head coach, and was a full 10% slower than the eleven described above.

Does that mean speed is not important in the NFL? Of course not. But it does mean that it is not the only thing that is important, and it's probably not even the most important.

The same, it turns out, is true for product development. Getting products to market faster is better, *everything else being equal*. But everything else is not always equal.

A recent exploration of the impact of speed on product development success demonstrated this point.[635] There was, at best, mixed evidence regarding the correlation of speed and success. As the authors put it, "From this analysis, indeed from the sum of the previous research done on NPD cycle time and success,[636] it is unclear which construct, speed or success, is the cart, and which is the horse. We cannot conclude whether faster development speed leads to improved NPD success, or whether companies that are more successful at developing new products also become speedier than others due to their development capabilities."

The study revealed some definite maybes regarding speed as a competitive advantage, though.

First, there may be some industries where speed is king. Software comes to mind. In other industries – say, for example, industrial valves – speed is a not-so-much. Look within your industry to see what kind of factor it may be. To paraphrase the research conclusions, before setting off on a unilateral corporate program to reduce NPD cycle time, get some data to support that implementing such a program will actually add value.

Second, a situation in which speed may be beneficial is when the window of opportunity for a successful launch is narrow. While working on office products, my team and I had to deal with launch calendars tied to our customers' annual catalogue release dates. Missing those dates meant waiting

---

[635] Pinar Cankurtaran, Fred Langerak and Abbie Griffin, "Consequences of New Product Development Speed: A Meta-Analysis," *Journal of Product Innovation Management*, May 2013.

[636] NPD=New Product Development.

an entire year to launch in the next catalogue. That's the kind of narrow window for which reduced cycle time would be helpful.

However, if you are in a business where it doesn't much matter to the success of your launch if it takes place this month or next, then reducing cycle time is not as likely to help. It's more important to get the product right than to get it launched fast.

Third, you must consider context before arbitrarily looking for ways to increase development speed. Go all the way back to your organizational culture.[637] Does it support the decision-making processes required for speed? Consider your strategy.[638] Is speed-to-market a critical aspect? Do your customers need you to be fast? Are competitive forces demanding more speed out of you?

There is another factor that makes speed potentially detrimental that many innovators overlook: the ability of customers to accept an innovation.[639] Customers can be resistant to change. The greater the change, the greater the resistance. Even an amazing new widget with fantastic customer benefits may not get accepted because it is too different from what they know and are comfortable with. A product ahead of its time may need to wait a bit for success.

Remember that there is no such thing as a free lunch.[640] Reducing cycle time will not come without some sort of cost. It won't magically happen because word comes down to the masses from on high. It won't happen without work and the invariable challenges of implementing change. The value may well be worth those costs, but ensure that it is before arbitrarily setting off to make it so.

---

[637] See the chapter on "Culture" for more information, page 58.

[638] See the chapter on "Strategy" for more information, page 92.

[639] Jiyao Chen, Richard R. Reilly and Gary S. Lynn, "New Product Development Speed: Too Much of a Good Thing?" *Journal of Product Innovation Management*, March 2012.

[640] I always thought that the free lunch quote was a Milton Friedman thing, but it's just another common saying attributed on the internet to a few dozen historical figures. For all I know, Sophocles included it in one of his Athenian plays.

Cloudy Crystal Ball

Have you ever gotten up in the morning, and known exactly how your day was going to turn out? Traffic was exactly what you expected and planned for; meetings were always on time and worked out exactly as you thought they would; you received the expected number of phone calls and emails from the expected people on the expected topics at the expected times; you arrived home to family and/or friends who all had the expected news and topics of conversation; and you went to bed at the expected time and got a restful night of sleep in advance of a repeat of expectations the following day?

That doesn't happen to anyone very often. I personally don't know anyone that it's happened to, ever. And that's just one day. Roughly sixteen awake hours.

Extrapolate that over weeks, months, and years of work in a constantly changing and unpredictable world – how are you supposed to forecast the five-year sales growth of Project X?

Look at all the variables involved: how will company performance impact spending on marketing, sales incentives, advertising, customer support, quality control, engineering, etc.? What counter response will the competitors have? What happens if the housing market collapses again? What if Greece actually does default on their debts? Is that trendy new thing all the kids are using going to replace your product in the hearts of your middle-aged customers, or will that just be a fad like parachute pants in the 1980's? How will the project be managed when the project lead leaves the company to pursue her/his lifelong dream of playing backup accordion for Weird Al Yankovich?[641]

Forecasting new product success is like shooting fish in a barrel, if the barrel is made of a steel/graphite/ceramic composite and you're shooting a bb gun from 100 meters.

And don't expect that simply asking experts will necessarily help. There are tons of quotes out there from experts of ages past that were so very, very wrong:[642]

---

[641] To see one of the king-of-musical-parody's videos, I suggest getting online and going to https://www.youtube.com/watch?v=zq7Eki5EZ8o. But there are many more to choose from!

[642] As with all internet quotes, many of the more famous ones out there simply aren't true. Bill Gates never said "640K should be all the memory anyone ever needs," nor any variation of it. Ken Olson did say "There is no reason anyone would want a computer in their home," but he

- "The advancement of the arts, from year to year, taxes our credulity and seems to presage the arrival of that period when human improvement must end." ~Commissioner of the US Patent Office, Henry L. Ellsworth, 1843.[643]
- "The idea of installing 'telephones' in every city is idiotic... This 'telephone' has too many shortcomings to be seriously considered as a means of communication. The device is inherently of no value to us." ~Western Union internal memo, 1876.
- "This is typical Berlin hot air. The product is worthless" ~Heinrich Dreser, head of Bayer's Pharmacological Institute, rejecting aspirin as a pain killer, 1897.
- "Who the hell wants to hear actors talk? The music! - That's the big plus about this." ~H.M. Warner, regarding adding sound to movies, 1927.
- "Computers in the future may weigh no more than 1.5 tons." ~Popular Mechanics, 1949.
- "We don't like their sound, and guitar music is on the way out." ~Decca Recording Company rejecting the Beatles, 1962.
- "900,000 subscribers." McKinsey & Company forecast for cell phone penetration in the USA by the year 2000, made in 1980. (The actual figure turned out to be about 109 Million)
- "There's no chance that the iPhone is going to get any significant market share. No chance." ~Steve Ballmer, 2007.
- "We simply do not know what the future holds." ~Peter L. Bernstein, investment guru and first editor of the *Journal of Portfolio Management*.

Okay, that last one you can trust. He got that right.

---

says that was in reference to the mainframes that his company, Digital Equipment Corp., manufactured. And for that, he was absolutely right. Remember what Abraham Lincoln said: ""Most of the quotes you find on the internet are wrong." Or was that Ben Franklin?

[643] You may have heard that Charles H. Duell, Commissioner of US patent office in 1899, said that "everything that can be invented has been invented." He didn't. In fact, in 1902 he said the opposite: "In my opinion, all previous advances in the various lines of invention will appear totally insignificant when compared with those which the present century will witness. I almost wish that I might live my life over again to see the wonders which are at the threshold." How did he ever gut such a bum rap?

So if the super-enlightened don't have a crystal ball, how is anyone supposed to do forecasting?

It is inherently impossible to do with precision. Many complex methods have been created to improve the accuracy of forecasts, but none have proven to be worth the resource input.[644] They were no more accurate – and often less accurate – than predictions based on simple analyses.[645]

So what are you to do? As with everything else in this book, keep it simple.

This will not go over well with many people. Some simply cannot deal with ambiguity.[646] They are comforted by the thought that very smart people spent a great deal of time and energy to input a lot of numbers into a complicated computer algorithm to generate a number down to the penny. They don't want to hear about variables and uncertainty. Uncertainty gives them a rash. Decimal points are the only ointment that relieves the itch.

But the reality is that simple works better, costs less, and keeps the team alert. False security in false certainty lulls people to sleep. Consciously dealing with and managing the uncertainty forces them to stay awake.

Some research has offered insights on how to do simple forecasting well, depending on the type of innovation you are forecasting.[647]

For incremental innovations in stable markets, leveraging historical data of similar product launches is most effective.[648] Yep, that simple. Say your project, Incremental X, got a set of product test metrics similar to previous products, Incremental A, Incremental B, and Incremental C. If you plan to support

---

[644] Kesten C. Green and J. Scott Armstrong, "Simple Versus Complex Forecasting: The Evidence," *Social Science Research Network*, March 1, 2015. Details of their conclusions were referenced in the "Why Simple?" section, page 18. Not that you would have skipped that part, of course.

[645] A great video to watch about why complex models go awry, featuring Peter L. Berstein, can be found at http://www.mckinsey.com/insights/risk_management/peter_l_bernstein_on_risk. He also discusses the investment concept of options – which is essentially what product development projects are. Watching is a good way to spend about fourteen minutes of your life.

[646] There's a brief story of people unable to deal with ambiguity in the "Why Simple" section, page 18, too.

[647] Matthias Seiffert, Enno Siemsen, Allegre L. Hadida, and Andreas B. Eisingerich, "Effective Judgmental Forecasting in the Context of Fashion Products," *Journal of Operations Management*, May 2015.

[648] For more on incremental, evolutionary, and radical innovation types, go to the "What the #&#! Is Innovation, Anyway?" section of the opening chapter, page 4.

Incremental X with similar launch resources, then your best forecast is going to be in the neighborhood of how Incremental A, Incremental B, and Incremental C performed.

As the innovations get more radical, and/or the markets get more unpredictable, however, historical data can actually get in the way of making good predictions. Oh great. So now what do we do?

The Delphi Method

In these cases, you should leverage "contextual data:" those things that ought to correlate with success, but may be more subjective and qualitative. For example, you may want to take a SWAG[649] at the expected efficacy of a marketing spend, anticipated competitive response, or the impact of key influencers' reactions to your product.

In the case of using contextual data, it is best to have a group evaluation, to try and eliminate individual biases and leverage the "wisdom of crowds."[650] The best way to do that in the case of innovation forecasting with a high level of uncertainty is the Delphi Method. [651]

This method was developed by the Rand Corporation in the 1950's and 1960's to forecast political and social changes around the globe. In the subsequent half century, it has proven itself to have application in many areas, not least of which include innovation forecasting. While we are talking here specifically about forecasting the potential sales, demand, rate of acceptance, or other criteria specific to an innovation project, the technique can also be applied to forecast other environmental changes that affect your organization.

The way the Delphi Method works is simple (a key criterion for everything presented in this book):

---

[649] SWAG stands for "Scientific Wild-[Expletive Deleted] Guess." Yes, it's a guesstimate, but at least it's one with some thought behind it. You'd be surprised at how much intuition can be relied upon in such situations.

[650] An entertaining read on the subject is a book by that very name: James Surowiecki, *The Wisdom of Crowds*, Anchor Publishing, 2005.

[651] For a really, really deep dive into the Delphi method (even including a thorough discussion of the underlying philosophy of the process from Leibnizian, Kantian, Lockean, Hegelian, and Singerian perspectives!), check out *The Delphi Method: Techniques and Applications*, edited by Harold A. Linstone and Murray Turoff, Addison-Wesley Educational Publishers Inc.,1975.

- A small forecasting team explains a situation to a larger respondent group. For an innovation, "explaining the situation" may mean describing the innovation, what it does, who it does it for, features, test results, etc.
- The respondent group is then polled individually on a question to forecast – for example, in the case of a new product launch by a for-profit company, initial sales volume, trial and repeat rates, etc. You'll need to choose the right metrics[652] for your organization and innovation specifics.
- The results are collected and summarized by the forecasting team.
- The larger group is allowed to see the summary of results, and is then given a chance to revise their answers based on the summary. In some cases, this is done individually, and in others, it may be done in an open forum to allow for discussion on controversial points. Determine which approach is right for your organizational culture.
- A consensus forecast is (hopefully) reached. If not among the whole respondent group, then among the smaller forecasting team. If not among them, then it may fall to a responsible individual for a final decision.[653]

This method can take some time and energy, but it's simple and effective. At least it is when it is done well.

But what if it's not done well? Just like any other process, garbage in, garbage out. The Delphi process can be susceptible to failure when:

- Preconceived beliefs about the project are conveyed to the respondent team;
- Poor capturing of the respondent group's thoughts after the first round of evaluation, such that important points are misrepresented, or under/overstressed;
- Failure to understand and address points of disagreement among respondents;

---

[652] For more on innovation metrics, go to the sections on "Innovation for Fun and Profit" (page 389) and "Innovation for Fun and Not-for-Profit" (page 403).

[653] Such responsibility should be defined for each team using the RAPID process, discussed in the Teams chapter, page 310.

- Domination of a discussion by an individual or small subset of the group, such that dissenting viewpoints are lost;
- Failure to compensate the respondents in some way. This may not be a problem the first time the process is tried, but in future efforts, people may be unwilling to do the hard work of full participation without some recognition or compensation.

The Pre-Mortem

Even after all the hard work of coming up with the best possible forecasts, you already know that they are going to be wrong. You can leverage the differing perspectives and discussions of the Delphi Method to be prepared in advance for those times when things go differently than anticipated.

The pre-mortem[654] is a fantastic contingency planning tool. And, best of all, it's simple.

Like the Delphi method and ideation techniques, this is best done individually before bringing people together. You'll get the best perspectives this way.

The approach is straightforward:

1) Imagine that you are in the future in a specified time frame, and the project has failed.
2) Conduct in your mind a hypothetical After Action Review.[655]
3) Capture the lessons hypothetically learned as potential contingency plans.
4) Repeat for a different specified time frame.

The time frames you choose will be specific to the project, but should follow the rough guidelines of short, medium, and long term. In some cases, that might be three months, six months, and one year. In other cases, it might be one year, five years, and ten years. The team leader should determine those specifications before the exercise.

---

[654] Olivier Serrat, "The Premortem Technique," *Asian Development Bank Knowledge Solutions*, March 2012.

[655] Which will be explained in detail at the end of this chapter.

Once people have gone through the exercise individually, the project manager can collate the results, then bring the team together for a discussion. The objective for such a discussion is to emerge with specific if-then-else contingency plans, which can then be communicated and, if necessary, approved by management.

The pre-mortem can help not only to prepare for the future unfolding in unexpected ways, but can also help avoid obstacles in the first place. It is a very powerful planning tool.

If you want to take the pre-mortem to the next level, then consider doing a full-blown Failure Modes and Effects Analysis (FMEA). That's a little beyond the scope of this book, but my experience with it has always been good. It's worth researching if you are interested.[656]

Managing a Budget

In setting a budget, the thinking is "What resources do I need to accomplish objectives A, B, and C?" Once the budget is set, the question for the execution team should become, "Within this level of resources, how do we best accomplish projects X, Y, and Z?"

Your responsibility for creative thinking doesn't end with the "what" of your innovation efforts. You must also be innovative with the "how." Just because you justified a budget with a set of planned activities doesn't mean you have to do those activities if you come up with a more efficient way of doing them. Heck, most of the time the budgets get adjusted along the way, anyway. It's a two-way street.

The uncertainty of innovation efforts means that deviations from planned budgets are unavoidable. The key to managing those deviations is transparency.[657] Communicate what needs to change, why it needs to change, and how the change will be managed. Communicate that message up, down, and across the organization.

---

[656] The American Society of Quality offers a nice summary of the process, as well as books and other resources for a dive deep into the topic. http://asq.org/learn-about-quality/process-analysis-tools/overview/fmea.html

[657] Admittedly, this works best in an organizational culture that can handle transparency. Better yet, one that encourages transparency.

Performance against budget should then be incorporated into portfolio decisions about which projects continue to move forward and which ones get either killed or put on hold. In some instances, you would want to kill a project that needs more resources than originally budgeted. In other cases, you would want to kill a different project in order to move resources to the project that now needs more. In any case, such decisions should be made in a portfolio context, not just on an individual project level.

Turning Assumptions into Knowledge

Innovation projects start with a big set of assumptions. "If this trend continues, then..." "If this technology is commercialized..." "If we can build awareness like this..." "But then again, if..."

If "ifs" and "buts" were candy and nuts, it'd be a party every day.

As projects move along over time, the job of the innovator is to test those assumptions, learn from the results, revise the hypotheses, and continue to learn all the way through a solid execution. Every innovation investment is made in learning. The more innovative the project, the more value that will be derived from learning. With learning, innovation project directions often have to change – the "pivot" in modern business parlance. Organizations need to monetize what they learn, and the knowledge gained often becomes monetized in very different ways from those initially conceived.

In many ways, it's learning by doing, and on the job training.

This requires flexibility in project management. Managing an innovation project needs to be done differently than managing a capital project. Innovation is not a linear, step-by-step undertaking. It is more like a series of increasingly defined learning objectives, in which developers are learning what needs to be learned in each new step.[658] If you are managing an innovation project, expect that your Gantt chart will need to be updated more often than a Chicago politician's criminal record.[659]

To manage the changes that will be required, do three things:

---

[658] Armand Hatchuel, Pascal Le Masson and Benoit Weil, "The Development of Science-Based Products: Managing by Design Spaces," *Creativity and Innovation Management*, December 2005.

[659] Corruption is a long-standing tradition in Chicago.
http://www.chicagobusiness.com/article/20150528/BLOGS02/150529813/chicago-is-still-no-1-for-public-corruption

1) Keep the team focused clearly on the end objective at all times;
2) Be ready, willing, and able to adjust and adapt anywhere within the system to achieve the objective;
3) Communicate the impact of changes to those impacted.

To illustrate these points, permit me to use an analogy.

Say you have a friend that you haven't seen in a while. You give them a call, and decide that it would be nice to hang out. You decide to meet for dinner, planning a date, time, and location to meet.

When that evening arrives, the weather is terrible, with high winds and rain. That wasn't in the plan, but you go ahead and hop in your car, setting off for the restaurant.

Along the way, you see a line of brake lights ahead. A tree has fallen across the road, preventing passage. This road was your best route for getting to the restaurant, but that route is now impassable.

Do you say, "oh well, I guess I'll cancel the plan and go home?"

Of course not. You consult the GPS routing app on your phone, and it suggests an alternate route to you. It's not one that is familiar to you, but you decide to take it.

After a turn here and a turn there, more brake lights appear. Cars are reversing course. Flooding across the road ahead has made it, too, impassable. What bad luck you are having! All you wanted to do was to hang out with a friend you haven't seen in a while.

Now do you say, "oh well, I guess I'll cancel the plan and go home?"

Of course not. Even though there's no way you are going to make it to the restaurant on time, you keep trying. You give your friend a call to let them know you are going to be a little late. You and your GPS app look for an alternative route.

The bad weather has led to a number of accidents, slowing you down even more than the poor visibility already has. You tell your friend that a little late will actually be a lot late. Your friend is really hungry, so you tell them to go ahead and eat.

Now do you say, "oh well, I guess I'll cancel the plan and go home?"

Of course not. You decide that you'll meet someplace else a little later. You had planned on getting to bed early that night, because you have an early morning meeting the next day, but you revise that. Getting a chance to see your friend is more important to you than eight hours of sleep. You'll compensate with an extra cup of coffee (or two) in the morning.

When you finally meet your friend, you curse the weather and the traffic. Then you start catching up, doing whatever laughing or crying that you hoped to be able to do in the first place. That goal accomplished, you go home, a little later than planned, but feeling fulfilled.

Awwwww, I love a happy ending.

Obviously, the scenario was made up, and will never win a Hemingway prize for compelling fiction, but it illustrates the point of project management. The plan is nothing. Planning is everything.

The important thing was not following the route to the restaurant as planned. The important thing was not eating at the particular restaurant. The important thing was not getting eight full hours of sleep that night. The important thing was making the connection with your friend.

Innovation projects run into the figurative rainstorm all the time. Effective project management is not about avoiding the rainstorms, but about continuing to make progress toward the goal in spite of them.

Keeping focus on the real goal is the most critical thing. It is easy to get sidetracked by focusing on the wrong goal. The fundamental purpose of any project is to create value.[660] Hitting milestones, following procedures, meeting budget targets, etc., are all important *pathways* to creating value, but they are subservient to the objective. They are not objectives in themselves. Don't let your organization get that relationship backwards.

Managing the individual innovation project should not be done in pieces, nor in isolation. To be successful with innovation projects, with all their unpredictability and uncertainty, is best done in the context of systems thinking.[661] Focusing on the end goal, and all that is associated with it, helps keep the thinking on the systems level.

---

[660] Thomas Gillier, Sophie Hooge, and Gérald Piat, "Collaborative Design of Value in Creative Projects: An Expansive Value Management Model," *i3 First Interdisciplinary Innovation Conference*, December 2013.

[661] Maria Kapsali, "Systems thinking in innovation project management: A match that works," *International Journal of Project Management*, May 2011.

The project needs to be managed as one among many objectives of the organization, just as connecting with your friend had to be managed against the need for sleep. Within a project, a step has to be managed as one among many, not as an end within itself. If plans were made to do steps in series, but events don't go according to plan, it may be necessary and wise to do those steps in parallel instead.

The project manager is responsible for working out such changes, negotiating them with the development team, and communicating any updates to the relevant stakeholders. That includes not only changes to the timeline, but also changes to the risk profile, investment requirements, new assumptions, etc.

Getting Products to Market

In the language of project managers, the planning process begins with the Work Breakdown Structure (WBS).[662]   As the name would imply, this is a breakdown of all the work that needs to be done to accomplish the objectives, structured in a way that makes sense for the project, for the team, and for the organization.

There are many ways to break it all down, and getting into the whole project management body of knowledge[663] is way beyond the scope of this book. But let's look at some of the critical things that go into a WBS – what I will call the project plan.

- The end game – the main objective of all the work, with timing of execution.
- Milestones along the way – critical points that need to take place before the end game can be reached.
- Steps along the path – all of the individual activities that need to be completed in order to reach the milestones and the ultimate end, broken down to an appropriate level of detail.[664]

---

[662] *A Guide to the Project Management Body of Knowledge: PMBOK Guide 5th Edition*, Project Management Institute, 2013.

[663] That's the job of the Project Management Institute, and they do it well already.

[664] You and your organization will have to decide what is "appropriate." The more detail-oriented will want more steps identified. If you get down to the point of planning bathroom breaks, though, you've probably gone too far.

- Dependencies – sometimes one thing absolutely, positively must happen before something else can happen. Those are dependencies, because they depend on that first thing happening.
- Responsibilities – who will be held accountable for achieving a particular step.
- Resource requirements – what inputs will be necessary to achieve a particular step.

These elements can be presented in a variety of ways. I'm personally fond of Gantt charts, but others like spreadsheet-style tables. Whatever your preference, get the project plan in front of people so they are clear on what they need to do by when.

The above is necessarily just at an overview level, in order to keep this a) simple, and b) generalizable to any industry, from nonprofit food pantries to residential construction to high-tech medical devices. But the principles are generally applicable.

One of the biggest questions a project planner will face is "how long do things take?" This is especially challenging on innovation projects, with uncertain futures, unproven assumptions, and undefined specifications. The best thing to do is to do the best you can, based on past data and experience under similar circumstances.

Start with an idealized plan that gets you where you need to go by the time you need to get there. Actually, if you can, plan to get there before you need to be there, incorporating a buffer that can absorb some of the unexpected bumps in the road.

But manage the buffer carefully. It will be very tempting early on to rely on that slack, and let things take a little longer than they need to. Then, as the timeline moves along, the buffer gets eaten up before the time when it is really needed. And by then, you are stuck. The buffer should be labeled with a big "for emergency use only" sign.

The next biggest question a project planner will face is "what is *really* dependent on something else?" When the project plan is being laid out, people will tell the planner that step 37 has to be complete before they can do step 38. But when push comes to shove, the reality is that they would *like* to have step 37 done first, and it really would be helpful, but it isn't actually *necessary*.

Let's say step 37 is eating your vegetables, and step 38 is eating dessert. As a parent, I will tell my kids that they can't do step 38 before they do step 37, but the reality is that they *can*...I just don't want them to do so.[665] That's not strictly a dependency. What they can't do is eat their dessert before we actually possess the dessert. That is a strict dependency.

In organizations doing innovation projects, what people really mean, but don't articulate, is that having step 37 done first will reduce the risk that they face doing step 38. That is a critically important perspective that allows for flexibility, while demanding communication, effective decision-making, and creative risk management.

Plan the Work, then Work the Plan

Once the original plan is in place, what does "managing the innovation project" mean? It means coordinating the efforts of the team, tracking progress, adjusting plans, communicating with stakeholders...it's a little like trying to carry a filled waterbed mattress. It requires heavy lifting and constant adjustment as it shifts its weight and changes its shape.

Like all project management, innovation project management consists of a number of interrelated efforts, including project scope management, personnel management, timeline management, cost management, quality management, risk management, and communication management.[666] The difference for innovation projects is the need to keep things flexible.

For most project managers, the main objectives are to deliver on time, on quality, and on budget. That works because those things are more predictable and manageable than they are for innovation projects. Yes, an innovation project manager needs to pay attention to cost, quality, and timing, but the one thing that is certain about those things is that they will change as the future unfolds. The innovation manager needs to adjust to those changes, communicate them well, while focusing on delivering the business objective that started the whole innovation initiative in the first place.

---

[665] And if they do, boy are they gonna get it.

[666] *A Guide to the Project Management Body of Knowledge: PMBOK Guide 5th Edition*, Project Management Institute, 2013.

Simple Meetings

Part of managing the project is managing the connections between people on the team. That is often done through the tool we all know and love: meetings.

So tell me...Are you suffering from a lack of meetings? Would you like to have more of them? Or maybe have them last longer?

I didn't think so.

A variety of surveys[667] confirm that people spend too much time in meetings, wasting productive time. Innovation teams are no exception. So let's stop wasting so much time.

But how?

Replace as many of your meetings as possible with just two types: the conflict/coordination meeting, and the working meeting.

Conflict/Coordination Meetings

As Al Pittampalli says so eloquently in his book *Read This Before Our Next Meeting*, "the Modern Meeting focuses on the only two activities worth convening for: conflict and coordination."[668] A meeting should not be a data dump, filled with a variety of updates by everyone on the team. If people want to make presentations and hear themselves speak, they can join Toastmasters International. The rest of the team does not need to be their captive audience when there is work to be done.

Coordination is one of the most important factors in being able to execute against a strategy effectively.[669] You can lay out a brilliant strategic plan, and have everyone in the organization aligned in saying "yes, this is the way to go, and we are fully committed to the strategy." But if the efforts everyone makes are not coordinated, the execution can break down.

---

[667] For example, several are referenced in Ray Williams, "Why Meetings Kill Productivity: Cancel 50 percent of your meetings and you'll get more work done," *Psychology Today*, April 15, 2012.

[668] Al Pittampalli, *Read This Before Our Next Meeting*, Do You Zoom, Inc., 2011.

[669] Donald Sull, Rebecca Homkes, and Charles Sull, "Why Strategy Execution Unravels—and What to Do About It," Harvard Business Review, March 2015.

Conflict, as we have discussed, is not only inevitable for teams, but is actually necessary for high performance. Conflict and coordination meetings are the place and time to deal with those conflicts in a healthy manner.

The one meeting that I will unequivocally recommend to a project team (or a portfolio team) is the weekly stand-up review. This is a conflict and coordination meeting held for the full team to identify where things stand and what must happen in the next week to keep things on track. It is NOT an update meeting in the sense of every team member reciting what they did, where they are, and what they were going to do next.

Instead, the team reviews tasks on a publicly-displayed board. Simple green (on track), yellow (attention needed) and red (off track – emergency!) color coding assigned by the project manager alerts everyone as

Stand-Up Team Meeting Task List Project _____
Date/Version_____

Status	Task	People	Date Due	Coordination/Conflict Issues?

Figure 91: A simple team project chart identifies where things are and where they need to go, quickly, easily, and publicly.

to status of various tasks. Conflicts and coordination needs are identified, along with the people required to resolve those issues. Those people, and only those people, work on the resolution, outside of the review session. You never allow two or three people to start discussing resolution while a dozen others sit there idle. That's the kind of time-wasting meeting that the world needs to eliminate.

Why do people stand up? It makes the meeting go faster. No one wants to stand for an hour or more.

I have used this kind of meeting in several organizations, and it is generally the most effective that I've been involved with.[670] The meeting takes no more than fifteen to thirty minutes, even if twenty people are reviewing thirty line

---

[670] And I've had more than one participant provide the unsolicited feedback that it's their favorite meeting.

items. Everyone sees clearly how things are going, what they need to do, and how their piece fits into the holistic picture.

If everyone is collocated, hold this kind of meeting in a place where the project chart can be prominently displayed and visited at any time. Those familiar with lean principles may know such a place as an "oobeya room."[671] Others may be familiar with the concept of a War Room. Whatever you call it, it's a great concept, and a great place to hold both stand-up team meetings and working meetings.

Figure 92: An Oobeya Room centrally locates the materials a team needs to collaborate effectively. And it's fun to say.

Such a room can take on a variety of styles, but generally it will have walls. Duh. These walls can then be used for displaying critical project information that the team needs, such as a schedule, task list, team responsibilities, issues, metrics,[672] and drawings or prototypes for reference.

If you want to keep things simple, all it needs is a big wipe board, some dry erase markers, and an eraser. On the board, create the simple project chart. If you are space-constrained and can't devote a room to the cause, use someone's office – the team leader's, the project manager's, the champion's, or that of whoever else has the space and the capability to make their office a part-time oobeya room.

If your team is geographically dispersed, create an electronic version of the project chart that all can share. Conduct meetings in real time by video or audio conference, with changes to the chart being made in real time for all to see.

Similar meetings can take place for other parts of the organization. Focusing on conflict resolution and coordination needs is a powerful way to cut the amount of time wasted in meetings.

---

[671] Fara Warner, "In a Word, Toyota Drives for Innovation," *Fast Company*, August 2002.

[672] For more on innovation metrics, go to the sections on "Innovation for Fun and Profit" (page 389) and "Innovation for Fun and Not-for-Profit" (page 403).

So now you've quickly identified conflicts and coordination needs. What's next?

The Working Meeting.

The working meeting is exactly what it says it is. It's for doing the work when individuals can't do the work alone. I hate to even call these meetings.

These "gatherings of people doing the work that needs to be done"[673] can be held anywhere that the work would be best accomplished. This might be in a lab, on a manufacturing floor, in an office, at a coffee shop, or in the Wrigley Field bleachers during a Cubs game. The only important thing about the location is that it enables collaborative work to get done efficiently.

These meetings should involve only the people that need to be involved to accomplish the task at hand. They should be about getting work done, accomplishing milestones, or making progress on a project, not about talking and updating.

They are that simple.

Meeting Rules So Crazy They Just Might Work

Here's a couple of crazy rules that I recommend when it comes to meetings. Be warned, that traditionalists will want you bound in a straightjacket for even suggesting them...

1) **Meeting attendance is 100% voluntary.**

    What?!? Then no one will show up! To that objection, I say "good!" If they aren't showing up, that's a sign that the meeting has no value, or at least that there is something else that is of significantly higher value. That puts the onus on the meeting organizer to make the meeting valuable and not to waste anyone's time. It keeps the invitation list from expanding to all those copied on a "just in case" basis.

    What about those people who just blow off meetings because they don't feel like going? Two things. First, if meetings are really valuable, people will either start attending because of the value, or

---

[673] Okay, that's a mouthful. I'll stick with "working meetings."

they will start attending because the rest of the team will have them drawn and quartered if they don't. Second, if they are just the kind of people looking for an excuse to blow off work, then you have much bigger problems than making meetings voluntary. Have the candid discussion with them that they need to start working or start the search for alternative employment.

2) **Never, ever, ever, schedule a meeting for one hour.**

"But Brad," you say, "that's the default on my Outlook Calendar!" I don't care. Schedule meetings for how long they are going to need to take. Put some thought into that. Remember Parkinson's Law:[674] "work expands so as to fill the time available for its completion." Schedule a meeting for an hour, and by golly, you will fill every femtosecond of that hour. More often, it will last 65 minutes, causing you to be seven minutes late for your next back-to-back hour long meeting, which will run 65 minutes, so that you are now seventeen minutes late for the next meeting, given that you absolutely had to stop in the restroom because of all the coffee you drank to stay awake for the previous meetings.

If you think a meeting should take 30 minutes, schedule it for 25. If you think it would be an hour, schedule it for 50. Plan for transition time between consecutive meetings, and account for the possibility of overage. Then work to beat the clock, not just meet it.

3) **Allow people to be distracted.**

Let them do email on their smart phones or do work on their tablets in the middle of the meeting. "But that's rude to the speaker!" you say. Not if it's an accepted and expected behavioral norm. If I see you playing *Minecraft: Pocket Edition* on your phone, I need to take that as feedback that you are unneeded (at least for that part of the meeting), and either make it relevant for you, or let you get back to work.

It may be counterintuitive, but since I started using this rule in all of my project team presentations, I find that I have dramatically *better* attention and focus among participants. No longer are they

---

[674] Cyril Northcote Parkinson, "Parkinson's Law," *The Economist*, November 19, 1955.

pretending to be engaged while actually being on another planet in their minds; no longer are they trying to sneak peeks at their mobile devices, having their attention not only diverted by what's on the screen, but also by the effort of trying not to get caught. Merely having the permission to check the smart phone makes it less tempting to do so, too.

The After Action Review

I am a stickler for this one. If you don't do anything else mentioned in this chapter, adopt the After Action Review. Oh, and do the Project Charter. Do those two things. Always.

Some people like to call it the "post mortem." I'm not among them. Post mortem implies death. It's such a bummer. Besides, not all projects die. Some get put on ice, to be resurrected later. Others become living, thriving products in the marketplace.

Some people call it the Post Project Review (PPR). That's better, but it limits the scope to only being about projects, and only after a project is terminated. What about learning from some portion of a project, or some part of a process? Especially in larger, more complex projects, couldn't there be something to learn after a significant process step? Heck, there's opportunity to learn after every meeting on how to run the meetings better.

All projects involve action, and after significant action, it's important to review what happened. So for me, After Action Review, or AAR, is how it's going to be.

How does it work?

The best thing you can do with the AAR is to keep it simple. By now, you must have known that I was going to say that.

I believe that there are three reasons the AAR isn't done on a regular basis in most organizations. First, the value is uncertain and long-term. The uncertain long-term will almost always get trumped by the more certain short-term. If I have to get something done on Project Simpleton by tomorrow because Executive Smith has requested it, my attention is going to be on Project

Simpleton and not on a review of a project that is done and forgotten by the masses.

Another reason is that if AARs have ever been done in the past, they resulted in having to prepare an 87-slide PowerPoint deck that got presented to a sleeping audience, then filed away somewhere never to be seen again. Finding Jimmy Hoffa would be easier than finding those reports.

And the final reason AARs are not done is that they are wrongly

The After Action Review

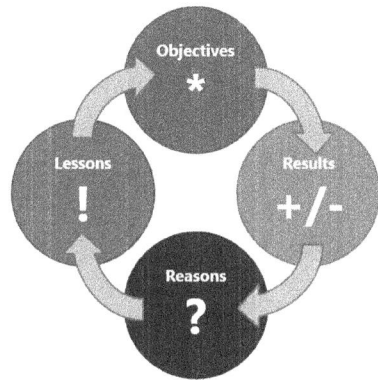

Figure 93: The flow of the simple After Action Review

perceived as modern day witch-hunts, in which the objective is to identify who is to blame for anything and everything that went wrong, rally the villagers to pick up their torches and pitchforks, and publicly burn the guilty at the organizational stake.

Those are all valid concerns. We've all seen those things happen in the past. The simple After Action Review process that follows addresses all three of those problems.

The simple AAR model provides a framework for learning from past actions that can be easily communicated both within the team and across the organization. The approach is simple (of course) – you review the objectives of the action, you identify what actually occurred (factually and objectively – putting on DeBono's white hat),[675] you determine reasons for deviations between the objectives and the reality that took place, and then condense that down into lessons learned. See? Simple.

The review is scalable to the actions. It can be applied to an entire program with multiple objectives and actions that span months or years, or it can be applied to something as small as a meeting. The level of detail and formality can be adjusted accordingly.

---

[675] For more on DeBono's six thinking hats, refer to the "Thinking Caps" section of the Mental Game of Innovation chapter, page 245.

Unfortunately, in numerous interactions with people from all sorts of industries – even the ones that I expected to be most buttoned-up when it comes to process – the AAR, regardless of what it is called, is almost never done. I can almost cross out the "almost" in that sentence, it's done so rarely.

So if nobody does it, how can I think it's so valuable?

Because of the two things that come from the AAR: learning and meaning.

Learning by Having Done

Learning by doing is good for the one who did the doing, but what about for the rest of the organization? Learning is the obvious point of the After Action Review, the reason it was created in the first place.

Military leaders have been reviewing what happened after battles pretty much since the first cave dweller threw a rock at the neighboring cave. Reviewing what actually occurred versus what you wanted to take place is nothing new. Even Daffy Duck engaged in a sort of after-action review, although with considerably less learning than desirable.[676]

Individuals involved in the review will gain valuable knowledge from the AAR process. They will gain insights from the perspectives and explanations of the events that took place. They will more deeply learn and improve future performance by reviewing and discussing the reasons for various steps taken and why certain decisions were made.[677]

For the organization, the opportunity is to disseminate learnings from one part of the organization to others. This will be particularly effective in organizations with project management offices, in which the discipline of project management is centralized and developed. Even without a PMO, sharing of information between project managers is helpful. Experiential learning will also be shared as people move from project to project.

---

[676] To see Daffy Duck's post-failure learning experience, get online and go to https://www.youtube.com/watch?v=8cuihrjLNAo.

[677] John Dunlosky, Katherine A. Rawson, Elizabeth J. Marsh, Mitchell J. Nathan, and Daniel T. Willingham, "Improving Students' Learning with Effective Learning Techniques: Promising Directions from Cognitive and Educational Psychology," *Psychological Science in the Public Interest*, January 2013. Refer to the techniques of elaborative interrogation and self-explanation.

In order to maximize learning, the timing of the AAR is important. For smaller actions, it is best to conduct a review as soon as possible after an action is taken. That way, information is fresh and memories more reliable. For full project reviews, I recommend doing the AAR in two parts. One should take place immediately after the termination of the project, either by completed launch or by cancellation. That portion should be focused on the process – how things were done.

The second part of the review (for fully executed projects) should occur sufficiently later to have an assessment of how well the product performed in the market – did it meet the objectives and expectations? Bringing the two parts together will then help identify what parts of the process contributed most to the outcomes.

More on Meaning

I've talked a good deal about the importance of meaning already. There is loads of evidence from all sorts of research that creating meaningful work is critically important to successful innovation outcomes. If any evidence presented in this book is irrefutable, it's that.

So you work on a compelling mission. You build your strategy with engaged staff. You get in the minds and hearts of your customers. You do everything you can to focus people on achieving something important.

Then, after weeks, months, years of work, the project meets an untimely end. Circumstances changed, a trend fizzled out, a technology proved unfeasible. Whatever the reason, the project is cancelled. And the next day, the members of the team simply get reassigned to something else.

Talk about meaninglessness.

When the work you've been doing during most of your awake hours for all that time ends up getting tossed aside like a tissue after a sneeze, it's pretty darn depressing. And it sucks the meaning right out of the job.

A variety of behavioral economic research has demonstrated just how valuable meaning is to us.[678] People are willing to work longer and do more at

---

[678] Dan Ariely, Emir Kamenica, and Drazen Prelec, "Man's search for meaning: The case of Legos," *Journal of Economic Behavior & Organization*, January 2008.

a lower rate of pay when their effort has even a little bit of meaning. People would rather work on a task with a bit of meaning than be given free money for a meaningless task.[679] Meaning matters.

Yet we kill meaning every time we kill projects. At least we do when we kill them without anything to show for the effort.

That is the unheralded, but perhaps most important element of an After Action Review. It's an opportunity for a team to derive meaning from their work, even when the work doesn't get to the marketplace.

Even in the relatively few organizations that tolerate, accept, or even encourage failure, failure still hurts. The After Action Review gives the whole cross-functional team a chance to mitigate that suffering by contributing to organizational learning and their own personal growth.

I'm not a big proponent of celebrating failure. I am a proponent of celebrating efforts that dare greatly, even if they come up short. I am a proponent of celebrating learning, the most valuable intangible asset[680] that an organization can have.

The best way to maximize the value of AARs is to maximize learning and meaningfulness. Do this by engaging the entire cross-functional team to participate and really think about the lessons to be drawn from their experience. Have the team present the learnings to both management and other parts of the organization. This helps to both disseminate the knowledge, and serve as recognition for the team's knowledge creation. Such presentations have more impact and meaning than reports which are easily filed in the I'll-get-to-that-later-but-really-I-know-that-I-won't file. It's all the better if specific actions can be taken on current projects to improve their chances of success based on the AAR outcomes.[681]

The only way an organization really fails is when they fail to fail well. When life hands you lemons, what should you do? An After Action Review, that's what. Make some learning lemonade, and quench the organization's thirst for the knowledge they need to be more successful.

---

[679] Ibid.

[680] Or is learning the most intangible valuable asset? Probably both are true.

[681] Ursula Koners and Keith Goffin, "Learning from Postproject Reviews: A Cross-Case Analysis," *Journal of Product Innovation Management*, May 2007.

And the AAR is not just for failed projects. It's for all significant action. Learn from success. Learn from failure. Learn from experience. And derive meaning from it as a result.

Simple Study Guide – Project Management

- What are the characteristics of effective project management?
- How does a phase-and-gate approach to project management work?
- How does a lean/agile approach to project management work?
- What are ways to keep project management flexible?
- What are the elements of a Project Charter?
- How can a project charter be used throughout a project?
- What is the value of speed-to-market?
- What is a pre-mortem and how does it work?
- How does the Delphi process work? When should it be used?
- What is a Work Breakdown Structure?
- How can meetings be simplified?
- How does an After Action Review work?
- What are the benefits of an After Action Review?

Where do you want to go from here?

Control	Creation	Conversion
Mission (page 40)	Voice of the Customer (page 175)	Innovation Teams (page 310)
Culture (page 58)	Minds of Innovators (page 217)	Project Management (page 347)
Strategy (page 92)	Ideation (page 279)	For-Profit Metrics (page 389)
Portfolio Management (page 146)		Nonprofit Metrics (page 403)
Change Management (page 411)		

Or just turn the page to keep reading...

Innovating for Fun and Profit (For-Profit Metrics)

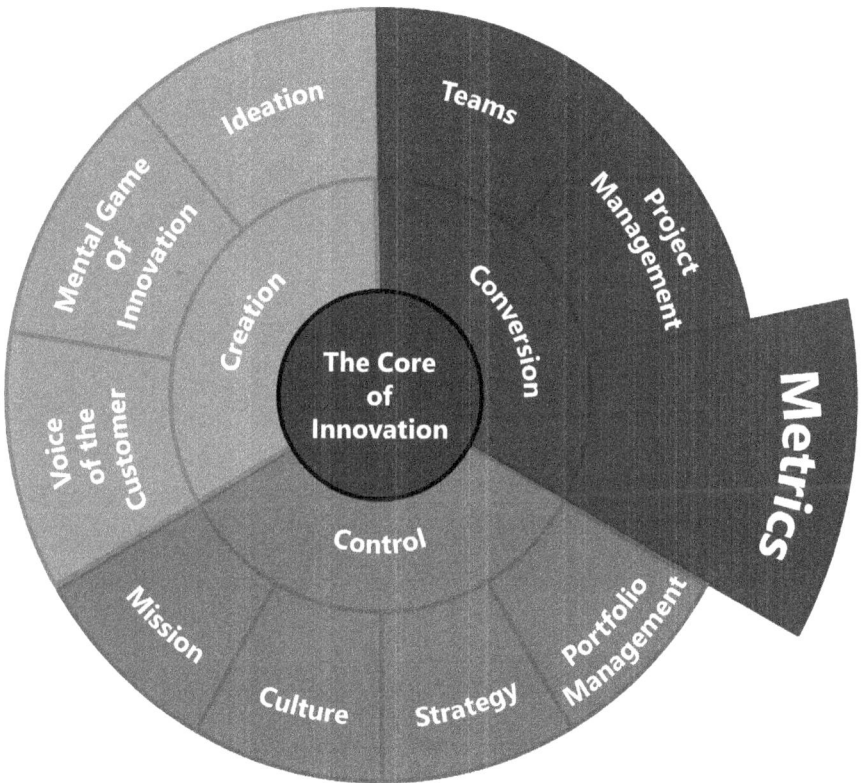

Simple Self-Assessment – For-Profit Metrics

Rate yourself on the following questions. To benchmark yourself against others, go to www.3point14Innovation.com and click the "Self-Assessments" menu.

- ### Does your organization have clear definitions of success?

When the beatings stop, we think we are succeeding   We all know what winning is about

1	2	3	4	5	6	7	8	9	10

- ### Does your organization have established metrics to measure success?

I think I have a ruler somewhere   Several diverse measures

1	2	3	4	5	6	7	8	9	10

- ### Does your organization use unique metrics specific to its mission?

That requires too much thought   Exactly what we need to do what we do

1	2	3	4	5	6	7	8	9	10

- ### Do your guidance metrics correlate to your review metrics?

There are different kinds?   Like light correlates with day

1	2	3	4	5	6	7	8	9	10

- ### Do you have a balanced set of metrics that ensures strong overall performance?

It's easier to just measure one thing   It ain't easy, but it's balanced

1	2	3	4	5	6	7	8	9	10

- ### Do people game the metrics at the expense of real performance?

Oh no, no, no... okay, yes.   Perhaps, but with balance, it's not easy to do.

1	2	3	4	5	6	7	8	9	10

- ### How much of your innovators' compensation is tied to metrics?

All of it; 100% commission-based.   Enough to reward, but not so much to inhibit innovation

1	2	3	4	5	6	7	8	9	10

Simple Summary – For Profit Metrics
Key take-aways you should get out of this section:

- "What gets measured gets done. What gets measured and fed back gets done well. What gets rewarded gets repeated." Without metrics, there is no way to help guide people on where to go and how to get there. It's like driving without a dashboard. Or windows.
- You need to have a clear understanding of what defines success. Understand how to "win," and understand what contributes to "winning." Don't confuse the two, though. Maintain a holistic view, to avoid optimizing the parts at the expense of the whole.
- Make sure you leverage both guidance metrics (those that guide you in real time) and review metrics (those that determine after the fact if you made it to your goal). Make it an ongoing part of your After Action Reviews to determine how well the guidance metrics get you to your review metrics.
- Beware of unintended consequences to your metrics. In some cases, people may try to "game the system" to achieve metrics at the expense of actual organizational performance. Even if there is no malicious intent, metrics will impact behaviors. A measure may seem like it is connected to the needs of the organization, but when pursued, it ends up leading things astray. This is a major reason to ensure that you use a balanced set of multiple, uncorrelated metrics.
- Include behavioral, values-oriented measures, in addition to your financial ones.
- Be careful with the psychological impact of incentives on innovation. Mental work can respond very differently to incentives than physical work. Overly stressing your innovation team with a high level of compensation tied to innovation outcomes can adversely impact those outcomes in a variety of ways, both short- and long-term.

Get Out Your Rulers

Metrics matter.[682] How things are measured changes the way people play the game.[683]

Tennis is a great example. How do you win a match? By winning the most sets in the match. Not by winning the most points or the most games, but the most sets. It's not uncommon for one player to win more total points in a match, or more total games, but still lose the match.

In such a case, it makes sense at times to relax a bit. If the loss of one set is almost certain, maybe you don't work quite so hard in the final game, so that you can start the next set with the advantage of first serve. You give up on points and games to maximize the chance of winning sets.

The US Presidential election with its Electoral College system is another example. You win elections by winning electoral votes, which means winning states. So you give up on a state with fewer electoral votes and where you are polling way behind, in order to fight for a 50/50 state with lots of electoral votes. Sorry, North Dakota, but you'll not earn the title "battleground state" anytime soon.

So the metrics you set up for your innovation projects *will* impact how people behave, and the kinds of decisions that they will make.

---

[682] "Metrics" are also known as "Key Performance Indicators," or KPIs.

[683] Remember the quote about "What gets measured gets done. What gets measured and fed back gets done well. What gets rewarded gets repeated." Find more about this in the "Communicating for Execution" section of the Strategy chapter, page 143.

So how should metrics be set to best guide the innovation outcomes you want?

Let's start by talking about how *not* to set metrics.

Metric-setting don'ts:

- Don't measure just one thing, no matter how important you think it may be.
- Don't measure everything that is measurable, no matter how much you'd like to measure it all.[684]
- Don't measure things just because all the cool organizations are measuring them. Don't be a Disney lemming.[685]
- Don't choose metrics that aren't directly relevant to your mission, your strategy, your product innovation charter, your customer, or your projects.

Okay, so knowing what not to do, now we can talk about what *to* do.

Money Ball

The example of the Oakland A's was made famous in the book and movie *Moneyball*. Baseball has been a sport of statistics since its inception. It's entirely possible that Abner Doubleday was an amateur statistician who created the sport to practice his math.[686]

The "important" statistics stayed the same for decades: batting average, hits, doubles, triples, home runs, on-base percentage, stolen bases, runs batted in, earned run average, strikeouts, saves (and blown saves) complete games,

---

[684] There is a potential caveat to this. In the days of "big data" and the increasing ease with which we can measure and record everything from the number of steps between the office and the Burger Barn up the street to the number of key strokes entered on a given keyboard every minute of every day, measuring everything without people knowing is tempting. Or maybe they know, but there is no consequence to the measurements. In such a case, it is possible to envision analyzing the data over time to find the things that best drive product success. Then again, as soon as they get measured with tangible consequences, behaviors will change and you may not get the outcomes you want, anyway. So really, this is a long-winded way of saying keep it simple, and don't measure everything.

[685] For more about Disney's cruel and deceptive role in the lemming myth, check out the footnotes on the bandwagon effect, page 229.

[686] Except for the fact that he didn't really invent baseball. He was, however, the president of the Theosophical Society, and I heard there was a time that he stayed at a Holiday Inn Express.

fielding percentage... every bubble gum card had the same numbers for every player. And scouts used the bubble gum cards to evaluate talent.[687]

Then came sabermetrics. The concept is actually much older than the Oakland A's of the early 2000s, but like Semelweiss and handwashing, it took decades to be accepted (and traditionalists are still fighting it).[688] The A's leveraged statistics that others ignored to create a highly competitive team with one of the lowest salary lines on their P&L.

Now, baseball has a host of new statistics: weighted runs created, wins above replacement, on base plus slugging, fielding independent pitching, ultimate zone rating, and batting average on balls in play,[689] to name a few.

While your organization probably does not operate in a sabermetric world, the lesson here is to measure the things that matter. Just because a measure has been used traditionally, doesn't mean that it's the right thing to measure. For example, one common innovation metric is the percentage of revenues (or profits) from new products. The reality is that such a metric has not been shown to drive innovation. A better metric intended to get at the same kind of information is the R&D Effectiveness Index, which is the ratio of the increase in profits from new products to investments in new product development. [690]

Of course, just because something is a traditional measure doesn't mean that it's the wrong thing to measure, either. You need to determine if it is right for your organization.

---

[687] Not really. But they used the same numbers.

[688] See, for example, David Wade, "Death to sabermetrics," *The Hardball Times*, April 1, 2011. Although that one was written for fools. Or check out the (presumably) for real blog, "Sabermetrics Suck: One man's fight against the statistical revolution in baseball."

[689] BAPIP is my favorite acronym. It reminds me of my favorite snack food, Spap Oop. That's what you get when you turn a box of doo dads upside down.

[690] Serdar S. Durmuşoğlu, Regina C. McNally, Roger J. Calantone and Nukhet Harmancioglu, "How Elephants Learn the New Dance When Headquarters Changes the Music: Three Case Studies on Innovation Strategy Change," *Journal of Product Innovation Management*, July 2008. The index is computed as (New Product Revenue%) x (Net Profit% + R&D%) ÷ (R&D%), where the percentages are stated as a percentage of revenue. You want the ratio to be greater than 1.

And that's the bad news: there is no single set of metrics that is universally right for anyone and everyone trying to innovate.[691] Across organizations, the proper metrics simply must be different. Your metrics should be set to fit with your mission, your culture, your strategy, your industry, your technologies, and your capability.[692]

That is probably obvious. What may be less obvious – and what makes the bad news worse – is that within an organization, you should use different metrics for different types of projects.[693] Good metrics must be finely tailored to the specifics of a project.

And as long as we are on the subject of bad news... Innovation metrics are likely to come in conflict with operational metrics. The effectiveness of operations is measured by speed, consistency, and profitability, while innovation pushes all the boundaries of the organization in an iterative and conflict-filled process, with uncertain returns even when done well. [694]

So what's the good news? Well, there are simple guidelines to setting metrics that you can follow.[695]

1) **Measure both "guidance metrics" and "review metrics."** Guidance metrics are those that you collect in real time to see how you are doing. They serve the purpose of helping you know whether you are going to reach your intended objective on time, on budget, and on quality. They are like a speedometer in a car, telling you how fast you are going during the trip.

    Review metrics are measures collected at the end of the journey, to determine if you achieved your objective. Did the product launch

[691] Abbie Griffin and Albert L. Page, "PDMA Success Measurement Project: Recommended Measures for Product Development Success and Failure," *Journal of Product Innovation Management*, November 1996.

[692] John R. Hauser, "Metrics thermostat," *Journal of Product Innovation Management*, May 2001.

[693] Serdar S. Durmuşoğlu, Regina C. McNally, Roger J. Calantone and Nukhet Harmancioglu, "How Elephants Learn the New Dance When Headquarters Changes the Music: Three Case Studies on Innovation Strategy Change," *Journal of Product Innovation Management*, July 2008.

[694] Gina Colarelli O'Connor and Mark P. Rice, "New Market Creation for Breakthrough Innovations: Enabling and Constraining Mechanisms," *Journal of Product Innovation Management*, March 2013.

[695] Do I need to remind you that simple does not mean easy?

on time? Were the sales what were expected? Are customers happy with the product? Does it uniquely meet their needs better than alternatives? Were the costs in line with budgets? All of those must be determined after the project is complete.

2) **Use measuring sticks other than just financial ones**. Yes, even as a for-profit organization. Ultimately, you want to make money. But purely financial metrics cloud perspectives on the route to making that money, especially in the long run.

3) **Select 3-9 guidance metrics for a project, and capture them on a one-page dashboard.** Have you ever seen a commercial airliner cockpit? There are very few people who can fly these planes well.[696] To do so requires thousands of hours of training and practice to understand what all the instruments mean and what to do when they have whatever readings they have. Do you want to have to put all of your innovators through such training for them to understand the dozens of metrics that you want to use? Do you want to incur the expense of doing all the measuring for those metrics? Make it more like driving a car, which more people are able to do well.[697] A few dials and indicators to help you get where you want to go safely, and to alert you when trouble is brewing.

At a bare minimum, you should be measuring money, time, and performance with one measure each. Better to do two or even three each. Keep it to single digits, though, or you start looking like an airplane cockpit.

4) **Tie the metrics to the project.** The best innovation organizations not only use a variety of metrics, but they also make those metrics flexible enough to adjust to the requirements of individual products.[698] Involve

---

[696] Do I really need a citation for that assertion?

[697] Please remind me that I said that when you catch me engaged in road rage during a Chicago rush hour.

[698] Kenneth B. Kahn, Gloria Barczak, John Nicholas, Ann Ledwith and Helen Perks, "An Examination of New Product Development Best Practice," *Journal of Product Innovation Management,* March 2012. The authors of the article will hopefully forgive me for dodging the term "best practice."

the people who will be responsible for execution in determining the success measures.

5) **Make the metrics relevant to project success.** That seems like an obvious statement, but consider it carefully. Organizations will often pick the metrics that they are likely to meet, rather than the metrics that are likely to distinguish true success against the mission.[699] While this may be done maliciously ("my bonus depends on hitting the number, so I'm going to measure a number I know I'm going to meet"), the more common cause is choosing the metrics that have always been measured. Because they've always been measured, they've always been worked on. Because they've always been worked on, the organization has gotten good at doing them. Measuring only what you already do well will not lead to improvement, learning, and innovative growth. A few keys to relevance:

- Tie your metrics to your customer – their needs that you are trying to meet and their problems that you are trying to solve. Customer satisfaction is critical to the success of your innovation, so measure it in some way on all projects.

- Tie metrics to the overall portfolio in addition to the project. Remember, each project is a part of an overall effort designed to achieve a single overlying mission, following a defined overarching strategy. Optimizing a single project in isolation can lead to sub-optimizing the overall organization. Reference the portfolio scorecard[700] when creating project metrics.

6) **Measure and reward innovation-driving behaviors**, not just outcomes. The role of culture and subculture to product development success is bigger than most people appreciate. Even when metrics are established and reward systems are tied to them, behaviors will still generally not violate cultural norms. If strategy is the omelet that

---

[699] Wayne Mackey, "Metrics that Matter to New Product Development: Measuring Actions, Getting Results," *The PDMA Toolbook for New Product Development 3*, Edited by Abbie Griffin and Stephen M. Somermeyer, John Wiley and Sons, 2007.

[700] For more on the project portfolio scorecard, see "Scorecards" in the Portfolio Management chapter, page 167.

culture eats for breakfast, then metrics are the toast. Whether you are trying to drive cultural change or reinforce an existing culture of innovation, you need to observe behaviors and attach clear consequences to those behaviors. Reward the ones you want. Redirect the ones you don't.

Admittedly, measuring behavior is not as objective as measuring the amount of money spent on fitting a gizmo onto a widget. But it can – and should – be done. Employ 360 reviews, team interviews, and mid-project AARs[701] to get this done.

7) **Think about how you measure, not just what you measure.** Make sure the *purpose* of the measurement is clearly communicated, not just the metric itself. Adjust the measures if you observe that achieving the targets for a particular metric is still not achieving the purpose for measuring it in the first place.[702]

8) **Use metrics that aren't correlated, and maybe even conflict.** Why on earth would you want conflicting metrics? To ensure a balanced approach. A common example of such metrics would be customer-perceived performance and time-to-market. You may be able to launch a garbage product tomorrow, or a perfect product three years from now...which is the right choice? Or is the best choice launching a good-enough product in a year? Having varied metrics that can come into conflict ensures that the team is making conscious decisions, and that the organization is focused on overall mission fulfillment.

An analogy would be measuring both acceleration and gas mileage on a car. Faster acceleration will adversely impact gas mileage, but slow acceleration to optimize gas mileage may be annoying, time-consuming, or even unsafe. You have to find the balance between the opposing metrics to determine optimum overall performance.

---

[701] For more on AARs (After Action Reviews) go to that section in the Project Management chapter, page 382.

[702] John R. Hauser, "Metrics thermostat," *Journal of Product Innovation Management*, May 2001.

Suggestion Box

If, after all those guidelines, you are scratching your head and thinking "that's all fine and good, but I still don't know what to measure," here are some common types of innovation metrics:

For Guidance

- Development budget (actual versus forecast, for example)
- Development headcount (numbers, total expense)
- Milestone completion (absolute and against plan)
- Customer test performance (liking, purchase intent, etc.)
- Product costs
- Manufacturability test results
- Quality testing (conformance, performance, reliability, etc.)

For Review

- Timeliness (percent of projects completed on time, for example)
- Efficiency (percent of projects completed on budget, for example)
- Total return on development investment (absolute and against forecasts)
- Time to Market (average, range, by type, etc.)
- Market penetration
- Trial and repeat purchasing rates
- Cannibalization of existing business[703]
- Percentage of internal versus external development (for open innovation)
- Business from new launches (as a percentage of revenue, for example)
- Break-even Time (absolute and against plan)
- Revenue from uncommercialized development (licensing, for example)
- Customer satisfaction
- And on, and on, and on...

---

[703] Note that cannibalization is not always bad: better to cannibalize your own business and keep your customers, than to let someone else take those customers away from you.

There are obviously many options for measuring innovation progress and success. To go ahead and be a broken record on the topic, you'll have to figure out the ones that are right for you and your projects.

Metrics, Incentives, and Rewards

After you define the metrics of success, you then have to figure out what the consequences will be, both for meeting and for missing targets. Your rewards and recognition systems, and even your organizational structure, should be aligned with your metrics.[704] But for that, I have some controversial advice.

Don't tie too much personal financial reward to the innovation metrics.

Pay-for-performance has indeed been shown, on average, to boost performance. There is evidence that the belief about financial rewards hindering creativity and other thinking tasks is a myth.[705] So why not attach greater financial rewards to project performance?

Three reasons: the conditions surrounding innovation efforts, the possibility of "learned helplessness," and effective team collaboration.

Innovation is a thinking game. While pay-for-performance can drive increased productivity in some tasks, there are others where it can have a detrimental effect: such as when goals are difficult to achieve, tasks are highly complex, and when the outcomes are long-term.[706] These all apply to innovation efforts. The stress imposed by high rewards tied to innovation performance can actually inhibit the ability to think and focus attention appropriately. In such instances, increasing incentives beyond an optimum will hinder performance, not enhance it.[707]

---

[704] Ibid.

[705] G. Douglas Jenkins, Jr., Atul Mitra, Nina Gupta and Jason D. Shaw, "Are Financial Incentives Related to Performance? A Meta-Analytic Review of Empirical Research," *Journal of Applied Psychology*, September 1998.

[706] Sarah E. Bonnera and Geoffrey B. Sprinkle, "The effects of monetary incentives on effort and task performance: theories, evidence, and a framework," *Accounting, Organizations and Society*, November 2002.

[707] Dan Ariely, Uri Gneezy, George Lowenstein, and Nina Mazar, "Large Stakes and Big Mistakes," *Review of Economic Studies*, 2009.

Add to that stress the inherent uncertainty of innovation, and the impact could be multiplied. "Learned helplessness" is a well-documented psychological condition that results from repeated painful experiences that are out of the individual's control.[708] Tying too much reward to metrics that can be significantly impacted by unforeseeable and uncontrollable circumstances can kill future motivation, and certainly discourages risk-taking in the first place.

Finally, consider team-based incentives, rather than individual incentives, at least when it comes to cross-functional innovation projects. Team incentives have been shown to be able to stimulate cooperative innovation, reduce costs, and improve productivity.[709] Other experiments have shown group incentives to enhance group cohesion, the desire to collaborate, and the willingness to build on each other's ideas.[710]

Also beware of the unintended consequences of your metrics. Remember that quote about what you measure impacting what gets done? In general, people will try to minimize the efforts required for the maximum rewards, and they will tend to be risk averse when big rewards are involved. So if you decide to measure something like revenue from new products, you'll find that "new products" will include low risk line extensions, like changing the widget color form blue to greenish-blue. Even that "R&D efficiency" metric can lead to such gaming of the system, contrary to the needs of the organization.

Setting good metrics isn't easy. Keep them simple, diverse, well-tailored, and relevant.

---

[708] Martin E. P. Seligman, "Learned Helplessness," *Annual Review of Medicine*, February 1972.

[709] Andrea R. Drake, Susan F. Haka, and Sue P. Ravenscroft, "Cost System and Incentive Structure Effects on Innovation, Efficiency and Profitability in Teams," *The Accounting Review*, July 1999.

[710] Clara Xiaoling Chen, Michael G. Williamson, and Flora H. Zhou, "System Design and Group Creativity: An Experimental Investigation," *The Accounting Review*, November 2012.

Simple Study Guide – For-Profit Metrics

- What are metrics?
- How do metrics impact what people do?
- What defines ultimate success for your organization?
- What are guidance metrics? What are review metrics? How are they different? How are they related?
- What are unintended consequences?
- How does pay-for-performance differ for physical vs. mental labor?
- How can incentive pay affect innovation efforts?

Where do you want to go from here?

Control	Creation	Conversion
Mission (page 40)	**Voice of the Customer** (page 175)	**Innovation Teams** (page 310)
Culture (page 58)	**Minds of Innovators** (page 217)	**Project Management** (page 347)
Strategy (page 92)	**Ideation** (page 279)	**For-Profit Metrics** (page 389)
Portfolio Management (page 146)		**Nonprofit Metrics** (page 403)
Change Management (page 411)		

Or just turn the page to keep reading...

Innovating for Fun and Not-For-Profit (Nonprofit Metrics)

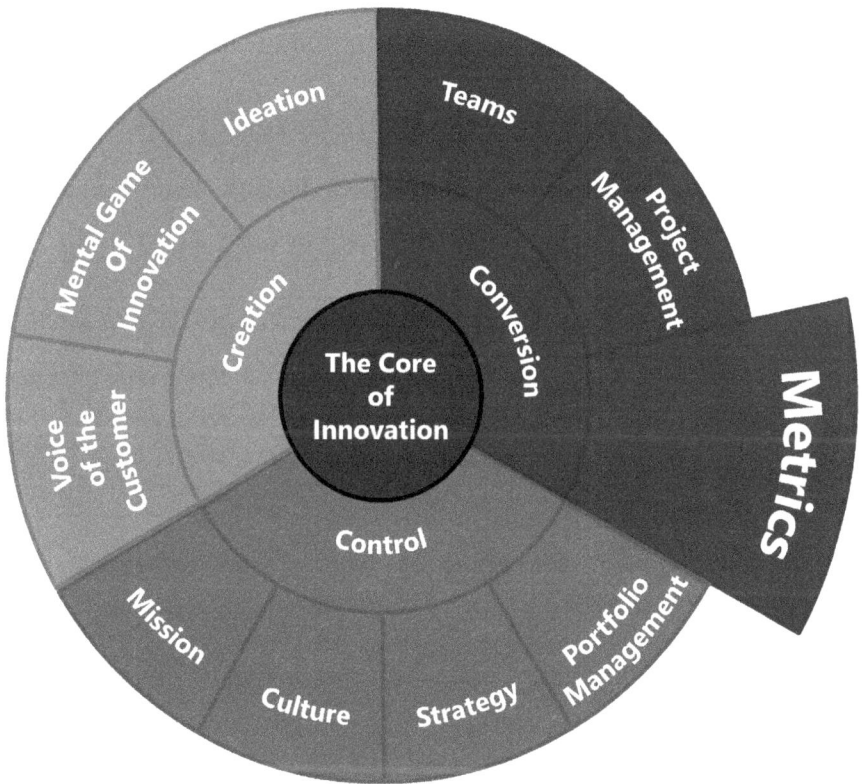

Simple Self-Assessment – Nonprofit Metrics

Rate yourself on the following questions. To benchmark yourself against others, go to www.3point14Innovation.com and click the "Self-Assessments" menu.

- **Do you follow the guidelines for metrics presented to for-profit organizations?**

  Um, we sorta skipped that part...   To the best of our ability

1	2	3	4	5	6	7	8	9	10

- **Does your organization monitor how focused your innovation efforts are?**

  We just do whatever comes to mind next   We make hard decisions to focus

1	2	3	4	5	6	7	8	9	10

- **How well do you know both those you serve and those who give you resources?**

  It's hard enough to focus on one   We know both very well

1	2	3	4	5	6	7	8	9	10

- **Do you segment the types of funders and volunteers your organization targets?**

  A donor is a donor, right?   Yep, and we tailor our efforts accordingly.

1	2	3	4	5	6	7	8	9	10

Simple Summary – Nonprofit Metrics

Key take-aways you should get out of this section:

- Non-profit readers, please don't skip the "for-profit metrics" section. Even if your organization was not created for the purpose of making money, you need to pay attention to financial performance. Plus, there is a bunch of non-financial metric advice in there that you need to know.

- The differences between for-profits and nonprofits does require a little special thought. One difference is that with non-profits, it can be even harder than in business to focus on a narrow set of projects. When every idea is for doing social good, it's awfully hard to say, "Let's not do that." So a key metric for all non-profits should be established around keeping project efforts within the means of their resources.

- Non-profits need to recognize that they have two distinct customer bases. They tend to be very good at recognizing and serving those with the social need for which they got into the non-profit gig in the first place. They tend to forget that those who provide the resources for their operations – volunteers and funders – are also customers. They, too, need to receive a benefit for their time and money.

- Both funders and volunteers of a nonprofit organization come in different shapes and sizes. Not all provide their time or money for the same reasons. Even if you think they should consider the good feeling of having donated to a worthy cause as their benefit, you need to do all that you can to provide that benefit in abundance. For other providers that you target, however, that may not be sufficient. You need to deliver value for those folks, too.

It's Not a Business...Or is it?

If you are a nonprofit innovator, and you skipped to this section thinking the for-profit metrics don't apply to you...well, go back and read that section anyway.

Nonprofits, whether they like it or not, need to be run with financials in mind. Even an all-volunteer workforce is going to need some resources beyond just their time and energy at some point. The better you manage your financial challenges, the better you'll be able to deliver on your mission.

Also, you may be surprised to know that not all of the for-profit metrics advice is financially related. Most, in fact, is not.

While the common advice to nonprofits is that they need to be run more like businesses, I offer the counter-advice to most for-profit businesses: they should be run more like non-profits. Consider one of the comments of Lars Sørensen, highlighted in his *Harvard Business Review* interview as 2015's top CEO in the world: "I tell my employees, 'If we wind up curing diabetes, and it destroys a big part of our business, we can be proud, and you can get a job anywhere. We'll have worked on the greatest social service of any pharmaceutical company, and that would be a phenomenal thing.'"

That's the kind of thing I'm talking about when I say for-profits should think more like nonprofits. Nonprofits tend to be very good at clearly articulating their missions, communicating those missions to their stakeholders, and leveraging those missions to drive decisions around their activities. [711]

What's the Difference?

But it is true that nonprofits are different, and not just in how they are treated by the tax collectors.

Even for large, established nonprofits, structured innovation is not the norm. New goods and services tend to come ad hoc, with little testing and

---

[711] Gloria Barczak, Kenneth B. Kahn and Roberta Moss, "An Exploratory Investigation of NPD Practices in Nonprofit Organizations," *Journal of Product Innovation Management*, November 2006.

business planning. In the realm of "shooting puppies,"[712] programs are rarely killed, because they are viewed as filling a social need. A particularly weak area is metrics, both in the short term, where the metrics of impact are weakly defined, and in the long term, where the success criteria are often intangible and difficult to track.[713]

Finding solid, reliable metrics is important for nonprofits. This is true not only for the sake of better innovation success, but for the ability to attract and retain donors, grants, and other sources of funding.

Which brings up one of the critical points about nonprofits that most don't consider: a key challenge for nonprofits is that they have two very different customer bases.

The obvious customers that they pay attention to are the ones whose suffering is what they are trying to relieve. They are very familiar with such people's needs. Those needs are what called them to service. It's difficult enough to come up with the right metrics for those customers.[714] But then there is the other set of customers.

The other customers are the people who provide the resources for all of the service activities the organization undertakes. Those resources are provided in the form of funding and volunteer time.

That's where many nonprofits fall flat in the creation of programs. They fail to recognize funders and volunteers as types of customers, and they focus little attention on serving them as such.

To make things even more complicated, funders and volunteers do not come in "one size fits all" wrappers, either. For funders, different sources of

---

[712] No, that's not specific to evil animal shelters. "Shooting puppies" refers to the hard decisions organizations must make. For more on that analogy, go to the "Tough Choices" section of the Portfolio Management chapter, page 154.

[713] Gloria Barczak, Kenneth B. Kahn and Roberta Moss, "An Exploratory Investigation of NPD Practices in Nonprofit Organizations," *Journal of Product Innovation Management*, November 2006.

[714] Don't let that stop you, though. If you simply *assume* that your programs are doing good without following-up to find out, well...go to the section on "Muddy Communication" in the Teams chapter to find out what happens when we assume (page 331).

revenue have different motives for giving. One study[715] breaks down the types of donors as:

- **Contented Benefactors** – those who have been long time donors, and are satisfied with their level of giving.
- **Busy Idealists** – People who want to do more, but are overwhelmed by demands for their time and money.
- **Cautious Strivers** – Believers in giving back, but who are concerned about not getting over-stretched; they are lacking the resources to give back as much as they'd like.
- **Unaware Potentials** – Giving is not a high priority; they assume that their giving is similar to others, and they are focused on other priorities.
- **Unengaged Critics** – Giving is not important; they are unengaged with and skeptical about nonprofits.

So one metric to look at is how your donors break out into these categories. That can guide both where to focus your energies for further giving (hint: the middle three), and help you know how to serve them. For example, a busy idealist might be addressed by programs that make donations fast and easy, so they don't have to spend time on the effort. Unengaged critics might join in for a social media challenge, bake sale, or black tie gala, in which they get entertainment value for their donation (which they see more as the price of admission to a good time). Directing endless pleas to Contented Benefactors will likely fail to increase their support, and may even prove to be irritating.

Volunteers are also customers. Yes, customers. They are not employees, although that is the more common way for nonprofits to treat them.

Like donors, volunteers are also not one-size-fits-all customers. They have different reasons for volunteering their time. A similar segmentation has been done for volunteers,[716] dividing them into five groups:

---

[715] Camber Collective, *Money for Good 2015: Revealing the voice of the donor in philanthropic giving.*

[716] Melanie J. Randle, Bettina Grun, Sara Dolnicar, "Segmenting the Volunteer Market: Learnings from an Australian Study," *Proceedings of the European Marketing Academy (EMAC) Conference,* Reykjavic, Iceland, 2007.

- **Enthusiastic Volunteers** – they are highly self-motivated to volunteer for a wide variety of reasons. They do not respond to external motivation, but rather seek out volunteer opportunities on their own.
- **Social Volunteers** – they are more motivated by receiving benefits for themselves, such as the opportunity to meet different people, to socialize, to keep active, to take their mind off of other concerns, to receive recognition, to build networks, or to help develop professional and career prospects.
- **Community Volunteers** – they are motivated to improve the community (or society as a whole), to support a cause they believe to be important to their local area, or to maintain community services.
- **Altruistic Volunteers** – they are motivated to help others, to "give something back" to society, to volunteer without regard to personal reward, and to set a good example for others to follow.
- **Not Interested** – the descriptor says it all. This group is not motivated to donate their time as a volunteer at all.

Clearly, these different types of volunteers will respond differently to what you offer them. Different services you provide may attract different types of volunteers. To be most effective, you must evaluate what kind of volunteers you have, what kinds of volunteers you want, and deliver customer benefits to them accordingly.

Also, provide the donors of both time and money with a return on their investment in you. Again, remember that return may take different forms depending on the donor.

Someone who gives anonymously may be most concerned with the donation doing the maximum amount of good for a cause in which they believe, so share the impact of your programs. Others may be concerned with recognition, and receive a return in the form of recognition on donor lists, or naming a campus building after them. The point is, you need to provide them with a return for the contributions they provide, and that requires you to know them as much as you do your other customers.

Simple Study Guide - Nonprofit Metrics

- What defines ultimate success for your organization?
- What kind of metric should nonprofits establish to efficiently use their resources?
- What are the two types of customers that nonprofits typically have?
- What types of funders are there for nonprofits?
- What types of volunteers are there for nonprofits?

Where do you want to go from here?

Or just turn the page to keep reading...

ENGINE OIL (Change Management)

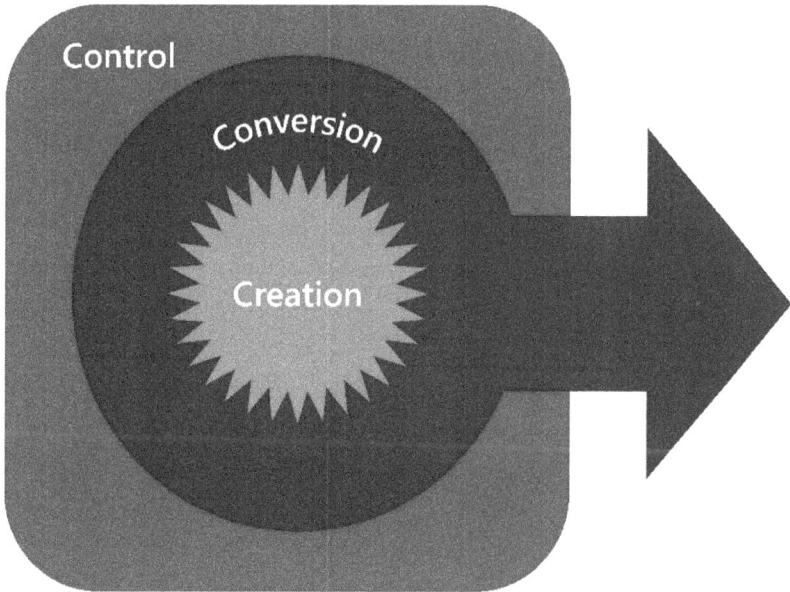

Simple Self-Assessment – Change

Rate yourself on the following questions. To benchmark yourself against others, go to www.3point14Innovation.com and click the "Self-Assessments" menu.

- ### How committed is your organization to innovation?

  We are totally committed, when we have time.   It guides our every action.

1	2	3	4	5	6	7	8	9	10

- ### How committed is your organization to decomplexification?

  Now you're just making words up.   Perfect word to describe us.

1	2	3	4	5	6	7	8	9	10

- ### How committed is your organization to change?

  We love nickels, dimes, quarters, pennies...   Determined to do what it takes

1	2	3	4	5	6	7	8	9	10

- ### Does your organization actively manage change?

  Que sera, sera   Intentional change is good change

1	2	3	4	5	6	7	8	9	10

- ### Do you focus on change at the individual as well as organizational level?

  Nah, the minions will follow when told to.   Group change is a collection of individual changes

1	2	3	4	5	6	7	8	9	10

- ### Do you pay attention to the emotional and social drivers of change?

  This is a business, not a therapy group.   Since those are what really drive change, yes, we do.

1	2	3	4	5	6	7	8	9	10

Simple Summary – Engine Oil
Key take-aways you should get out of this section

- Change is hard.
- Change takes non-stop vigilance
- Create awareness for the need to change with facts, but support change emotionally: attitude, social norms, and reinforcement.
- Pay attention to stages of change, and adjust your approach to individuals with recognition of where they are in the change process. The stages of change include pre-contemplation, contemplation, preparation, action, and maintenance.
- You must rely on emotions, feelings, and motivations to actually create and sustain change. Logic and reason alone will not do it.
- Plan out change management just like a project, keeping the change processes and objectives in mind. Manage the change actively.

Making the Complex Clear

Innovation in any organization is a complex process done in an even more complex world. Making innovation simple is not the same as making it easy – easy innovation is going to be bad innovation. Simple, on the other hand, is about clarity.

The objective of this book was to provide clarity for the various aspects of the innovation process, and to provide some simple tools for execution. Not easy – simple.

Learning to make all the different parts of the process work together reminds me of learning to drive a stick shift. At first, there were so many things to think about – where all the gears were in the gear box, timing of pressing and releasing the clutch and the gas pedals, all while paying attention to my speed, keeping an eye on the traffic lights, reading street signs, avoiding the cars in the other lanes, watching the kids playing near the street up ahead, and not hitting that – squirrel! – trying to get that acorn laying in the road.

I stalled out frequently at first. That turned into grinding the gears. That evolved into not progressing to the right gear at the right time. But, eventually, I was able to get where I was going without such errors. And after that, I became one with the car, unconsciously shifting and maneuvering safely to my destinations, even before the days of GPS directions telling me to turn in 350 feet.

If you are new to systematic innovation, you may feel like there is too much to think about all at once, like me when I was new to manual transmissions. That's okay. Stick with it. Keep it simple, and keep progressing until it becomes part of your professional being.

If you are an experienced innovator, I hope this book offered some insights on how to decomplexify[717] any aspects of what you do that are unnecessarily complex.

What I hope you did not get out of this is any impression that you must do X, Y, and Z, or that you should copy any practices just because other people have done it. I am not preaching an innovation orthodoxy. Rather, I am encouraging innovation orthopraxy.

---

[717] Another word I've "innovated."

"What the heck is 'orthopraxy?'" you ask. "Is that just another word you made up?

No, that one is a real word. Father Richard Rohr captures its meaning best: "We don't think ourselves into a new way of living; we live ourselves into a new way of thinking." You don't read a book, even one as entertaining and informative as this one has been,[718] and suddenly change how you do things, achieving previously unimagined levels of success. You practice those things, try and fail, learn some more, get better at what works for you, and drop what doesn't. That's innovation orthopraxy.

Inspiring Changes

Innovation requires behavioral change. But change is hard! That's a fact that has been understood for hundreds of years (if not more). Ever seen this quote posted on a wall at the office?

> "There is nothing more difficult to take in hand, more perilous to conduct, or more uncertain in its success, than to take the lead in the introduction of a new order of things. For the reformer has enemies in all those who profit by the old order, and only lukewarm defenders in all those who would profit by the new order, this lukewarmness arising partly from fear of their adversaries ... and partly from the incredulity of mankind, who do not truly believe in anything new until they have had actual experience of it."
> ~Niccolo Machiavelli, *The Prince*

So change is hard, even for princes. That makes it rarer than it ought to be. When organizations have been successful, it is easy for them to get complacent, thinking that everything has been working well so far. Why mess with it? Or if change is tried, it's given meager support and poorly executed.[719]

---

[718] Please, please, oh please think it was entertaining and informative. Not necessarily in that order.

[719] Michael L. Tushman, Philip C. Anderson, and Charles O'Reilly, "Technology Cycles, Innovation Streams, and Ambidextrous Organizations: Organization Renewal through Innovation Streams and Strategic Change," from *Managing Strategic Innovation and Change*, edited by Michael L.

Organizational leaders, relying on what has worked in the past to continue working into the future, become "stale in the saddle."[720] They fail to recognize change in the competitive environment, or fail to change from their tried and true responses until it is too late.

But even if this occurs at the corporate level, surely those responsible for innovation can see past this, right? Well, not so much. Research specific to new product development shows that even innovators within an organization can get rigidly attached to the values, skills, and systems that served them well in the past, but have become inappropriate for a new environment.[721]

So if even the innovators of the world struggle to change with the times, how is any organization to institute real change? Fortunately, there's research for that, too.

In order to achieve broad behavioral change, you should pursue positive strategies that are both motivational and informative, rather than punitive or threatening.[722] Three factors in particular are critical for enticing effective change:

- Attitude - belief about what will happen if behavior changes;
- Social norms – belief about what others should do, or about what others think about behaviors;
- Self-efficacy - confidence in one's own ability to achieve something.

Change is a process, not an event. It does not happen with a sudden epiphany or lightning bolt out of the sky. It need not be as dramatic as the former, nor as painful as the latter.

Tushman and Philip Anderson, Oxford University Press, 1997. Please don't confuse Dr. Charles O'Reilly with Charles Nelson Reilly. They are very different people.

[720] Danny Miller, "Stale in the Saddle: CEO Tenure and the Match between Organization and Environment," *Management Science*, January, 1991.

[721] Dorothy Leonard-Barton, "Core Capabilities and Core Rigidities: A Paradox in Managing New Product Development," *Strategic Management Journal*, Summer 1992.

[722] Thomas Llewelyn Webb and Paschal Sheeran, "Does Changing Behavioral Intentions Engender Behavior Change? A Meta-Analysis of the Experimental Evidence," *Psychological Bulletin*, April 2006.

The Process of Changing

Research into how people change entrenched behaviors shows that the process of change is consistent. [723] The time it can take to change will vary from person to person, and the time a person spends within a particular stage can vary, but the overall process is the same. There are five stages that people will go through: [724]

1. **Pre-contemplation** – no real intention to change behavior in the foreseeable future.
2. **Contemplation** – recognition that the problem exists, but the pros and cons of change are still in doubt and being evaluated. There is not a commitment to change – like they say, though, admitting you have a problem is the first step toward recovery.[725]
3. **Preparation** – the intention is there to take action in the near future, and some initial steps toward change have started. Full commitment, though, is still elusive. They've stepped to the edge of the diving board, and maybe started bouncing on it, but they have not yet taken the plunge.
4. **Action** – actual behavioral change takes place, with considerable commitment of time and energy. This is where external recognition of the change first becomes apparent. It is important to recognize not only the change, but also the effort required to get through the preparation stages. Those stage are the most psychologically difficult, but the effort often goes unnoticed and unrecognized.
5. **Maintenance** – the new behavior becomes the new norm, but still requires commitment to avoid relapse. With many long-term behaviors, even those most detrimental to our well-being, relapse is the rule, not the exception. Maintenance should be viewed as a

---

[723] James O. Prochaska and James O. Prochaska, "Chapter 2: Behavior Change," from *Population Health: Creating a Culture of Wellness*, edited by David B. Nash, JoAnne Reifsnyder, Raymond J. Fabius, and Valerie P. Pracilio, Jones and Bartlett Learning, LLC, 2011.

[724] James O. Prochaska, Carlo C. DiClemente, and John C. Norcross, "In Search of How People Change: Applications to Addictive Behaviors," *American Psychologist*, September 1992.

[725] I have no idea who "they" are, but since I've heard this often enough to remember it, I know they are out there. If you see them, tell them I said "hello."

continuation of the change, not as a reaching of the proverbial finish line. There is some evidence that recovering from relapses actually strengthens the desired behavior, as people learn from mistakes and take a better approach in the future.[726]

In order to really change a culture, each person within the organization will need to go through these stages. And, like the innovation process, it's not a linear thing. People will often have to repeat and recycle through some stages before getting to the end.

As a leader of change, you need to recognize where people are in these stages, and tailor your encouragements accordingly. People in the pre-contemplation and contemplation stages need motivating information raising the awareness of the problem. Once people move into the preparation and action stages, more information is not better. Insight and data by themselves do not drive behavioral change. That's where the attitude, social norms and self-efficacy encouragements come in.

Several action plans for changing behaviors have been proposed. For example, Dan and Chip Heath, in their book *Switch: How to Change Things When Change Is Hard*, give three principles based on a "rider and elephant" model. The "rider" is our capacity for reason. The "elephant" is our emotions (remember, even in the professional world, we are not entirely rational creatures). When someone is riding an elephant, they do what they can to control it. If that elephant determines it's going to do something else, though, it's gonna do it, and there is little that the rider can do about it. Similarly, under normal circumstances, reason (as the rider) may have control, but under stress, emotions (as the elephant) will do what they will, and there is little that the rational mind will be able to do about it.

To create change, then, the Heath brothers offer three guidelines:

1) **Direct the Rider.** What looks like resistance is usually a lack of clarity. If the riders don't know where to go, they can spin their elephants in circles. To direct the riders, create a crystal clear vision of the outcome. Use the CLEAR communication technique to ensure that they

---

[726] Especially if they do an After Action Review! (for more on that topic, see page 382)

understand what needs to be done, and the RAPID decision model to ensure that everyone knows their roles and responsibilities.

2) **Motivate the Elephant.** What looks like laziness is often exhaustion. Make your audience *feel* the need for change. Analytical appeals won't cut it. Just knowing is not enough. Get beyond the knowing and make it possible for people to feel the impact. Win the heart, and the mind will follow. Help people to imagine a world in which they are successfully employing the change you want to see in them.

   Note that although fear is an emotion, it only works as a short-term motivator, and not one that motivates innovation effectively. Telling everyone that the beatings will continue until innovation improves will not have the best of outcomes.

3) **Shape the Path.** What looks like a people problem is often a situation problem. Make it easy for people to embrace the change. Make instructions simple with step-by-step guidance. Provide support groups. Create training. Pair people up with mentors. Remember, behavior is contagious.

A related point of view comes from Alan Deutschman, in his book *Change or Die*. He points out that upwards of 9 out of 10 people don't successfully change their lifestyles, even when their lives depend upon it. Smokers continue smoking even after painful lung disease. Heart attack victims stop exercising and go back to eating junk foods, in spite of their doctor's dire warnings.

Deutschman points out that people often make two common mistakes when they try to motivate others to change: they rely on fear, and they rely on facts. Fear may work, but only for a brief time. Then the old behaviors come right back. Facts just don't work at all. Facts don't appeal to emotions and desires. Denial takes hold, and the facts are lost, even when they are clearly understood.

He suggests that the way to effect meaningful, sustainable change involves three R's:

1) **Relate:** Help people to form a new, emotional relationship with a person or community that inspires change. Again, there's that emotion thing. It really is critical.

2) **Repeat:** The new relationship helps people learn, practice, and master the new habits and skills that they'll need. This is where reason comes into play. This is where the CLEAR communication technique and RAPID decision model will help.

3) **Reframe:** The new relationship and repeated behaviors (remember that "orthopraxy" term) helps people to learn new ways of thinking about a situation. This breaks the old "way we do things around here" to generate a new "way we do things around here."

These two models have subtle differences, but they have a common lesson. You must rely on emotions, feelings, and motivations to actually create and sustain change. Logic and reason will not do it. Emotion will drive the why. Only when the "why" is firmly established can you then work with reason to drive the "who," "what," "when," "where," and "how."

So plan out your change management just like a project, keeping these processes and objectives in mind. Manage the change actively. Do not expect it to happen magically on its own, or to happen exactly as you want, without a good deal of guidance.

Now, knowing how to change, let's review what to change.

The Principles

From the start, I have intended to communicate general principles that you should follow to maximize your chances of successful innovation. To make it simple to know exactly what those principles are, let's list 'em out here...

Simplicity

- When faced with a choice between simplicity and complexity, choose simplicity.
- Simple is not the same as easy – making something simple can be hard work.
- Simplicity is making the complex clear. Clarity can grow with practice and experience.
- Innovation occurs at the intersection of creativity, significance, and execution.

- Understand the fundamental principles of innovation, then apply them to your specific circumstances for a customized and optimized approach.
- Manage your expectations. There is no such thing as innovation utopia.

Mission

- Define a mission by what to achieve, within what constraints, and why people should want to achieve it.
- Communicate that mission through both words and actions, to improve both innovation and overall organizational performance.
- Align organizational structures, systems, and processes to the mission.
- Involve as many stakeholders as possible in the process of mission development.

Culture

- Fit your culture with your strategy, programs, and processes. Culture is more powerful, and more influential on the organization, than any strategy or program.
- Manage the organizational culture to best achieve the mission – perhaps not fully control, but manage.
- Use tools to assess and define the culture you have, and the culture you want.
- Celebrate innovative behaviors and organizational learning, even in failure.
- Cultural fit should be an important part of both hiring and firing decisions.
- Create and leverage an innovation subculture when the overall culture does not support innovation well.

Strategy

- Strategy is a leader's plan for the use of available resources to uniquely create value that supports a higher mission.
- The greatest value of a strategic plan is the planning process itself.
- Start strategic planning with clear focus on the mission.
- Use simple tools to analyze your situation, then to create a plan to achieve the objectives that best serve the mission.

- Capture and communicate your strategy simply. A simple one-page communication tool that people use is better than a binder full of strategic prose that no one ever looks at.
- Open innovation is a continuum, not an on/off switch. Determine where your organization best fits on the continuum, then plan accordingly.

Portfolio Management

- Innovation efforts are investments, and should be managed as such.
- Balance and diversification are the keys to good portfolio management.
- Portfolio management is the implementation of the strategic plan – it must always be linked directly to the strategy.
- Live within your means – pay attention to your resource constraints and do not overstretch the limited resources that you have.
- The toughest choices are always between two goods. Have the courage to make the difficult decisions.
- Never forget that there is risk to inaction as well as to action.
- Portfolio management is not a one-time event, but an ongoing process.
- Be flexible and adaptable to changing circumstances.

Voice of the Customer

- Customer understanding is the foundation of all innovation efforts.
- Start innovation efforts by clearly defining the problem that you are going to solve.
- Design thinking is most valuable at the front end of the innovation process, and should be incorporated throughout the process. Design is not limited to aesthetic work tacked on at the end of a project.
- "Voice of the Customer" means getting into the minds and hearts of customers to really, thoroughly understand their needs. It's not just listening to their requests.
- Thinking in terms of "jobs to be done" is an effective way to think about customer problems.
- Filter VoC data for relevance, then organize it to make sense of it all before starting the innovation process.

- The perceptions of your customers are their reality.
- Involve customers in the solution process, at least through frequent feedback on your solution efforts.

The Mental Game of Innovation

- Innovation is fundamentally a mental process. You need to understand how the human mind works – both its amazing abilities and its hard-wired shortcomings – to manage the innovation process well.
- Multitasking doesn't work. Don't do it, and don't expect others to do it.
- Innovators need thick skin, and thick skulls, to withstand the challenges they face.
- Innovators should have an attitude of "respectful irreverence" for existing products around processes.
- Innovators must be able to handle ambiguity and uncertainty.
- Mindfulness exercises will improve innovation capabilities.
- Create an environment in which you and your team can get into the psychological state of "flow."

Developing Ideas

- The lone innovator whose "eureka!" moment suddenly generates the one brilliant idea that becomes the next big thing is a myth. And a detrimental one.
- Classic brainstorming doesn't work. Use tools that really deliver solutions.
- When thinking of ideas, start with customer problems.
- Leverage outside viewpoints during the ideation process.
- Avoid feature creep. Keep innovations focused on a particular customer need.
- Define your ideas according to a formal value proposition.
- Simplify the communication of an idea with a formal concept statement, and use it to seek out customer feedback.

Teams

- Innovation is a team sport.
- Teams need to have a complete set of both professional skills and teamwork skills to be successful.
- Create frequent, effective, real-time communication opportunities for teams, especially if geographically dispersed.
- Maintain a common shared team identity that all members can embrace.
- Clearly define roles and responsibilities for all team members.
- Promote strong relationships between team members.
- Encourage healthy conflict within teams.
- Find a transformational leader to maximize team effectiveness.

Project Management

- Follow a structured yet flexible process for getting innovations from ideas to market.
- Create a Project Charter for every project, and leverage it to guide the team throughout the process.
- Balance speed to market with ensuring customer satisfaction and product quality.
- Use simple forecasting methods, and don't waste time with ineffective complex forecasting models.
- Develop contingency plans during the planning process.
- Simplify your meetings so people can get their work done.
- Do the After Action Reviews.

Metrics

- "What gets measured gets done. What gets measured and fed back gets done well. What gets rewarded gets repeated."
- Measure more than one thing, but don't measure everything.
- Customize your metrics for your organization, and for each project.
- Choose metrics that are relevant for your culture, mission, strategy, and customer.
- Use both guidance and review metrics.

- Use a blend of metrics that are unrelated or even conflicting.
- Beware unintended consequences.

Change Management
- Change is hard and requires non-stop vigilance
- Drive change with emotional levers: attitude, social norms, and reinforcement.
- Understand that change comes in stages, and adjust your approach to individuals based on where they are in the change process.

Simple Study Guide-The Engine

- Why is change hard?
- What is required for lasting change to take hold?
- What is the change process?
- What is the *Switch* model of change?
- What is the *Change or Die* model of change?
- How can you actively manage organizational change?

Where do you want to go from here?

Control	Creation	Conversion
Mission (page 40)	Voice of the Customer (page 175)	Innovation Teams (page 310)
Culture (page 58)	Minds of Innovators (page 217)	Project Management (page 347)
Strategy (page 92)	Ideation (page 279)	For-Profit Metrics (page 389)
Portfolio Management (page 146)		Nonprofit Metrics (page 403)
Change Management (page 411)		

Or just turn the page to keep reading...

Help me to Help You

Now to turn the tables. I want to know your thoughts, not just throw mine at you.

After working your way through this book,[727] I really want to know what you thought. Good or bad. Positive or negative. Serious or humorous. Pithy or verbose. Here's two ways for you to get your revenge on me for making you read this stuff:

Option 1:

Go to www.3point14Innovation.com/ContactUs/.

Feel free to leave questions, criticisms, comments, compliments, requests, concerns, and, of course, comedy jokes. Who knows, if there's enough commentary, maybe I'll start a sharing community for simple innovators.

Option 2:

The online survey at www.3point14Innovation.com/KIS-Feedback/.

This is just a four-question survey, and you only have to answer one of them before being allowed to click the "submit" button. The other three are all optional, but gratitude will spill from my heart like meatballs from a toddler's high chair if you answer any or all of them, too. Feel free to take more than one-minute. You will not be timed.

As discussed in the "If You Must" section of the Voice of the Customer chapter,[728] I think that there is little worse than all of those surveys that go on and on with 873 questions, getting into such excruciating detail about

---

[727] Congratulations!

[728] Which can be found on page 195, if you must go back and read it. See what I did there?

your experience that you forget what the experience even was before you finish the thing.[729, 730, 731, 732f]

Thank you for plowing through all of this. I sincerely hope it has been worth your time, and will continue to be of value going forward from here.

That's all. There is no more. Now go innovate.

---

[729] For example, "Question 743) On a scale from 1 to the square root of the largest known prime number, what color underwear were you wearing while reading this book?"

[730] The largest known prime number is 17,425,170, and the square root of it is approximately 4174.35.

[731] Actually, there are many things worse than this, but they are way too graphic to describe in this book. If you want to play a game of "Would You Rather" or "Cards Against Humanity" with me some time, though, maybe we can go there.

[732] Last footnote. I promise.

Acknowledgements

First, some props to people I've never met and don't know, but who unwittingly provided extraordinary help to me in the writing of this book...

Thanks to Larry Page and Sergey Brin for the Google, and particularly for Google Scholar. Thanks also to Jimmy Wales and Larry Sanger for Wikipedia, and to all those who have made contributions to it (I will not attempt to list them all out by name – you know who you are). What amazing resources.

Thanks to Guy Kawasaki and Shawn Welch for their book *APE: Author, Publisher, Entrepreneur*. I recommend it highly to anyone setting out to do some "artisanal publishing." The sharing of their insights and experience relieved more headaches than all the ibuprofen in my local pharmacy possibly could have.

And now for the people I do know (or at least with whom I've personally interacted)...

Thanks to the Product Development and Management Association for the opportunity to meet so many thought leaders, and to work on the managerial publication *Visions*. I will forever cherish my experience in and with the organization, and I will always be grateful for the interactions with so many people so much smarter than me.

Thanks to all of the academic researchers whose work I have referenced throughout this text. The curiosity, intellect, patience, determination, and courage required to formulate important questions, design clever test methods, collect and analyze data, write up conclusions, and defend them to your peers are all beyond impressive.

Thanks to Dr. Liz Perl, who repeatedly helped me regain my sanity when I was on the edge of losing it. God rest her soul. I miss her.

Thanks to Dr. Garson O'Toole, "The Quote Investigator." Any quote collectors (like me) out there who (like me) prefer to confirm the veracity of their attributions, should store Dr. O'Toole's website QuoteInvestigator.com in their browser favorites. It is like a gift from the Olympian gods. He was even kind enough to investigate a particular quote for which I could find no verified source. I am grateful for his service.

Thanks to Dr. Abbie Griffin, my all-time favorite professor, for teaching me – in an operations management class of all things – that innovation can be sexy, and for entrusting me with *Visions* magazine for a few years.

Thanks to Dr. Steven Markham for the education and encouragement. I've always enjoyed our talks and debates, and respect his point of view highly. Even when (perhaps especially when) we have different perspectives.

Thanks to Dr. Dan Zhang, whose thorough review of my early drafts was so helpful and encouraging. Her intellect, design skills, and artistic eye were filled with insight, and her thoughtful encouragement were good for my ego. I'm so glad that we both attended that Doctoral Consortium all those years ago.

Thanks to Dan Adams for being the first to send in feedback on the full-length draft, and for helping me to feel good about what I was doing and the direction I was heading. Thanks to all the others who participated in my Voice of the Customer efforts, from early casual conversations to outline reviews to title polls to cover design feedback to beta testing...they all helped my baby to grow up.

Thanks to Richard Brooks, Meta Brown, and Bryan Mattimore for the no-holds-barred candid feedback. They sparked some great ideas for reorganization, topics, editing...whipping things into far better shape than I originally offered.

Thanks to Deb Loftus, for helping me to write in a way that actually makes sense (at least on occasion). I greatly appreciate the candid, collaborative feedback and suggestions that push me to do better, always delivered in the most caring of ways. Thanks also for the insights into mankind's psychology and spirituality, which not only helped me with this book, but go on helping me in my daily life.

Thanks to Yolanda Harris, Maggie Burns, Daria Moore, Lindsey Pinkerton, Jack Stone, and Whitney Williams at The Keynote Group, for insisting that I make this as professional a publication as possible, elevating its quality, and not allowing me to be too much of an amateur do-it-yourselfer author.

Thanks to Kim Hall of Inhouse Design Studio for the cover design, which captures the primary message of the book simply and elegantly. Thanks also for putting up with my nearly endless string of nit-picky adjustment requests.

Thanks to Lisa Coughlin for the non-stop encouragement throughout a process that took way, way longer than I ever anticipated it would, and for frequently reminding me to get over my obsessive perfectionism and just publish the damn thing.

Thanks to Francis Boyle, my editor-in-chief. He caught everything from stupid phrasing (not in the sense that they use "phrasing" in *Archer*), to silly typos, to irrelevant rants, to missed opportunities for historical references and TV/movie clips that perfectly illustrate particular points in the text. All while offering dozens of ways to improve the writing. And providing comic relief with *Fawlty Towers* episodes. He demonstrated the courage and passion required of the dictum "no passion in the world, no love or hate, is equal to the passion to alter someone else's draft."

Thanks to Angie Boyle, the aforementioned Jello-Head, for serving as the ultimate grammarian, arbiter of proper phraseology, and manipulator of the useful but often frustrating tool that is Microsoft Word. While I curse that extra IQ point that she has over me, I am grateful to her for using it to help straighten out my manuscript. Any and all errors remaining are in spite of her knowledge and advice.

I must again thank my parents for the love and support that made this book possible. Through five decades, they've been pushing me to be my best, while always being there to pick me up when I fell. There is truly no way to express my gratitude sufficiently. I love you guys!

And finally, thanks go up, down, and sideways to that Higher Power of the Universe, by whatever name He/She/It may be known. I will continue to seek the one ultimate Truth, and use the blessings given to me (however imperfect they may be) to the best of my ability, according to my duty. I appreciate the patience, guidance, and gentle (or not-so-gentle) corrections along the way.

Gratefully,

BRAD

About the Author

Brad Barbera has over twenty-five years of innovation experience, bringing hundreds of successful new products and services to market in a variety of industries and business models. He founded Pi Innovation LLC in 2009 to help leaders of businesses and nonprofits structure their innovation efforts so that they can stop just throwing things against the wall to see what sticks. He is a certified New Product Development Professional (NPDP), has served as the Executive Director of the Product Development and Management Association (PDMA), and is currently the Editor-in-Chief of PDMA's *Visions* magazine, the flagship managerial publication for innovation professionals. He's also a proud dad of two, a competitive stair climber, and a moderately competent chess player (with ambitions of mastery).